Introduction to Financial Modelling

How to Excel at Being a Lazy [That Means Efficient!] Modeller

FIRST EDITION

Dr. Liam Bastick

www.sumproduct.com

Published in 2018 by SumProduct Pty Limited.
Level 9, 440 Collins Street, Melbourne, Vic 3000, Australia.

Published in the United States by Holy Macro! Books, PO Box 541731, Merritt Island FL 32953
ISBN 978-1-61547-066-2 (Print) 978-1-61547-152-2 (Digital)

About the Author

Dr. Liam Bastick FCA FCMA CGMA MVP

Starting off as a university lecturer, Liam has over 30 years' experience in financial model development / auditing, valuations, M&A, strategy, training and consultancy. He has considerable experience in many different sectors (e.g. banking, energy, media, mining, oil and gas, private equity, transport and utilities and has worked in many countries including Australia, Belgium, Denmark, France, Germany, Hong Kong, Indonesia, Malaysia, New Zealand, Singapore, Switzerland, United States, United Kingdom and Vietnam, with many internationally recognised clients, constructing and reviewing strategic, operational and valuation models for many high profile International Public Offerings (IPOs), Leveraged Buyouts (LBOs) and strategic assignments.

With over 1,000 articles written for the accounting profession, he is a regular contributor to the American Institute of Certified Public Accountants (AICPA), Chartered Accountants Australia and New Zealand (CAANZ), Certified Practising Accountants Australia (CPAA), the Chartered Institute of Management Accountants (CIMA), the Institute of Chartered Accountants in England and Wales (ICAEW), Finance 3.0 and various LinkedIn specialist discussion groups. Liam is a Fellow of the Institute of Chartered Accountants (ICAEW), a Fellow of the Institute of Chartered Management Accountants (CIMA), a Chartered Global Management Accountant and is also a professional mathematician. Since 2012, he has been recognised by Microsoft as a Most Valuable Professional (MVP) in Excel, one of 104 such awardees worldwide (as at the time of writing).

Unfortunately, he follows Derby County and the England cricket team.

Preface

So, I finally managed it: I wrote this book. Over the years, like many of you, I have been frustrated about the content and detail of many texts supposedly on financial modelling. I'm a practitioner with 30 years' experience and I kept seeing theoretical books that didn't address the sorts of pragmatic issues that occur in reality.

Hence, I got off my backside and decided to do something about it. I have been writing in many accounting journals and on websites for years regarding common issues those working in in finance and forecasting face day in, day out. I decided it was time to go the whole hog and write a simple book on how to get started in financial modelling in such a way that you can easily have financial statements talking to each other and a Balance Sheet balancing readily and easily. It's intended out for those starting on their journey to develop their modelling prowess and for more advanced users who are seeking a simpler way to put financial statements together, especially key practical tips and tricks to avoid the common pitfalls that bedevil the unwary.

I have been lucky enough to be appointed a Most Valuable Professional (MVP) by Microsoft for services to Excel – one of 104 so-recognised "experts" as at the time of writing. Now I know an "ex" is a has-been and a "spurt" is a drip under pressure, but I hope you'll see me as a farmer – someone out(-)standing in their field! It takes thousands of mistakes to get good at something. This book is intended to show you how to avoid many of these traps.

I'd like to thank those that helped contribute to this book over the years (this has been 10 years in the making). Thanks to Bill Jelen for getting me to actually write it (even if we didn't end up joining forces), Tim Heng for technically editing it and not deleting all my bad puns, Cecile Nguyen and Jonathan Liau for firming up the examples, and most importantly my immediate family, Nancy and little Layla, who have always supported me – even when I have gone many months spreading the word around the globe at the expense of a home life. To that end, I let my nine-year old daughter, Layla Bastick, have the last (fore)word:

"This book is a great source of information for people who are hoping to learn more about Excel and financial modelling. Liam Bastick has an amazing talent which helps people who read books like these to have a better understanding of modelling. This book is also inspiring for many of us thinking about becoming an expert in financial modelling or Excel. I am so proud of you daddy."

Liam Bastick, March 2018

www.sumproduct.com

Editor's notes

It's entirely possible that I have spent more time than Liam did on this book – partly because he's extremely good at what he does and condensed a lifetime of experience into a few weeks of furious book writing, and partly because I've spent a few minutes at every bit of humour that he's written, wondering if we would be sued if I left it in. Suffice to say, you don't need a PhD to see how the numbers work out there.

The challenge in writing a book about financial modelling is that the core of any modelling example is in the Excel files themselves. A picture may show a thousand words, but it's incredibly hard to convey exactly how a formula or a set of calculations work without seeing the overall context of the model and being able to drill into the formula itself. With that in mind, we have set up a page on our website for further reference, where we will (for as long as our website and the internet as we know it still exists) provide files containing examples that we have used throughout this book, as well as any supplementary materials that we think may be useful: www.sumproduct.com/book-resources.

Although financial modelling has remained relatively consistent over the last few decades, there is always room for improvement, just as it is with this book. As with any text of this nature, there are bound to be typos, images that need improving, Excel features we've recommended that become deprecated, and new tips and ideas that demand to be included in the next edition of this book. Please let us know if you discover any errors, if you have any new ideas, or if you can think of better ways to present and explain the material that we have. We welcome any comments, best received via email at contact@sumproduct.com.

Tim Heng, Microsoft Excel MVP

www.sumproduct.com

Contents

Chapter 10: Example Model Build 185

Chapter 11: Self Review 291

Chapter 12: Ratio Analysis 301

Appendix 315

Index 324

Chapter 0: Introduction

At last we meet.

I have been meaning to write this book for more years than I care to remember and you have decided that maybe there is a better way of building financial models that doesn't involve trying to find Balance Sheet errors at 2am on a Saturday morning. It has always frustrated me that there's never been a really practical book – heck, maybe a manual – that helps newcomers and the experienced alike to build better financial models. I just hope this one ticks some, if not all, of the boxes for you.

You may feel a little daunted looking at both the title and the thickness of this book. Hey, you're worried – I've had to write this thing! For those of you unlucky enough to have met me, you'll know I get bored very easily and you'll also know I have a truly terrible sense of humour. Therefore, let's make a pact: I am going to make this as easy and as practical a read as I can – and you're going to tolerate my jokes. Deal..?

So what's this book about? Well, I am going to assume that you, dear reader, have a basic understanding of Excel: I assume you are alive, you know how to open Excel, you know where the Ribbon is, you have used a keyboard before and that you can both read and type (sometimes even at the same time). I am also going to assume your work requires you to work in "finance" and that you have to work with financial projections or forecasts (most likely, you are charged with their preparation). This is who I am aiming this book at.

The plan is therefore as follows:

- **Key Excel functions:** Before we go anywhere, let's do a refresher on the key functions most commonly required in financial modelling. That way, we are all on the same page. For the more advanced amongst you, may I suggest you read this section as well, as there's stuff in here that many just don't appreciate.

- **Key Excel functionalities:** There are other attributes that we need to take for granted too. In this section, I will discuss key functionalities such as absolute referencing, number formatting, conditional formatting, Data Tables, data validation, range names, hyperlinks and the like. OK, these features will be taken out of context, but it will make for an easier read when we talk about building the model.

- **"Best Practice" methodology:** There's so much literature out there on this hotly-debated topic. Many academics and practitioners alike get hot under the collar just thinking about a model's flexibility (maybe I could have phrased that better, but I did warn you about my sense of humour). I have even been involved in writing some of these said texts, but hey, I was young and I needed the money… However, we do need a conceptual framework and I propose something very simple – something I call **CRaFT.**

- **Layout tips:** Everyone always ploughs straight into Excel and seldom gives thought as to how to put a worksheet – never mind a workbook – together. Where should a heading go? Why? Should we use a convention for sheet tabs? Should we be pedantic about spacing? Citing units? Formatting? Copying? (The answer is yes; otherwise this will be a very short section…).

- **Time series analysis:** If we are going to build a model, we will have to work with dates – and that's perhaps not quite as straightforward as you might think. In this section, I will explain how dates ought to be constructed and why – including periodicity issues – and where they should be positioned both in a worksheet and within the workbook to avoid errors.

- **Error checks**: Talking of errors, error checks are often added as an afterthought in a model. They shouldn't be. In this section, I will explain why they should be at the forefront of your model development and implementation will just make your life – and the model user's life – easier.

- **Base template:** No, I don't mean, here's a model I used last time and I will add a row here, delete a column there and deal with the *#REF!* errors and other model integrity issues when someone points them out to me. No; I accept all models are different, but they do share common attributes. It's this foundation which I can translate into a base template to use at the outset of developing a financial model.

- **Financial statement theory:** It's no secret that it was the phrases "double entry" and "working with models" that attracted me to this profession. How disappointed was I? On a serious note though, I want to revisit the key outputs of a financial model to fully understand what "three-way integrated" means and the ramifications for the modeller. Further, I actually go back to understand what is an Income Statement, a Balance Sheet and a Cash Flow Statement. Yes, you may know what they are – but I want to do it from the perspective of understanding the purpose of each statement so that it guides you in determining the order of building a financial model. No matter what you build, the derived order may be applied to all future model developments.

- **Control accounts**: How often have I mentioned debits and credits so far? Who said I haven't? I just did in the first sentence. Debits and credits are the accountants' way of keeping the mystery alive in finance. Hey, I think the bigger mystery more commonly encountered is, why doesn't my Balance Sheet balance? If you choose to use control accounts, Balance Sheet errors will become a thing of the past.

- **Example of a model build**: Oh yes, might be an idea to actually build a model. This may be a small paragraph here, but it's a big part of the book as we explain the four methods of model input, calculation tips *etc.* building in the order derived in the **Financial statement theory** section.

- **Reviewing the model**: Here, I talk about the difference between a "self-review" and a "model audit" and why the latter is very important. I present some common tips and tricks for checking your models – without any fancy add-in software – and even leave you with a suggested checklist and a discussion on ratio analysis.

Providing someone reads this book, future texts will cover "further reading", such as what-if analysis, debt and the cash waterfall, valuations modelling and other corporate finance stories including mergers and acquisitions and project finance.

Before I proceed, let me stress one last thing: this book is a practical book. There are lots of supporting Excel models to play with and use, grouped by chapter / section, to visualise the important concepts discussed here. So no excuses, make sure you are sitting comfortably and open up Excel. There's examples aplenty and the best way to understand is to do. Enjoy!

Chapter 1: Key Excel Functions

This chapter is dedicated entirely to going over the key functions most commonly used when developing a financial model in Excel. And you might be surprised regarding what's on my shopping list:

- SUM
- IF
- IFERROR
- SUMIF
- SUMIFS

- SUMPRODUCT
- VLOOKUP / HLOOKUP
- LOOKUP
- INDEX and MATCH
- CHOOSE

- OFFSET
- MOD
- EOMONTH and EDATE
- MAX and MIN

Yes, they're pretty straightforward: too often people show off using horror functions and formulae of length Tolstoy would have been proud. For me, financial modelling has one basic rule:

KEEP IT SIMPLE STUPID

That's it. A colleague of mine once talked about the **Rule of Thumb**: Excel formulae in your formula bar should be no longer than your thumb:

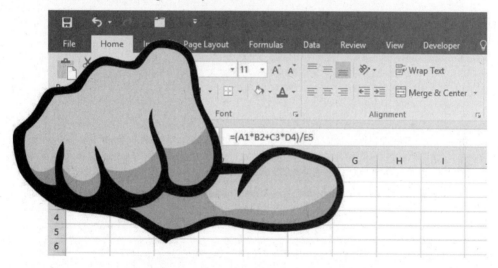

I love this idea. It means the modeller – *i.e.* you – is forced into stepping out the logic making it easier for others to follow and more difficult for you to stuff up. I used to run a large Financial Model Audit team and I trained my staff to always be on the look-out for overly-complex formulae: the chances are the logic would contain errors and it may be that the model user might be trying to hide something too. Try not to fall into that trap.

OK, so with no further ado, let's take a look at our function list in more detail.

CHAPTER 1.1: SUM

Is there really anyone out there that hasn't encountered the **SUM** function? Given this book is intended to be about financial modelling rather than an introduction to Excel functions, is there anything new for me to tell you about **SUM...**?

Well, let me try.

SUM adds things up. It may include cells, numbers or ranges. In the context of financial modelling, summations are usually of numbers either directly above or to the left of the cell in question:

G5			X	✓	f_x	=SUM(C5:F5)	

◢	A	B	C	D	E	F	G
1	**Summary**						
2							
3			Product A	Product B	Product C	Product D	
4	Business Unit 1		54	46	78	31	**209**
5	Business Unit 2		40	72	25	47	**184**
6	Business Unit 3		91	82	76	80	**329**
7	Business Unit 4		79	12	28	92	**211**
8			**264**	**212**	**207**	**250**	
9							
10							

There is a great keyboard shortcut available on most PC's (PC = *proper computer*). If you select the cell directly to the right or below the values to be aggregated and then use the shortcut **ALT + =** you will see that the range is summed automatically. If you find this doesn't work for you, make sure you keep the **ALT** button held down on your keyboard.

I use this all of the time in modelling. It's a fast shortcut, it ensures you don't miss cells within the range, it requires the range to be contiguous and you can't leave blank cells. This shortcut actually forces you to build in a manner that will reduce the number of errors you might make. This reinforces one of my on-going themes:

A lazy modeller is to be encouraged; lazy modelling isn't.

Let me be clear what I mean by a **"lazy modeller"**: this is someone who finds a way to keep formulae and constructs simple, so that their models are highly efficient and can be reproduced in seconds. It encourages flexibility, transparency and robustness – three key qualities of a "Best Practice" model (*more on that later*).

Lazy modelling may include typing in hard code, changing a formula on a cell by cell basis when it doesn't quite work and refusing to add error checks to ensure model integrity. Lazy modelling always comes back to bite you. It may take longer initially to develop your model, but it will pay off many times over as the model continues to be used.

Be careful with **SUM**. Consider the following example:

E9					f_x	=E3+E4+E5+E6+E7	
	A	B	C	D	E	F	G
1							
2					Values		
3					1		
4					2		
5					3		
6					4		
7					5		
8			Using SUM		15	=SUM(E3:E7)	
9			Using +		15	=E3+E4+E5+E6+E7	
10							

In this example, I have totalled the values in cells **E3:E7** in two distinct ways: the first uses the aforementioned **SUM** function with **ALT + =**, the other has added each cell individually using the '+' operator. Are you thinking you'd be mad to use the alternative (second) approach – especially if there were many more rows?

Well, take another look:

E9					f_x	=E3+E4+E5+E6+E7	
	A	B	C	D	E	F	G
1							
2					Values		
3					1		
4					2		
5					3		
6					4		
7					5		
8			Using SUM		12	=SUM(E3:E7)	
9			Using +		15	=E3+E4+E5+E6+E7	
10							

In this example, cell **E5** has been modified. It has been stored as text, even though it looks like the number 3. **SUM** treats this as having zero value whereas the more convoluted addition carries on regardless. Simplest may not always be bestest.

In an example like the one above, this may be easy to spot, but would you stake your life that the sum here:

B23				f_x	=SUM(B2:M21)							
	A	B	C	D	E	F	G	H	I	J	K	L	M
1													
2		49	88	67	21	29	93	77	82	71	24	46	5
3		20	81	56	36	86	26	74	57	11	52	18	28
4		37	9	63	7	11	83	82	12	95	90	81	91
5		60	14	99	29	81	73	55	42	64	84	25	58
6		33	45	38	49	56	99	76	31	89	77	86	8
7		60	65	22	19	42	42	33	41	93	91	57	21
8		57	94	79	43	68	65	83	37	63	75	67	70
9		52	30	45	57	23	13	26	67	77	2	17	83
10		54	78	78	76	45	34	47	30	63	37	78	59
11		52	90	59	80	76	38	4	97	52	17	39	48
12		41	21	92	77	68	4	96	37	97	23	52	47
13		28	78	15	79	17	67	3	52	77	77	13	77
14		17	34	6	7	95	42	44	70	79	60	34	62
15		71	63	39	94	58	54	57	75	44	30	29	41
16		38	50	9	43	58	45	20	99	31	13	88	20
17		100	30	83	6	47	87	52	97	37	71	39	4
18		90	26	1	21	93	10	87	18	49	51	90	63
19		43	45	12	55	19	59	87	63	9	13	97	40
20		21	98	47	88	85	17	55	20	92	77	44	90
21		21	57	91	97	59	16	43	49	76	21	12	100
22													
23		12,566											
24													

...is correct?

There is a simple way to check using the **COUNT** function. **COUNT** counts the number of numbers in a range, so we can use it to spot numbers that aren't actually numbers:

G5					f_x	=1-COUNT(E5)		

	A	B	C	D	E	F	G	H	I
1									
2					Values				
3					1		-		=1-COUNT(E3)
4					2		-		=1-COUNT(E4)
5					3		1		=1-COUNT(E5)
6					4		-		=1-COUNT(E6)
7					5		-		=1-COUNT(E7)
8			Using **SUM**		12				=SUM(E3:E7)
9			Using +		15				=E3+E4+E5+E6+E7
10									

Here, the formula in column I highlights when a number is not a number. Note how it reports by exception: if the cell in question contains a number then **COUNT(Cell_Reference)** equals 1 and **1-COUNT(Cell_Reference)** equals zero. Only non-numbers will be highlighted – it's better to know I have two errors rather than 14,367 values working correctly.

If you don't think this applies to you, have you ever worked with PivotTables? This book isn't about PivotTables, but as an aside, for those of you who have ever worked with this Excel feature, have you ever been frustrated when the following has happened?

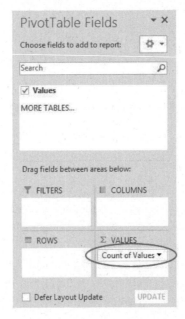

You want your aggregation of values to default to **SUM** but instead they display as **COUNT**. This could be highlighting that some of your data is non-numerical and / or blank. Just a thought.

CHAPTER 1.2: IF

So what's the most Important Function in Excel? Any takers for **IF**? The syntax for **IF** demonstrates just how useful this function is for financial modelling:

> **=IF(Logical_test,[Value_if_TRUE],[Value_if_FALSE])**

This function has three arguments:

- **Logical_test:** this is the "decider", i.e. a test that results in a value of either TRUE or FALSE. Strictly speaking, the **Logical_test** tests whether something is TRUE; if not, it is FALSE.

- **Value_if_TRUE:** what to do if the **Logical_test** is TRUE. Note that you do not put square brackets around this argument! This is just the Excel syntax for saying that this argument is optional. If this argument is indeed omitted, this argument will have a default value of TRUE.

- **Value_if_FALSE:** what to do if the **Logical_test** is FALSE (strictly speaking, not TRUE). If this argument is left blank, this argument will have a default value of FALSE.

This function is actually more efficient than it may look at first glance. Whilst the **Logical_test** is always evaluated, only one of the remaining two arguments is computed, depending upon whether the **Logical_test** is TRUE or FALSE. For example:

f_x	=IF(Denominator=0,,Numerator/Denominator)				
D	E	F	G	H	I
	Numerator	3			
	Denominator	-			
	Decimal	-			

In this example, the intention is to evaluate the quotient **Numerator / Denominator**. However, if the Denominator is either blank or zero, this will result in an #DIV/0! error. Excel has several errors that it cannot evaluate, *e.g.* #REF!, #NULL, #N/A, #Brown, #Pipe. OK, so one or two of these I may have made up, but **prima facie** errors should be avoided in Excel as they detract from the key results and cause the user to doubt the overall model integrity. Worse, in some instances these errors may contribute to Excel crashing and / or corrupting. Note to self: prevent these errors from occurring.

This is where **IF** comes in. In my example above, **=IF(Denominator=0,,Numerator/Denominator)** tests whether the **Denominator** is zero, If so, the value is unspecified (blank) and will consequently return a value of zero in Excel. Otherwise, the quotient is calculated as intended.

This is known as creating an **error trap**. Errors are "trapped" and the 'harmless' value of zero is returned instead. You could put "n.a" or "This is an error" as the **Value_if_TRUE**, but you get the picture.

It is my preference not to put a zero in for the **Value_if_TRUE**: personally, I think a formula looks clearer this way, but inexperienced end users may not understand the formula and you should consider your audience when deciding to put what may appear to be an unnecessary zero in a formula. The aim is to keep it simple **for the end user**.

An **IF** statement is often used to make a decision in the model, *i.e.*

> =IF(Decision_Criterion=TRUE,Do_it,Don't_Do_It)

This automates a model and aids management in decision making and what-if analysis. **IF** is clearly a very powerful tool when used correctly. However, sometimes it is used when another function might be preferable. For example, if you find yourself writing a formula that begins with:

> =IF(IF(IF(IF...

then I humbly suggest you are using the wrong function. **IF** should never be used to look up data: there are plenty of functions out there to help with that problem, but we will come to that in time. However, sometimes your **Logical_test** might consist of multiple criteria, *e.g.*

> =IF(Condition1=TRUE,IF(Condition2=TRUE,IF(Condition3=TRUE,1,),),)

Here, this formula only gives a value of 1 if all three conditions are true. This nested **IF** statement may be avoided using the logical function **AND(Condition1,Condition2,...)** which is only TRUE if and only if all dependent arguments are TRUE, *i.e.*

> =IF(AND(Condition1,Condition2,Condition3),1,)

This is actually easier to read. There are two other useful logic functions sometimes used with **IF**:

- **OR(Condition1,Condition2,...)** is TRUE when at least one of the arguments is TRUE

- **NOT(Condition)** gives the opposite logic value, so that if the **Condition** is TRUE the result will be FALSE and vice versa.

Even using these logic functions, formulae may look complex quite quickly. There is an alternative: **flags**. In its most common form, flags are evaluated as

> =(Condition=TRUE)*1

Condition=TRUE will give rise to a value of either TRUE or FALSE; the brackets will ensure this is evaluated first; multiplying by 1 will provide an end result of zero (if FALSE, as FALSE*1 = 0) or one (if TRUE, TRUE*1 = 1). I know some modellers prefer TRUEs and FALSEs everywhere, but I think 1's and 0's are easier to read (when there are lots of them) and more importantly, easier to sum when you need to know how many issues there are, *etc.*

Flags make it easier to follow the tested conditions. Consider the following:

D9						f_x	=PRODUCT(D4:D7)								
	A	B	C	D	E	F	G	H	I	J	K	L	M	N	O
1															
2	Counter			1	2	3	4	5	6	7	8	9	10		
3															
4	Divisible by 3			-	-	1	-	-	1	-	-	1	-	=(MOD(Counter,3)=0)*1
5	Greater than 4			-	-	-	-	1	1	1	1	1	1	=(Counter>4)*1
6	Less than or equal to 9			1	1	1	1	1	1	1	1	1	-	=(Counter<=9)*1
7	Is not 6			1	1	1	1	1	-	1	1	1	1	=(Counter<>6)*1
8															
9	Product			-	-	-	-	-	-	-	-	1	-	=PRODUCT(D4:D7)
10															

In this illustration, you might not yet understand what the **MOD** function does (more on that later), but hopefully, you can follow each of the flags in rows 4 to 7 without being an Excel guru. Row 9, the product, simply multiplies all of the flags together. This produces an **AND** flag. If I wanted the flag to be a 1 as long as one of the above conditions is TRUE (similar to **OR**), that is easy too:

D9						f_x	=MAX(D4:D7)								
	A	B	C	D	E	F	G	H	I	J	K	L	M	N	O
1															
2	Counter			1	2	3	4	5	6	7	8	9	10		
3															
4	Divisible by 3			-	-	1	-	-	1	-	-	1	-	=(MOD(Counter,3)=0)*1
5	Greater than 4			-	-	-	-	1	1	1	1	1	1	=(Counter>4)*1
6	Less than or equal to 9			1	1	1	1	1	1	1	1	1	-	=(Counter<=9)*1
7	Is not 6			1	1	1	1	1	-	1	1	1	1	=(Counter<>6)*1
8															
9	MAX			1	1	1	1	1	1	1	1	1	1	=MAX(D4:D7)
10															

Flags frequently make models more transparent and this example provides a great learning point. Often we mistakenly believe that condensing a model into fewer cells makes it more efficient and easier follow. On the contrary, it is usually better to step out a calculation. If it can be followed on a piece of paper (without access to the formula bar), then more people will follow it. If more can follow the model logic, errors will be more easily spotted. When this occurs, a model becomes trusted and therefore is of more value in decision-making.

I'd like to finish on a word of caution. Sometimes you just <u>can't</u> use flags. Let me go back to my first example in this section – but this time using the flag approach:

f_x	=(Numerator/Denominator)*(Denominator<>0)				
D	E	F	G	H	I
	Numerator	3			
	Denominator	-			
	Decimal	#DIV/0!			

Here, the flag does not trap the division by zero error. This is because this formula evaluates to

$$=\#DIV/0! \times 0$$

which equals *#DIV/0!* If you need to trap an error, you <u>must</u> use an **IF** function.

CHAPTER 1.3: IFERROR

IFERROR first came into being back in Excel 2007. It was something users had asked Microsoft for, for a very long time. But let me go back in time first and explain why.

At the time of writing, there are 12 **IS** functions, i.e. functions that give rise to a TRUE or FALSE value depending upon whether a certain condition is met:

1. **ISBLANK(Reference):** checks whether the **Reference** is to an empty cell

2. **ISERR(Value):** checks whether the **Value** is an error (*e.g. #REF!, #DIV/0!, #NULL!*). This check specifically excludes #N/A

3. **ISERROR(Value):** checks whether the **Value** is an error (*e.g. #REF!, #DIV/0!, #NULL!*). This is probably the most commonly used of these functions in financial modelling

4. **ISEVEN(Number):** checks to see if the **Number** is even

5. **ISFORMULA(Reference):** checks to see whether the **Reference** is to a cell containing a formula

6. **ISLOGICAL(Value):** checks to see whether the **Value** is a logical (TRUE or FALSE) value

7. **ISNA(Value):** checks to see whether the **Value** is #N/A. This gives us the rather crude identity **ISERR + ISNA = ISERROR**

8. **ISNONTEXT(Value):** checks whether the **Value** is not text (N.B. blank cells are not text)

9. **ISNUMBER(Value):** checks whether the **Value** is a number

10. **ISODD(Number):** checks to see if the **Number** is odd. Personally, I find the number 46 very odd, but Excel doesn't

11. **ISREF(Value):** checks whether the **Value** is a reference

12. **ISTEXT(Value):** checks whether the **Value** is text.

You get the idea. As mentioned previously, sometimes you need to trap errors that may originate from a formula that is correct most of the time. Where possible, you should be specific with regard to what you are checking, *e.g.*

> **=IF(Denominator=0,Error_Trap,Numerator/Denominator)**

In this example, I am checking to see whether the **Denominator** is zero. I could use this formula instead:

=IF(ISERROR(Numerator/Denominator),Error_Trap,Numerator/Denominator)

The difference here is that this will check for anything that may give rise to an error:

f_x	=IF(ISERROR(Numerator/Denominator),"Kebab",Numerator/Denominator)						
D	E	F	G	H	I	J	K
	Numerator	Dog					
	Denominator	4					
	Decimal	Kebab					

Do you see the problem here? I have to put the same formula in *twice*. If that is a long formula, then the calculation becomes doubly long. This is where **IFERROR** comes in; it halves the length of the calculation but still achieves the same effect:

=IFERROR(Calculation,Error_Trap)

Essentially, this formula is the bastard lovechild of **IF** and **ISERROR**. It checks to see whether the **Calculation** will give rise to a *prima facie* error. If it does, it will return **Error_Trap**; otherwise, it will perform the said **Calculation**, *e.g.*

f_x	=IFERROR(Numerator/Denominator,"Kebab")				
D	E	F	G	H	I
	Numerator	Dog			
	Denominator	4			
	Decimal	Kebab			

You shouldn't just sprinkle **IFERROR** throughout your models like your formulae are confetti. Used unwisely, **IFERROR** can disguise the fact that your formula isn't working correctly and that modifications to the logic may be required. Try to use it sparingly.

Sometimes you have to use **IF** and **ISERROR** in combination anyway:

=IF(ISERROR(Calculation),Error_Trap,Different_Calculation)

In this example, the formula is checking to see whether a particular **Calculation** gives rise to an error. If it does, the **Error_Trap** will be referenced in the usual way, but if not a **Different_ Calculation** (not the **Calculation** used for the test) will be computed.

These two methodologies should be mastered. You will create more robust and flexible models once your error become a thing of the past. Not just the model – but your own expertise – will become more trusted in your organisation if users never encounter *prima facie* errors in your model.

CHAPTER 1.4: SUMIF

If you are unfamiliar with this function, you can still probably guess what **SUMIF** does: it combines **SUM** with **IF** to provide conditional summing, *i.e.* where you wish to add numerical values provided they meet a certain criterion. For example, imagine you were reviewing the following data summary:

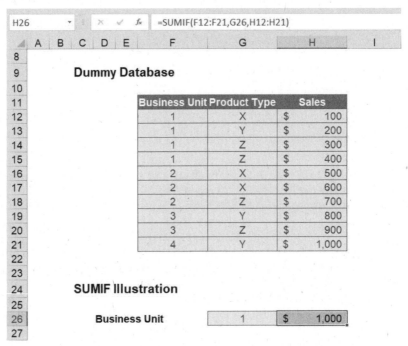

The function **SUMIF(Range,Criterion,Sum_range)** is ideal for summing data based on one requirement:

- **Range** is the array that you wanted evaluated by the criterion (in this instance, cells **F12:F21**)

- **Criterion** is the criterion in the form of a number, expression, or text that defines which cell(s) will be added, *e.g.* "X", 1, **G26** or **"<>"&G27** (this last one means "not equal to the value in cell **G27**")

- **Sum_range** are the actual cells to be added if their corresponding cells in **Range** match the Criterion.

So, to find the sales for Business Unit 1 in the above example, you can use the formula **=SUMIF(F12:F21,1,H12:H21)** (which is $1,000), or to find the total sales of Product X, the formula could be modified to **=SUMIF(G12:G21,"X",H12:H21)** (which is $1,200). Note that any text must be in inverted commas.

SUMIF is fine when there is only one condition. However, how would you find the total sales of Product Z in Business Unit 1 using this function? That's two criteria and **SUMIF** does not work with multiple conditions. There are various alternatives using other functions, but it is possible to solve this problem simply using **SUMIF**.

It is often possible to cheat with SUMIF by making a 'mega-criterion' out of multiple criteria. This works on joining criteria together usually by using the ampersand (**'&'**) operator.

Let's consider our example, slightly revised, from above.

| G29 | | ▾ | : | × | ✓ | fx | =SUMIF(H12:H21,G26&G27,I12:I21) |

◢	A	B	C	D	E	F	G	H	I	J
8										
9		**Dummy Database**								
10										
11						Business Unit	Product Type	Mega-Criterion'	Sales	
12						1	X	1X	$ 100	
13						1	Y	1Y	$ 200	
14						1	Z	1Z	$ 300	
15						1	Z	1Z	$ 400	
16						2	X	2X	$ 500	
17						2	X	2X	$ 600	
18						2	Z	2Z	$ 700	
19						3	Y	3Y	$ 800	
20						3	Z	3Z	$ 900	
21						4	Y	4Y	$ 1,000	
22										
23										
24		**SUMIF Illustration**								
25										
26			Business Unit				1			
27			Product Type				Z			
28										
29			Solution				$700			
30										

A new column has been inserted (column **H**), with a formula combining the contents of columns **F** and **G** (*e.g.* the formula in cell **H12** is =F12&G12). Provided that all possible combinations are unique (*i.e.* no duplicates can be generated), a simple **SUMIF** can then be applied, *e.g.*

=SUMIF(H12:H21,"1Z",I12:I21).

This is by far and away the simplest solution – *if it works*. It can fall down though (in another example, the concatenation "111" might refer to Product 1 in Business Unit 11 or Product 11 in Business Unit 1).

As I say, there are other ways to solve this issue...

CHAPTER 1.5: SUMIFS

SUMIFS is similar to the **SUMIF** function. The syntax might not look similar when you first inspect it:

> =SUMIFS(Sum_range,Criterion_range1,Criterion1,...)

If you think about it, the syntax is consistent with **SUMIF**. This function allows various ranges **(Criterion_range1, Criterion_range2, ...)** to be assessed against multiple criteria **(Criterion1, Criterion2, ...).** The key difference is that the range to be conditionally summed, **Sum_range**, is the first argument of the function rather than the last. This is so there is never any confusion regarding what is to be totalled.

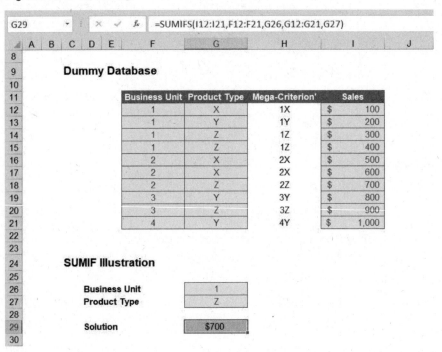

Unlike the solution proffered in the **SUMIF** section, the helper column (column **H**) is no longer required. In some ways, this makes the function more straightforward, but it should remember that this function only arrived with the advent of Excel 2007 and therefore will not work with earlier versions of Excel.

There is another problem too – and this affects **SUMIF** as well. In fact, it's an issue that harks back to our original discussion with the **SUM** function. **SUM, SUMIF** and **SUMIFS** have an Achilles' Heel: numbers that look like numbers but are considered text (a common problem with data imported from management information systems) are treated as zero. This can lead to "right formula wrong result":

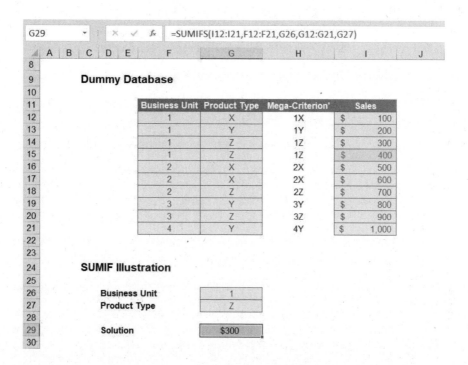

There is only difference between this example and the previous one: cell **I15** has now been entered as text. Therefore, the $400 is not recognised as a value and the summation has been reduced by this amount accordingly.

Care needs to be taken with these functions if conditional summations are to be relied upon in a financial model (the same may be said for PivotTables too).

But there's a more robust alternative...

CHAPTER 1.6: SUMPRODUCT

I must admit this is one of my favourite functions in Excel – so much so our company was named after it (time for a shameless plug)!

At first glance,

SUMPRODUCT(Vector1,Vector2,...)

appears quite humble. Before showing an example, though, let's look at the syntax carefully:

- A **vector** for Excel purposes is a collection of cells either one column wide or one row deep. For example, **A1:A5** is a column vector, **A1:E1** is a row vector, cell **A1** is a unit vector and the range **A1:E5** is not a vector (it is actually an array, but more on that later). The ranges must be contiguous; *and*

- This basis functionality uses the comma delimiter (,) to separate the arguments (vectors). Unlike most Excel functions, it is possible to use other delimiters, but this will be revisited shortly below.

So before I continue, I think it's time to have a moan and reminisce about how I have been ripped off in the past. Just a couple of years ago, back when I was 18 (*the Editor does not believe a word of this*), I supported my studies by working at a petrol station. The hours were long (12 hours per day) and my boss would not buy an electronic till (yes, electricity had been invented back then), so all sales were recorded manually. Consequently, all sales had to be kept in a tally chart, *i.e.* the pricing points were listed in the first column and the sales were then noted in the second column. At the end of the day, I would have to calculate the total revenue and reconcile it with the payments received:

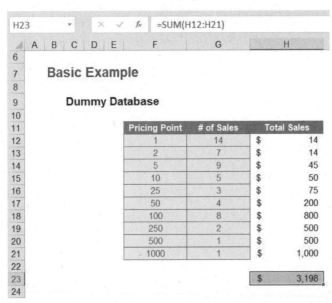

The sales in column H are simply the product of columns F and G, *e.g.* the formula in cell **H12** is simply **=F12*G12**. Then, to calculate the entire amount cell **H23** sums column **H**.

This could all be performed much quicker using the following formula:

=SUMPRODUCT(F12:F21,G12:G21)

i.e. **SUMPRODUCT** does exactly what it says on the tin: it <u>sums</u> the individual <u>products</u>.

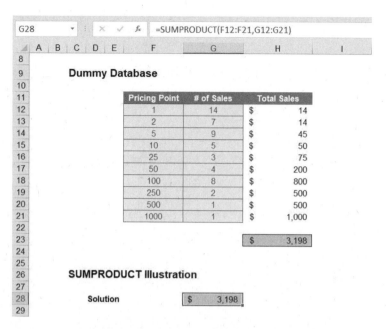

I mentioned the comma delimiter earlier. You can multiply the vectors together instead.

=SUMPRODUCT(F12:F21*G12:G21)

will produce the same result. However, there is an important difference. If you think back to our earlier example:

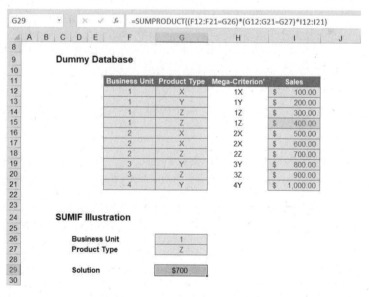

SUMPRODUCT will work with numbers that aren't really numbers. However, if you look at the formula in the example, you can be forgiven for not understanding the formula. Let me explain.

Where **SUMPRODUCT** comes into its own is when dealing with multiple criteria. This is done by considering the properties of TRUE and FALSE in Excel, namely:

- TRUE*number = number (*e.g.* TRUE*7 = 7); and

- FALSE*number = 0 (*e.g.* FALSE*7=0).

Consider the following example:

	E	F	G	H	I
10					
11		Business Unit	Product Type	Sales	
12		1	X	$ 100	
13		1	Y	$ 200	
14		1	Z	$ 300	
15		1	Z	$ 400	
16		2	X	$ 500	
17		2	X	$ 600	
18		2	Z	$ 700	
19		3	Y	$ 800	
20		3	Z	$ 900	
21		4	Y	$ 1,000	
22					

we can test columns **F** and **G** to check whether they equal our required values. **SUMPRODUCT** could be used as follows to sum only sales made by Business Unit 1 for Product Z, *viz.*

=SUMPRODUCT((F12:F21=1)*(G12:G21="Z")*H12:H21).

For the purposes of this calculation, **(F12:F21=1)** replaces the contents of cells **F12:F21** with either TRUE or FALSE depending on whether the value contained in each cell equals 1 or not. The brackets are required to force Excel to compute this first before cross-multiplying.

Similarly, **(G12:G21="Z")** replaces the contents of cells **G12:G21** with either TRUE or FALSE depending on whether the value "Z" is contained in each cell.

Therefore, the only time cells **H12:H21** will be summed is when the corresponding cell in the arrays **F12:F21** and **G12:G21** are both TRUE, then you will get TRUE*TRUE*number, which equals the said number.

Note also that this uses the * delimiter rather than the comma, analogous to TRUE*number, *etc.* If you were to use the comma delimiter instead, the syntax would have to be modified thus:

=SUMPRODUCT(--(F12:F21=1),--(G12:G21="Z"),H12:H21)

Minus minus? The first negation in front of the brackets converts the array of TRUEs and FALSEs to numbers, albeit substituting -1 for TRUE and 0 for FALSE. The second minus sign negates these numbers so that TRUE is effectively 1, rather than -1, whilst FALSE remains equals to zero. This variant often confuses end users which is why I recommend the first version described above.

You can get more sophisticated:

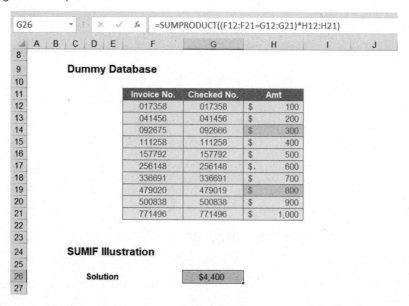

In this scenario, the end user pays invoices only where the invoice number matches the number "checked" on an authorised list. In the illustration above, two invoices (highlighted in red) do not match. **SUMPRODUCT** can be used to sum the authorised amounts only as follows:

=SUMPRODUCT((F12:F21=G12:G21)*H12:H21)

The argument in brackets only gives a value of TRUE for each row when the values in columns **F** and **G** are identical.

SUMPRODUCT and **SUMIFS** truly part company in the following comprehensive example. Consider the following:

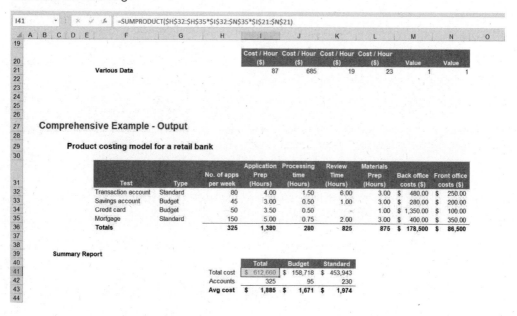

So far, I have only considered **SUMPRODUCT** with vector ranges. Using the multiplication delimiter (*), it is possible to use **SUMPRODUCT** with arrays (an array is a range of cells consisting of both more than one row and more than one column).

In the above example, **SUMPRODUCT** has been used in its elementary form in cells I36:N36. For example, the formula in cell I36 is:

=SUMPRODUCT($H$32:$H$35,I$32:I$35)

and this has then been copied across to the rest of the cells.

To calculate the total costs of this retail bank example, this could be calculated as:

=SUMPRODUCT($I$36:$N$36,$I$21:$N$21)

However, the formula in cell **I41** appears more – and unnecessarily – complicated:

=SUMPRODUCT($H$32:$H$35*$I$32:$N$35*$I$21:$N$21)

The use of the multiplication delimiter is deliberate (the formula will not work if the delimiters were to become commas instead). It should be noted that this last formula is essentially

=SUMPRODUCT(Column_Vector*Array*Row_Vector)

where the number of rows in the **Column_Vector** must equal the number of rows in the **Array**, and also the number of columns in the **Array** must equal the number of columns in the **Row_Vector.**

The reason for this extended version of the formula is in order to divide the costs between Budget and Standard costs in my example. For example, the formula in cell **J41** becomes:

=SUMPRODUCT($H$32:$H$35*$I$32:$N$35*$I$21:$N$21*($G$32:$G$35=J$40))

i.e. the formula is now of the form

=SUMPRODUCT(Column_Vector*Array*Row_Vector*Condition)

where **Condition** uses similar logic to the TRUE / FALSE examples detailed earlier. This is a powerful concept that can be used to replace PivotTables for instance.

There are valid / more efficient alternatives to **SUMPRODUCT** in some instances. For example, dealing with multiple criteria for vector ranges, the **SUMIFS** function is up to six times faster, but will only work with Excel 2007 and later versions. Further, it cannot work with arrays where the dimensions differ such as in the example above.

Over-use of **SUMPRODUCT** can slow the calculation time down of even the smallest of Excel files, but it is a good all-rounder. Used sparingly it can be a highly versatile addition to the modeller's repertoire. It is a sophisticated function, but once you understand how it works, you can start to use **SUMPRODUCT** for a whole array of problems (pun intended!).

CHAPTER 1.7: VLOOKUP / HLOOKUP

Often you will need to look up data in a table – and two functions most modellers are very familiar with are **VLOOKUP** and **HLOOKUP**. But do you realise it's very easy to make a mistake with these functions? For those unsure of these functions, let me first start with a refresher.

> ## VLOOKUP(Lookup_value,Table_array,Col_index_num,[Range_lookup])

has the following syntax:

- **Lookup_value:** What value do you want to look up?

- **Table_array:** Where is the lookup table?

- **Col_index_num:** Which column has the value you want returned?

- **[Range_lookup]:** Do you want an exact or an approximate match? This is optional and to begin with, I am going to ignore this argument exists.

HLOOKUP is similar, but works on a row rather than a column basis (**h**orizontal rather than **v**ertical).

I am going to use **VLOOKUP** throughout to keep things simple. **VLOOKUP** always looks for the **Lookup_value** in the first column of a table (the **Table_array**) and then returns a corresponding value so many columns to the right, determined by the **Col_index_num** column index number.

In this above example, the formula in cell **G25** seeks the value 2 in the first column of the table **F13:M18** and returns the corresponding value from the eighth column of the table (returning 47). Pretty easy to understand – so far so good. So what goes wrong? Well, what happens if you add or remove a column from the table range?

Adding gives us the wrong value:

With a column inserted, the formula contains hard code (8) and therefore, the eighth column (**M**) is still referenced, giving rise to the wrong value.

Deleting a column instead is even worse:

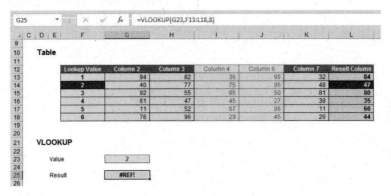

Now there are only seven columns so the formula returns *#REF!* Oops.

It is possible to make the column index number dynamic using the **COLUMNS** function:

COLUMNS(Reference) counts the number of columns in the **Reference**. Using the range **F13:M13**, this formula will now keep track of how many columns there are between the lookup column (**F**) and the result column (**M**). This will prevent the problems illustrated above.

But there's more issues. Consider duplicate values in the lookup column. With one duplicate, the following happens:

Here, the second value is returned, which might not be what is wanted.

With two duplicates:

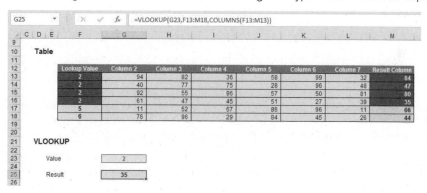

Ah, it looks like it might take the last occurrence. Testing this hypothesis with three duplicates:

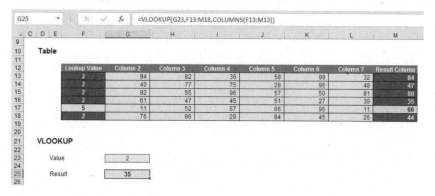

Yes, there seems to be a pattern: **VLOOKUP** takes the last occurrence. I had better make sure:

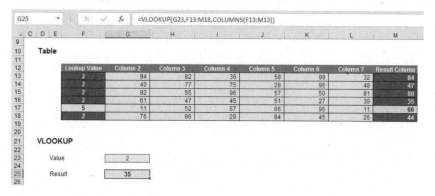

Rats. In this example, the value returned is the fourth of five. The problem is, there's no consistent logic and the formula and its result cannot be relied upon.

It gets worse if we exclude duplicates but mix up the lookup column a little:

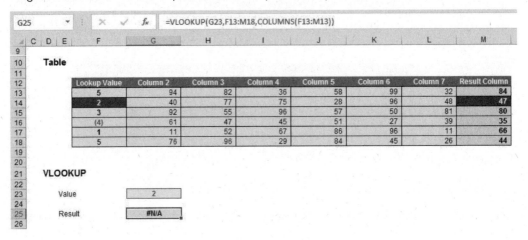

In this instance, **VLOOKUP** cannot even find the value 2!

So what's going on? The problem – and common modelling mistake – is that the fourth argument has been ignored:

> **VLOOKUP(Lookup_value,Table_array,Col_index_num,[Range_lookup])**

[Range_lookup] appears in square brackets, which means it is optional. It has two values:

- **TRUE:** this is the <u>default</u> setting if the argument is not specified. Here, **VLOOKUP** will seek an approximate match, looking for the largest value less than or equal to the value sought. There is a price to be paid though: the values in the first column (or row for **HLOOKUP**) must be in <u>strict ascending</u> order – this means that each value must be larger than the value before, so no duplicates.

  This is useful when looking up postage rates for example where prices are given in categories of kilograms and you have 2.7kg to post (say). It's worth noting though that this isn't the most common lookup when modelling.

- **FALSE:** this has to be specified. In this case, data can be any which way – including duplicates – and the result will be based upon the <u>first</u> occurrence of the value sought. If an exact match cannot be found, **VLOOKUP** will return the value #N/A.

And this is the problem highlighted by the above examples. The final argument was never specified so the lookup column data <u>has to</u> be in strict ascending order – and this premise was continually breached.

The robust formula needs both **COLUMNS** and a fourth argument of **FALSE** to work as expected:

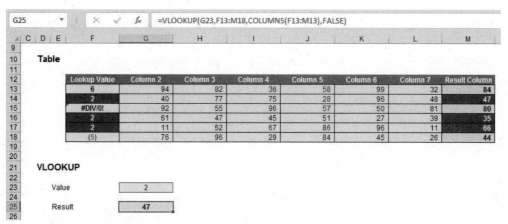

This is a very common mistake in modelling. Using a fourth argument of **FALSE, VLOOKUP** will return the corresponding result for the first occurrence of the **Lookup_value**, regardless of number of duplicates, errors or series order. If an approximate match is required, the data must be in strict ascending order.

VLOOKUP (and consequently **HLOOKUP**) are not the simple, easy to use functions modellers think they are. In fact, they can never be used to return data for columns to the left (**VLOOKUP**) or rows above (**HLOOKUP**). So what should modellers use instead..?

CHAPTER 1.8: LOOKUP

Now that I have taken **VLOOKUP** and **HLOOKUP** to task, some of you may have considered **LOOKUP** is conspicuous by its absence. It may seem a less versatile function upon first glance, but it is quite useful for modelling. Allow me to explain.

LOOKUP has two forms: an <u>array</u> form and a <u>vector</u> form. As a reminder:

- An **array** is a collection of cells consisting of at least two rows and at least two columns

- A **vector** is a collection of cells across just one row (row vector) or down just one column (column vector).

The diagram should be self-explanatory:

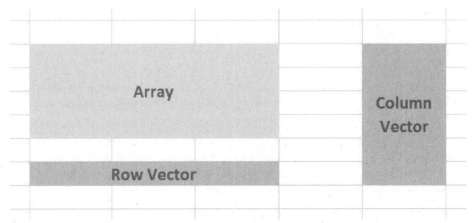

The array form of **LOOKUP** looks in the first row or column of an array for the specified value and returns a value from the same position in the last row or column of the same array:

LOOKUP(Lookup_value,Array)

where:

- **Lookup_value** is the value that **LOOKUP** searches for in an array. The **Lookup_value** argument can be a number, text, a logical value, or a name or reference that refers to a value

- **Array** is the range of cells that contains text, numbers, or logical values that you want to compare with **Lookup_value**.

The array form of **LOOKUP** is very similar to the **HLOOKUP** and **VLOOKUP** functions. The difference is that **HLOOKUP** searches for the value of **Lookup_value** in the first row, **VLOOKUP** searches in the first column, and **LOOKUP** searches according to the dimensions of array.

If **Array** covers an area that is wider than it is tall (*i.e.* it has more columns than rows), **LOOKUP** searches for the value of **Lookup_value** in the first row and returns the result from the last row. Otherwise, **LOOKUP** searches for the value of **Lookup_value** in the first column and returns the result from the last column instead.

The alternative form is the vector form:

LOOKUP(Lookup_value,lookup_vector,[result_vector])

The **LOOKUP** function vector form syntax has the following arguments:

* **Lookup_value** is the value that **LOOKUP** searches for in the first vector

* **Lookup_vector** is the range that contains only one row or one column

* **[Result_vector]** is optional – if ignored, **Lookup_vector** is used – this is the where the result will come from and must contain the same number of cells as the **Lookup_vector**.

Like the default versions of **HLOOKUP** and **VLOOKUP**, **Lookup_value** must be located in a range of strictly ascending values, *i.e.* where each value is larger than the one before and there are no duplicates.

So why do I advocate for **LOOKUP** when I said don't use the other functions just recently? Well, it's because it is simpler to use, doesn't rely on row or index column numbers and allows modellers to create inputs that do not need to be specified for all periods modelled. Let me demonstrate with the following example:

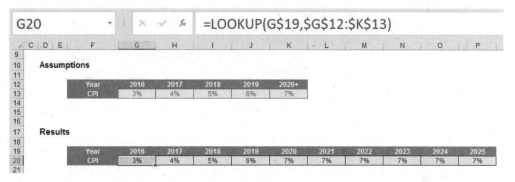

Imagine you have an annual model forecasting for many years into the future. Creating inputs will be time consuming if data has to be entered on a period by period basis. But there is a shortcut.

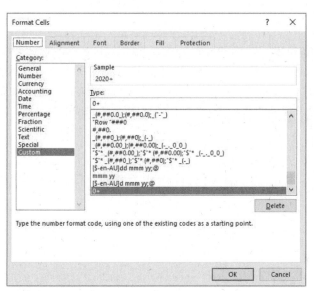

Do you see the data table in cells **F12:K13** above? The value in the final cell of the first row is actually "2020" not "2020+". It appears that way due to custom number formatting (**CTRL + 1**):

The syntax "0+" adds a plus sign to the number although Excel still reads the value as 2020. Number formatting is discussed in more detail later on.

The formula uses the array version of **LOOKUP**, looking up the year in the first row of the data table and returning the corresponding value from the final row. When a year is selected which is greater than 2020, the 2020 value is used as **LOOKUP** seeks out the largest value less than or equal to the value sought. Therefore, we don't need to have lengthy data tables – once we assume inputs will be constant thereafter, we can just curtail the input section.

Using the array form of **LOOKUP** is dangerous though. What if someone accidentally inserts rows? The lookup will "flip" to look the first and last columns instead, which is not what is required. Using the vector form is safer:

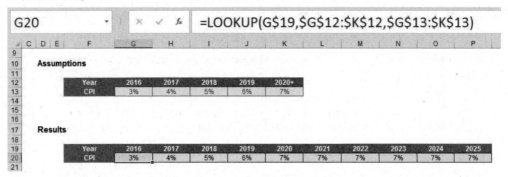

Whilst the formula contains one more argument, the formula is more stable. Further, the **Lookup_vector** and the **Result_vector** do not need to be in the same worksheet or even the same workbook. In fact, as long as there are the same number of elements in each, one can be a row vector and the other a column vector.

LOOKUP is very useful when the **Lookup_vector** contains data in strict ascending order. Where do we find this? Dates in time series – **LOOKUP** is very useful for financial modelling / forecasting. Just be careful though; consider the following scenario:

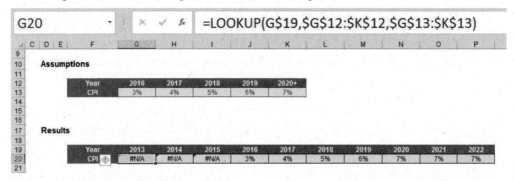

Here, the same formula generates an #N/A error. This is because the date is smaller than the smallest value in the data range. **LOOKUP** is not quite clever enough to use the first value unprompted, but a simple tweak of the formula will suffice:

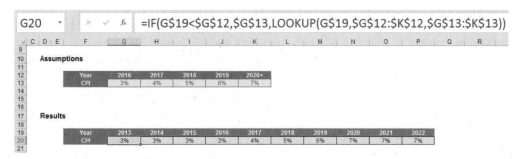

Here, the formula has been modified to:

=IF(G$19<$G$12,$G$13,LOOKUP(G$19,$G$12:$K$12,$G$13:$K$13))

The added **IF** statement checks to see if the year is smaller than the first year in the data table and if so, returns the first result. Simple. It is with this final modification – in its vector form – that I usually use **LOOKUP** to return values for certain time periods where I do not want to have an input for each period modelled. Very useful!

CHAPTER 1.9: INDEX AND MATCH

INDEX and **MATCH** – as a combination – are two of the most useful functions at a modeller's disposal. They provide a versatile lookup in a way that **LOOKUP**, **HLOOKUP** and **VLOOKUP** simply cannot. The best way to illustrate this point is by means of an example.

Here is a common problem. Imagine you have built a financial model and your Balance Sheet – ahem! – contains misbalances. You need to fix it. Now I am sure you have never had this mistake yourself, but you have "close friends" that have encountered this feast of fun: solving Balance Sheet errors can take a *long* while. One of the first things modellers will do is locate the first period (in ascending order) that has such an error, as identifying the issue in this period may often solve the problem for all periods. Consider the following example:

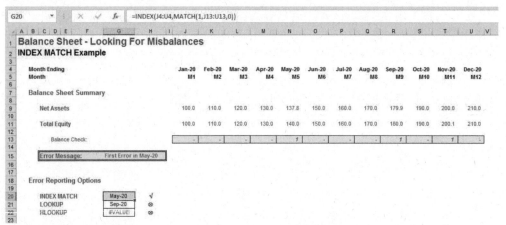

This is a common modelling query. The usual suspects, **LOOKUP** and **HLOOKUP** / **VLOOKUP** do not work here:

- **LOOKUP(Lookup_value,Lookup_vector,[Result_vector])** gives the wrong date as the balance checks are not in <u>strict</u> ascending order (*i.e.* ascending alphanumerically with no duplicates); *whilst*

- **HLOOKUP(Lookup_value,Table_array,Row_index_num,[Range_lookup])** gives *#VALUE!* since the first row must contain the data to be 'looked up', but the Balance Check is in row 13 in our example above, whereas the dates we need to return are in row 4 – hence we get a syntax error.

There is a solution, however: **INDEX MATCH**. They form a highly versatile tag team, but are worth introducing individually.

Index

Essentially, **INDEX(Array,Row_num,[Column_num])** returns a value or the reference to a value from within a table or range (list). For example, **INDEX({7,8,9,10,11,12},3)** returns the third item in the list {7,8,9,10,11,12}, *i.e.* 9. This could have been a range: **INDEX(A1:A10,5)** gives the value in cell **A5**, *etc*.

INDEX can work in two dimensions as well (hence the **Column_num** reference). Consider the following example:

		1	2	3	4	5	6	7
		F	G	H	I	J	K	L
1	11	1	2	3	4	5	6	7
2	12	8	9	10	11	12	13	14
3	13	15	16	17	18	19	20	21
4	14	22	23	24	25	26	27	28
5	15	29	30	31	32	33	34	35
6	16	36	37	38	39	40	41	42
7	17	43	44	45	46	47	48	49
8	18	50	51	52	53	54	55	56
9	19	57	58	59	60	61	62	63
10	20	64	65	66	67	68	69	70
11	21	71	72	73	74	75	76	77

INDEX(F11:L21,4,5) returns the value in the fourth row, fifth column of the table array **F11:L21** (clearly 26 in the above illustration).

Match

MATCH(Lookup_value,Lookup_vector,[Match_type]) returns the relative position of an item in an array that (approximately) matches a specified value. It is <u>not</u> case sensitive.

The third argument, **Match_type**, does not have to be entered, but for many situations, I strongly recommend that it is specified. It allows one of three values:

- **Match_type 1 [default if omitted]:** finds the largest value less than or equal to the **Lookup_value** – but the **Lookup_vector** must be in strict ascending order, limiting flexibility;

- **Match_type 0:** probably the most useful setting, **MATCH** will find the position of the first value that matches **Lookup_value** exactly. The **Lookup_array** can have data in any order and even allows duplicates; and

- **Match type -1:** finds the smallest value greater than or equal to the **Lookup_value** – but the **Lookup_array** must be in strict descending order, again limiting flexibility.

When using **MATCH**, if there is no (approximate) match, *#N/A* is returned (this may also occur if data is not correctly sorted depending upon **Match_type**).

MATCH is fairly straightforward to use:

	E	F
12	1	a
13	2	b
14	3	a
15	4	c
16	5	b
17	6	d
18	7	d
19	8	e
20	9	f
21	10	a
22	11	c

In the figure to the left, **MATCH("d",F12:F22,0)** gives a value of 6, being the relative position of the first 'd' in the range. Note that having **Match_ type** 0 here is important. The data contains duplicates and is not sorted alphanumerically. Consequently, using **Match_type** 1 and -1 would give the wrong answer: 7 and *#N/A* respectively.

Index Match

Whilst useful functions in their own right, combined they form a highly versatile partnership. Consider the original problem:

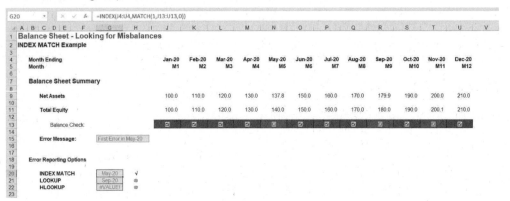

MATCH(1,J13:O13,0) equals 5, *i.e.* the first period the balance sheet does not balance in is Period 5. But we can do better than that. **INDEX(J4:O4,5)** equals May-20, so combining the two functions:

INDEX(J4:O4,MATCH(1,J13:O13,0))

equals May-20 in one step. This process of stepping out two calculations and then inserting one into another is often referred to as "staggered development". No, this is not how you construct a financial model late in the evening after having the odd drink or two!

Do note how flexible this combination really is. We do not need to specify an order for the lookup range, we can have duplicates and the value to be returned does not have to be in a row / column below / to the right of the lookup range (indeed, it can be in another workbook never mind another worksheet!). With a little practice, the above technique can be extended to match items on a case sensitive basis, use multiple criteria and even 'grade'.

CHAPTER 1.10: CHOOSE

Do you choose to use **CHOOSE**? Certainly it is a function used in modelling, but perhaps it is not used as regularly as some of the others discussed. This is useful for non-contiguous references:

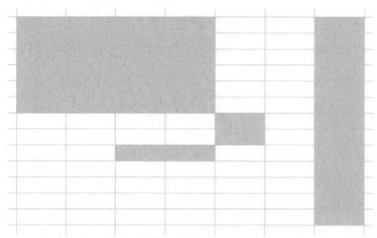

Just so that we are clear on jargon: a **non-contiguous** range (with reference to Excel) means a range that cannot be highlighted with the mouse alone. In the image above, to highlight the cells coloured you would have to press down the **CTRL** key as well.

INDEX, **LOOKUP**, **VLOOKUP** and **HLOOKUP** all require contiguous references. They refer to lists, row vectors, column vectors and / or arrays. **CHOOSE** is different:

=CHOOSE(Index_Num,Value1,[Value2]...)

This function requires an index number, **Index_num**, to make a selection out of the ensuing list **Value1**, **Value2**, ... and so on. The values may be numbers, cell references, defined names, formulae, functions or text. There is a restriction on the number of items in the list though: 254 (Excel 2007 onwards) or 29 (Excel 2003 and earlier). **Index_num** has to be a number between 1 and one less than the total number of arguments, otherwise you can expect an #*VALUE!* error. **Index_num** rounds down if it is not an integer.

This function allows references to different calculations, workbook / worksheet references, *etc*. Try to use the function appropriately. For instance, a well-known Excel website proposes the following formula for calculating the US Thanksgiving date. Assuming cell A1 has the year:

=DATE(A1,11,CHOOSE(WEEKDAY(DATE(A1,11,1)),26,25,24,23,22,28,27))

To understand this formula, note that **DATE(Year,Month,Day)** returns a date and **WEEKDAY(Date)** returns a number 1 (Sunday) through 7 (Saturday). But doesn't this formula look horrible? It is full of hard code and it contains an unnecessary number of arguments. The formula could exclude **CHOOSE** *viz*.

=DATE(A1,11,28-MOD(WEEKDAY(DATE(A1,11,1))+1,7))

Now let me be clear here. I am not saying this is a simple, transparent formula (I am going to discuss **MOD** shortly). Test it. They both provide the same answer. **CHOOSE** – and plenty of additional hard code – has been used unnecessarily.

That's not to say there isn't a time and a place for **CHOOSE**. It is useful when you need to refer to cells on different worksheets or in other workbooks. Some argue that it is useful when a calculation needs to be computed using different methods, *e.g.*

=CHOOSE(Selection_Number,Calculation1,Calculation2,Calculation3,Calculation4)

I disagree. Let me explain. In the example below, I have created a lookup table in cells **E10:E13** which I have called **Data** (I will explain how to create range names later). The calculations are all visible on the worksheet, rather than hidden away in the formula bar. The selection, **Selection_Number**, is input in cell **E2**. The result?

E4			× ✓ f_x	=INDEX(Data,Selection_Number)		
	A	B	C	D	E	F	G
1							
2				Selection	3		
3							
4				Result	88		
5							
6							
7				*Calculations*			
8							
9					Data		
10				Calculation 1	17		
11				Calculation 2	94		
12				Calculation 3	88		
13				Calculation 4	53		
14							
15							

It's identical, but easier to follow

=INDEX(Data,Selection_Number)

I have taught financial modelling to many gifted analysts over the years and a common mistake made by many is that they build models that are easy to build rather than *models that are easy to understand*. The end user is the customer. It should be simple to use: taking shortcuts invariably only helps the modeller – and even then, more often than not, shortcuts will backfire.

CHOOSE can lead to opaque models that need to be rebuilt and are often less flexible to use. You have been warned!

CHAPTER 1.11: OFFSET

The older I get, the more invaluable **OFFSET** becomes. The syntax for **OFFSET** is as follows:

> **OFFSET(Reference,Rows,Columns,[Height],[Width]).**

The arguments in square brackets (**Height** and **Width**) can be omitted from the formula (they both have a default value of 1 which is explained further below).

In its most basic form, **OFFSET(Ref,x,y)** will select a reference **x** rows down (**-x** would be **x** rows up) and y columns to the right (**-y** would be **y** columns to the left) of the reference **Ref**. For example, consider the following grid:

	A	B	C	D	E	F
1	1	2	3	4	5	6
2	7	8	9	10	11	12
3	13	14	15	16	17	18
4	19	20	21	22	23	24
5	25	26	27	28	29	30
6	31	32	33	34	35	36

OFFSET(A1,2,3) would take us two rows down and three columns across to cell **D3**. Therefore, **OFFSET(A1,2,3)** = 16, *viz*.

	A	B	C	D	E	F
1	1	2	3	4	5	6
2	7	8	9	10	11	12
3	13	14	15	16	17	18
4	19	20	21	22	23	24
5	25	26	27	28	29	30
6	31	32	33	34	35	36

OFFSET(D4,-1,-2) would take us one row up and two rows to the left to cell **B3**. Therefore, **OFFSET(D4,-1,-2)** = 14, *viz*.

	A	B	C	D	E	F
1	1	2	3	4	5	6
2	7	8	9	10	11	12
3	13	14	15	16	17	18
4	19	20	21	22	23	24
5	25	26	27	28	29	30
6	31	32	33	34	35	36

We can use these mechanics to construct a very simple scenario table:

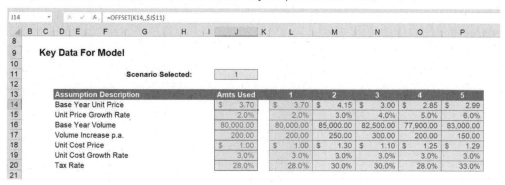

| J14 | | | fx | =OFFSET(K14,,$J$11) | | | | | | | | | |

	B C D E	F	G	H	I	J	K	L	M	N	O	P
8												
9	**Key Data For Model**											
10												
11		Scenario Selected:				1						
12												
13	**Assumption Description**				**Amts Used**		**1**	**2**	**3**	**4**	**5**	
14	Base Year Unit Price			$ 3.70		$ 3.70	$ 4.15	$ 3.00	$ 2.85	$ 2.99		
15	Unit Price Growth Rate			2.0%		2.0%	3.0%	4.0%	5.0%	6.0%		
16	Base Year Volume			80,000.00		80,000.00	85,000.00	82,500.00	77,900.00	83,000.00		
17	Volume Increase p.a.			200.00		200.00	250.00	300.00	200.00	150.00		
18	Unit Cost Price			$ 1.00		$ 1.00	$ 1.30	$ 1.10	$ 1.25	$ 1.29		
19	Unit Cost Growth Rate			3.0%		3.0%	3.0%	3.0%	3.0%	3.0%		
20	Tax Rate			28.0%		28.0%	30.0%	30.0%	28.0%	33.0%		
21												

Essentially, the assumptions used in this illustration are linked from cells **J14:J20** (in yellow). These values are drawn from the scenario table to the right of the highlighted yellow range (*e.g.* cells **L14:L20** constitute Scenario 1, cells **M14:M20** constitute Scenario 2).

The Scenario Selector is located in cell **J11**. Using **OFFSET**, scenarios may be selected at will. For example, the formula in cell **J14** is simply **OFFSET(K14,,$J$11)**; that is, start at cell **K14** and displace zero rows down and the value in **J11** columns across. In the image above, the formula locates the cell one column to the right, which is Scenario 1.

The advantage of **OFFSET** over other functions such as **INDEX**, **CHOOSE** and **LOOKUP** functions is that the range of data can be added to. Whilst the other functions require a specified range whereas we can keep adding scenarios without changing the formula / making the model inefficient.

OFFSET can be used for other practical uses in Excel, taking advantage of the **Height** and **Width** arguments. Consider the **OFFSET** example from earlier. If we extend the formula to **OFFSET(D4,-1,-2,-2,3)**, it would again take us to cell **B3** but then we would select a range based on the **Height** and **Width** parameters. The **Height** would be two rows going up the sheet, with row 14 as the base (*i.e.* rows 13 and 14), and the **Width** would be three columns going from left to right, with column **B** as the base (*i.e.* columns **B**, **C** and **D**).

Hence **OFFSET(D4,-1,-2,-2,3)** would select the range **B2:D3**, *viz.*

	A	B	C	D	E	F
1	1	2	3	4	5	6
2	7	8	9	10	11	12
3	13	14	15	16	17	18
4	19	20	21	22	23	24
5	25	26	27	28	29	30
6	31	32	33	34	35	36

Note that typing in **OFFSET(D4,-1,-2,-2,3)** equals *#VALUE!* since Excel cannot display a matrix in one cell, but it does recognise it. However, if after typing in **OFFSET(D4,-1,-2,-2,3)** we press **CTRL + SHIFT + ENTER**, we turn the formula into an array formula: **{OFFSET(D4,-1,-2,-2,3)}** (do not type the braces in, they will appear automatically as part of the Excel syntax). This gives a value of 8, which is the value in the top left hand corner of the matrix, *but Excel is storing more than that*. This can be seen as follows:

- **SUM(OFFSET(D4,-1,-2,-2,3))** = 72 (*i.e.* **SUM(B2:D3)**)

- **AVERAGE(OFFSET(D4,-1,-2,-2,3))** = 12 (*i.e.* **AVERAGE(B2:D3)**).

Indeed, you may construct a simple depreciation calculation or transpose references using **OFFSET**'s **Height** and **Width** functionalities. But more on that later...

There are a couple of problems with **OFFSET**:

• Values returned by an **OFFSET** function confuse Excel. Only the original **Reference** is recognised as a precedent reference to the formula by Excel's auditing tools.

The result returned is most likely to come from another cell which will not be highlighted by this technique. If you think about it, this actually makes sense as potentially all of the cells on a worksheet are potential precedents.

To take account of this, I suggest you give the **Reference** a **range name**. Range names are discussed in detail later in this book, but for now to name a cell, click on the cell and then type the desired name in the **Name box** in Excel:

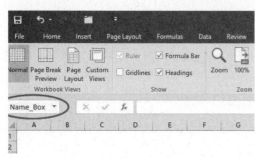

This range name should start with **BC_**. This prefix stands for "Base Cell" and makes it easier to sort / locate range names later. When users or model auditors alike inspect a formula with a **Reference** starting with **BC_** for Base Cell (e.g. **BC_Example_Reference**), this can alert them to the fact that the model may be using cells in the region of this **Reference** that do not appear to have any dependents.

• The other issue is that **OFFSET** is what is known as a **volatile** function. A volatile function is one that causes recalculation of the formula in the cell where it resides every time Excel recalculates. This can really slow down your model if there are too many **OFFSET** functions, for example.

Aside: Volatile Functions

As stated above, a **volatile function** is one that causes recalculation of the formula in the cell where it resides every time Excel recalculates. This occurs regardless of whether precedent cells / calculations have changed, or whether the formula also contains non-volatile functions. One test to check whether your workbook is volatile is close a file after saving and see if Excel prompts you to save it a second time (this is an indicative test only). This can really slow down your model if there are too many **OFFSET** functions, for example.

Just because a function is volatile in one version of Excel does not mean it is volatile in all versions. Perhaps the best example of this is **INDEX**, which was volatile prior to Excel 97. Microsoft still states this function is volatile, but this does not appear to be the case except when used as the second part of a range reference, for example **$A$1:INDEX($A$2:A$10,4)**, will also cause the reference to be flagged as "dirty" (*i.e.* needs to be recalculated) when the workbook is opened only.

Another common 'semi-volatile' function is **SUMIF**, which has been so since Excel 2002. This function becomes volatile whenever the size of the first range argument is not the same as the second (**Sum_range**) argument, *e.g.* **SUMIF(A1:A4,1,B1)** is volatile whereas **SUMIF(A1:A4,1,B1:B4)** is not.

IF and **CHOOSE** do not calculate all arguments, but if any of the arguments are volatile – regardless of whether they are used – the formula is deemed to be volatile. Therefore, **IF(1>0,1,RAND())** is always volatile, even though the **Value_if_false** argument will never be calculated. It is not quite as simple as this though. If the formula in cell **A1** is **=NOW()** then this cell will be volatile, but **IF(1>0,1,A1)** will not be.

In essence, direct references or dependents of volatile functions will always be recalculated, whereas indirect ones will only recalculate when activated or in certain other functions that always calculate all arguments such as **AND** and **OR**.

Does **MOD** cause division amongst the financial modelling community? Well, the [bad] jokes keep coming I'm afraid. The **MOD** function, **MOD(Number,Divisor)**, returns the remainder after the **Number** (first argument) is divided by the **Divisor** (second argument). The result has the same sign as the **Divisor**.

For example, 9 / 4 = 2.25, or 2 remainder 1. **MOD(9,4)** is an alternative way of expressing this, and hence equals 1 also. Note that the 1 may be obtained from the first calculation by (2.25 – 2) x 4 = 1, i.e. in general:

$$\text{MOD(n,d)} = \text{n - d*INT(n/d)},$$

where **INT()** is the integer function in Excel.

This function has various uses and I provide three common examples below:

1. **Obtaining "residuals":** In some instances in modelling, you need the integer part of a number, *e.g.* how many payments fall between two dates may calculate as 9.94 – but that's nonsense. In this instance, you would have only made nine payments, *i.e.* **INT(9.94)**.

   Similarly, you might want to accrue the fee for payments not yet made. Using **MOD(9.94,1)** = 0.94, i.e. the number after the decimal place. Note that **9.94 – INT(9.94)** gives the same result here; the **MOD** approach is simply shorter.

2. **Calculations at regular time intervals:** Consider tax payments as an example. Many companies make tax payments quarterly (*i.e.* once every three months). If we assume these payments are made in March, June, September and December then we can formulate the payment as **IF(MOD(Month_Number)=0,Make_Payment,0)**, *etc.*

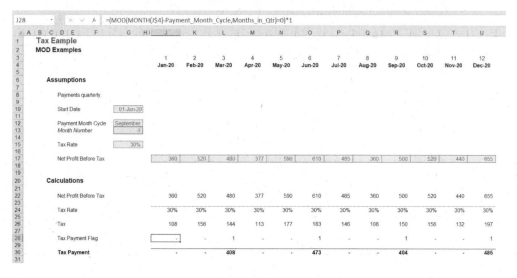

3. **Summing every nth row:** It is not uncommon for users to want to sum every **n**th cell (*e.g.* second, third, fourth,...) in a spreadsheet. Excel has no standard function which will do this, but **MOD** can come to the rescue. For example, the array formula

{=SUM(IF(MOD($E$19:$E$48,$G$13)=0,$F$19:$F$48,0))}

was used in cell **H53** in the following example:

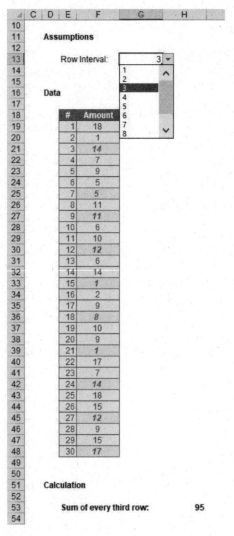

Arrays using large ranges can cause calculations to slow down considerably. This is why I used a counter rather than the volatile **ROW()** function (volatile functions calculate each time you press **ENTER** or **F9**).

If accuracy is vital, be careful with **MOD** as it may give very slightly erroneous results:

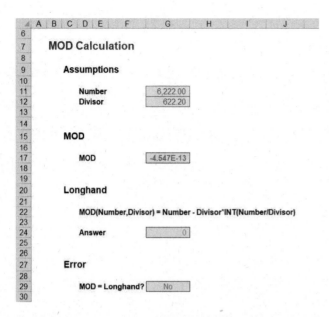

The result for **MOD** in cell **G17** might seem inconsequential, but imagine you were making calculations based on **MOD(Number,Divisor)=0**. In this case **MOD** would not equal zero and the calculation would not work.

This issue tends to occur more commonly when working with non-integers.

The problem here isn't really **MOD**. Calculations are performed in binary [1,0] format and most floating point numbers have no exact binary representation (just as 1/3 has no exact decimal representation). In this instance, 10 times the binary approximation to 622.2 is 6222.0000000000004547....

i.e. you may need to use the **ROUND(Number,Num_digits)** as part of your formula too in order to round your **Number** to **Num_digits** number of digits (after the decimal point).

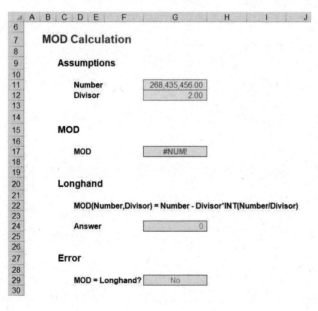

Another weird anomaly is if the number is 134,217,728 (2^{27}) times greater or more than the divisor this gives rise to a #NUM! error *viz.*

Some texts suggest that you could use the formula

=MOD(MOD(Number,134217728*Divisor),Divisor)

This will solve for larger numbers much larger than the limit for **MOD**, but theoretically will hit the same problem when the number being evaluated reaches 134,217,728*134,217,728***Divisor**. For most uses, this is limit is large enough that it will never be reached, but I suggest sticking with Microsoft's recommended solution which is calculating the "longhanded" result as illustrated above (cell **G24**).

Also, when using the **MOD** function with one negative number and the expected result is the numerator, **MOD(9,-10)** actually returns -1, whereas you could argue the correct result should be 9:

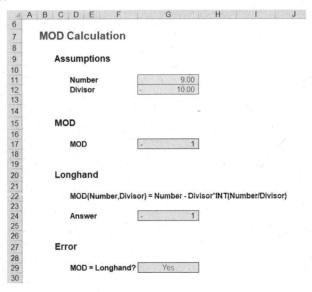

Note that the longhand approach also gives a result of -1.

Microsoft explains that this approach has been taken deliberately in order to be consistent with the dBase MOD function. If you always need **MOD** to deliver a value of **x** where $0 \leq x <$ divisor, then use the adjusted formula:

=IF(MOD(Number,Divisor)<0,ABS(Divisor)+MOD(Number,Divisor)).

Common Example with MOD and OFFSET

Now that I have explained **MOD**, I can show you a really good use of this function for a situation which causes many working in finance plenty of consternation. The solution works in conjunction with **OFFSET**. For those that skipped that section, the syntax of **OFFSET** is as follows:

OFFSET(Reference,Rows,Columns,[Height],[Width]).

The arguments in square brackets (**Height** and **Width**) can be omitted from the formula in this instance. In its most basic form, **OFFSET(Reference,x,y)** will select a **Reference x** rows down (**-x** would be **x** rows up) and **y** rows to the right (**-y** would be **y** rows to the left).

Imagine you have set up a scenario table in Excel to determine which inputs should be used in your model (*i.e.* "what-if? Analysis"):

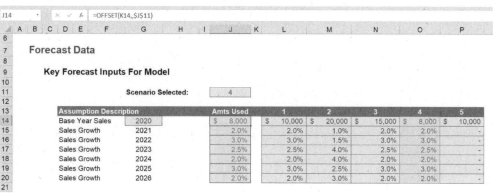

This method allows for various scenarios to be modelled easily with a different set of input data inserted into each column (from column L onwards in this illustration). A selector (cell **J11** in the figure above) is used to select the active scenario, which may be highlighted using conditional formatting (see later).

The data used to drive the model is then highlighted in column **J** (here, emphasised in yellow) using the follow formula for cell **J14** for example:

=OFFSET(K14,,$J$11)

In other words, this formula looks up data **x** columns to the right of column **K**, where **x** is specified as the value input in cell **J11** (here, this value is 4 so column **O**'s data is selected).

Clearly, using a columnar approach here makes it very straightforward to set the various scenarios out. However, most financial models are displayed with dates going from left to right across columns rather than down the page using rows. This requires us to transpose the data, and again we may use **OFFSET** to 'flip' the data:

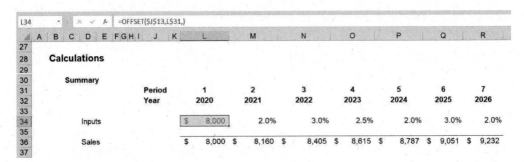

Here, the period numbers specified in row 31 make it easy for us to transpose the data. For example, the formula in cell **L34** would be:

=OFFSET($J$13,L$31,)

i.e. insert the data **x** rows down from cell **J13** in the first graphic, where **x** is again specified as the value input in cell **J11**.

Take care, however, if using an amount followed by growth rates approach for forecast / budget data. The amounts using these examples should be as follows:

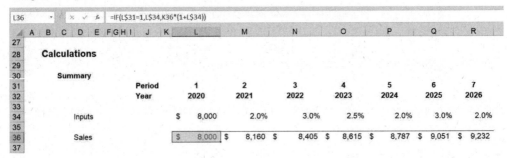

The correct formula here is:

=IF(L$31=1,L$34,K36*(1+L$34))

for cell **L36** (say), *i.e.* if it is the first period take the amount, otherwise take the amount calculated in the preceding period and multiply it by (1 + growth rate specified in the current period <u>not</u> the next period).

When actual data is input into a model, frequently it replaces the original information, and therefore management loses the ability to see how accurate forecasts were originally and how budgeting may be improved. One way around this would be to simply have "Actuals" as one of the scenarios so that all forecasts are retained. This is often all that is required, and if so, simply do that – Keep It Simple Stupid (KISS).

However, often we may wish to undertake variance analysis by comparing actual data with the original budgeted information. In this case, I would suggest the following approach.

	L23		✕ ✓ *fx*	=IF(L$18<>"",L$18,IF(L$3=1,L$11,K23*(1+L$11)))						

	A B C D E	F	G H I	J	K	L	M	N	O	P	Q	R
3				Period		1	2	3	4	5	6	7
4				Year		2020	2021	2022	2023	2024	2025	2026
5												
6												
7	**Actual Data to be Used for Calculations**											
8												
9		Part 1 - Budget / Forecast Data Used										
10												
11		Inputs				$ 8,000	2.0%	3.0%	2.5%	2.0%	3.0%	2.0%
12												
13		Sales				$ 8,000	$ 8,160	$ 8,405	$ 8,615	$ 8,787	$ 9,051	$ 9,232
14												
15												
16		Part 2 - Actual Inputs										
17												
18		Actual Data Override		If blank, then unused			$ 9,000	$ 8,500				
19												
20												
21		Part 3 - Reforecast Data										
22												
23		Reforecast Data				$ 8,000	$ 9,000	$ 8,500	$ 8,713	$ 8,887	$ 9,153	$ 9,336
24												

Rows 9 to 13 of this illustration simply reiterate the calculations already detailed above regarding the original forecasting. Note row 18 however: this is where actual data is added instead. In my example, I simply use hard coded inputs for my data, but it only requires a simple variation to this methodology to revise growth rates, etc.

Using my logic, we simply use actual data where it is available; otherwise we fall back on the original data and calculations. This is achieved by the formula in row 23 in my example, which is (for cell **L23**):

> **=IF(L$18<>"",L$18,IF(L$3=1,L$11,K23*(1+L$11))),**

i.e. if there is data in the corresponding cell in row 18 use it; if not, if it is the first period take the original input value, otherwise simply inflate the prior period amount by (1 + growth rate for that period). It may include a nested **IF** statement, but it is still a relatively simple and straightforward calculation.

Performing the calculations is only half of the battle. Modellers often have difficulty comparing the original outputs with the reforecast counterparts in an effective and efficient manner. If sufficient, the following would be relatively straight forward:

	A B C D E	F	G H I	J	K	L	M	N	O	P	Q	R
1	**Simple Outputs Example**											
2												
3												
4				Counter		1	2	3	4	5	6	7
5				Year		2020	2021	2022	2023	2024	2025	2026
6						$	$	$	$	$	$	$
9												
10												
11	**Simple Outputs Example**											
12												
13		Sales										
14			Budget			$8,000	$8,160	$8,405	$8,615	$8,787	$9,051	$9,232
15			Act. / Refcast			$8,000	$9,000	$8,500	$8,713	$8,887	$9,153	$9,336
16			Variance	*Favourable / (Unfavourable)*		-	$840	$95	$98	$100	$103	$105
17												

This is very easy to put together, but alas, more often than not, the following presentation is required by senior management instead:

Bad Outputs Example

	Counter	1	2	3	4	5	6	7	8	9	10
	Year	2020	2020	2020	2021	2021	2021	2022	2022	2022	2023
	Description	Budget	Act / Ref'cast	Variance	Budget	Act / Ref'cast	Variance	Budget	Act / Ref'cast	Variance	Budget
Bad Outputs Example											
Sales		$8,000	$8,000		$8,160	$9,000	$840	$8,405	$8,500	$95	$8,615

Seem familiar? I have been a model reviewer for many a year and seen this type of output on an extremely regular basis. Many senior management teams like it this way and it is not my role to challenge the status quo – it doesn't stop me from trying though!

The problem with this layout is that it lends itself to promoting poor practice. Modellers tend to use a large number of unique formulae across a row, which in turn slows down model construction and increases the potential for mistakes, such as referencing errors.

If you have to use this layout, create the simple summary elsewhere (maybe on an input page):

Part 4 - Summary

	Year No.		1	2	3	4	5	6	7
Budget		$	8,000 $	8,160 $	8,405 $	8,615 $	8,787 $	9,051 $	9,232
Act. / Ref'cast		$	8,000 $	9,000 $	8,500 $	8,713 $	8,887 $	9,153 $	9,336
Variance		$	- $	840 $	95 $	98 $	100 $	103 $	105

Look carefully at this graphic. The shading in cell **K28** above may appear innocuous, but it is the most important cell on the worksheet and has been named **BC_Sales_Summary** accordingly (**BC** means "Base Cell" for an **OFFSET** function). Consider:

- For every column moved to the right, the cursor is in a different year. One column across is Year 1, two columns across is Year 2 and so on

- For every row moved down, the cursor reports a different figure. One row down is the Budget data, two rows down is the Actual / Reforecast data and three rows down is the Variance. The depth of this table (three rows) has been defined as **List_Depth** so that it may be used in formulae.

Now, if we return to the outputs worksheet and modify it slightly by inserting two additional lines, using the **OFFSET** function once more may make your potential troubles a thing of the past, *viz.*

| L13 | ▼ | : | ✕ | ✓ | *fx* | =OFFSET(BC_Sales_Summary,L$7,L$8) |

A B C D E F G H I	J	K	L	M	N	O	P	Q	R	S	T	U
1 Better Outputs Example												
2												
3												
4	Counter		1	2	3	4	5	6	7	8	9	10
5	Year		2020	2020	2020	2021	2021	2021	2022	2022	2022	2023
6	Description		Budget	Act. / Ref'cast	Variance	Budget	Act. / Ref'cast	Variance	Budget	Act. / Ref'cast	Variance	Budget
7	Selector		1	2	3	1	2	3	1	2	3	1
8	Year No.		1	1	1	2	2	2	3	3	3	4
9												
10												
11 **Better Outputs Example**												
12												
13 **Sales**			$8,000	$8,000	-	$8,160	$9,000	$840	$8,405	$8,500	$95	$8,615
14												
15												

You will see that each row of the revised output example contains only one unique formula copied across, making it easy to edit, extend and review. This is achieved by adding two rows:

- **Selector (row 7):** identifies whether the column should be reporting the budget information, the actual data or the variance. The equation used makes use of the **MOD** function:

=MOD(L$4-1,List_Depth)+1

As stated above, List_Depth is the number of selections (Budget, Act / Ref'cast, Variance) permissible – in this case three. =MOD(L$4,List_Depth) takes the counter and converts each one to 1, 2 and zero (i.e. the remainder upon dividing the counter by three). By subtracting one inside the MOD function and adding it once more outside, this simply forces a zero to a three instead, so that the Selector reports the values 1, 2 and 3 alternately.

- **Year No. (row 8):** simply notes which year the column is reporting using the formula:

=IF(L$7=1,K8+1,K8)

i.e. **the year increases the period that the counter in row 7 equals 1 (in this example).**

Therefore, in my example, row 13 requires a very simple formula to generate the required outputs:

=OFFSET(BC_Sales_Summary,L$7,L$8).

For example, cell **Q13** equals **OFFSET(BC_Sales_Summary,3,2)**, which would refer to the Year 2 Variance figure of $840.

Easy!

CHAPTER 1.13: EOMONTH AND EDATE

Dates are commonplace in models and usually run across one of the top rows in an Excel worksheet as part of a time series analysis:

In this example, a monthly model has been constructed starting in July 2020. The dates in cells **J5** onwards are formatted to show only the month and year. This can be performed easily by selecting the date (here, 31 July 2020) and then formatting the cell (**CTRL + 1**).

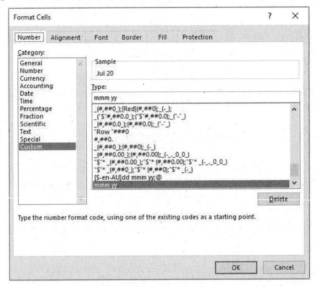

More interestingly, if the General category were to be selected instead, we note that the Sample (circled in red) would be displayed as follows.

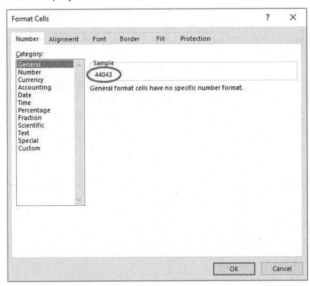

In other words, 31 July 2020 is no more than a number: 44,043. Microsoft Excel for Windows supports what is called the 1900 date system. This means that 1 January 1900 is considered to be day 1 by Excel, 2 January 1900 is day 2 and so on.

Extrapolating, 31 July 2020 would be day 44,042 (not 44,043). The reason that the 1900 date system views it as one day later is because this system considers 1900 to be a leap year – which it wasn't! Years ending in '00' have to be divisible by 400 to be a leap year, so 1 March 1900 in this system was day 61 rather than day 60.

Most modellers are not concerned about how the days are numbered as long as Excel calculates correctly. However, early Macintosh computers used a different start date to prevent issues with the 1900 leap year and used 1 January 1904 as the start date. This is known as the 1904 date system and the date values can be calculated as:

=1900 date system value – 1,462

Care has to be taken with Excel files opened on both PCs and Macs, as the date systems may vary. You can force Excel to use a particular date system as follows:

- Go to Excel Options (alternatively, **ALT + T + O** still works)

- Select 'Advanced' from the left hand column

- Scroll down to the eighth section, 'When calculating this workbook'

- Check / uncheck 'Use 1904 date system' as desired

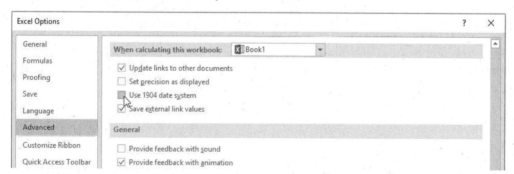

Clearly, dates are not as easy to manipulate as you might think. Extracting the day, month or even the year from any given date is not straightforward because the date is really a number known as a serial number. (If I were to delete a date, would this make me a serial killer?)

To extract the day, month or a year has to be undertaken using the following three functions:

- **v(serial_number)** gives the day in the date (for example, **DAY(31-Jul-20)** = 31)

- **MONTH(serial_number)** gives the month in the date (for example, **MONTH(31-Jul-20)** = 7)

- **YEAR(serial_number)** gives the year in the date (for example, **YEAR(31-Jul-20)** = 2020).

It is just as awkward the other way round. If the day, month and year are already known, the date can be calculated using the following function:

DATE(Year,Month,Day) (for example, DATE(2020,7,32) = 1 August 2020, *etc.*).

Since dates are nothing more than serial numbers, they behave just like formatted numbers in Excel, for example, 31-Jul-20 + 128 = 6-Dec-2020.

This is all great, but time series still cause us problems. If we want to have the month end date in each column, we cannot simply take the previous month's date and add a constant to it, since the numbers of days in months vary. Fortunately, there is a function in Excel that will perform this calculation for us:

EOMONTH(Specified_date,Number_of_months)

The "End of month" function therefore calculates the end of the month as the **Number_of_ months** after the **Specified_date**. For example:

- **EOMONTH(31-Jul-20,0)** = 31-Jul-20

- **EOMONTH(3-Apr-05,2)** = 30-Jun-05

- **EOMONTH(29-Feb-08,-12)** = 28-Feb-07

Although the examples use typed in dates, for it to work in Excel, it is best to have the **Specified_date** either as a cell reference to a date or else use the **DATE** function to ensure that Excel understands it is a date (otherwise the formula may calculate as *#VALUE!*).

In some instances (for example, appraisal of large scale capital infrastructure projects), the dates may need to be for the same day of the month (for example, the 15th) rather than for the month end. The **DATE** function can often be used to calculate these dates – unless it is near the end of the month as problems may arise with February, April, June, September and November.

A function similar to **EOMONTH**, **EDATE** can be used instead:

EDATE(Specified_date,Number_of_months).

The 'Equivalent day' function therefore calculates the date that is the indicated **Number_of_ months** before or after the **Specified_date**. For example:

- **EDATE(15-Jul-20,2)** = 15-Sep-20

- **EDATE(3-Apr-05,-2)** = 3-Feb-05

- **EDATE(29-Feb-28,-12)** = 28-Feb-27

If an equivalent date cannot be found (as in the last example), month end is used instead.

Similar to **EOMONTH**, it should be noted that although these examples also use typed in dates, for it to work in Excel, it is best to have the **Specified_date** either as a cell reference to a date or else use the **DATE** function to ensure that Excel understands it is a date (otherwise the formula may calculate as *#VALUE!*).

Certain functions are not in the 'main library' of Excel functions and will give rise to *#NAME?* errors in Excel if not recognised. Unfortunately, **EOMONTH** and **EDATE** were two such functions in Excel 2003 and earlier versions.

To ensure they work / are recognised correctly, the Analysis ToolPak had to be added in. To ensure it is, in all versions, use the keyboard shortcut **ALT + T + I** to load up the Add-Ins dialog box:

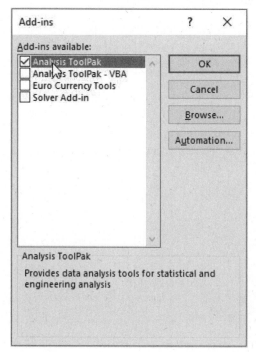

It is important that model developers and end users alike have this ToolPak added in for all versions of Excel up to and including Excel 2003, otherwise these functions will not work.

Since Excel 2007, **EOMONTH** and **EDATE** have been added to the 'standard' functions database in Excel so it is not necessary to ensure that the Analysis ToolPak has been added in. This avoids our first common problem, but unfortunately, it sometimes causes a bigger one due to an apparent compatibility issue between Excel 2007 and earlier versions of Excel.

If Excel 2003 Analysis ToolPak functions such as **EOMONTH** or **EDATE** are used in a file created in Excel 2003 (or earlier) that is then opened in Excel 2007 (or later), the formulae that incorporate these functions may be replaced by **=#/N/A** or simply *#N/A*. Some experienced users believe that if you ensure the Analysis ToolPak is switched on in Excel 2007 <u>before</u> you open the file (albeit in compatibility mode), the problem will be avoided, but the modelling community as a whole is not sure this is the case necessarily.

The only sure fire way I have found to avoid this problem is to not use these functions if the file will be opened in Excel 2007 or later <u>and</u> earlier versions of Excel. This means that you need to find equivalent formulae that do not use Analysis ToolPak formulae.

For developers and users in this predicament you might wish to consider the following alternative formulae. For **EOMONTH(Specified_date,Number_of_months)** use:

=DATE(YEAR(Specified_date),MONTH(Specified_date)+IF(Number_of_
months,ROUNDDOWN(Number_of_months,0),)+1,)

For **EDATE(Specified_date,Number_of_months)** use:

=MIN(DATE(YEAR(Specified_date),MONTH(Specified_date)+ROUNDDOWN(Number_
of_months,0),DAY(Specified_date)),DATE(YEAR(Specified_date),MONTH(Specified_
date)+ROUNDDOWN(Number_of_months,0)+1,0))

CHAPTER 1.14: MAX AND MIN

There isn't really that much to say about **MAX** and **MIN**. These functions take the maximum and the minimum of their references respectively. But it's going to be a very short section if I leave it there. How about we consider a slightly more sophisticated application of these functions?

Consider the following:

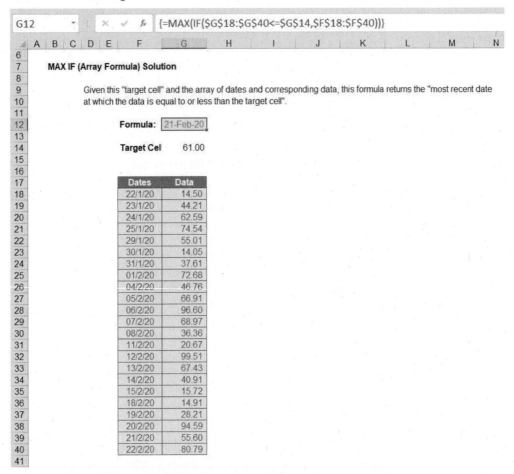

The problem here is to create a simple formula (cell **G12**) which will return the most recent date at which the corresponding data was less than or equal to the value in the 'Target' cell (cell **G14**).

In this example, it can be assumed that there will be at most one data point for each date, but the dates may not necessarily be in ascending order.

One possible solution (displayed above) is by using an array function:

={MAX(IF($G$18:$G$40<=$G$14,$F$18:$F$40))}

Common mistakes here might include using the **LOOKUP** function (this requires the dates to be in strict ascending order) and getting the inequality the wrong way round.

So What is an Array Function?

In Excel, an **array** is a contiguous set of items in a single row (called a one-dimensional horizontal array or vector), or in a single column (a one-dimensional vertical vector), or in a table consisting of at least two rows and two columns (a two-dimensional array). If you need more dimensions, you are better served with relational databases such as MS Access.

Array formulae perform multiple calculations on one or more of the items in an array. Array formulae can return either multiple outputs or a single result. There are two types:

- Formulae that work with an array or series of data and aggregate it, typically using **SUM, AVERAGE, MIN, MAX** or **COUNT**, to return a single value to a single cell. Microsoft calls these **single cell array formulae**.

- Formulae that return a result in to two or more cells (there are various formulae that will do this including **MINVERSE, LINEST** and **TRANSPOSE**). These types of array formulae return an array of values as their result and are referred to as **multi-cell array formulae**.

  Multi-cell formulae can cause problems as the range of cells to hold your results must be selected before you enter the formula. Once entered, the contents of an individual cell in a multi-cell array formula cannot be edited and / or deleted. Only Chuck Norris may change part of an array.

Some functions, such as **SUMPRODUCT, INDEX** and **OFFSET** will allow you to work with an array in a single cell by just pressing **ENTER**. However, Excel often needs to know you are working with an array formula, and this is performed by entering the formula using **CTRL + SHIFT + ENTER**. This will result in the formula appearing in braces ({}). These braces cannot be typed in.

Array formulae allow you to perform tasks that would require multiple cells.

The problem here requires working with a list to return a single value, *i.e.* using a single cell array formula on a column vector. So, returning to our solution:

$$\{=MAX(IF(\$G\$18:\$G\$40<=\$G\$14,\$F\$18:\$F\$40))\}$$

The central formula, **IF($G$18:$G$40<=$G$14,$F$18:$F$40)**, checks to see which data is less than or equal to the target value (**$G$14**) and returns the corresponding dates (otherwise it provides a default value of FALSE since the **Value_if_false** in the **IF(Logical_test,[Value_if_true],[Value_if_false])** syntax is not defined).

Hence we get an array in the form {Date_1,FALSE,FALSE,Date_2,...}. **MAX** simply takes the largest value, *i.e.* the most recent date – easy!

End users may not understand your array formulae. How many basic Excel users would understand the **MAX(IF)** array explained above? Advanced users will all too often use an array function when there are simpler, easier to understand alternatives. Further, large array formulae can slow down calculations significantly. Worse still, they can simply stop calculating with no error message provided.

In conclusion, array formulae can be very powerful but they may be a weapon of last resort.

Chapter 2: Key Excel Functionalities

Congratulations, you made it! Whether you are a novice or last year's Financial Modelling World Champion *(someone needs to explain that title to me)*, hopefully you learned something as we braved the common functions used in financial modelling.

I make no apologies that certain functions were not there, such as **FACTDOUBLE**, **IPMT**, **IRR**, **MIRR**, **NPV**, **PMT**, **PPMT**, **RATE**, **ROMAN**, **XIRR** and **XNPV** (and plenty more) were not discussed. Many of them have issues; others are just simpler to derive from first principles; some just couldn't make the final cut for this book. Having said that, I might leave you with one final tip. If profits are way down on budgets, rather than issue profit warnings, have you considered producing your lacklustre outputs using the **ROMAN** function?

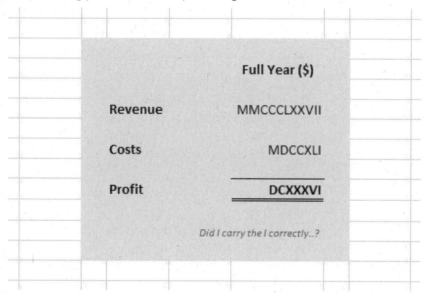

	Full Year ($)
Revenue	MMCCCLXXVII
Costs	MDCCXLI
Profit	DCXXXVI

Did I carry the I correctly..?

Jokes aside, maybe we should move on.

Apart from functions, you should also familiarise yourself with various key functionalities of Excel often required for developing financial models. Just as with functions, I am going to discuss some aspects that you may consider you understand fully already. Again, I'd like to encourage you to stick with the programme, as whether you are a novice or an expert, hopefully, there may be some useful tips for all.

In this section, I plan to explain the merits (or otherwise) of each of the following:

- Absolute referencing
- Number formatting
- Styles
- Conditional formatting
- Range names

- Data validation
- Data Tables
- Goal Seek and Solver
- Hyperlinks.

If nothing else, this should provide useful reference material as we make sure we have the complete toolkit for putting together a "Best Practice" financial model.

CHAPTER 2.1: ABSOLUTE REFERENCING

As my editor said to me recently, "are you absolutely sure you need this section?" *(I said no such thing – Editor.)* Some people say that financial modelling may be all about the dollar signs – well, they may be possibly right in more ways than one.

Consider the following situation:

| C14 | | ▾ | ⋮ | ✕ | ✓ | *fx* | =C4 |

◢	A	B	C	D	E	F	G	H
1								
2		**Data**						
3								
4			1	2	3	4	5	6
5			7	8	9	10	11	12
6			13	14	15	16	17	18
7			19	20	21	22	23	24
8			25	26	27	28	29	30
9			31	32	33	34	35	36
10								
11								
12		**Formula**						
13								
14			1					
15								

In this example, I have created data in cells **C4:H9** inclusive and then written a formula in cell **C14** linking to cell **C4** (a bit of an incendiary reference, I know). If I were to copy this formula down and across over a similarly dimensioned range, I would get the following result:

| H19 | | ▾ | ⋮ | ✕ | ✓ | *fx* | =H9 |

◢	A	B	C	D	E	F	G	H
1								
2		**Data**						
3								
4			1	2	3	4	5	6
5			7	8	9	10	11	12
6			13	14	15	16	17	18
7			19	20	21	22	23	24
8			25	26	27	28	29	30
9			31	32	33	34	35	36
10								
11								
12		**Formula**						
13								
14			1	2	3	4	5	6
15			7	8	9	10	11	12
16			13	14	15	16	17	18
17			19	20	21	22	23	24
18			25	26	27	28	29	30
19			31	32	33	34	35	36
20								

As the formula is copied down and / or across, so the reference moves in a corresponding fashion. This is known as **relative referencing** and forms the cornerstone of formula construction whenever a modeller refers to another location in the <u>same</u> workbook.

This is not what happens when you refer to another workbook:

| C14 | ▼ | ⋮ | × | ✓ | *fx* | =[Book2]Sheet1!$A$1 |

◢	A	B	C	D	E	F	G	H
1								
2		Data						
3								
4			1	2	3	4	5	6
5			7	8	9	10	11	12
6			13	14	15	16	17	18
7			19	20	21	22	23	24
8			25	26	27	28	29	30
9			31	32	33	34	35	36
10								
11								
12		Formula						
13								
14			99					
15								

becomes

| H19 | ▼ | ⋮ | × | ✓ | *fx* | =[Book2]Sheet1!$A$1 |

◢	A	B	C	D	E	F	G	H
1								
2		Data						
3								
4			1	2	3	4	5	6
5			7	8	9	10	11	12
6			13	14	15	16	17	18
7			19	20	21	22	23	24
8			25	26	27	28	29	30
9			31	32	33	34	35	36
10								
11								
12		Formula						
13								
14			99	99	99	99	99	99
15			99	99	99	99	99	99
16			99	99	99	99	99	99
17			99	99	99	99	99	99
18			99	99	99	99	99	99
19			99	99	99	99	99	99
20								

once copied down and across as before. The default for external references is this **absolute referencing**.

It is the dollar ($) signs that do the damage. These can be added or removed by directly typing them into the cell reference or else clicking in the formula bar (alternatively, use the **F2** function key) to enable Edit mode and highlight the relevant references and press the **F4** function key repeatedly

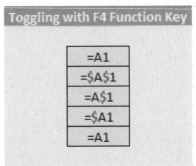

Toggling with F4 Function Key
=A1
=$A$1
=A$1
=$A1
=A1

The dollar sign makes the reference to the right of the sign constant, *viz.*

=A1	Relative referencing
=$A$1	Column and row static, *i.e.* absolute referencing
=A$1	Row constant (column will change), *i.e.* semi-absolute referencing
=$A1	Column constant (row will change), *i.e.* semi-absolute referencing
=A1	Relative referencing

It is important that all would-be modellers master this referencing. It is an essential skill as you need to be able to copy formulae down and across ranges with little effort. If you are unsure, try the following exercise. Create the following spreadsheet:

| E7 | ▼ | ⋮ | ✕ ✓ | *fx* | =D7*E6*C3 |

	A	B	C	D	E	F	G	H	I	J
1	**Absolute v Relative Referencing Example**									
2										
3		*Multiplier*		2						
4										
5										
6					**x**	**1**	**2**	**3**	**4**	**5**
7					**1**	2				
8					**2**					
9					**3**					
10					**4**					
11					**5**					
12										

In this example (assuming you have set up the spreadsheet identically to the one illustrated), the aim is to create a "times table" in cells **E7:I11** inclusive. The numbers should be equal to

Column Header Number x Row Header Number x Multiplier

So that the formula in the first cell is **=D7*E6*C3**. All you need to do is add dollar signs to these cell references so that the formula may be copied across and down the range correctly. Have a go now without peeking.

Have you had a go? Here's my solution below:

E7	▼	⋮	✕	✓	*fx*	=$D7*E$6*$C$3

◢	A	B	C	D	E	F	G	H	I	J
1	**Absolute v Relative Referencing Example**									
2										
3		*Multiplier*		2						
4										
5										
6				**x**	**1**	**2**	**3**	**4**	**5**	
7				**1**	2	4	6	8	10	
8				**2**	4	8	12	16	20	
9				**3**	6	12	18	24	30	
10				**4**	8	16	24	32	40	
11				**5**	10	20	30	40	50	
12										

The formula I constructed was:

=$D7*E$6*$C$3

i.e. the first reference has the column anchored (so that it always references the correct Row Header), the second reference has the row anchored (so that it always references the appropriate Column Header) and the final reference is fully anchored (that is, it is an absolute reference).

Let's get a little more sophisticated and deal with more of a real world problem. Imagine you had the following sample business data:

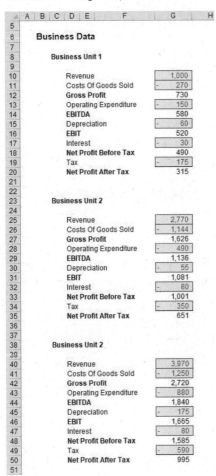

You might wish to create an output which summarises the revenue by business unit. You will need to construct formulae such as

='Business Data'!G10

='Business Data'!G25

='Business Data'!G40, ... etc.

If you had, say, 500 of these business units you would have a busy but boring morning ahead of you. Surely there is a simpler way that does not require the implementation of macros?

Actually, I can think of two ways of dealing with this common query and I present both solutions next.

Method 1: Text Little Time

This approach requires the first two formulae to be entered into the output sheet as usual, *viz.*

SUM	▼	⋮	✕ ✓ *fx*	='Business Data'!G25

◢	A	B	C	D	E	F	G
1							
2		1000					
3		2770					
4							
5							
6							

In our example, cell **B2** contains the formula **='Business Data'!G10** and cell **B3** contains the formula **='Business Data'!G25** (displayed). Next, edit both formula by typing an apostrophe (') before the equals sign in each formula:

B3	▼	⋮	✕ ✓ *fx*	'='Business Data'!G25

◢	A	B	C	D	E	F
1						
2		='Business Data'!G10				
3		='Business Data'!G25				
4						
5						

Now, these formulae are treated as text and are displayed in the two cells. If you then highlight cells **B2:B3** together and copy the formulae down, Excel's AutoFill feature will copy the cells similar to below:

B2	▼	⋮	✕ ✓ *fx*	'='Business Data'!G10

◢	A	B	C	D	E	F
1						
2		='Business Data'!G10				
3		='Business Data'!G25				
4		='Business Data'!G40				
5		='Business Data'!G55				
6		='Business Data'!G70				
7						
8						
9						
10						

Now, all we need to do is remove the apostrophes. The first idea that comes to mind is to use 'Replace...' (**CTRL + H**) and replace '= with =. Unfortunately, this does not work in all versions of Excel as 'Replace...' does not seem to recognise apostrophes in certain instances.

There is a very simple trick to circumvent this problem. With this data still selected, click on the 'Text to Columns' button in the 'Data Tools' group of the 'Data' tab on the Ribbon (**ALT + D + E** for all versions of Excel or **ALT + A + E** in Excel 2007 onwards):

This launches the 'Text to Columns Wizard' dialog box. In the first step, ensure that the '...file type that best describes your data...' is set to 'Delimited':

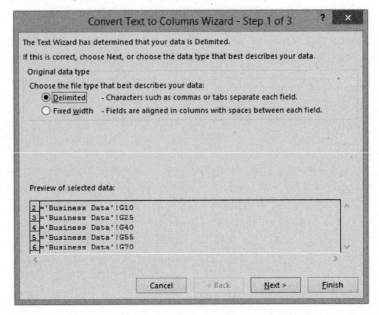

Then, simply depress the 'Finish' button. The spreadsheet will then reinstate the formulae, *viz.*

Simple!

Now this approach is fairly simple, but has two major drawbacks:

1. This method only works with rows. Using **R1C1** formula notation it is possible to create a similar approach for columns, but this technique can be confusing.

2. Once the formulae have been reinstated it is not simple to extend the formulae if necessary. This can be cumbersome where the output summaries may differ period to period for example.

The **OFFSET** approach counters these issues.

Method 2: OFFSET from the Outset

For all those similar to me with the memories of a goldfish (I had to look that up, because I keep forgetting it), the syntax for **OFFSET** is as follows:

OFFSET(Reference,Rows,Columns,[Height],[Width]).

The arguments in square brackets (**Height** and **Width**) can be omitted from the formula. In its most basic form, you will recall **OFFSET(Reference,x,y)** will select a reference **x** rows down (**-x** would be **x** rows up) and **y** rows to the right (**-y** would be **y** rows to the left) of the reference **Reference**.

Applying this idea to our example:

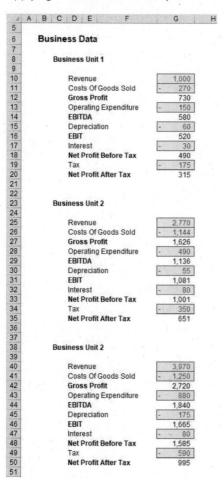

Note that the Business Unit data is 15 rows apart (*e.g.* the first block begins in row 8 and ends in row 22, taking the blank rows into account).

Therefore, I can therefore create one formula I may copy down:

| B2 | ▼ | : | ✕ | ✓ | *fx* | =OFFSET('Business Data'!$G$10,ROWS('Business Data'!$C$8:$C$22)*(ROWS($A$2:$A2)-1),) |

▲	A	B	C	D	E	F	G	H	I	J	K	L	M	N
1														
2		1000												
3		2770												
4		3970												
5		660												
6		8400												
7														
8														

In this example, we have started the formula in cell **B2** and copied it down to cell **B6**. The formula in cell **B2** is:

> **=OFFSET('Business Data'!$G$10,ROWS('Business Data'!$C$8:$C$22)*(ROWS($A$2:$A2)-1),)**

The first reference is the Revenue for Business Unit 1. The **Rows** reference takes the depth of each block (defined here by **ROWS('Business Data'!$C$8:$C$22)**) multiplied by **ROWS($A$2:$A2)-1**, *e.g.* in row 2 this factor will be zero, in row 3 it will be 1, in row 4 it will be 2, *etc.* This ensures that the next Revenue item is referred to in the next row down.

This may seem complex to begin with, but with practice this idea can be adapted for columns to be skipped as well and to allow for other line items (*e.g.* Gross Profit, Tax) to be selected instead.

CHAPTER 2.2: NUMBER FORMATTING

Given that one of the primary purposes of financial modelling is to present numerical data, it is important how numerical data is presented. Cells may be individually formatted using **CTRL + 1** or **ALT + O + E** in all versions of Excel:

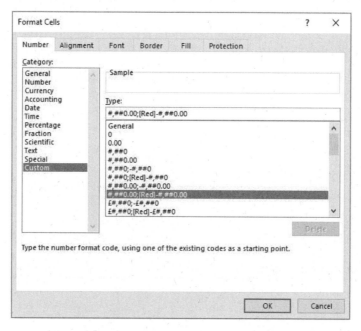

Formatting only changes the appearance, not the underlying value, of a cell. For example, if cells **A1** and **B1** had the number '1.4' typed in but were formatted to zero decimal places, then if cell **C1 = A1 + B1**, you would truly have 1 + 1 = 3 (well, 1.4 + 1.4 = 2.8 anyway).

This should not be confused with 'Set precision as displayed' (from the Ribbon, **File -> Excel Options -> Advanced -> When calculating this workbook -> Set precision as displayed**).

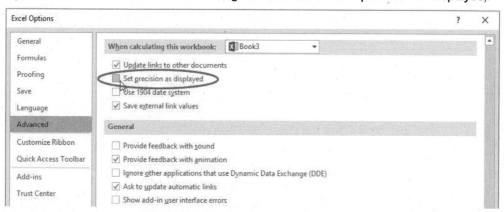

Selecting this option and clicking 'OK' will <u>permanently</u> change stored values in cells to whatever format has been selected, including the number of decimal places (*e.g.* 15.75 formatted to one decimal placed would become precisely 15.8).

From the above diagram, Excel has many built-in number formats that are fairly easy to understand, *e.g.* Currency, Date, Percentage. The default format is 'General' where Excel will endeavour to provide the most appropriate format for the contents. For example, typing '3 3/4' into a cell will result in Excel selecting a mixed format.

But what do you do if you can't find an appropriate format?

Selecting the 'Custom' category activates the 'Type' input box and allows between 200 and 250 custom number formats in a particular workbook, depending upon the language version of Excel that has been installed.

The 'Type' input box allows up to four aspects of formatting to be specified in a cell. These aspects are referred to as sections and are separated by a semi-colon (;). To ascertain what is contained in each section depends on the total number of sections used, *viz.*

No. of Sections	Section Details (assuming no conditions)
1 (min)	All numerical values
2	Non-negative Numbers; Negative Numbers
3	Positive Numbers; Negative Numbers; Zero Values
4 (max)	Positive Numbers; Negative Numbers; Zero Values; Text

To the uninitiated, coding custom number formats may appear incomprehensible. However, understanding the following tables from Microsoft soon puts things into perspective.

Number Code	Description
General	General number format
0	Digit placeholder (if no number, a '0' will be used to 'pad')
#	Digit placeholder (does not display extra zeros)
?	Digit placeholder (leaves space for extra zeros, but does not display them)
. (decimal point / full stop)	Decimal point!
%	Percentage displayed
, (comma)	Thousands separator
/	Used to delineate numerator from denominator in Fraction category
E+ e+ E- e-	Scientific notation

Text Code	Description
$ - + / ( ) : space	These characters are displayed in the number.
"text"	For other characters, in order to ensure Excel does not misinterpret them, it is best to use enclose the character(s) in quotation marks…
\character	…or precede it with a backslash
*	Repeats the next character in the format to fill the column width. Only one asterisk per section of a format is allowed
_character	Skips the width of the next character. In particular, this syntax is often used with the closing parenthesis, _) , in a positive number format (when the negative format includes brackets). This allows the values to line up at the decimal point
@	Text placeholder

Date Code	Description
m	Month as a number without leading zeros (1 to 12)
mm	Month as a number with leading zeros (01 to 12)
mmm	Month as an abbreviation (Jan – Dec)
mmmm	Unabbreviated month (January – December)
mmmmm	First letter of month (J, F, M, A, M, J, J, A, S, O, N, D)
d	Day without leading zeros (1 to 31)
dd	Day with leading zeros (01 to 31)
ddd	Week day as an abbreviation (Sun – Sat)
dddd	Unabbreviated week day (Sunday – Saturday)
y or yy	Year as a two digit number (e.g. 09, 97)
yyy or yyyy	Year as a four digit number (e.g. 2009, 1997)

Time Code	Description
h	Hours as a number without leading zero (0 to 23)
hh	Hours as a number with leading zero (00 to 23)
m	Minutes as a number without leading zero (0 to 59)
mm	Minutes as a number with leading zero (00 to 59)
s	Seconds as a number without leading zero (0 to 59)
ss	Seconds as a number with leading zero (00 to 59)
[h]	With times only, will increment hours to 24 and beyond
[m]	With times only, will increment minutes to 60 and beyond
[s]	With times only, will increment seconds to 60 and beyond
AM/PM am/pm	Time based on the 12-hour clock [24-hour clock is the default]

Miscellaneous Code	Description
[Black], [Blue], [Cyan], [Green], [Magenta], [Red], [White], [Yellow]	Displays the characters in the specified colours
[Color n]	Displays the characters in a specified colour, where n is a value from 1 to 56, and refers to the nth colour in the color palette
;	Delineates a section
[Condition Value]	Condition may be any one of the comparison operators, <, >, =, <=, >=, <> and Value may be any number.
	A number format may contain up to two conditions

Allow me to go through several examples.

Example 1: Comprehensive

[Blue]$* _(#,##0.0,_0_);[Red]$* (#,##0.00,);[Color 7]\-_._0_0_);[Cyan]@*."is text"

Comprehensive Example

Distinguishing between positive numbers, negative numbers, zero values and text.

Format	[Blue]$* _(#,##0.00,_0_);[Red]$* (#,##.0.00,);[Color 7]\-_._0_0_);[Cyan]@*."is text"

Cell Value	Appearance
123456789	$ 123,456.8
-123456789	$ (123,456.7.89)
0	-
This is text	This is text..is text

This format has all four sections, so the first section, **[Blue]$* _(#,##0.0,_0_)**, specifies the formatting for positive numbers. In this case, positive numbers will be formatted blue and be preceded with a $ sign. Note the use of the asterisk followed by a space: this means that the cell width will be 'padded out' with spaces so that the dollar sign will be pushed to the very left of the cell and the number formatting will be to the very right. _(is not necessary, strictly speaking, but ensures there is space made for an open bracket, even though there is no such character shown. #,##0.0, ensures positive numbers contain thousand separators (where needed) and displays the number to the nearest 0.1 of a thousand. Two commas at the end would have the number displayed to the nearest 0.1 of a million, and so on. Finally, the _0_) requires Excel to maintain enough space at the right end of a cell for a digit (not necessarily zero) and a close bracket. It should be noted that a separate underscore is required for each character that is to be allowed for.

The second section, **[Red]$* (#,##0.00,)**, specifies the formatting for negative numbers. It is similar to the first section, but colours the number red, reports numbers to 0.01 of a thousand and encloses it in brackets.

The third section, **[Color 7]\-_._0_0_)**, specifies the formatting for zero values. This colours zero values "Color 7" which is a delightful pink in Excel's standard color palette. I am a great believer in using a dash, generated by using \- here, to denote zero as it distinguishes a zero value from something that is approximately zero, which can be useful for error checking. The final four underscored characters, _._0_0_), ensure that the dash will line up with the units value of a positive or negative value.

Finally, the fourth section, **[Cyan]@*."is text"**, defines how text is to be formatted. If omitted, text is simply formatted as 'General', but here it will be coloured cyan. The @ symbol specifies the relative location of the text within the cell (left-hand side of the cell), the ***.** will 'fill' the cell with period characters and **"is text"** will add these words to the end of the text, right-aligned (note no '&' concatenation is required since these words appear in the formatting only).

Example 2: Hiding the Contents of a Cell

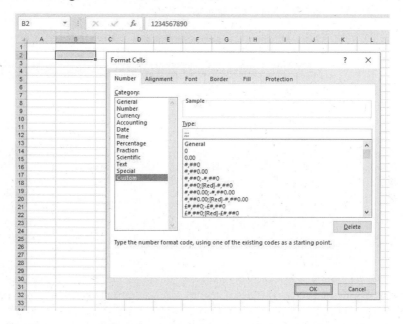

Colouring the font and the background the same may hide a cell's contents on screen, but it will often reappear when printed out (especially if 'black and white printing' is selected). By choosing the above formatting (three semi-colons), numbers and text are simply 'blanked out' and will only appear in Excel's formula bar instead.

Example 3: Formatting Based on Conditions

[>=1000000]#,##0,,"M";[>=1000]#,##0,"K";0

Thousands Etc. Format Examples

Various ways of representing larger numbers.

Format   [>=1000000]#,##0,,"M";[>=1000]#,##0,"K";0

Number	Appearance
0.1	0
1	1
10	10
100	100
1,000	1K
10,000	10K
100,000	100K
1,000,000	1M
10,000,000	10M
100,000,000	100M
1,000,000,000	1,000M

Earlier, I mentioned what the four sections mean most commonly. This third example highlights that this is not always the case. Custom number formats allow up to two conditions to be specified. This is because only four sections are allowed for custom number formatting and two are reserved. The fourth section always specifies text formatting and one other section is required to detail how 'everything else' (numerically) will be formatted. It is a bit like conditional formatting (see later), just for numbers.

The conditions are included in square brackets such that if the condition is true, the following formatting will be applied. In this example, there are only three sections, so text will be formatted as 'General'. The first section, **[>=1000000]#,##0,,"M"**, will format all numbers greater than or equal to a million to the nearest million and add an "M" to the end of the number. Note that the commas effectively make it look like each divided by 1,000.

The second section will only be considered if the first condition is not true, so the order of the two 'conditional formats' needs to be thought through. Here, the second section, **[>=1000]#,##0,"K"**, will format all numbers greater than or equal to a thousand (but necessarily less than a million) to the nearest thousand and add a "K" to the end of the number.

The third and final section, **0**, will format all other numbers (every value less than 1,000) to the nearest integer without thousands separator(s).

Use with Caution

Using lots of custom number formats in a single workbook uses considerable memory and can slow down the calculation time of an Excel file unnecessarily. Many of these formats are created accidentally. Each time a custom number format is edited, it will generate an additional listing for Custom Category Types. Any custom formats created inadvertently in this manner (that are not being used in the file) should be deleted; good house-keeping is essential.

CHAPTER 2.3: STYLES

Do you know the difference between formats and styles, other than formatting is what you do in Excel and style is what I lack? Take the illustration below. How easy is it to find the key data, or see which cells should be changed to facilitate updated information? Have you ever noticed that spreadsheets built by colleagues do not look similar to your own? How easy are these things in your own spreadsheets? Have I asked enough questions in this paragraph? No?

	A	B	C	D	E
1	Sample Data				
2		Q1	Q2	Q3	Q4
3	Revenue	3700	4142	4099	5008
4	Costs Of Goods Sold	-1577	-1746	-1680	-1931
5	Gross Profit	2123	2396	2419	3077
6	Rent	-440	-440	-440	-440
7	Electricity	-212	-240	-242	-308
8	Other Operating Expenditure	-770	-790	-745	-977
9	Total Operating Expenditure	-1422	-1470	-1427	-1725
10	EBITDA	701	926	992	1352
11					

Later on, I will discuss the four key qualities of a "Best Practice" model, but as a taster, two of these key qualities are consistency and transparency.

Examples of consistency:

- formulae are copied without amendment across rows

- cells with a common purpose (for example, inputs that are assumptions, such as inflation rates) are formatted similarly

- titles are positioned in the same cells in different worksheets

- assumption cells (cells containing data that can be changed by the user to affect model outputs) are unlocked, where all other cells are locked, so that only the assumption cells can be changed.

Examples of transparency:

- assumptions are formatted to be instantly recognisable

- key outputs (for example, totals) can be identified immediately, with their derivation made obvious.

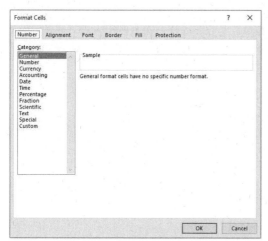

Excel's 'Styles' features can assist with both transparency and consistency. Frequently, the words 'formats' and 'styles' are used interchangeably, but they are not the same thing. To see this, select any cell in Excel and apply the shortcut keystroke **CTRL + 1**. As mentioned previously, this shortcut brings up the 'Format Cells' dialog box:

Excel has six format properties: Number, Alignment, Font, Border, Fill and Protection. A style is simply a pre-defined set of these various formats. With a little forethought, these styles can be set up and applied to a worksheet cell or range very easily.

Creating your own styles is straightforward with Excel's Style dialog box. Simply go to the Home tab, click the arrow in the bottom right corner at the very right-hand corner of the 'Styles' section:

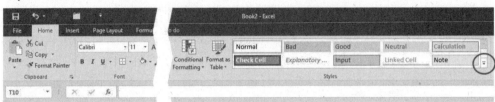

This expands the section:

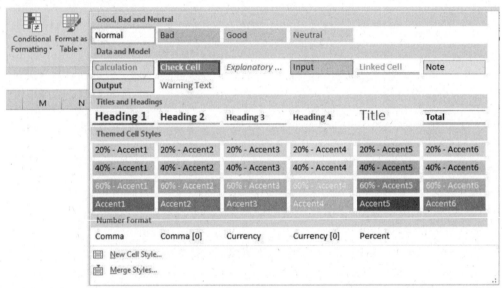

You can then select a New Cell Style (see the list at the bottom of the pop-up or **ALT + H + J + N**), use an existing style or modify an existing style (right-click with the mouse). If you decide to create a new style or edit an existing one, the following dialog box will appear:

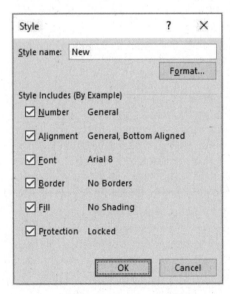

Let's create an assumption format for entering data in dollars. First, select a cell or range of cells. Then, call up the above dialog box by selecting "New Cell Style". We'll change the name to 'Dollar Assumptions" and click the 'Modify' or 'Format' button (depending upon the version of Excel you have).

The 'Format Cells' dialog box reappears:

- **Number:** select the Currency category, with zero decimal places and apply the '$' symbol

- **Alignment:** Horizontal – Right (Indent) with zero indent

- **Fill:** select an 'easy-on-the-eye' colour such as pale green

- **Protection:** uncheck the Locked check box (allows the cell to be changed in a protected worksheet)

- Click 'OK' to return to the Style dialog box.

Note that no formats have been ascribed for Font or Border in this example. We don't want the style to control (that is, overwrite) these properties, so the 'Style Includes' check boxes for these two format properties should be unchecked:

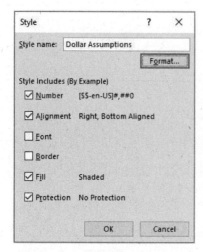

This allows you to combine multiple formatting properties in one cell, although there is no point having more than six as you will be overwriting an earlier style otherwise. Returning to the graphic, click on 'OK' or 'Add'. Now that this style has been added, you simply select the range and then click on the style in the Styles gallery on the Home tab.

The main difference between formats and styles becomes obvious when you realise you want to change (update) a style. Call up the Style dialog box in the usual way, modifying the style as required. Click 'OK' when finished. Note that every cell in the open workbook that uses this style has automatically updated. Once you start using styles, you will never look back!

You will only want to set up styles once. When you're finished, simply save the file as a template (.xltx) using **File-->Save As** (you may wish to delete or remove formatted cells first so that you have a blank workbook). Using **File-->New** will call up your saved styles.

With very little practice, you will find yourself being able to style worksheets faster than you can say "floccinaucinihilipilification" (I am impressed my spell checker recognises this word!). Returning to our original example, which do you prefer?

Before Styles

	A	B	C	D	E
1	Sample Data				
2		Q1	Q2	Q3	Q4
3	Revenue	3700	4142	4099	5008
4	Costs Of Goods Sold	-1577	-1746	-1680	-1931
5	Gross Profit	2123	2396	2419	3077
6	Rent	-440	-440	-440	-440
7	Electricity	-212	-240	-242	-308
8	Other Operating Expenditure	-770	-790	-745	-977
9	Total Operating Expenditure	-1422	-1470	-1427	-1725
10	EBITDA	701	926	992	1352

After Styles

	A	B	C	D	E
1	**Sample Data**				
2		Q1	Q2	Q3	Q4
3	Revenue	3,700	4,142	4,099	5,008
4	Costs of Goods Sold	- 1,577	- 1,746	- 1,680	- 1,931
5	**Gross Profit**	2,123	2,396	2,419	3,077
6	Rent	- 440	440	- 440	440
7	Electricity	- 212	240	242	308
8	Other Operating Expenditure	- 770	790	- 745	977
9	**Total Operating Expenditure**	- 1,422	1,470	- 1,427	1,725
10	**EBITDA**	701	926	992	1,352

Should you have the Styles you want in another workbook, there is a quick way to copy them in. Simply have both workbooks open. Then, in the workbook in which you would like to import the Styles, go to 'Merge Styles…' *viz.*

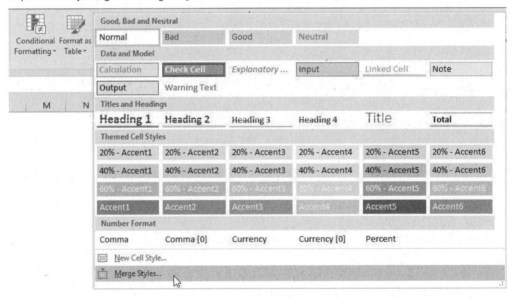

A dialog box will pop up from which you may select the workbook with the Styles you require.

Click on the correct workbook and then on 'OK' and all of the Styles from that workbook will be imported (including any duplicates).

This leads me on to mentioning one issue with Styles. If worksheets or ranges are copied from other workbooks, the Styles from that workbook may be copied across too, leading to hundreds – if not thousands – of Styles you don't want, artificially bloating the size of your financial model. To delete Styles, you right-click on the Style of your choice and select 'Delete' – but this has to be performed *one at a time*. Yuck!

There are two workarounds to this issue:

- When copying from another workbook, copy the range to be imported (**CTRL + C**) and then paste special twice. First, in the destination workbook, select where you want the data to go and Paste Special as Formulas (**ALT + E + S + F + ENTER**) and then Paste Special as Formats (**ALT + E + S + T + ENTER**).

- Use a macro to delete Styles.

I provide an example of such a macro below. This one allows you to choose which custom (*i.e.* not those that are built in) Styles should be deleted in the workbook:

```
Sub RemoveStyles()

    Dim StyleCustom As Style

    Dim ReturnedInteger As Integer


    For Each StyleCustom In ActiveWorkbook.Styles

        If Not StyleCustom.BuiltIn Then

            ReturnedInteger = MsgBox("Delete style '" & StyleCustom.
Name & "'?", vbYesNo)

            If ReturnedInteger = vbYes Then StyleCustom.Delete

        End If

    Next StyleCustom

End Sub
```

Macros

This book is not about macros, so forgive me if I only mention them in passing here and there. Essentially, a **macro** is a coded procedure using the language Visual Basic for Applications (**VBA**) often used to automate actions. Since Excel 2007, files must not be saved as *.xlsx files (these Excel workbooks will not allow macros). Your best bet is to use a macro-enabled workbook - *.xlsm.

Even then, because macros may execute all sorts of undesirable code, Excel's default setting is set so that macros will not run automatically. To ensure the macro below will work, when you open the file, make sure that you click on "Enable Content" or "Enable Macros" when prompted.

To enter a typed (rather than recorded) macro, open the Visual Basic Editor (**ALT + F11**), select the file (if more than one open) from the Project Explorer (top left-hand window) and then from the menu, click **Insert->Module** and type your code into the right-hand pane.

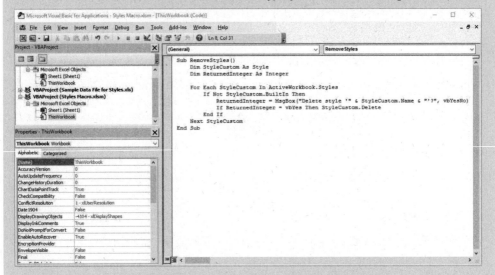

To run the macro, you can go to the View tab and click on the Macros button.

CHAPTER 2.4: CONDITIONAL FORMATTING

With Excel's **IF** function, the contents of a cell can be modified depending upon (a) certain condition(s) being met (*i.e.* held to be TRUE). However, the formatting or style of the cell cannot be changed in this manner.

Macros are not needed.

First introduced in Excel 97, Conditional Formatting is an Excel feature that indeed allows you to apply formats to a cell or range of cells, and have that formatting change depending on the value of the cell or the value of a corresponding formula. This was one of the features that was given a major overhaul in Excel 2007.

Accessed from the 'Home' tab (or **ALT + O + D**), conditional formatting formats the cell(s) selected depending upon whether a condition is TRUE. In Excel 2003 and earlier versions, conditional formatting would work as follows:

```
If Condition1 = True Then
     Apply Format1
Else
     If Condition2 = True Then
          Apply Format2
     Else
          If Condition3 = True Then
               Apply Format3
          Else
               Apply DefaultFormat
          End If
     End If
End If
```

Essentially, as soon as Excel finds a condition that is held, it formats accordingly and stops. If none of the three conditions is met, the underlying format (*i.e.* the fourth format) is retained.

As explained above, conditional formatting was completely revamped and reinvented in Excel 2007. Located in the 'Styles' group of the 'Home' tab, the conditional formatting feature has had a raft of new features added:

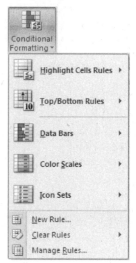

For instance, inspecting 'Highlight Cells Rules' is akin to many of the "Cell Value Is" functionalities of its predecessor, such as Greater Than, Less Than, Between, Equal To, or even More Rules:

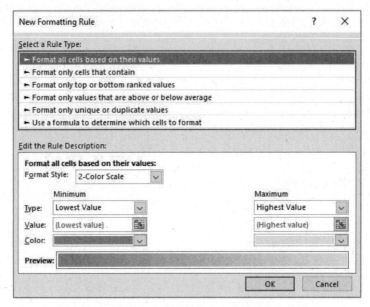

Other options are also available: Date Occurring and Duplicate Values. All you have to do is highlight the list, select the option and colour scheme required. No need to concoct hideous formulae such as **=IF(COUNTIF($A:$A,$A1)>1,COUNTIF($A$1:$A1,$A1)>1)** for locating duplicates, for example.

Users should not be fooled by the easy-to-use Top / Bottom Rules either. Top 10 Items, Top 10%, Bottom 10 Items and Bottom 10% all highlight items that conform to these labels. However, the '10' can be changed to a number of the user's choice. Who could possibly live without the Bottom 37% Debtors Report, for instance?

Above average and below average data can be highlighted also in one or two clicks and even graded shading of a cell as well. For example, if cells **A1:A10** had the values 10, 20, 30, ..., 100 respectively, the cells could be filled in as follows:

Using Data Bars

	A
1	10
2	20
3	30
4	40
5	50
6	60
7	70
8	80
9	90
10	100

Using Color Scales

	A
1	10
2	20
3	30
4	40
5	50
6	60
7	70
8	80
9	90
10	100

Clearly, looking at the Color Scales example, conditional formatting lends itself neatly to traffic light reporting. This is compounded by Icon Sets that will stratify data into three to five sections using various icons (such as the red, amber and green traffic lights). Given that conditional formatting now permits cells to be sorted dependent upon their background colour (**ALT + D + S**, then choose 'Cell Color' in 'Sort On' field), you can make monthly reporting a colourful adventure!

Conditional formatting in Excel 2007 does differ logically from its predecessor.

With Excel 2003 and earlier, as soon as Excel finds a condition that is held it formats accordingly and stops. This can be performed for up three conditions. These days, there is 'no limit' and testing does not have to stop (more than one format can be applied in a cell at a time), *i.e.*

```
If Condition1 = True Then
        Apply Format1
End If
If Condition2 = True Then
        Apply Format2
End If
If Condition3 = True Then
        Apply Format3
End If
```

To highlight this, consider the following data set before and after multiple conditional formatting:

Before Multiple Conditional Formatting

	A
1	11
2	20
3	29
4	40
5	51
6	60
7	79
8	80
9	91
10	100

After Multiple Conditional Formatting

	A
1	11
2	20
3	29
4	40
5	51
6	60
7	79
8	80
9	91
10	100

No less than four conditional formats have been applied, as can be seen by opening up the Conditional Formatting Rules Manager (**ALT + O + D**):

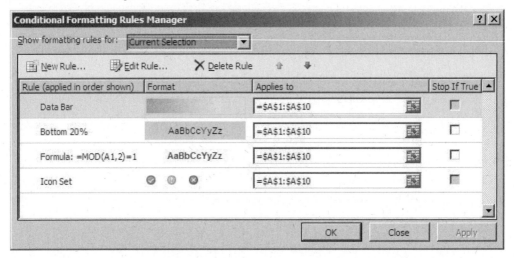

Using the blue up and down arrows can reorder the sequence and the sequence can be stopped if certain conditions are true (simply check the box in the fourth columns). This gives conditional formatting significantly greater flexibility these days

One tip though: always try to add conditional formatting after completing all of the calculations in your model. This is because conditional formatting sometimes misbehaves when rows or columns are deleted and / or inserted. Trust me, it's less work to add it at the end!

CHAPTER 2.5: RANGE NAMES

If you were to ask modelling professionals about the merits of using range names you will find that opinion is strongly divided. In spreadsheets, used appropriately and sparingly, great value can be obtained from using range names, as it can make formulae easier to read. In macros (not discussed here), they are vital. Overuse, on the other hand, can lead to end user confusion.

There are various ways range names may be created in Excel. One way is to use the **Name Box**:

Note that range names must start with a letter or an underscore character (_) and cannot be mistaken for a cell reference (can you imagine the fun you would have calling cell **A1 D3** *etc*?). Spaces are not allowed either.

Space: the Final Frontier?

There is a very good reason that spaces are not allowed in range names. Not many modellers – even advanced ones – seem to appreciate the following functionality. Consider the following extract:

Space (" ") is actually the **intersect** operator in Excel. This is why you should never put spaces in formulae in Excel – the software may inadvertently try to intersect your ranges. If you do need to break out a formula, use **ALT + ENTER** instead: this will put line breaks in instead.

Regarding range names, if you need to make a name readable, I suggest using the underscore (_) character, *e.g.* **Range_name**.

Remaining characters in the name can be letters, numbers, periods, and underscore characters. Spaces are not allowed but two words can be joined, or with an underscore (_) or period (.). For example, to enter the Name 'Cash Flow' you should enter 'Cash_Flow' or 'Cash.Flow.'.

There is no limit on the number of names you can define, but a name may only contain up to 255 characters (why on earth you would want something this long is beyond me). Names can contain uppercase and / or lowercase letters. Excel does not distinguish between uppercase and lowercase characters in names. For example, if you have created the global name 'Profit' and then create another global name called 'PROFIT' in the same workbook, the second name will replace the first one.

It is not a syntax issue, but I strongly recommend thought is given to adding prefixes to range names. When I discussed **OFFSET** earlier, I recommended using the prefix '**BC_**' (**B**ase **C**ell). Similarly, I use '**LU_**' for **L**ook **U**p lists and so on. By using these prefixes, I understand the purpose of the range name and so that names with a common purpose are grouped together in a list. This is not to say all range names should contain a prefix. 'Tax_Rate', for instance, makes sense on its own and adding a prefix would only detract from the name given, potentially confusing the end user.

Once you have decided upon a name for your range, perhaps the quickest way of all to add and edit a range name is using the Name Manager (**CTRL + F3**):

This is where you go to delete range names – one of the most common questions I am asked in financial modelling!!

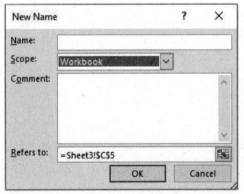

If you click on 'New...' (above), the dialog box to the left appears.

Note the highlighted section (Scope). All names have a scope, either to a specific worksheet (also called the local worksheet level) or to the entire workbook (also called the global workbook level). The scope of a name is the location within which the name is recognised without qualification.

For example, if you have defined a range name as 'Profit' with its scope as Sheet1 (say) rather than 'Workbook', then it will only be recognised in Sheet1 as 'Profit' (*i.e.* without qualification). To use this local name in another worksheet, you must qualify it by preceding it with the localised worksheet name:

=Sheet1!Profit

If you have defined a name, such as 'Cashflow', and its scope is the workbook, that name is recognised for all worksheets in that workbook (but not for any other workbook).

A name must always be unique within its scope. Excel prevents you from defining a name that is not unique within its scope. However, you can use the same name in different scopes. For example, you can define a name, such as 'Profit' that is scoped to Sheet1, Sheet2 and Sheet3 in the same workbook. Although each name is the same, each name is unique within its scope. You might do this to ensure that a formula that uses the name 'Gross_Profit' (say) is always referencing the same cells at the local worksheet level.

You can even define the same name, 'Profit' for the global workbook level, but again this scope is unique. In this case, there may be a name conflict. To resolve this conflict, Excel uses the name that is defined for the worksheet by default. The local worksheet level takes precedence over the global workbook level. This can be circumvented by adding the following prefix to the name, *e.g.* rename it 'WorkbookFile!Profit' instead.

It is possible to override the local worksheet level for all worksheets in the workbook, except for the first worksheet. This will always use the local name if there is a name conflict and cannot be overridden.

From experience, I strongly recommend that you never duplicate a range name within a workbook. It can cause formulaic errors. For similar reasons, I also suggest that you try never to have range names on a worksheet that may be copied.

There is a nifty shortcut for creating range names using existing names. Consider the following list:

	M	N
V33		

	M	N
11		
12		Phonetic Alphabet
13		A for 'orses
14		B for Dam
15		C for Miles
16		D for Effort
17		E for Brick
18		F for Vescent
19		H for ID purposes
20		I for an Eye
21		L for Leather
22		M for CIMA
23		P for Test Sample
24		Q for Sales
25		R for Kilo
26		T for Two
27		U for Mism
28		

Imagine you were to highlight cells **N12:N27** in the above example and then use the shortcut **CTRL + SHIFT + F3**:

Create Names from Selection ? ×

Create names from values in the:

- ☑ **T**op row
- ☐ **L**eft column
- ☐ **B**ottom row
- ☐ **R**ight column

[OK] [Cancel]

With the first check box ('Top row') checked, by clicking on 'OK' the range **N13:N27** (not **N12:N27**) will be named 'Phonetic_Alphabet' (*i.e.* the underscore will be added automatically). Ranges across rows can be named in seconds similarly using 'Left column' similarly.

The reason this dialog box uses check boxes (rather than option buttons) is to allow users to select more than one at a time. For example, consider the following data:

	M	N	O	P	Q	R
30						
31			Jan	Feb	Mar	Apr
32		Sales	7,000	8,000	9,000	10,000
33		Costs	(2,270)	(3,817)	(4,522)	(5,712)
34		Gross Margin	4,730	4,183	4,478	4,288
35						

Highlighting cells **N31:R34** and then employing the keyboard shortcut **CTRL + SHIFT + F3** would generate the following dialog box:

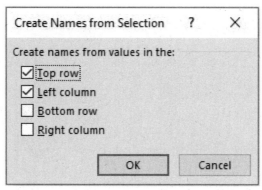

Highlighting **N31:R34** and using the keyboard shortcut **CTRL + SHIFT + F3** once more should generate the Create Names dialog box as above with both 'Top row' and 'Left column' checked. This means that **O32:O34** will be called 'Jan', **O33:R33** will be called 'Costs' and so on. This would take considerably longer to perform manually.

This example also reinforces why spaces are illegal characters in range names (and for that matter, should not be added to formulae either). Space is the ***intersect operator i***n Excel. If you were to type the following formula:

=Gross_Margin Feb

Excel would return the value in cell **P34** (the intersection of the two ranges, above), *i.e.* $4,183. This can be a powerful yet quick and simple analytical tool for key outputs.

One of the reasons I like using the **CTRL + F3** shortcut is that it is part of the **F3** 'Names family of shortcuts'. We have just seen how **CTRL + SHIFT + F3** can be useful – and so can **F3** on its own. Perhaps superseded by the fact that Excel will now prompt as you type formulae, **F3** has been very useful in the past as the 'Paste Names' shortcut. For example, as you type a formula you can refer to a range name by simply typing **F3** to get the Paste Names dialog box, *viz.*

Selecting one of the cells and clicking 'OK' inserts the range name. However, look closer at the dialog box. The 'Paste List' button in the bottom left hand corner, if depressed, will paste the list and their definitions into a pre-selected range of cells in an Excel worksheet which can be invaluable for model auditing purposes.

Sometimes, formulae have been written before the range name was created. In some circumstances, it is possible to apply these names retrospectively using 'Apply Names' within the 'Defined Names' group of the 'Formulas' tab, *viz.*

Note that the keyboard shortcut **ALT + I + N + A** will work in all versions of Excel. Selecting the required range names in the resulting dialog box will see formulae on the active worksheet(s) updated accordingly.

Deleting Range Names

If I got paid just $1 for every time I have been asked how to delete range names I would probably have nearly $10 by now. This was chiefly attributable to the counter-intuitive menu in Excel 2003 and earlier versions:

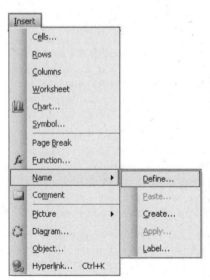

From the resulting dialog box, you would then select the range name (unfortunately, only one at a time could be selected) and hit 'Delete', *viz.*

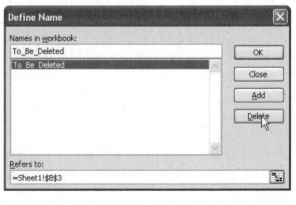

Excel 2007 onwards makes this much simpler. Users can now go to the 'Name Manager':

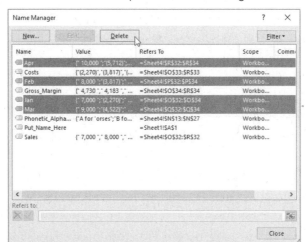

The other marked improvement is that multiple names may be deleted simultaneously by using the **CTRL** or **SHIFT** buttons to make multiple selections before hitting the 'Delete' button. In fact, range names may be even filtered to find names with errors, scoped to the workbook, scoped to the worksheet *etc*.

Relative Referencing

By default, range names are referenced absolutely (i.e. contain the **$** sign so that references remain static). However, imagine a scenario where you are modelling revenue and you wish to grow the prior period value by inflation (already given a range name, say cell **C3** on Sheet1). Simply click on any cell (for example, I will use **D17** arbitrarily), then define the new range name as follows:

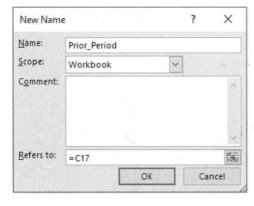

Note the 'Refers to:' entry. Cell **C17** (the cell to the left of **D17**) has been chosen without the dollar signs. This is a relative reference. Once we click on 'OK', the range name '**Prior_Period**' will be defined as the cell immediately to the left of the active cell. We can then inflate values easily by copying the formula

$$=Prior\_Period*(1+Inflation)$$

across the row.

Other Types of Names

Most of us use the terms 'names' and 'range names' synonymously. However, this is not strictly true. We can create names simply using hard coded values, *e.g.*

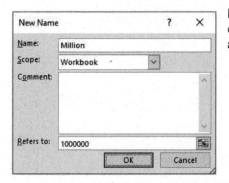

Names may also refer to functions, dates and constants in order to avoid inserting hard code into a formula.

Another useful type is what are called **dynamic ranges**. These ranges vary in size depending upon how they are defined. Consider the following range:

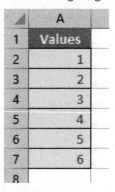

Let's define the following range name (**CTRL + F3**, then 'New'):

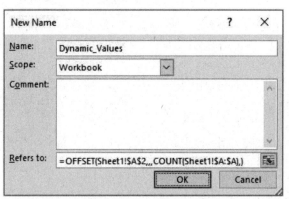

Here, the range name has been defined by an **OFFSET** formula:

=OFFSET(Sheet1!$A$2,,,COUNT(Sheet1!$A:$A),)

This formula creates a range in cell A2 with a depth of how many numbers there are in column **A**. In our example, there are six numbers so the range extends to **$A$2:$A$7**.

This can be useful for creating versatile ranges for lists or charts, for example. It should be noted that these type of range names will not be visible in the Name Box and will not work with all Excel functions – trial and error is very much recommended!

One interesting quirk of names relating to range names is what happens if you actually reduce the scale of Zoom View (**ALT + W + Q**) to 39% or below:

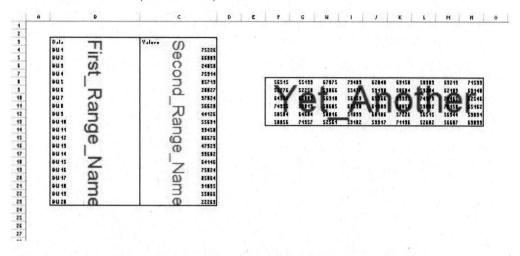

It can be a simple way of tracking down some of those pesky critters.

This section discusses just the tip of the Names iceberg. Experimenting can pay dividends. The aim is not to go overboard, as a preponderance of names in a work book may actually make formulae – and hence your model – more difficult to follow.

Further, be careful if you name ranges that are then deleted. The range names will not be deleted (even though they will no longer appear in the Name Box). They will need to be deleted as described above in order to cause potential errors in formulae, *etc.* These types of errors (known as **redundant range name errors**) can cause significant issues and have been known to crash and / or corrupt Excel files on occasion.

CHAPTER 2.6: DATA VALIDATION

Another useful Excel functionality is data validation. This feature restricts what end users may type into a cell. I must admit that this is one of Excel's functionalities I am guilty of assuming everyone knows. However, it's like Styles: many aren't aware of this in Excel, but once you use this functionality and understand what it can do for you, you never go back to whatever it was you were doing before.

To access data validation, from any cell in Excel:

- On the Data tab of the Ribbon, go to the Data Tools group and click the Data Validation icon (**ALT + A + V + V**)

- **ALT + D + L** still works from earlier versions of Excel.

This brings up the following dialog box:

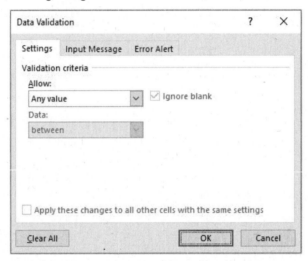

The default setting for all cells in Excel is to allow any value (pictured). This can be changed by changing the selection in the 'Allow' drop down box. It may be modified to any of the following:

Most of these criteria do exactly what they say on the tin: by choosing 'Decimal', the input must be a number, whereas 'Whole Number' allows for integers only. However, making a selection from the 'Allow' drop down box is only the first part of the data validation process.

Once a selection has been made (for example, I will use 'Whole Number'), the dialog box will change appearance, *viz*.

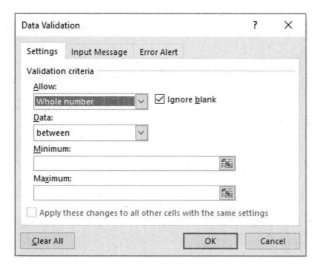

The 'Ignore blank' check box is no longer greyed out. This allows blank cells to be 'valid' regardless of the criteria selected. The remainder of the dialog box is governed by the 'Data' drop down box. There are various selections that may be made:

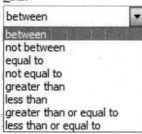

Depending upon the choice made, the box will prompt for values (*e.g.* Minimum and Maximum in the illustration above) which can be typed in, or else the values can refer to cell references directly or indirectly via range names.

One the choices have been made, you might wish to utilise the other two tabs of the Data Validation dialog box.

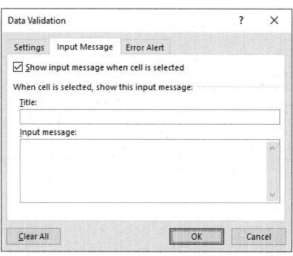

With the 'Show input message when cell is selected' checked, if the end user selects the data validated, cell the message typed in here will appear. This can make data inputs in a model much simpler as end users are 'spoon fed' with a pop-up box detailing what to do. In the example below, the 'Input Restrictions' comment only appears when the cell is selected:

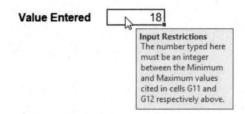

The third tab selects what to do if invalid data is entered in the cell:

This alerts the end user when an invalid entry has been made (*e.g.* typing "dog" when a number is expected) – as long as the 'Show error alert after invalid data is entered' check box is ticked.

There are three styles available:

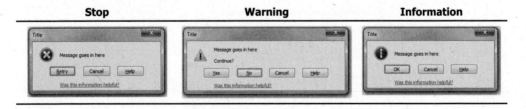

The three styles provide differing treatment of invalid data:

- **Stop** – the value will not be accepted and the end user will be prompted to retry;

- **Warning** – the end user will be warned that the data is invalid, but be asked whether it is OK to continue; *and*

- **Information** – the end user will be advised that the data is invalid but that the data has been accepted.

If the 'Show error alert after invalid data is entered' check box is not ticked, no prompt will occur and invalid data will be accepted in the cell without any warning.

Other Types of Data Validation

Whole Number, Decimal, Date, Time and Text Length are all relatively straightforward, albeit very similar in nature. This leaves just two remaining categories to consider.

List

This functionality allows the end user to select from a list.

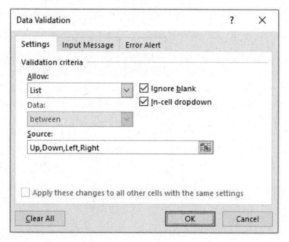

With 'List' selected, the dialog box prompts for a source for the list. In the illustration, the entries have been typed in, separated by a comma (the delimiter). However, the data can use cell references which are in a column – or a row – as long as the cells are on the same worksheet in versions of Excel up to and including Excel 2007. This can be limiting and a viable workaround is to name a row or column of data (using the prefix '**LU_**' for **L**ook **U**p) and then use the range name here (which may be pasted in using the **F3** function key).

For lists, I strongly recommend using the 'In-cell dropdown' which provides a dropdown list of valid entries once the cell has been selected.

Custom

As you become more experienced, you may find the functionality limiting. This is where the final 'Allow' category comes in useful, as you design your own data validation. My recommendation is to experiment with the other types first and then graduate to this classification once you realise validation may not be created using the built-in options.

Data Validation is Reactive Not Proactive

Data validation will not solve all of your data entry problems. If data has already been entered into a cell and data validation is applied retrospectively such that the contents of the cell would be deemed invalid, no warning will ensue. Similarly, if the contents of a list are altered, any cells that selected the changed value will not update automatically.

To counter these issues, invalid data may be identified on a worksheet as follows:

- On the Data tab of the Ribbon, go to the Data Tools group and click the drop down menu next to the Data Validation icon

- Select 'Circle Invalid Data' (**ALT + A + V + I**)

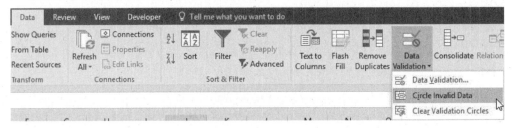

This will circle all invalid data on the worksheet.

One other issue is locating cells that have been data validated in the first place (i.e. no longer allow 'any value'). The simplest way to do this is through the 'Go to' dialog box (**F5**), click on the 'Special…' button and then select 'Data Validation' (either all data validated cells on the worksheet or else those validated similarly to the cell(s) presently selected):

Select 'Special…' on the Go To Dialog Box   **Choose Data Validation**

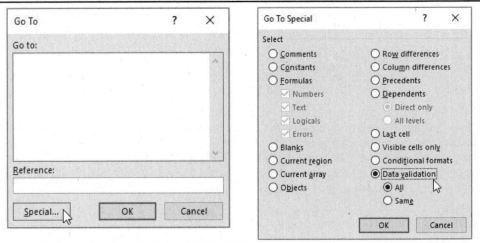

Best Excel Tip Ever..?

Our company produces a monthly newsletter (feel free to subscribe). A short while ago, we polled our readers for their Best Excel Tip ever – and I think it revealed more about the psyche of our average reader than it ever did about improving efficiencies and effectiveness in the workplace...

As discussed above, data validation is a useful way to control what end users can type into a worksheet cell. You can use this functionality to play a trick. Please use this at your own risk: if you get fired, you will get no sympathy here.

If someone is unfortunate to leave a spreadsheet unprotected, simply highlight the whole worksheet and then activate Data Validation (**ALT + D + L**).

In the 'Settings' tab, select settings similar to the following (the aim is to pick a number the user won't use):

Then, select the 'Error Alert' tab:

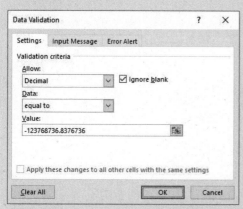
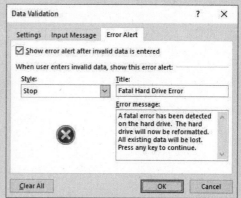

Now, de-select the range and wait for your victim to use the worksheet. As soon as they type an invalid entry, they will be greeted with the following error alert:

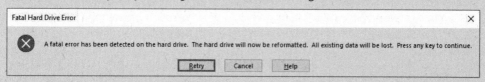

Who says spreadsheets can't be fun..?

CHAPTER 2.7: DATA TABLES

The next built-in feature I'd like to address assists with what-if analysis and is an alternative to copy and paste macros. Just to be clear, when I refer to "sensitivity analysis" here, I mean the flexing of one or at most two variables to see how these changes in input affect key outputs. Excel has various built-in features that assist with this type of analysis, but here we will focus on **Data Tables**.

Data Tables are ideal for executive summaries where you wish to show how changes in a particular input affect a key output. However, as always with modelling, Keep It Simple Stupid (KISS). If you can achieve the same functionality without using Data Tables in a simple, straightforward fashion, then do it that way. Consider the following example:

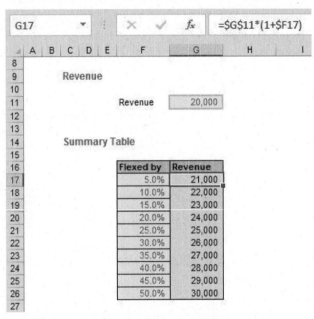

In this illustration, the key output revenue has been given in cell **G11**. We want to summarise what happens if we increase ("flex") this figure by a given percentage, with the inputs specified in cells **F17:F26**. This can be simply computed by using the formula

$$=\$G\$11*(1+\$F17)$$

in cell **G17** and simply copying this calculation down.

Data Tables should really be used when such simple calculations are not possible and you want to flex one variable (known as a "one-variable" or "one-dimensional (**1-D**)" Data Table) or two (known as a "two-variable" or "two-dimensional (**2-D**)" Data Table).

I will now consider each in turn.

1-D Data Tables

This is best illustrated using the following example.

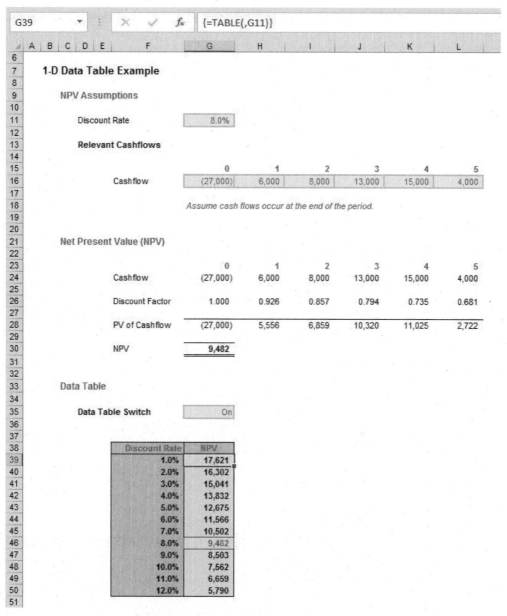

Now I do appreciate this example could be constructed using a similar technique to our revenue example using the **NPV** function: I just wanted to construct a slightly more complex alternative that could still be followed!

Here, a simple Net Present Value calculation calculated for a total of six periods (0 to 5 inclusive). If you don't understand what this is, don't worry, the point is, we are building a calculation. The output for a discount rate of 8.0% (cell **G11**) is +$9,482 (cell **G30**). But what if I wanted to know how the NPV would change if I varied the discount rate?

It is very easy to construct a table (a Data Table) similar to the one displayed in cells **F38:G50** above. The required discount rates are simply typed into cells **F39:F50**, but the headings in cells **F38:G38** are not what they seem.

For a 1-D Data Table to work using a columnar table similar to the one illustrated, the top row has to contain the reference to output cell in the right hand cell (**G38** must be **=G30**). Many modellers will do this, putting the headings in the row above instead and then they may or may not hide row 38 in order to compensate.

There is a crafty alternative (employed above).

Using **CTRL + 1** or **ALT + O + E** to Format Cells, if we go to the 'Number' tab we can still type the formulae in but change the outward appearance of the cell. For example, cell **F38** is formatted as follows:

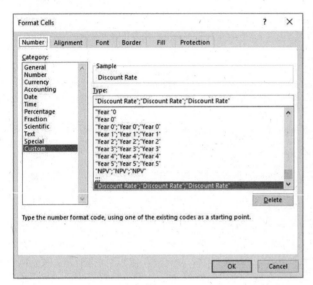

Here, I have typed in "Discount Rate";"Discount Rate";"Discount Rate". Custom number formatting was explained in detail earlier, but essentially this syntax forces Excel to display any numerical output as "Discount Rate". Note that simply typing "Discount Rate" here once would be insufficient: e.g. if the output were negative, the cell would be displayed as "-Discount Rate". **G38** is formatted similarly.

Once row 38 has been finalised, highlight cells **F38:G50** and then create the Data Table as follows:

- Click on the 'Data' tab on the Ribbon

- In the 'Data Tools' group, click on the 'What-If Analysis' icon and select 'Data Table..."
  (**ALT + D + T** or **ALT + A + W + T**).

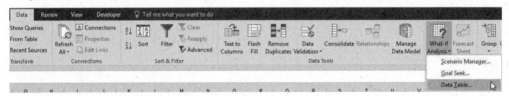

This gives rise to the following dialog box:

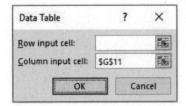

In a 1-D Data Table only one of these two input cells should be populated. When the table is of a columnar format, the column input cell should be populated, referring to the input cell, as above.

If the table had been across a row instead, ensure that the input values are in the top row, and that the 'headings' are in the first column (i.e. transpose the example table above). Then, you would populate the 'Row input cell:' box above instead.

Once 'OK' has been clicked, the Data Table will populate showing what the NPV would be for alternative discount rates. The formula should be noted: {=TABLE(,G11)} shows this is an array function with **G11** as the column input cell. The use of array functions here means that once constructed, the Data Table may not be modified partially.

1-D Data Tables do not need to be simply two columns or two rows. It is entirely possible to display the effects on more than one output at the same time provided you wish to use the same inputs throughout the sensitivity analysis, *viz.*

	B	C	D	E	F	G	H	I	J	K	L	M
32												
33		Data Table										
36												
37									Present Values			
38					Discount Rate	NPV	Year 0	Year 1	Year 2	Year 3	Year 4	Year 5
39					1.0%	17,621	(27,000)	5,941	7,842	12,618	14,415	3,806
40					2.0%	16,302	(27,000)	5,882	7,689	12,250	13,858	3,623
41					3.0%	15,041	(27,000)	5,825	7,541	11,897	13,327	3,450
42					4.0%	13,832	(27,000)	5,769	7,396	11,557	12,822	3,288
43					5.0%	12,675	(27,000)	5,714	7,256	11,230	12,341	3,134
44					6.0%	11,566	(27,000)	5,660	7,120	10,915	11,881	2,989
45					7.0%	10,502	(27,000)	5,607	6,988	10,612	11,443	2,852
46					8.0%	9,482	(27,000)	5,556	6,859	10,320	11,025	2,722
47					9.0%	8,503	(27,000)	5,505	6,733	10,038	10,626	2,600
48					10.0%	7,562	(27,000)	5,455	6,612	9,767	10,245	2,484
49					11.0%	6,659	(27,000)	5,405	6,493	9,505	9,881	2,374
50					12.0%	5,790	(27,000)	5,357	6,378	9,253	9,533	2,270
51												

2-D Data Tables

These Data Tables are similar in idea: they simply allow for two inputs to be varied at the same time. Let's extend the 1-D example as follows:

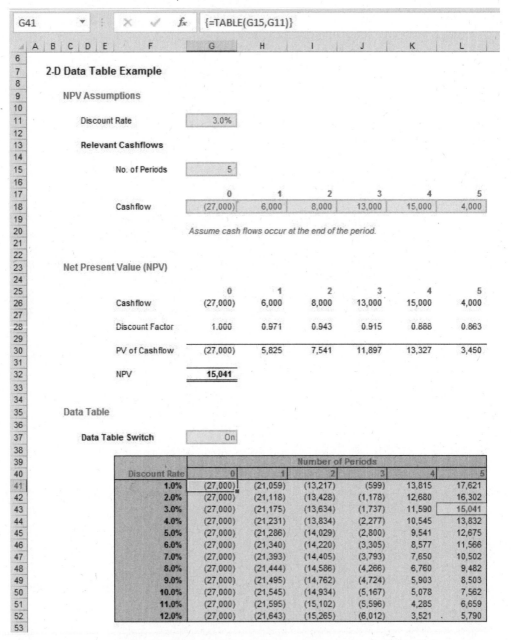

This example is similar, but only calculates the NPV for a certain number of periods – specified in cell G15. Our 2-D Data Table (which is cells **F40:L52**, not **F39:L52**) can answer the question, "What is the NPV of our project over **x** periods with a discount rate of **y**%?". It also displays the current value in blue using conditional formatting. Again, if you don't follow, it doesn't matter – the point is, there's a sophisticated calculation here dependent upon two inputs and the output may be summarised easily.

If anything, a 2-D Data Table is simpler than its 1-D counterpart since there is little confusion over row and column input cells. The formula for analysis is always positioned in the top left-hand corner of the Data Table (in this example, this is cell **F40**). Again, the output needs to be in the table, this time it must be in the top left hand corner of the array. In our example, it is disguised as "Discount Rate" using similar number formatting to that described earlier.

The inputs required now form the remainder of the top row and the first column of the Data Table. With cells **F40:L52** highlighted, the Data Table dialog box is opened as before:

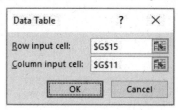

Since the top row are the inputs for the Number of Periods, the 'Row input cell:' should reference **$G$15**, whilst the discount rate inputs ('Column input cell:') should link to **$G$11** once more.

Once 'OK' is depressed, the Data Table will populate as required – simple!

Important Considerations

Data Tables can be really useful for executive summaries, but there are drawbacks to consider:

- The variable inputs to be flexed should always be hard coded, since formulae may not work as envisaged with this feature. This is due to the fact that these calculations may be dependent upon calculations that may vary for differing inputs, which may change as the Data Table calculates. This can prove cumbersome if you wish to change the Data Tables regularly;

- Data Tables can slow down the file calculation time dramatically. For example, if you have just three 2-D Data Tables, each with ten inputs on each axis, the model calculation time could increase by a factor of up to 300 (= 3 x 10 x 10).

   Microsoft has recognised this issue and allows you to change Excel's Calculation option (found in **ALT + T + O**, under 'Calculation') to 'Automatic except tables':

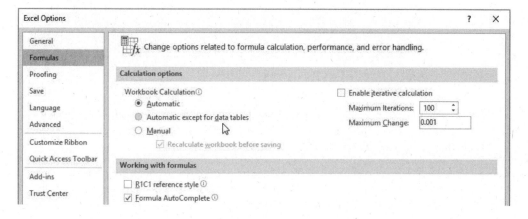

I strongly recommend you do not implement this option. End users tend to assume Excel is always calculating everything automatically and some do not know how to check / modify this functionality.

Instead, I would build in 'On / Off' switches next to the Data Tables themselves. These are transparent and intuitive and have the same effect. All that is required is that the output formula is revised to be

=IF(Switch="On",Calculation,)

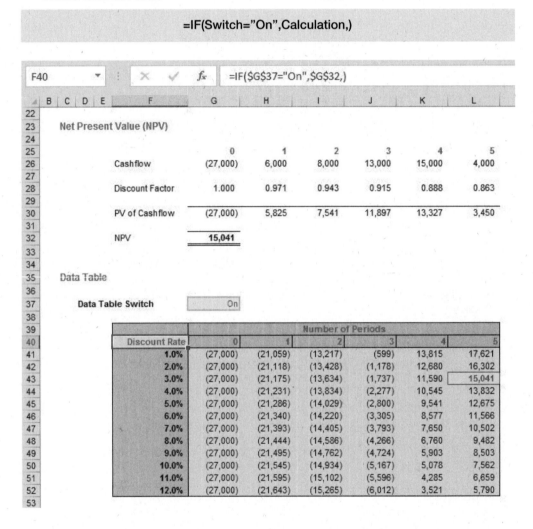

- Data Tables will only flex one or two variables at a time. If more variations are changed, consider using Excel's **Scenario Manager** or the **Solver add-in** (depending upon your requirements, not discussed here);

One other point to note is that although there are workarounds, in general the inputs and outputs should be on the same worksheet as the Data Table. This is not always ideal, but this Excel restriction may be circumvented as follows.

Data Table on Other Sheets

I have a saying that anything is possible in Excel. Maybe one day I may come unstuck, but today is not that day. The issue is that Excel restricts where the referred inputs must be located, *i.e.* they must be positioned on the same page. If you try and reference cells on another worksheet, or become cunning and use range names which refer to cells on another worksheet (a useful workaround on many occasions), you will encounter the following error message:

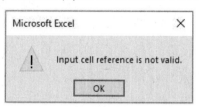

Most financial modellers will recall the mantra of keeping inputs separate from calculations separate from outputs. Data Tables force you to put outputs on the same worksheet as the inputs which can confuse end users and make it difficult to put all key outputs together.

So how can you get round this? My solution assumes you do not wish to hide Data Tables on the input sheet and then link them to another worksheet (this is cumbersome and can make the model less efficient).

To make things more "difficult", I will assume that you have already built your financial model and the Data Tables are to be incorporated as an afterthought. There could be two inputs to incorporate. I will explain how to create one of them (you then just have to follow this process twice).

Firstly, create a "dummy" input cell on the same worksheet as the Data Table. This needs to be protected such that data cannot be entered into this cell. I will assume that this cell is **W44** (say) on the **Sheet2** worksheet, *i.e.* the same sheet as the Data Table.

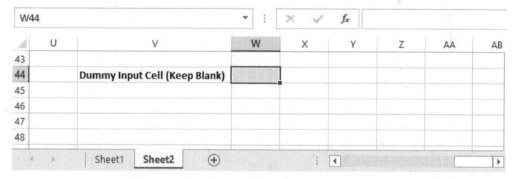

Secondly, link the Data Table (**ALT + D + T**) to this dummy input (in the illustration here I assume that the Data Table is a 1-dimensional Data Table):

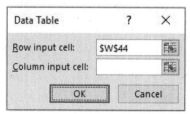

Thirdly, let us assume you want actually want the Data Table to link to "Input 1" (cell **D4**) on **Sheet1**:

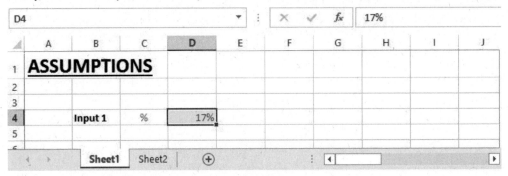

Fourthly, since we have already built the model this input will already be linked throughout the model. Since I do not wish to change all the dependent formulae, I first cut (NOT copy) the input into an adjacent cell:

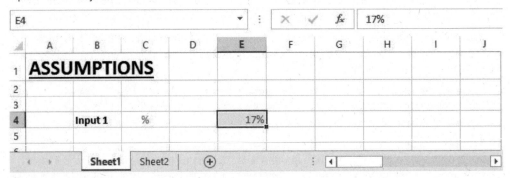

Fifthly, a copy is pasted back into the original cell (here, this was cell **D4**):

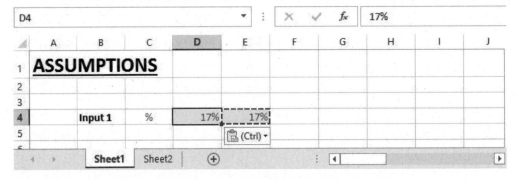

Finally, the value in cell E4 is replaced with the following formula

=IF(Sheet2!W44="",D4,Sheet2!W44)

and then formatted / protected to ensure end users do not actually type into this cell:

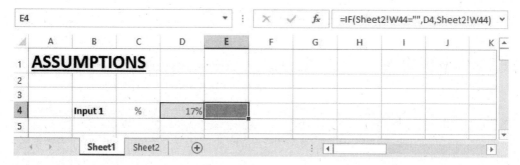

The Data Table will now work. This is because:

- The Data Table links directly to a cell on the same sheet as the Data Table, but indirectly to the input on the other worksheet;

- Cell **E4** on **Sheet1** is now the cell that drives all calculations throughout the model, even though it appears to have been added;

- Cell **D4** on **Sheet1** still appears to be – and acts like – the original input it replaces.

CHAPTER 2.8: GOAL SEEK AND SOLVER

Three accountants go for a job interview. The first one goes in and is handed a glass of water, precisely half-filled. The interviewer asks him to describe the contents to which he replies, "It's half empty". "Thank you," replies the interviewer, "We will let you know". The accountant walks out and shrugs his shoulders as he walks past the remaining two candidates.

The second accountant walks in and is asked the same question. She thinks for a second and then responds, "It's half full". "Thank you," replies the interviewer, "We will let you know". The second accountant walks out. She scratches her head quizzically as she walks away from the final interviewee.

The third accountant – who is also a financial modeller – walks in and is asked the very same question. "What would you like it to be?" the modeller enquires. "When can you start?" asks the interviewer.

Ever since spreadsheets and calculators were invented there have been two types of forecasting task: those that seek accurate forecasting and those that, well, seek the number first thought of. It is commonplace in modelling for users to ascertain what value an input must have in order to achieve a desired outcome. Modellers need to possess the skills to facilitate this even with the most complex spreadsheets. Luckily, there are tools available.

Consider the following example:

10-Jan-20	27-Mar-20	02-Sep-20	02-Sep-21	27-Oct-21	28-Oct-23	26-Apr-24	27-Apr-26
–	(50,000)	18,750	12,412	57	1,655	19,451	–

Here, let's imagine we have been asked to calculate the internal rate of return (**IRR**) on these cash flows (*i.e.* imagine you could put money in the bank and either invest or pay interest at the same compounding rate. IRR would be the rate which would make the totals including all interest add up to zero).

NPV and IRR

The **Present Value (PV)** of a cashflow is defined as "what it is worth today". Some describe it as compound interest in reverse. If you were to deposit $100 in the bank today at an interest rate of 10% p.a. then in one year's time it would be worth $110, in two years' time it would be worth $121 and in three years' time it would be worth $133.10, *etc.*

With a **discount factor** of 10%, the present value of $110 in one year's time would be $100 today; the present value of $121 in two years' time would be $100 now; the present value of $133.10 in three years' time would also be $100 today.

The sum of all present values, both positive and negative is known as the **Net Present Value (NPV)**. Theoretically, if you invest in a project with a particular discount rate – also known as the cost of capital – you should only proceed with the project (from a financial perspective) if the NPV is greater than zero. This is known as **value accreting**.

The **Internal Rate of Return (IRR)** is the discount rate which makes the NPV precisely zero.

It will probably not surprise you that I have deliberately chosen a set of values which cause problems for Excel. Excel has two functions which calculate the IRR: **IRR** (when cashflows occur on a regular / periodic basis) and **XIRR** (when cashflows do not occur on a regular basis). Neither will work on the above:

- **IRR** will not work as the periods are not equidistant;

- **XIRR** gives an incorrect answer (0.00%). If this were correct, then the sum of the cash flows excluding any interest effects (known as the **undiscounted cashflows**) must equal zero. They do not:

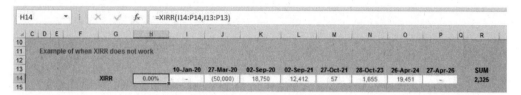

You may have noted that the valuation functions **IRR, XIRR, NPV** and **XNPV** have neither been demonstrated nor explained fully anywhere in this book. This is because they do not always calculate correctly. I am a keen advocate of taking these computations back to first principles instead so that everyone may understand how the results have been derived.

So allow me to take this example back to first principles. Here, I have created an elementary Net Present Value calculation:

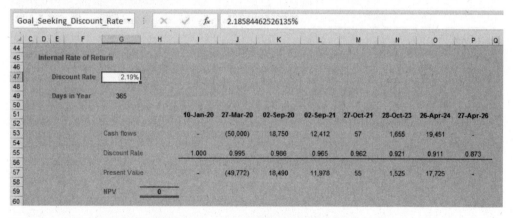

To generate the value in cell **G47**, I have manually kept changing it to try to get a zero NPV in cell **H59**. I did this as follows:

- Typed in a rate of 0%: NPV was $2,325 (positive)

- Tried a higher rate of 10%; NPV was negative, ($6,650)

- Tried a rate of 5% (mid-point between the two rates): NPV was still negative, ($2,666) (still negative)

- Tried a rate of 2.5% (mid-point between 0% and 5%): NPV was ($315) (negative, but getting smaller)

- Tried a rate of 1.25% (mid-point of 0% and 2.5%): NPV was $966 (positive)

- *etc.*

After a gazillion attempts (look it up, it's a technical term), I will get very close if I keep bisecting the two rates that provide the smallest positive and smallest negative NPVs. You can imagine this will become heavily time consuming and I will have less time to do the things I would rather do than this – like pulling out my toe nails…

The general rule with financial modelling is whenever you catch yourself doing the same thing over and over again, it's very likely you haven't realised there is an easier way to do whatever it is you are doing. Like here. I can use Excel's Goal Seek functionality to derive the discount rate that will make the NPV zero:

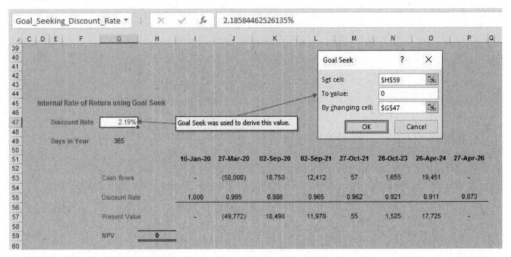

Goal Seek (**ALT + T + G**, or else go to the 'Data' tab on the Ribbon, then in the 'Data Tools' group, select 'What-If Analysis' and then choose 'Goal Seek…') requires three inputs:

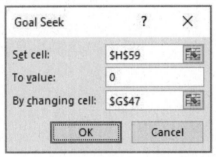

The 'Set cell' value is the NPV output here, 'To value' is the desired outcome (e.g. zero) and 'By changing cell' defines the variable input (e.g. discount rate). So what happens if you want to set the 'To value' to refer to a cell value rather than a typed-in number?

I have a very simple response: you can't.

So what can you do instead..?

Introducing Solver

Excel includes a (hidden) tool called **Solver** that uses techniques from the operations research to find optimal solutions for all kind of decision problems. It is not situated in the standard loadset: it has to be loaded from Excel's add-ins.

In any version of Excel, a simple way to access add-ins is to use the keystroke shortcut **ALT + T + I**:

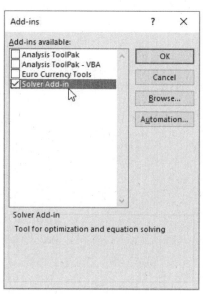

Checking the Solver add-in will add Solver to the 'Data' tab of the Ribbon:

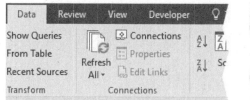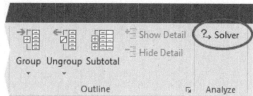

Solver is often used to optimise / minimise outputs. Consider the following example:

	C	D	E	F	G	H	I
10							
11		**Maximising Product**					
12							
13					kg	Profit / kg ($)	Profit ($)
14				Product A	100	$ 9.00	$ 900.00
15				Product B	50	$ 10.00	$ 500.00
16				Product C	475	$ 11.00	$ 5,225.00
17				Product D	375	$ 12.00	$ 4,500.00
18					**1,000**		**$ 11,125.00**

Imagine you run a company with four products: A, B, C and D. Your intention is to maximise company profits, but you only have 1,000kg of raw material necessary for these four products. If this is all there is to the problem, then it would be simple – only produce Product D. However, imagine you had the following operational constraints:

- For every kilogram of Product B produced, you have to manufacture at least two kilograms of Product A;

- You must produce at least 50kg of Product B;

- Product C is a by-product of Products A and D: the total weight of Products A and D must equal the number of kilograms of Product C produced.

The above graphic shows the optimal solution; the question is, how did I derive it?

To recreate the solution, open the Solver dialog box:

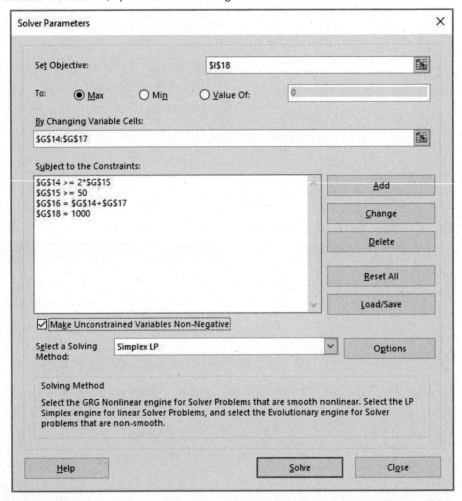

The "objective" here would be the output, i.e. total profit (cell **I18** in the example) and the aim is to maximise it (note the other two alternatives of minimisation or trying to generate a particular output value). This is achieved by selecting which cells may be varied (here the kg produced), subject to the constraints specified.

Constraints are simple to include – merely click the 'Add' button:

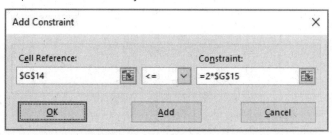

In Excel 2010 and later versions, Solver explicitly allows one of three Solving methods:

- **Simplex Method:** this method is used for solving linear problems (i.e. where the relationship between variables could be charted using a straight line). Our example above is one such instance;

- **GRG Nonlinear:** this is used for solving smooth nonlinear problems;

- **Evolutionary Solver:** this approach uses genetic algorithms to find its solutions. While the Simplex and GRG solvers are used for linear and smooth nonlinear problems, the Evolutionary Solver can be used for any Excel formulas or functions, even when they are not linear or smooth nonlinear. Spreadsheet functions such as **IF** and **VLOOKUP** fall into this category.

In summary, Solver is a more powerful variant of Goal Seek, allowing forecasters to derive inputs to achieve specific goals and objectives. However, upon first inspection, Solver still does not appear to allow the value to be set to be a cell reference.

Therefore, you need to employ a simple trick.

Using Solver with a Reference

In this example, I will return to the NPV example:

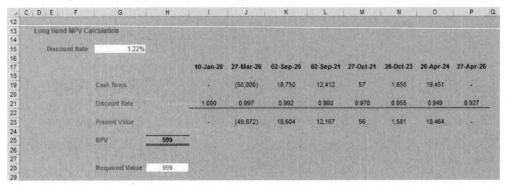

In this instance, I could have used Goal Seek as before, but instead I got out the heavy artillery:

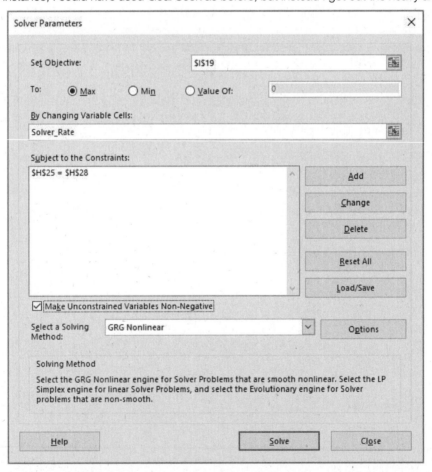

The discount rate (**Solver_Rate**) here is cell **G15**. You should notice two little tricks though: I have not used the NPV (cell **H25**) as the output, but a dummy value of cell **I19** (the first period's cash flow). This allows us to select a very useful constraint: that the NPV (cell **H25**) equals the required value (cell **H28**). It should also be noted that compounding discount rates is clearly a non-linear calculation technique so Simplex should not be used as a Solving Method.

This has allowed me to show you a neat trick, but I am not entirely convinced of this solution. I cannot help feeling we are cracking a walnut with a thermonuclear warhead and besides, you still have to activate the Solver – this method will not update values automatically as inputs change.

So is there another way..?

VBA Approach

Well, yes there is, although it involves VBA, which regular readers will note is a method I try to fall back on when all else fails. This could be argued (perhaps!) as one such instance.

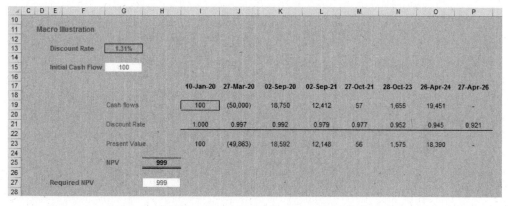

In this example, there are two inputs, initial cash flow and required NPV (cells **G15** and **H27** respectively). Typing a value in either cell will change the discount rate in cell **G13** so that the NPV (cell **H25**) equals the required value.

This was achieved using a macro.

I have included the macro code by right-clicking on the relevant worksheet tab and select 'View Code', *viz.*

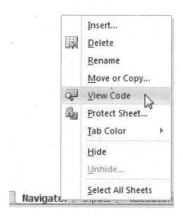

This will launch the Visual Basic Editor:

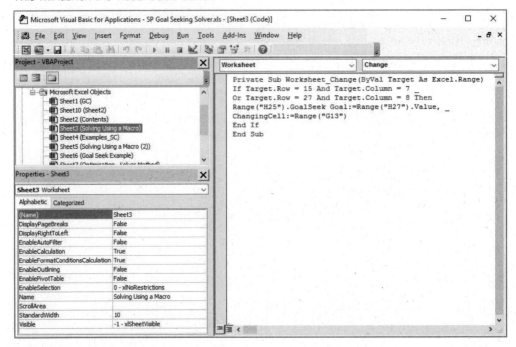

Not all of the above panes may be visible, but in the right hand pane paste in the following code (as shown in the graphic above):

```
Private Sub Worksheet_Change(ByVal Target As Excel.Range)
If Target.Row = 15 And Target.Column = 7 _
Or Target.Row = 27 And Target.Column = 8 Then
Range("H25").GoalSeek Goal:=Range("H27").Value, _
ChangingCell:=Range("G13")
End If
End Sub
```

It is very straightforward: if cell **G15** (row 15, column 7) or **H27** (row 27, column 8) is edited the macro is invoked and changes the discount rate in cell **G13** such that the NPV in cell **H25** equals the required output specified in cell **H27**.

Assuming macros are enabled (see earlier), this will change the discount rate without calling either Goal Seek or Solver. If you choose to use the macro solution, do remember to save the Excel file as a macro enabled workbook!

CHAPTER 2.9: HYPERLINKS

I commonly use hyperlinks in my Excel files as they are a great way to move around a file. If you create a central worksheet with hyperlinks to all of the other worksheets, you are only ever two clicks away from anywhere else in the workbook. They make life very easy for end users and once you know how to construct them, they take mere seconds to insert.

The 'Insert Hyperlink' dialog box is fairly straightforward to use and readily accessed via one of two keyboard shortcuts, either **ALT + I + I** or **CTRL + K**. Alternatively, from the Ribbon, select the 'Insert' tab, click on 'Hyperlink' in the 'Links' group:

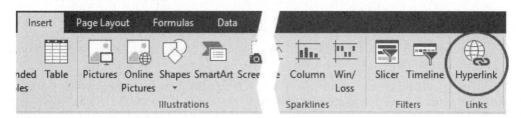

Hyperlinks can be used to link to a variety of places, but in this instance, I will focus on linking to elsewhere within the same workbook.

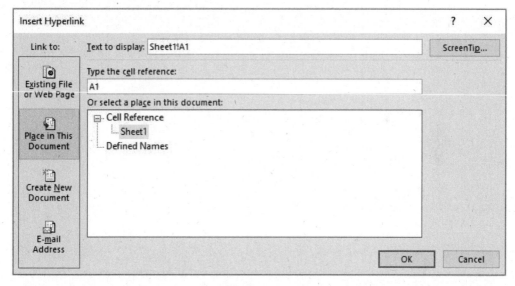

To create a hyperlink, first select the cell or range of cells that you wish to act as the hyperlink (*i.e.* clicking on any of these cells will activate the hyperlink). Then, open the Insert Hyperlink dialog box (above) and select 'Place in This Document' as the 'Link to:', which will change the appearance of the rest of the dialog box.

Insert the text for the hyperlink in the 'Text to display:' input box (clicking on the 'ScreenTip...' macro button will allow you to create an informative message in a message box when you hover over the hyperlink).

The next two input boxes, 'Type the cell reference:' and 'Or select a place in this document:', work in tandem – sort of:

- If you type a cell reference in the first input box without making a selection in the second input box, the hyperlink will link to the cell reference on the current (active) worksheet;

- If you type a cell reference in the first input box and select a worksheet reference in the second box, the hyperlink will link to the specified cell in the given worksheet. In my example above, this hyperlink will jump to **Sheet1** cell **A1**; *or*

- If you select a 'Defined Name' (*i.e.* a pre-defined range name) in the second input box, this will link to the cell(s) specified. This is the recommended option, where available, if you wish to link to cell(s) on another worksheet within the same workbook. This is because if the destination worksheet's sheet name were to be changed, the link would still work. I recommend that the range name should start with **HL_** for **H**yper **L**ink, to make it easier to sort through range names if necessary.

It should be noted that there is an Excel function, **HYPERLINK(link_location,[friendly_name])**. I tend not to use this as it is not so user-friendly.

Chapter 3: Best Practice Methodology

So far so good – so what? The whole intention of this book is to pretty much provide a text that can be handed to someone who is looking to build financial models as part of their role. Jokes aside, I am assuming for those of you with no more than a passing acquaintance with Excel, this book will get you – as the (would-be?) modeller – up to speed with the requirements and concepts associated with financial model development.

That's why I have spent a fair bit of time ploughing through the most common functions and functionalities in Excel that are employed time and time again. Even if you are a more experienced modeller, hopefully you have found some useful tricks and tips – assuming you haven't cheated and turned straight to this chapter!

Spreadsheeting is often seen as a core skill for accountants, many of whom are reasonably conversant with Excel. However, many modellers frequently forget that the key end users of a spreadsheet model (*i.e.* the decision makers) are not necessarily sophisticated Excel users and often only see the final output on a printed page, *e.g.* as an appendix to a Word document or as part of a set of PowerPoint slides.

With this borne in mind, it becomes easier to understand why there have been numerous high profile examples of material spreadsheet errors. I am not saying that well-structured models will ensure no mistakes, but in theory it should *reduce* both the number and the magnitude of these errors.

Modellers should strive to build "Best Practice" models. Here, I want to avoid the semantics of what constitutes 'best" in "Best Practice". "B and P" are in capitals deliberately as I see this as a proper noun insofar no method is truly "best" for all eventualities. There's plenty of texts out there that include copious amounts on what thou shalt and shalt not do regarding building a spreadsheet. And lo, by the seventh day, the reader was truly bored and sleepeth. Instead, I must admit that I have actually contributed to the odyssey of developing some of these epic tomes that Homer would have been truly proud of. But hey, I am a big fan of *The Simpsons*.

I would rather we consider the term as a proper noun to reflect the idea that a good model has four key attributes:

- **C**onsistency;
- **R**obustness;
- **F**lexibility; *and*
- **T**ransparency.

Our company calls this **CRaFT**. We try to keep it simple (how many times have I said that so far?). Looking at these four attributes in turn can help model developers decide how best to design financial models.

Consistency

Models constructed consistently are easier to understand as users become familiar with both their purpose and content. This will in turn give users more comfort about model integrity and make it easier to add / remove business units, categories, numbers of periods, scenarios *etc.*

Consistent formatting and use of styles cannot be over-emphasised. Humans take in much information on a non-verbal basis. Consider the following old 'Print' dialog box from *c.* Excel 2003:

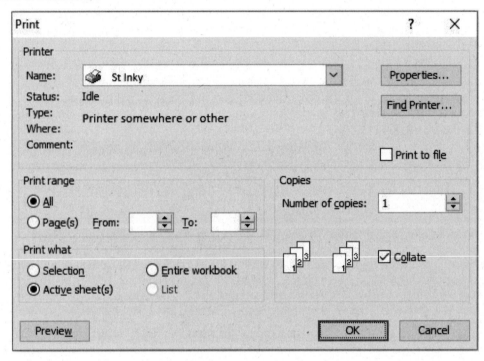

True, this interface has long since been replaced, but like Quasimodo, does it ring any bells..? Feast your eyes on the above dialog box. It has a dropdown box, check boxes, option buttons, scroll bars – all manner of data validation. You may have never seen this dialog box before in your life but you just *know* where you need to input data. We may not realise it but we have all been indoctrinated by Microsoft. Whilst the above dialog box appears quite flexible, we know the only things we are able to change are the objects in white (for example, I know I cannot print out a List from the above dialog box since the selection has been greyed out).

Those of you familiar with the models supplied with this book may now realise I exploit this mindset: the worksheets in my workbooks all contain objects or cells that may be modified by the user are readily identifiable without the reading of any instructions – we are all Pavlov's dogs!

H26	▼	:	×	✓	fx	=SUMIF(F12:F21,G26,H12:H21)

	A	B	C	D	E	F	G	H	I	J
8										
9			Dummy Database							
10										
11						Business Unit	Product Type	Sales		
12						1	X	$100		
13						1	Y	$200		
14						1	Z	$300		
15						1	Z	$400		
16						2	X	$500		
17						2	X	$600		
18						2	Z	$700		
19						3	Y	$800		
20						3	Z	$900		
21						4	Y	$1,000		
22										
23										
24			SUMIF Illustration							
25										
26			Business Unit				1	$1,000		
27										

There are other key elements of a workbook that should be consistent. These include:

- Formulae should be copied uniformly across ranges, to make it easy to add / remove periods or categories as necessary;

- Sheet titles and hyperlinks should be consistently positioned to aid navigation and provide details about the content and purpose of the particular worksheet;

- For forecast spreadsheets incorporating dates, the dates should be consistently positioned (i.e. first period should always be in one particular column), the number of periods should be consistent where possible and the periodicity should be uniform (the model should endeavour to show all sheets monthly or quarterly, etc.). If periodicities must change, they should be in clearly delineated sections of the model. If you do have a model where you want the first 12 months (say) to be monthly, then annually thereafter, always model everything at the lowest level of granularity (here, monthly) and then use **SUMIF** to aggregate months into years on output sheets later – it makes formulae so much easier to create and manipulate.

This should reduce referencing errors, increase model integrity and enhance workbook structure.

Robustness

Models should be materially free from error, mathematically accurate and readily auditable. Key output sheets should ensure that error messages such as *#DIV/0!*, *#VALUE!*, *#REF!* etc. cannot occur (ideally, these error messages should not occur anywhere).

My old boss used to promote the idea of "cockroach theory": once you saw one of these errors in a model, you would believe the model was infested and never trust it after that. Removing these *prima facie* errors is straightforward and often highlights that the modeller has not undertaken a basic review of his or her work after completing the task (see later).

When building, it is often worth keeping in mind hidden assumptions in formula. For example, a simple gross margin calculation may calculate profit divided by sales. However, if sales are non-existent or missing, this calculation would give #DIV/0! The user therefore has two options:

- Use an **IF** statement to check that sales are not zero (proactive test); or
- Construct an error check to flag if sales are zero (reactive test, not recommended in this instance).

However, checks are useful in many situations, and essentially each will fit into one of three categories:

1. **Error checks** – the model contains flawed logic or *prima facie* errors, *e.g.* Balance Sheet does not balance, cash in cashflow statement does not reconcile with the balance sheet, or the model contains #DIV/0! errors *etc*;

2. **Sensitivity checks** – the model's outputs are being derived from inputs that are not deemed to be part of the base case. This can prevent erroneous decisions being made using the "Best Case"; *and*

3. **Alert checks** – everything else! This flags points of interest to users and / or developers issues that may need to be reviewed: *e.g.* revenues are negative, debt covenants have been breached, *etc.*

Incorporating dedicated worksheets into the model that summarise these checks will enhance robustness and give users more confidence that the model is working / calculating as intended.

Error Checks Overall:	☑		

1. Error Checks

Summary of Errors

Assumptions

General

	Include?	
All Months included?	☑	Yes	☐

Division 1

Annual Balance Sheet free of errors	☑	Yes	☐
Annual Balance Sheet balances	☑	Yes	☐
Annual Balance Sheet solvent	☑	Yes	☐
Annual Operating Cash Flows reconcile	☑	Yes	☐
Annual Restated Balance Sheet free of errors	☑	Yes	☐
Annual Restated Balance Sheet balances	☑	Yes	☐
Annual Restated Balance Sheet solvent	☑	Yes	☐
Annual Restated Operating Cash Flows reconcile	☑	Yes	☐
External Revenue Cash Receipts OK	☑	Yes	☐
Spare Cash Receipts OK	☑	Yes	☐
Materials and Sundry Cash Payments OK	☑	Yes	☐
Subcontractor Cash Payments OK	☑	Yes	☐
Plant Hire Cash Payments OK	☑	Yes	☐
Salaries & Wages – Productive Cash Payments OK	☑	Yes	☐
Salaries & Wages – Unproductive Cash Payments OK	☑	Yes	☐
Repairs & Maintenance Cash Payments OK	☑	Yes	☐
Fleet Costs Cash Payments OK	☑	Yes	☐
Admin & Overheads Cash Payments OK	☑	Yes	☐
Corporate Overhead Recoveries Cash Payments OK	☑	Yes	☐
Spare Cash Payments OK	☑	Yes	☐

Summary of Errors	☑

The above is a sanitised screenshot from a real financial model. It is an extract from a worksheet with no fewer than 800 checks with the overall total included at the bottom (this links to the overall check at the top of the sheet, displayed in all worksheets throughout the model). Each check may be switched off if necessary and each check hyperlinks back to where the check is in the model. If you were the recipient of such a model, assuming the checks have been calculated correctly (!), would you feel more comfortable with this model compared to the usual fare received?

Flexibility

One benefit of modelling in a spreadsheet package such as Excel is to be able to change various assumptions and see how these adjustments affect various outputs.

Therefore, when building a model, the user should consider what inputs should be variable and how they should be able to vary. This may force the model builder to consider how assumptions should be entered.

The most common method of data entry in practice is simply typing data into worksheet cells, but this may allow a model's inputs to vary outside of scoped parameters. For example, if I have a cell seeking 'Volumes', without using data validation I could enter '3', '-22.8' or 'dog' in that cell. Negative volumes are nonsensical and being able to enter text may cause formula errors throughout the model. Therefore, the user may wish to consider other methods of entry including using drop down boxes, option buttons, check boxes and so on.

I strongly recommend that all inputs are entered as positive numbers, wherever possible, just change the descriptions accordingly. If I were to tell you that last year costs were $10,000 but they have increased 10% this year. You would understand me. But what would you make of me telling you costs were minus $10,000 and had increased by -10%!?

The aim is to have a model provide sufficient flexibility without going overboard.

Transparency

As stated above, many modellers often forget that key decision makers base their choices on printed materials: consequently, models must be clear, concise, and fit for the purpose intended. I always say if you can follow it on a piece of paper (*i.e.* no Formula bar), it's transparent.

Most Excel users are familiar with keeping inputs / assumptions away from calculations away from outputs. However, this concept can be extended: it can make sense to keep different areas of a model separate, *e.g.* revenue assumptions on a different worksheet from cost(s) of goods sold assumptions, and capital expenditure assumptions on a third sheet, and so on. This makes it easier to re-use worksheets and ringfence data. Keeping base case data away from sensitivity data is also important, as many modelling mistakes have been made from users changing the wrong, yet similar, inputs.

Aside from trying to keep formulae as simple as possible, it makes sense to consider the logical flow of a model at the outset too. Indeed, including a simple flowchart within an Excel workbook can be invaluable: as the saying goes, a picture is worth a thousand words, and can actually help to plan the structure and order of the spreadsheet build.

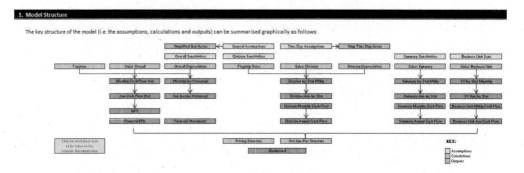

Again, this graphic comes from a genuine model, albeit modified. It should be noted that not only does this graphic show how the model flows, each box within the graphic is actually a hyperlink that takes you to the relevant section of the model, complete with documentation.

Similarly, a Table of Contents constructed with hyperlinks helps users and developers alike navigate through larger Excel models:

Navigator

Error Checks: ☑

Documentation / Instructions
Frequently Asked Questions
Style Guide

General Assumptions
Time Dependent Assumptions and Calculations

Simplified General Assumptions
Simplified Time Dependent Assumptions

Dashboard Summary
Pricing Structure
Standard Annual Pricing Structure

Financial Key Performance Indicators
Overall Financial Statements
Overall Annual Income Statement
Overall Annual Cash Flow Statement
Overall NPV Calculation
Overall Sensitivities

Division Annual Income Statement
Division Sensitivities

Summary Annual Income Statement
Summary Sensitivities

Business Unit Annual Income Statement
Business Unit Sensitivities

In summary, it's all about design and scoping. The problem is, we are all time poor in today's business environment with perpetual pressure on producing results more and more quickly. Consequently, we dust off old templates, fit square pegs in round holes and produce mistake-laden spreadsheets time and time again resulting in costly management decisions. The whole process is simply a false economy. Time spent on better scoping out the model and designing the layout will lead to fewer mistakes and greater efficiencies in the long term.

Hey, that leads me nicely into the next chapter…

Chapter 4: Layout Tips

In light of the discussion on "Best Practice", I want to provide some tips on laying out a typical worksheet in a financial model. I want to be clear: no one is holding a gun to your head and saying you *must* do it this way. I have been modelling for a long time (you'd think I would get the thing finished by now) and I'd like to pass on some of the things I have learned – more often than not, the hard way. I do not profess to be an expert (an "ex" is a has-been and a "spurt" is a drip under pressure). I see myself more as a farmer: a man outstanding in his field (get it?).

So where do I start? Before I start developing a worksheet, let me discuss setting up Excel in the first place. There are ways to make your life a little easier when setting up a spreadsheet – so allow me to set up some of the foundations…

Quick Analysis

You may have noticed I have been using Excel 2016 screenshots throughout this book. This allows me to stay hip and up to date (my daughter doesn't agree) and to show off some of the newer features. One such new addition came out in Excel 2013: **Quick Analysis**.

To ensure it is enabled, go to Excel Options (**ALT + T + O**) and select 'General' from the left hand column. Then, ensure 'Show Quick Analysis options on selection' from 'User Interface options' is ticked:

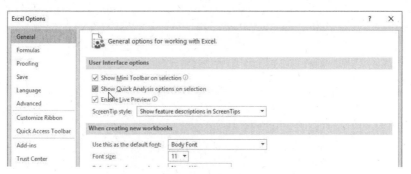

This feature is clearly aimed at those still feeling their way round some of the more sophisticated analytical tools in Excel. All you need to do is highlight the entire data to be analysed (including headings) and click on the Quick Analysis icon in the bottom right-hand corner, *viz.*

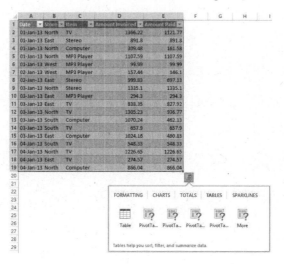

This generates a pop-up menu where the user can make simple selections regarding formatting, charts, totals, Tables, PivotTables and sparklines (charts in a cell). For example:

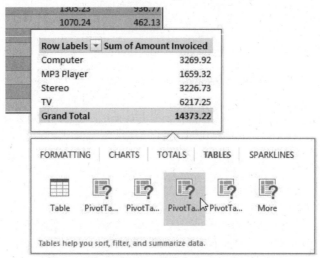

I recall when Excel 2013 first came out that I ought to be on commission for Microsoft. I used to demonstrate why this tool was so useful by creating a reasonably sophisticated chart with just a couple of clicks of the mouse. In seconds, I used to transform the example:

	A	B	C	D	E
1					
2					
3		Business Unit	Sales	Gross Margin	
4		A	$ 100	22%	
5		B	$ 80	18%	
6		C	$ 65	34%	
7		D	$ 125	25%	
8		E	$ 45	17%	
9		F	$ 140	30%	
10		G	$ 90	20%	
11		H	$ 105	22%	
12					
13					
14					

by clicking on the Quick Analysis tool and converting the data into the following chart:

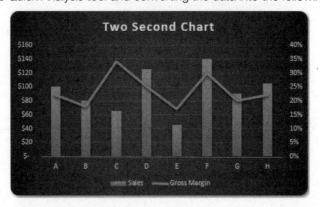

Now yes, I appreciate it isn't *that* difficult to construct that chart. The point I make here is that Excel can create it *immediately*.

New Workbook Defaults

I hate to admit it, but I find as I get older my eyes require longer and longer arms. Finding working on a 75-inch plasma screen a little impractical (and awfully warm!), there is a viable alternative. Go to Excel Options (**ALT + T + O**) and select 'General' from the left hand column. Then, consider the options in 'When creating new workbooks':

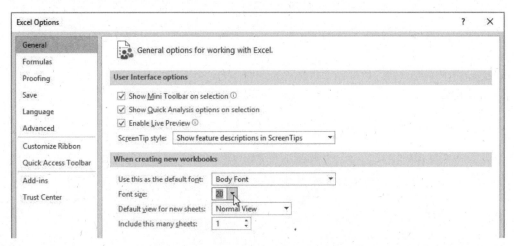

Changing the font size scales up the workbook fonts including – most importantly – the Formula toolbar. This is particularly useful for tired eyes, presentations and training.

The final option in this section, 'Include this many sheets' is also useful if you find yourself copying / deleting worksheets in a newly-created workbook on a regular basis.

Formulas Options

The options in Excel Options (**ALT + T + O**) -> **'Formulas'** are useful too.

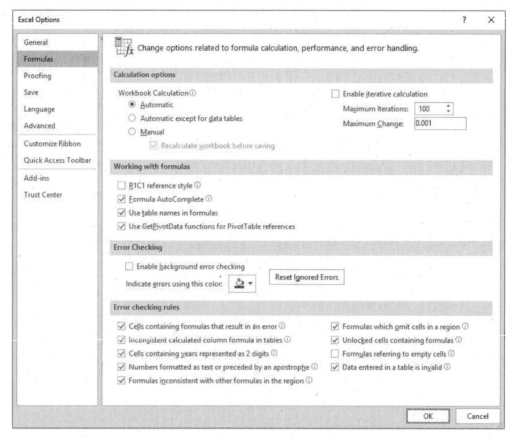

The Workbook Calculation in 'Calculation options' should <u>always</u> be set to 'Automatic'. No exception. Why? Well, how many times have you opened another's workbook, changed inputs and relied upon the outputs? On those occasions, how often did you check the model calculations were set to 'Automatic'? Exactly.

There are some professional modelling firms out there that advise you should set calculations to 'Automatic except for data tables'. Rubbish. Yes, Data Tables may slow a model down, but if you want to a Data Table to cease calculating, it should be done *transparently*. When I discussed Data Tables earlier, I explained how data validation could be employed to do this on the face of a worksheet, rather than hidden away in Excel Options.

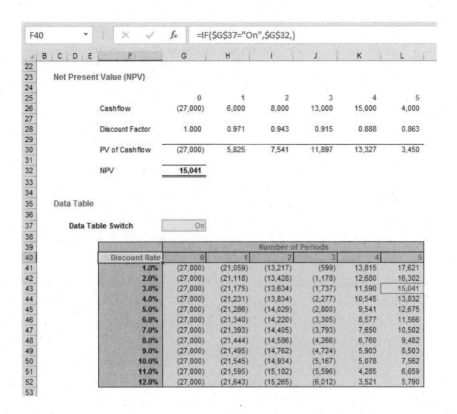

There are other functionalities to consider on this page of Excel Options as well. 'Formula AutoComplete' provides the prompt that has made entering calculations simpler since the advent of Excel 2007.

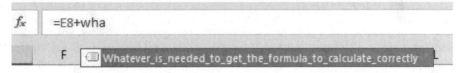

I would recommend keeping that option checked. 'Use table names in formulas' and 'Use GetPivotData functions for PivotTable references' do similar things. Given Tables and PivotTables may both change structure depending upon filters and the data added, linking to a structured reference such as

=GETPIVOTDATA("Amount Paid",$A$1,"Item","Stereo")

can ensure the correct reference is always applied no matter how the structure of the underlying Table or PivotTable may vary.

The last section in 'Formulas' concerns error checking. I strongly recommend that 'Enable background error checking' is selected. This allows Excel to identify and highlight common errors that modellers make and essentially protects you from yourself.

Save Options

The options in Excel Options (**ALT + T + O**) -> **'Save'** is another area to review.

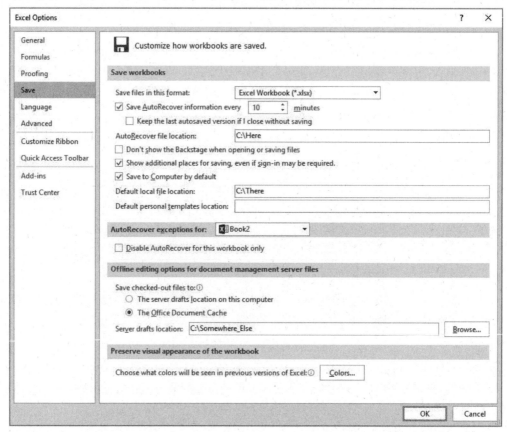

Note the default save format: it is as an Excel Workbook (***.xlsx**) file. This type of file does not permit macros. I can understand that Microsoft wants to err on the side of caution and therefore does not allow macros by default, but there are hidden dangers with selecting this option. If you receive an Excel file from a third party and open it, say, from Microsoft Outlook, when you try to save it, Excel will save it as an **xlsx** file. If there are macros contained within the workbook, these may be consigned to the great macro locker in the sky if the warning message when saving is not read properly. Therefore, it is arguably safer to modify the 'Save files in this format:' option to 'Excel Macro-Enabled Workbook (*.xlsm)' instead.

The next option down can also be troublesome. For years, scientists have been spending millions on developing AI (Artificial Intelligence). I really do not know why they have bothered. Microsoft perfected this nearly 30 years ago. Ever made a clanger in Excel and you were just about to undo when Excel automatically saved your file?

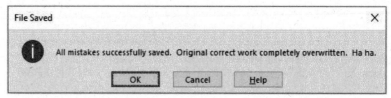

Microsoft has long since learned when it's the most inopportune time to save. In the middle of a long, complex formula? Presenting the results to the board? Trying to work out in a rush? No problem, Excel will autosave now, thank you very much. This can be very frustrating – but there is a remedy: either extend the duration or switch it off completely.

Now be careful here. I once recommended this to a group of accountants who the next time they bumped into me had brought along a tree, gallows and a noose. If you switch AutoSave off, *make sure you save regularly* or you may lose your work. Professional modellers tend to switch AutoSave off but train themselves to save every two to five minutes. Seriously. This way, you can save a file on your own terms.

Saving Files

It is a good idea to have a good nomenclature set up for file saving. I tend to use the format

'Meaningful Filename vLB1.01'.xlsm

Meaningful Filename is <u>not</u> 'INT RND OMG FG ex Crs' or 'Project Wildebeast'. I am a professional consultant and I have liaised on many confidential projects in my time. Not only have some of the codenames been a mite questionable over the years ('Project Herpes' anybody?), but 12 – 24 months later you cannot remember which project goes with which codename. It is better to keep your files in a secure location and call it 'Chess Pieces Sales Five Year Forecasts' so you can find it quickly when you need to.

LB simply represents my initials. Don't use mine, use yours. It's good to know who the author was as so few modellers bother to update this in File Properties. It gives the end user a fighting chance as to who they ought to approach should they have any queries.

v..1.01 is the version number. Rather than using dates, I use numbering. The date information is stored in the metafile in any case. I tend to add 0.01 to the numbering every two hours. This means that if a file were to corrupt, I never have to do too much re-work. It also helps in the consulting industry as I know vLB1.15 represents approximately 30 hours work.

I add 1 to the version number when something significant has happened. This may be to signify that the model has been presented to senior management, or that sales calculations were completely re-worked or that a particular subsidiary's data has been completely added / removed. These are "landmarks" and it is these changes that should be documented in a File Changes document (I am optimistic that you might be creating one of these!).

Another major source of irritation is trying to save a file for the first time and Excel spends six weeks thinking about it whilst it endeavours to connect to the Cloud. Checking 'Save to Computer by default' will save you tearing out all of your hair.

One last item on this page is 'Disable AutoRecover for this workbook only'. This should not be confused with AutoSave. This is the option whereby Excel will make a valiant attempt to save something of your file should Excel crash so that when you re-open the 'recovered' file will be available. It will not overwrite your existing work, but instead create a temporary recovery file for you to inspect and decide whether you wish to retain it.

Now this might seem like switching this option off is like buying a new car without brakes, but if your PC is struggling with memory issues, this may be a reason for considering disabling the option. I vehemently suggest you don't though: closing other applications down is immensely preferable. It may be better to live without iTunes for an hour or two rather than your friends or family for the weekend…

Advanced Options

The largest selection of options in Excel Options (**ALT + T + O**) is contained in the **'Advanced'** section. I could probably write a book just going through these options but I think it might be even more boring than this one.

It is worth perusing this section and changing options deciding upon personal preferences. Some of the multitude of options include:

- In 'Editing options', you can un-check 'Allow editing directly in cells'. This will mean all formulae when typed will appear in the Formula bar rather than in the worksheet making it easier to read and easier to select nearby cells with the mouse. Further, with this option unchecked double-clicking on a formula reveals precedent cells (the function F5 will take you back afterwards). This is always the first thing I do in Excel after installing a new edition.

- Checking 'Enable automatic percent entry' in the 'Editing options' section allows you to type percentages into Excel faster as you do not always have to hunt out the pesky % symbol.

- For those in other regions of the world where the decimal point is replaced by the comma and the comma replaced by the semi-colon for example, it's possible to change these settings without changing the regional settings on your computer. Simply uncheck 'Use system separators' in 'Editing options' and make your own choice.

- If you want to access the last few files in the Backstage are of your workbook, check 'Quickly access this number of Recent Workbooks' in the 'Display' section and specify the number of workbooks you wish to view.

- Sometimes graphics go missing in Excel. No one is quite sure why, but it does happen. To make these objects reappear, go to 'Display options for this workbook' and ensure 'For objects, show:' is set to 'All'.

- Don't want zeros to be displayed? This can be achieved with number formatting (see earlier) or else you can un-check 'Show a zero in cells that have zero value' in the 'Display options for this workbook' section.

- If you have a more powerful computer and / or you are using 64-bit Excel, you may require a bit more grunt for some of your formulae. In the 'Formulas' section, consider checking 'Enable multi-threaded calculation' to ensure you are availing yourself of all of your hardware's capabilities.

- Ever typed 'Jan' in one cell, 'Feb' in the next cell and then completed the rest of the months by highlighting both cells and using Excel's AutoFill feature? You are exploiting one of the built-in lists in Excel. If you want to add other lists, it's easy – simply click on the 'Edit Custom Lists…' button in the 'General' section and either type the list in manually or link to a pre-existing list in your spreadsheet.

Quick Access Toolbar

Everyone has favourite features / functions in Excel, some of which are buried away deep in the software. Let me give you an example. Ever closed that final file in Excel 2013 or later version only for the application to close down as well? There is a workaround.

In Excel 2013, simply right-click on the Quick Access Toolbar and select 'Customize Quick Access Toolbar…' *viz.*

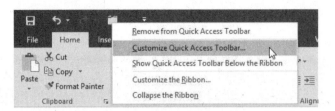

In the subsequent dialog box, select 'All Commands' in the 'Choose commands from' drop down box and then select 'Close File' (with the folder icon, please see the illustration below). Next, click on the 'Add>>' button to add it to the Quick Access Toolbar and finally click on 'OK' to exit the dialog box.

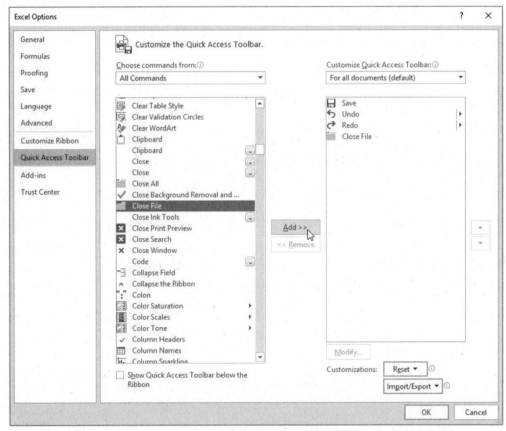

From now on, simply click on this 'Close' icon (Excel 2013 and earlier) / 'Close File' icon (Excel 2016) in the Quick Access Toolbar and you will never have to say goodbye to Excel again. In fact, you will see it has its very own keyboard shortcut too: press the **ALT** button in Excel and it will reveal the number (in the illustration below, it is **ALT + 4**):

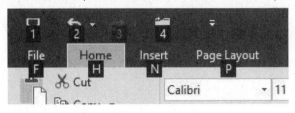

Breaking up can just be so very hard to do!

Layout Suggestions

Right, back to work I suppose. The aim of this chapter is to suggest layout tips for developing your model. To begin with then, here's something I *didn't* prepare earlier:

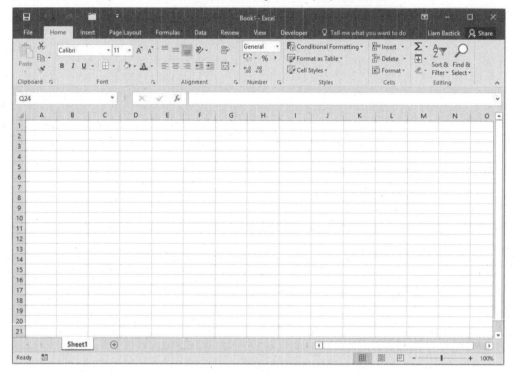

In summary, it's all about design and scoping. The problem is, we are all time poor in today's business environment with perpetual pressure on producing results more and more quickly. Getting a layout structure won't solve all of your problems but it's a start.

Let me show you how I develop this basic worksheet. Assuming this isn't a dashboard output page where column widths may be more critical, I tend to narrow the first few columns (highlight columns, then right-click):

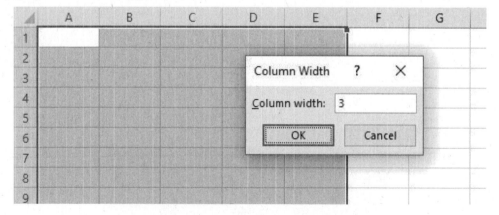

I choose a width of 3 as this effectively makes the cells in these columns square.

	A	B	C	D	E	F	G
1							
2							
3							
4							
5							
6							

You can elect to highlight more or less columns and you can modify the width too. There's two key points to this:

- Keep column **A** blank other than for the sheet headings (I will explain later)

- Be consistent, both with the widths of the columns narrowed here and with other worksheets within the same workbook (again, I will explain soon).

Next, let's put the Sheet Title in cell **A1**. This should be the same as the description in the sheet tab:

	A	B	C	D	E	F	
1	Sheet Title						
2							
3							
4							
5							
6							
7							
8							

Sheet Title ⊕

There are three reasons for this:

- Given sheet tab names cannot be infinitely long, sheet titles become more succinct and easier for the end user to understand

- Given the sheet title appears on the worksheet, the name has to be written formally and cannot be an incomprehensible abbreviation, similar to many sheet tab names out there

- This approach promotes consistency, one of the four key concepts of Best Practice modelling.

In cell **A2**, I will put the model name. This may surprise some of you as this is possible to put in the header or footer of each worksheet instead:

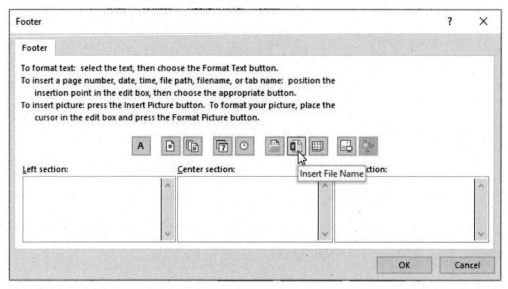

For a start, how many of you know how to locate this dialog box (**ALT + P + SP -> 'Header / Footer' tab -> 'Custom Footer...' button**)? This filename will only display when the worksheet is printed. What if it is an image on a PowerPoint slide or, say, as Appendix 4 in a Word document? This is why I keep the model name front and centre on my worksheets.

There's a formula too:

=IFERROR(MID(CELL("filename",A1),FIND("[",CELL("filename",A1))+1,FIND("]",
CELL("filename",A1))-FIND("[",CELL("filename",A1))-1),"")

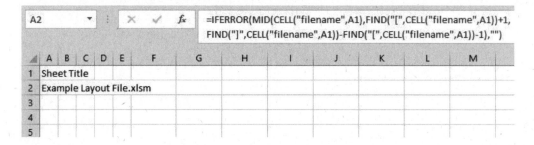

The formula is obvious, yes? I suspect I may need to explain it a little more. It revolves around the **CELL** function in Excel.

Padded CELL

This function returns information about the formatting, location, or contents of the upper-left cell in a reference (in our example, we will be using cell **A1** as our reference in the active worksheet, but this selection is entirely arbitrary). The syntax is

CELL(Information_type,[Reference])

and works as follows:

Information_type	Returns
"address"	Reference of the first cell in reference, as text.
"col"	Column number of the cell in reference.
"color"	1 if the cell is formatted in colour for negative values; otherwise returns 0 (zero).
"contents"	Value of the upper-left cell in reference; not a formula.
"filename"	Filename (including full path) of the file that contains reference, as text. Returns empty text ("") if the worksheet that contains reference has not yet been saved.
"format"	Text value corresponding to the number format of the cell. The text values for the various formats are shown in the following table. Returns "-" at the end of the text value if the cell is formatted in colour for negative values. Returns "()" at the end of the text value if the cell is formatted with parentheses for positive or all values.
"parentheses"	1 if the cell is formatted with parentheses for positive or all values; otherwise returns 0.
"prefix"	Text value corresponding to the "label prefix" of the cell. Returns single quotation mark (') if the cell contains left-aligned text, double quotation mark (") if the cell contains right-aligned text, caret (^) if the cell contains centred text, backslash (\) if the cell contains fill-aligned text, and empty text ("") if the cell contains anything else.
"protect"	0 if the cell is not locked, and 1 if the cell is locked.
"row"	Row number of the cell in reference.
"type"	Text value corresponding to the type of data in the cell. Returns "b" for blank if the cell is empty, "l" for label if the cell contains a text constant, and "v" for value if the cell contains anything else.
"width"	Column width of the cell rounded off to an integer. Each unit of column width is equal to the width of one character in the default font size.

We therefore use the syntax **=CELL("filename",A1)**. An example of a returned filename might be:

**C:\Documents and Settings\Liam\My Documents\Wretched Book\
Layout Chapter\[Example Layout File.xlsm]Sheet1**

This is not what is required, there's 'padding'. All we want is the actual filename, in this case 'Example Layout File.xlsm'. Therefore, we need to extract the filename from this worksheet directory path.

This will be a three-step process.

Step 1: FINDing the Beginning and the End

The directory path will vary for each file, so we need to spot a foolproof method of finding the beginning and the end of the workbook name. Fortunately, Excel assists us here. '[' and ']' are reserved characters in Excel's syntax and denote the beginning and the end of the workbook name.

The example returned filename above is 105 characters long. If we can find the position of the '[' and ']' we will be on our way.

FIND(find_text,within_text,start_num**)** is the function we need, where:

- **find_text** is the text you want to find;

- **within_text** is the text containing the text you want to find; and

- start_num (which is optional) specifies the character at which to start the search. The first character in **within_text** is character number 1. If you omit start_num, it is assumed to be 1.

So, in our example, **=FIND("[",CELL("filename",A1))** returns the value 74 and the formula **=FIND("]",CELL("filename",A1))** returns the value 99. In other words, for our illustration, if we can get Excel to return the character string in positions 75 to 99 inclusive (*i.e.* between the square brackets) we will have our workbook name.

Step 2: LEFT a bit, RIGHT a bit, Aim for the MID Section

There are various functions in Excel that will return part of a character string:

- **LEFT(Text,Num_characters)** returns the first few characters of a string depending upon the number specified (**Num_characters**). This is not useful here as we do not want the first few characters of our text string;

- **RIGHT(Text,Num_characters)** returns the last few characters of a string depending upon the number specified (**Num_characters**). This is not useful here either as we do not want the last few characters of our text string; and

- **MID(Text,Start_num,Num_characters)** returns a specific number of characters from a text string, starting at the position specified, based on the number of characters chosen.

Therefore, we should use the **MID** function here. In hard code form, our formula would be:

=MID(CELL("filename",A1),75,24)

where:

- 75 = position one character to the right of '[' (74 + 1); and

- 24 which is the length of the filename string, being the position of ']' less the position of '[' less 1, i.e. 99 − 74 − 1 = 24.

This gives us our filename 'Example Layout File.xlsm'.

The problem is we don't want hard code: a flexible formula is required. Using the concepts explained above, we derive:

=MID(CELL("filename",A1),FIND("[",CELL("filename",A1))+1,FIND("]", CELL("filename",A1))-FIND("[",CELL("filename",A1))-1)

And so we are done. Except we aren't.

Step 3: Error Trapping

A good modeller will always ensure that a formula will work in all foreseeable circumstances. The above formula will only work if the file has been named and saved. Otherwise, **CELL("filename",A1)** will return empty text (""), which will cause the embedded **FIND** formulae to return #*VALUE!* errors, and hence the overall formula will also return the #*VALUE!* error.

We therefore need an error trap, *i.e.* a check that ensures if the file has not yet been saved we just get empty text ("") returned. To do this, we can use the following formula:

> =IFERROR(MID(CELL("filename",A1),FIND("[",CELL("filename",A1))+1,
> FIND("]",CELL("filename",A1))-FIND("[",CELL("filename",A1))-1),"")

IFERROR(Formula,Error_trap) has been discussed earlier and prevents the #*VALUE!* error. It isn't pretty, it's not short, it's not transparent, but it's flexible and robust.

The formula above is intended to be copied – as is – straight into an Excel worksheet by pasting it directly into the Excel formula bar and pressing ENTER. In certain situations, it will not work due to the exact method of copying employed, fonts used or the set-up of the ASCII characters.

In this instance, try re-typing all of the inverted commas (" and ") in the formulae first. If that doesn't work, I apologise, but you will have to re-type it. C'est la vie.

Sheet Title Revision

You have to admit that is quite a comprehensive example. Assuming you are still awake, we can employ a very similar formula to the Sheet Title in cell **A1**:

> =IFERROR(RIGHT(CELL("filename",A1),
> LEN(CELL("filename",A1))-FIND("]",CELL("filename",A1))),"")

| A1 | ▼ | : | × | ✓ | *fx* | =IFERROR(RIGHT(CELL("filename",A1),LEN(CELL("filename",A1))-FIND("]", CELL("filename",A1))),"") |

	A	B	C	D	E	F	G	H	I	J	K	L	M	N
1	Sheet Title													
2	Example Layout File.xlsm													
3														
4														
5														

The aim is to automate as much as possible. It may not adhere to the "Rule of Thumb", but sometimes, you have to balance transparency against flexibility and robustness.

Back to Layout Tips

20,000 pages into this chapter and I am about to consider what to put on Row 3.

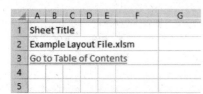

It looks like I have added a hyperlink in cell **A3**, right? Not quite. I am a little craftier than that. Actually, I have highlighted cells **A3:F3** and then merged the cells using Excel's **Merge Across** functionality (**ALT + H + M + A**):

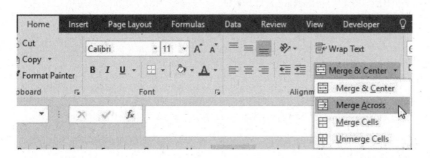

I have discussed how to create hyperlinks earlier in the book (**CTRL + K**). The intention is to set up a central Table of Contents worksheet where all of the hyperlinks to the other worksheets reside:

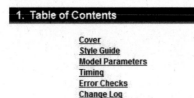

The hyperlink should link to cell **A1** of that worksheet and that cell should have a range name such **HL_TOC** for reasons explained previously. The reason cells **A3:F3** are merged is so that if the end user clicks anywhere in that range the hyperlink will activate; otherwise, the user will have to click on cell **A3** only for the hyperlink to work.

This brings us on nicely to cell **A4**:

	A	B	C	D	E	F	G
1	Sheet Title						
2	Example Layout File.xlsm						
3	Go to Table of Contents						
4	Error Checks:						
5							

Not much to say about typing text into cell **A4**, but there is more to do on this row:

	A	B	C	D	E	F	G	H	I	J	K	L	M	N
1	Sheet Title													
2	Example Layout File.xlsm													
3	Go to Table of Contents													
4	Error Checks:				OK	Units			Date 1	Date 2	Date 3	Date 4	Date 5	
5														
6														

Cell **F4** is not just the word "OK"; it actually links back to an Error Checks worksheet. I am going to talk about constructing error checks in a subsequent chapter, so imagine for the moment that cell **F4** is a formula to another worksheet. In reality, it will also be a hyperlink, but as I said, more anon.

In my layout, I have made column **G** my **Units** column: down this column I shall put in all of my units so end users may distinguish between numerical fields. How often have you seen an output and not known if it is in $, $'000, $m, kg or sliced dolphins? This will make this issue a thing of the past. It should be noted that this column is not always required. For instance, on an outputs worksheet, you may simply state near the top of the sheet, "All outputs are displayed in $m unless stated otherwise".

Cells **J4:N4** contain the date headings. In the next chapter, I will explain that you actually need more than one row of details for the dates, but that can keep for now. The dates should be periodic (*e.g.* monthly, quarterly, annually) and should always start and end in the same columns (and rows) on each forecast worksheet. That is not always possible: sometimes, you require some parts of your model to be annually forecast and other aspects monthly. Where this occurs, this should be in clearly delineated areas of the workbook.

Certainly, under no circumstances should the periodicity be inconsistent across any row of an input or calculations worksheet. It is foreseeable that an output sheet may summarise differently, but this should use a methodology such as **SUMIF** or **SUMIFS** *(see earlier)* to summarise data from other worksheets where the periodicity was consistent throughout, *e.g.*

D17				fx	=SUMIF($D$8:$AA$8,D$15,$D$10:$AA$10)											
	A	B	C	D	E	F	G	H	I	J	K	L	M	N	O	P	Q
1																	
2	*Input*																
3																	
4	Month No.			1	2	3	4	5	6	7	8	9	10	11	12	13	14
5	Month			M1	M2	M3	M4	M5	M6	M7	M8	M9	M10	M11	M12	M1	M2
6	Quarter			Q1	Q1	Q1	Q2	Q2	Q2	Q3	Q3	Q3	Q4	Q4	Q4	Q1	Q1
7	Year			Y1	Y1	Y1	Y1	Y1	Y1	Y1	Y1	Y1	Y1	Y1	Y1	Y2	Y2
8	SUMIF Ctr	=IF(D$7="Y1",IF(D$4<=6,D$5,D$6),D$7)		M1	M2	M3	M4	M5	M6	Q3	Q3	Q3	Q4	Q4	Q4	Y2	Y2
9																	
10	Sales			100	200	300	400	500	600	700	800	900	1,000	1,100	1,200	1,300	1,400
11																	
12																	
13	*Output*																
14																	
15	Period			M1	M2	M3	M4	M5	M6	Q3	Q4	Y2					
16																	
17	Sales	=SUMIF($D$8:$AA$8,D$15,$D$10:$AA$10)		100	200	300	400	500	600	2,400	3,300	22,200					
18																	

You may have noticed as well that there is a line inserted in between rows 4 and 5 of our image:

	A	B	C	D	E	F	G	H	I	J	K	L	M	N
1	Sheet Title													
2	Example Layout File.xlsm													
3	Go to Table of Contents													
4	Error Checks:					**OK**	**Units**			**Date 1**	**Date 2**	**Date 3**	**Date 4**	**Date 5**
5														
6														

This is not a drawn line. This is a frozen pane. Frozen panes break up the worksheet in to as many four pieces. Located in the 'Window' grouping of the 'View' tab of the Ribbon, there are three ways to create a frozen pane:

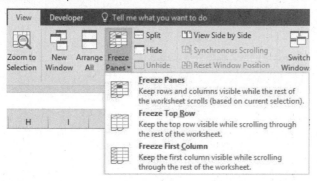

141

- **Freeze top row:** Keeps the top row visible no matter how far down the spreadsheet you scroll

- **Freeze first column:** Keeps the first column visible no matter how far to the right you scroll the spreadsheet

- **Custom (Freeze Panes):** Creates a frozen locus at the intersection of the top row and the first column of the cell(s) selected.

That final option is a little confusing. Essentially the frozen panes are created as follows:

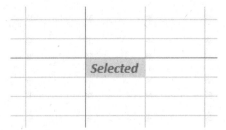

Frozen panes are created for the region the selection is in, the region directly above, the region to the immediate left and diagonally opposite the top left hand corner of the selection. If the selection were in column A, there would only be two frozen panes: the rows immediately above and the remainder. If the selection were in row 1, again, there would only be two frozen panes: the columns to the left and the remainder.

Splits

Splits are similar to frozen panes. They are created like Freeze Panes (keyboard shortcut: **ALT + W + S**). but create scrollbars in all quadrants, which means no section is truly fixed.

In our example, cell **A5** has been made the basis of the frozen pane, so that rows 1 to 4 will always be visible. This cell should be given a range name, *e.g.* **HL_Home**, as this is the cell hyperlinks to this sheet should link. This cell 'resets' the sheet and makes the model easier to navigate as a consequence.

Hyperlink Home Cell

The cell that effectively resets the worksheet can be readily identified. If there is a split or frozen pane on the worksheet, then the chances are cell **A1** is not the correct cell. The cell can be identified by the keyboard shortcut **CTRL + HOME**. It is always the top left hand corner of the bottom right hand quadrant of any frozen panes. It is the top left hand corner cell of the range selected to freeze panes in the first place.

Back to our example, headings should start in column **B**, not **A**, and then move out a column or two for sub headings and sub sub headings respectively. I then put data labels directly beneath sub sub headings:

	A	B	C	D	E	F	G	H	I	J	K	L	M	N
1	Sheet Title													
2	Example Layout File.xlsm													
3	Go to Table of Contents													
4	Error Checks:					OK	Units			Date 1	Date 2	Date 3	Date 4	Date 5
5														
6		Main Heading												
7														
8			Sub Heading											
9														
10				Sub Sub Heading										
11				Label										
12				Label										
13				Label										
14				Label										
15				Label										

I have called them "Headings" and "Sub Headings" *etc.* to make it clear, but if I develop a stutter I might be in column **Q** before you know it! Renaming the headings "Heading 1" and so on may be clearer. This also makes them consistent with pre-existing Style names *(hint, hint)*:

	A	B	C	D	E	F	G	H	I	J	K	L	M	N
1	Sheet Title													
2	Example Layout File.xlsm													
3	Go to Table of Contents													
4	Error Checks:					OK	Units			Date 1	Date 2	Date 3	Date 4	Date 5
5														
6		Heading 1												
7														
8			Heading 2											
9														
10				Heading 3										
11				Label										
12				Label										
13				Label										
14				Label										
15				Label										
16														
17														
18		Heading 1												
19														
20			Heading 2											
21														
22				Heading 3										
23				Label										
24				Label										
25				Label										
26				Label										
27				Label										

Aside from keeping column A clear, do you now see why I have narrowed columns **B**, **C** and **D** (I am keeping column **E** "just in case")? The narrowing of the columns effectively indents the headings and makes worksheets easier to read and navigate (especially if the gridlines, **ALT + W + VG**, are toggled off).

Take special note of the spacing: one blank row between headings; two lines between sections. That's my preference. You choose your own if you would prefer – just be consistent. This treatment will reap dividend as our financial model case study later will demonstrate.

Blank columns **H** and **I** are in existence in case we have any calculations, inputs or referred values that do not refer to a particular time period. If they are not required, I tend to narrow the columns to a width of 1 (say), so that they are still there in case they are needed later.

Adding labels, data and formulae:

	A	B	C	D	E	F	G	H	I	J	K	L	M	N
1	Sheet Title													
2	Example Layout File.xlsm													
3	Go to Table of Contents													
4	Error Checks:					OK	Units			Date 1	Date 2	Date 3	Date 4	Date 5
5														
6		Heading 1												
7														
8			Heading 2											
9														
10				Heading 3										
11				Label			Number			7481	2962	19411	8388	7157
12				Label			$/unit			3.8	3.81	3.82	3.83	3.84
13				Label			$/unit			2.95	2.94	2.93	2.92	2.91
14				Label			$/unit			4.5	4.5	4.5	4.5	4.5
15				Label			$/unit			3.75	3.7	4.1	3.9	4.22
16														
17														
18		Heading 1												
19														
20			Heading 2											
21														
22				Heading 3										
23				Label			Number			7481	2962	19411	8388	7157
24				Label			$'000			28427.8	11285.22	74150.02	32126.04	27482.88
25				Label			$'000			22068.95	8708.28	56874.23	24492.96	20826.87
26				Label			$'000			33664.5	13329	87349.5	37746	32206.5
27				Label			$'000			28053.75	10959.4	79585.1	32713.2	30202.54

It's starting to look more like a spreadsheet now. If we start adding / taking into account Styles (**ALT + H + J**),

these may be applied:

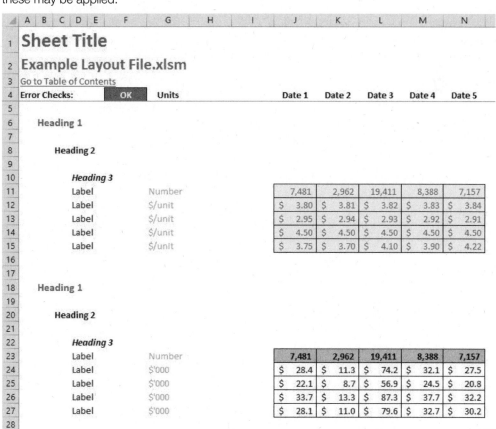

	Units		Date 1	Date 2	Date 3	Date 4	Date 5
Sheet Title							
Example Layout File.xlsm							
Go to Table of Contents							
Error Checks:	OK	Units	Date 1	Date 2	Date 3	Date 4	Date 5
Heading 1							
Heading 2							
Heading 3							
Label		Number	7,481	2,962	19,411	8,388	7,157
Label		$/unit	$ 3.80	$ 3.81	$ 3.82	$ 3.83	$ 3.84
Label		$/unit	$ 2.95	$ 2.94	$ 2.93	$ 2.92	$ 2.91
Label		$/unit	$ 4.50	$ 4.50	$ 4.50	$ 4.50	$ 4.50
Label		$/unit	$ 3.75	$ 3.70	$ 4.10	$ 3.90	$ 4.22
Heading 1							
Heading 2							
Heading 3							
Label		Number	7,481	2,962	19,411	8,388	7,157
Label		$'000	$ 28.4	$ 11.3	$ 74.2	$ 32.1	$ 27.5
Label		$'000	$ 22.1	$ 8.7	$ 56.9	$ 24.5	$ 20.8
Label		$'000	$ 33.7	$ 13.3	$ 87.3	$ 37.7	$ 32.2
Label		$'000	$ 28.1	$ 11.0	$ 79.6	$ 32.7	$ 30.2

Do you see? It's starting to look more like a spreadsheet already. I switch off gridlines on my spreadsheets so that the majority of my files appear to have a white background. There is more to this point than merely aesthetics. Adding a colour to the background of a spreadsheet can make a file significantly larger – unnecessarily.

The spacing is deliberate too. Not only does it look neater (remember, Excel 2007 onwards has 1,048,576 rows and 16,384 columns, *i.e.* it is 1,024 times larger than an Excel 2003 worksheet so there is plenty of room), but the space is functional too.

Want to navigate between the main headings in column **B**? Click on cell **B6**, go **CTRL + Down Arrow** and you will arrive at cell **B18**. Repeat this action and the next cell you will hit is cell **B1048576**, *i.e.* the very bottom of the spreadsheet because there is nothing else in this column.

Click on cell **D10** (**Heading 3**) and go **CTRL + Down Arrow** will take you to cell **D15**, the final cell in the contiguous range. **CTRL + Up Arrow**, **CTRL + Right Arrow** and **CTRL + Left Arrow** will all perform similar actions. Need to highlight a range? Click on any cell within the range and **CTRL + A** will select the whole contiguous range. This makes the model easier for developer and user alike to navigate and manipulate.

So why have I kept column **A** blank? The reason is to take into account work in progress. How often have you started creating a spreadsheet only to be interrupted, have to go to a meeting, take a telephone call, go home or go to sleep? The point is, when we are interrupted we need to remember how far along we were. If you design a spreadsheet similar to the one discussed here, imagine you are interrupted without notice. Before you turn your attention to the disruption, whichever row you are working on, press the **HOME** key which will take you to column **A** of that row. Type anything in that cell, *e.g.* "w" for "work in progress" or "check" and so on. That's it.

How does that help you? Before you hand the model to anyone else, we need to undertake some checks before saving and distributing. One of those checks will be to ensure there is nothing in column **A** of any worksheet after the frozen pane. I will explain how to do this when we discuss reviewing the model at the end of this book. I bet you can't wait…

Summary

That's all I wanted to say about layout. Keep it consistent, make it transparent, ensure there are checks to protect the robustness and that inputs are clearly marked to aid flexibility. See? I have developed a simple layout adhering to the **CRaFT** methodology.

Chapter 5: Time Series Analysis

There comes a time in most people's lives that they realise it's time to confront the world head-on, go out there and ask for a date. You can imagine asking a model for a date can be even more stressful. Well puns completed, it's not that difficult, but it does deserve its own chapter.

Most forecast models project key outputs over multiple periods. Typically, these periods are not headed "Time 1", "Time 2", etc. like in our example from the last chapter, but display end dates to assist users to understand payback periods, seasonality, trends and so on.

An example time series could contain some or all of the following:

Month Ending	Jan-20	Feb-20	Mar-20	Apr-20	May-20	Jun-20
Month	M12	M1	M2	M3	M4	M5
Period End Year	2020	2020	2020	2020	2020	2020
Financial Year	2020	2021	2021	2021	2021	2021
Days in Period End Year	366	366	366	366	366	366
Days in Financial Year	365	366	366	366	366	366
Financial Year Period	M12	M1	M2	M3	M4	M5
Start Date	1/1/20	1/2/20	1/3/20	1/4/20	1/5/20	1/6/20
End Date	31/1/20	29/2/20	31/3/20	30/4/20	31/5/20	30/6/20
Months in Month	1	1	1	1	1	1
Days in Period	31	29	31	30	31	30
Days in Month	31	29	31	30	31	30
Counter	1	2	3	4	5	6

The above is an example of time series data in a real-life financial model. My question is this though: are all of these rows absolutely necessary?

I would suggest not.

Essentially, three lines are necessarily needed when modelling (the rest may be derived as necessary):

- **Start date:** This will allow for models where the first period is not a "full" period (often called a 'stub' period), *e.g.* a business may wish to project its profits from now until the end of the calendar year for the first year;

- **End date:** This will define the end of the period and will often coincide with reporting dates, *e.g.* end of financial year or quarter ends. By having both the start date and end date defined, a modeller can determine the number of days / weeks / months in the period, which financial year the period pertains to and so forth;

- **Counter:** Start and end dates are insufficient. Constructing calculations based on consideration of a date is fraught with potential issues in Excel. This is because dates are really serial numbers in Excel which may differ depending upon the underlying operating system (*e.g.* Day 1 for Microsoft Excel for Windows is 1 January 1900, whilst Day 1 is 1 January 1904 for Microsoft Excel for the Macintosh). Further, if you are building a monthly model you may wish to divide an annual figure evenly instead of based on the number of days. This is also the easiest way to identify the first and last periods in a robust manner.

So, bearing this in mind, how do you build up the necessary formulae for these three line items allowing for the more common eventualities? Well, to begin with, there's only really one troublesome formula. This is because:

- The Counter is simply the last period's number plus one. I tend to use the formula **=N(Previous_Cell)+1**, where the **N()** function takes the numerical value in the previous cell. importantly, text is ignored so that *#VALUE!* errors will not arise;

- The Start Date is simply the Model Start Date for the first period and the day following the last period's end date otherwise. This can simply be written as **=IF(Counter=1,Model_Start_Date,Previous_Period_End_Date+1)**.

Therefore, we need only consider the formula for the Period End Date. Consider the following simple example:

1. Timing Assumptions

Data (do not change once modelling has commenced)

Model Start Date	17 Jan 20
Number of Months in a Full Period	3
Example Reporting Month	12 *e.g. 31–Dec-20*
Reporting Month Factor	3
Months per Year	12

I have selected an arbitrary start date (**Model_Start_Date**) of 17 January 2020, and assumed that the number of months in a full period (**Periodicity**) is 3. The third line item is a little more subtle: this specifies which periods are period ends by specifying one month that will be a period end month. For example, tax may be paid quarterly in the months of January, April, July and October. By entering a **Periodicity** of 3 and specifying an **Example_Reporting_Month** of any of 1, 4, 7 or 10, this will provide sufficient information to work out the quarter ends, i.e. 31-Jan, 30-Apr, 31-Jul and 31-Oct. The **Reporting_Month_Factor** is simply the minimum of these acceptable alternative values and is calculated automatically here. The approach I will use here requires that the periodicity is a divisor of the number of months in a year (**Months_in_Year**) – which is why my example only allows the **Periodicity** to be 1, 2, 3, 4, 6 or 12.

In the example above, we are building a quarterly model where December is one of the quarter ends. Therefore, the possible quarter end months are:

End Date Month
3
6
9
12

This example table allows for up to 12 month ends (*i.e.* for a monthly model).

So how do we derive the necessary formula? I will give you some insight into my simplistic view of the world. First, I would construct the following table:

Model Start Date Month	End Date Month	Addition Reqd
1	3	2
2	3	1
3	3	0
4	6	2
5	6	1
6	6	0
7	9	2
8	9	1
9	9	0
10	12	2
11	12	1
12	12	0

This simple table considers all 12 months of the year for the **Model_Start_Date** (first column). The middle column displays which month would be the first quarter, given the assumption regarding the month of the **Model_Start_Date**. Therefore, a start date in January, February or March will give rise to a March quarter end, etc.

I can use an array formula to calculate this month number dynamically. This is not necessary, and the values could just be typed in – remember, this table is simply a tool to ascertain how to construct the formula required.

The final column is then the difference between the end date month and the **Model_Start_Date** month. It is slightly more complicated than this as we need to consider what happens if the Model_Start_Date month exceeds the final end date month. For example, in my tax example above, tax arising in November (month 11) is after the final payment period of the year (month 10). This would be paid in month 1 of the following year instead.

The point is, the final column highlights the pattern of how many months after the **Model_Start_Date** the first reporting period will occur. We can now use two functions in tandem to derive this first period end date:

- **EOMONTH(Date,Months)** returns the last day of the month that is so many months from the date specified. For example, **=EOMONTH(11-Dec-20,14)** would be 28-Feb-22, *i.e.* the end date 14 months after the end of December 2020.

- **MOD(Number,Divisor)** returns the remainder when **Number** is divided by the **Divisor**. For example, **=MOD(17,6)** is 5, since 17/6 = 2 remainder 5.

With trial and error the number of months we need to add on can be calculated as follows:

=MOD(Perodicity+Reporting_Month_Factor-MONTH(Model_Start_Date),Perodicity)

and therefore if we call this equation our **Additive_Factor**, then the reporting end date will be:

=EOMONTH(Model_Start_Date,Additive_Factor)

In the example file, I have checked my workings, *viz.*

Model Start Date Month	End Date Month	Addition Reqd	Dates Calc	Verification
1	3	2	2	3
2	3	1	1	3
3	3	0	0	3
4	6	2	2	6
5	6	1	1	6
6	6	0	0	6
7	9	2	2	9
8	9	1	1	9
9	9	0	0	9
10	12	2	2	12
11	12	1	1	12
12	12	0	0	12

Furthermore, a robust yet flexible time series can be constructed:

F62		× ✓ *fx*	=EOMONTH(F61,MOD(Perodicity+Reporting_Month_Factor-MONTH(F$61),Perodicity))							

	C D	E	F	G	H	I	J	K	L	M
58										
59	With EOMONTH									
60										
61		Start Date	17-Jan-20	01-Apr-20	01-Jul-20	01-Oct-20	01-Jan-21	01-Apr-21	01-Jul-21	01-Oct-21
62		End Date	31-Mar-20	30-Jun-20	30-Sep-20	31-Dec-20	31-Mar-21	30-Jun-21	30-Sep-21	31-Dec-21
63		Counter	1	2	3	4	5	6	7	8
64										

Even allowing for flexible start dates and "Reporting Month Factors", the above will not work in all circumstances. Other periodicities may be sought, whilst some businesses require weekly reporting or 5-4-4 week period regimes. Nonetheless, the above approach can be modified and extrapolated to consider most complications.

Chapter 6: Error Checks

You may recall during our discussion on robustness, one of the four key qualities of a "Best Practice" model, I sang the praises of including as many checks as possible. I use the generic "error check" descriptor to cover three types of check:

1. **Error checks** – the model contains flawed logic or *prima facie* errors, *e.g.* Balance Sheet does not balance, cash in cashflow statement does not reconcile with the balance sheet, or the model contains #DIV/0! errors, *etc*;

2. **Sensitivity checks** – the model's outputs are being derived from inputs that are not deemed to be part of the base case. This can prevent erroneous decisions being made using the "Best Case"; *and*

3. **Alert checks** – everything else! This flags points of interest to a user's and / or developer's issues that may need to be reviewed: *e.g.* revenues are negative, debt covenants have been breached, *etc*.

Many modellers add checks as an afterthought. Basically, it is too late to create them then. While building a model, a developer knows what situation might break a formula. *That is when you should create the check*. When the issue is foremost in your mind, create the check there and then.

Let me give you an example. I am going to create the world's simplest Balance Sheet:

You may be a Fellow or one of the accounting institutes or you may know very little on financial reporting. In either case, one thing everybody knows: *Balance Sheets have to balance*.

So let me put a check in to ensure it balances:

The formula **=C6=C10** is pretty straightforward, but I don't recommend it. Any financial model we build will have many time periods and we will need a check for each period. Further, that's just one check out of many. How do you feel about reading through all of your error checks and making sure they all equal TRUE?

It is true you could use a **SUMIF** formula to count all of the TRUE responses, but surely there is an easier way? Of course there is; let me walk you through it. First thing is to put the formula in brackets and multiply the bracketed expression by 1:

C13		× ✓	fx	=(C6=C10)*1	
▲	A	B	C	D	E
1		**Simple Balance Sheet Example**			
2					
3			$m		
4		Total Assets	100		
5		Total Liabilities	30		
6		**Net Assets**	70		
7					
8		Shareholders' Equity	50		
9		Retained Earnings	20		
10		**Total Equity**	70		
11					
12					
13		Balance Check:	1		
14					

The requirement for brackets is due to the order of operations in a calculation using the **BODMAS** principle:

B rackets

p O wers

D ivision

M ultiplication

A ddition

S ubtraction

i.e. calculations in brackets are performed before raising numbers to powers (computing exponentials), before division, and so on.

The problem with this formula is that this will count all the times the Balance Sheet balances. Is it really that informative knowing that your Balance Sheet balances in 17,212 instances? Would it be preferable to learn that you have two errors? Of course it would. This is known as **reporting by exception**. To revise the formula:

C13		× ✓	fx	=(C6<>C10)*1	
▲	A	B	C	D	E
1		**Simple Balance Sheet Example**			
2					
3			$m		
4		Total Assets	100		
5		Total Liabilities	30		
6		**Net Assets**	70		
7					
8		Shareholders' Equity	50		
9		Retained Earnings	20		
10		**Total Equity**	70		
11					
12					
13		Balance Check:	-		
14					

The "**<>**" symbol means "is not equal to" so **=(C6<>C10)*1** flags (*i.e.* displays a '1') when Net Assets does not equal Total Equity. That sounds good, but this is not quite sufficient either. In additions and other calculations within Excel, sometimes Excel produces minor rounding errors simply due to the way the software has been programmed. This error may occur at the eighth or ninth decimal place and is not caused by the modeller's formula *per se*, more it is an anomaly in the coding of Excel itself. To circumvent this, I use the **ROUND** function:

> **ROUND(Number,Number_of_digits)**

This rounds **Number** to **Number_of_digits** decimal places, *e.g.* **ROUND(2.928,2)** equals 2.93.

	A	B	C	D	E
	C13		f_x	=(ROUND(C6-C10,5)<>0)*1	
1		Simple Balance Sheet Example			
2					
3			$m		
4		Total Assets	100		
5		Total Liabilities	30		
6		Net Assets	70		
7					
8		Shareholders' Equity	50		
9		Retained Earnings	20		
10		Total Equity	70		
11					
12					
13		Balance Check:	-		
14					

In this illustration, **=(ROUND(C6-C10,5)<>0)*1** alerts when **C6** (Net Assets) does not equal **C10** (Total Equity) to five decimal places.

Just before I continue, I am going to be pedantic here – with good reason. There are three hard coded values in that last formula, 5, 0 and 1. Some hard code (*i.e.* typed in numbers) is acceptable and some is not:

- '5' is essentially a variable. In this example, we are rounding to five decimal places, but this could be argued as an arbitrary choice. It is better to have this as an input value and to make its reference clearer, provide it with a range name, *e.g.* **Rounding_Factor**.

- '0' is not a variable. This is a **constant**. I am testing to see whether the difference between two values (given a **Rounding_Factor** tolerance) is zero. I am unlikely to want to change this so I may determine whether the difference between the two values is 44.8 *(say)*. Therefore, this value is acceptable in a formula.

- '1' is also a constant. This converts TRUE or FALSE values to 1's and 0's respectively so that they may be added together to determine the number of errors. For this reason, the use of the number 1 in this formula is also deemed acceptable.

Variables vs. Constants

When building models, we often forget to consider the nature of the inputs we include. Numerical data serves two key purposes:

- **Variables:** These are values that are entered for *flexibility* that we want the end user to be able to change (within reason) as required. This is the heart of a financial model. Inputs may include sales, growth rates, volume and taxation assumptions amongst much other numerical data.

  Values that are time-dependent (*e.g.* year-on-year growth rates, foreign exchange rates) should be entered for each period, whilst other data (*e.g.* test discount rate, percentage of business acquired) should be entered in a separate column so that users do not incorrectly believe they relate to a particular time period.

- **Constants:** These are values that are entered for *transparency* so that end users may understand certain constraints that the model is operating under. It is recommended that these constants are not only labelled but are also assigned range names.

  For example, the number 12 may relate to the number of calendar months in the year, the number of hours in half a day or the number of five-minute intervals in an hour. It is through both creating labelling and range names that an end user may truly understand a particular formula.

Typically, variables and constants should be entered in separate sections or separate worksheets of a financial model.

In this example, I will leave hard code in the previous formula alone, but perhaps a "better practice" version of the calculation might be **=(ROUND(C6-C10,Rounding_Factor)<>0)*1**. However, there is still a large issue. What if someone deletes a key reference?

C13		✕ ✓	f_x	=(ROUND(C6-C10,5)<>0)*1	
	A	B	C	D	E
1		**Simple Balance Sheet Example**			
2					
3			$m		
4		Total Assets	100		
5		Total Liabilities	#REF!		
6		**Net Assets**	#REF!		
7					
8		Shareholders' Equity	50		
9		Retained Earnings	20		
10		**Total Equity**	70		
11					
12					
13		Balance Check:	#REF!		
14					
15					

In example, the reference in cell **C5** no longer exists giving rise to an *#REF!* error. Unfortunately, this does happen in models. Even if you protect a worksheet (**ALT + T + P + P**), the end user may still delete the sheet! (Protecting the workbook – **ALT + T + P + W** – will prevent this, but the workbook can still be deleted.)

Therefore, if someone does manage to accidentally delete a key reference, we would want our error check to alert us accordingly. The problem is, in our example above, while our check may alert us, *#REF!* is not necessarily the ideal way to display this. I would prefer to be alerted using our 1 / 0 system already utilised:

⬛	A	B	C	D	E
1		**Simple Balance Sheet Example**			
2					
3			$m		
4		Total Assets	100		
5		Total Liabilities	#REF!		
6		**Net Assets**	**#REF!**		
7					
8		Shareholders' Equity	50		
9		Retained Earnings	20		
10		**Total Equity**	**70**		
11					
12		Prima Facie Check:	1		=IF(ISERROR(C6-C10),1,)
13		Balance Check:	0		=IF(C12,,(ROUND(C6-C10,5)<>0)*1)
14					

Now the checks are becoming more sophisticated. In cell **C12** *(above)*, I have added a check and modified the existing one in **C13**. The first check, **=IF(ISERROR(C6-C10),1,)**, provides the value 1 if Net Assets less Total Equity may not be evaluated. This is <u>not</u> the same as the formula

=IFERROR(C6-C10,1)

Whilst this formula will provide a value of 1 if the subtraction cannot be evaluated, the alternative is not necessarily zero. This formula is not intended to be my balance check, merely a check to ensure that my balance check will work. If I were to use **IFERROR** rather than **IF(ISERROR)** the values could be *anything*. I just want values of zero and one only.

Turning our attention to the second formula in cell **C13**, did you check out that this check contains a check to check the check can be checked? Did you just check out with that last sentence? I really should have been a poet – then even fewer would read my drivel…

Consider the following variant of the formula in cell **C13**:

=IF(C12<>0,0,(ROUND(C6-C10,5)<>0)*1)

To be honest, this is the formula I would probably use in a model as it is easier for users to understand. This checks to ensure that the error check in cell **C12** (the "prima facie check") has not been triggered before checking whether Net Assets equals Total Equity. I wrote the formula differently above, *i.e.* **=IF(C12,,…)**, to demonstrate two "shortcuts":

- Putting a cell reference or value in as the first argument in an **IF** statement is the same as checking whether the value is non-zero. All numerical values other than zero are treated as if they were TRUE by Excel, whereas a value of precisely zero is FALSE.

- Omitting a value (just putting two commas) in this instance is the same as assuming a **Value_if_TRUE** value of zero (0).

We don't have to stop there:

	A	B	C	D	E
1	**Simple Balance Sheet Example**				
2					
3			$m		
4		Total Assets	100		
5		Total Liabilities	130		
6		**Net Assets**	(30)		
7					
8		Shareholders' Equity	50		
9		Retained Earnings	(80)		
10		**Total Equity**	(30)		
11					
12		Prima Facie Check:	0		=IF(ISERROR(C6-C10),1,)
13		Balance Check:	0		=IF(C12,,(ROUND(C6-C10,5)<>0)*1)
14		Insolvency Check:	1		=IF(AND(C12=0,C13=0),(C6<0)*1,)
15					

With this third check, it may be getting see why order of checks is so important.

> ## =IF(AND(C12=0,C13=0),(C6<0)*1,)

checks to see if Net Assets are negative, but only if there are no *prima facie* errors in the output *and* the Balance Sheet balances. In fact, this last check is a different type of check. The first two are error checks, *i.e.* these highlight issues that <u>must</u> be resolved before the model may be relied upon. Materiality is not relevant. Until these issues are fixed, the model is not calculating correctly.

The insolvency check, on the other hand, is an example of an alert check. The model is calculating correctly and there appear to be no *prima facie* errors. However, if actuality coincides with the forecast, your business will become insolvent with more owing than owed. Warning!

This whole idea may be extrapolated further:

	A	B	C	D	E	F	G	H	I	J
1	**Simple Balance Sheet Example**									
2										
3					2020	2021	2022	2023	2024	
4					$m	$m	$m	$m	$m	
5		Total Assets			100	100	100	140	185	
6		Total Liabilities			30	130	90	100	130	
7		Net Assets			70	(30)	10	40	55	
8										
9		Shareholders' Equity			50	70	(30)	10	40	
10		Retained Earnings			20	(100)	40	30	15	
11		Total Equity			70	(30)	10	40	55	
12										
13		Prima Facie Check:	-	=MIN(SUM(E13:I13),1)	-	-	-	-	-	
14		Balance Check:	-	=MIN(SUM(E14:I14),1)	-	-	-	-	-	
15		Insolvency Check:	1	=MIN(SUM(E15:I15),1)	-	1	-	-	-	
16										
17										

In this illustration I have demonstrated how checks may be incorporated across periods of time. The checks in cells **E13:I15** are similar to those described above already, but the checks in column **C** are new. These are aggregator checks, summarising issues across their respective rows. The formula used in cell **C13**:

> ## =MIN(SUM(E13:I13),1)

adds up the total in each row and takes the minimum of that summation and one. This retains the structure of the checks: zero means no issues, whereas one signifies an issue to be investigated further.

These checks could be linked to an overall Error Checks worksheet at this stage or else there may be one additional step to take:

C16					f_x	=MIN(SUM(C13:C15),1)				
	A	B	C	D	E	F	G	H	I	J
1	**Simple Balance Sheet Example**									
2										
3					2020	2021	2022	2023	2024	
4					$m	$m	$m	$m	$m	
5	Total Assets				100	100	100	140	185	
6	Total Liabilities				30	130	90	100	130	
7	**Net Assets**				70	(30)	10	40	55	
8										
9	Shareholders' Equity				50	70	(30)	10	40	
10	Retained Earnings				20	(100)	40	30	15	
11	**Total Equity**				70	(30)	10	40	55	
12										
13	Prima Facie Check:		-	=MIN(SUM(E13:I13),1)	-	-	-	-	-	
14	Balance Check:		-	=MIN(SUM(E14:I14),1)	-	-	-	-	-	
15	Insolvency Check:		1	=MIN(SUM(E15:I15),1)	-	1	-	-	-	
16	**Overall:**		1	=MIN(SUM(C13:C15),1)						

Here, I have created an overall check for this section. The check in cell **C16** summarises the checks in column **C** above it, using a similar construct of the **MIN** function to create a check that may only ever be one or zero.

Adding conditional formatting, number formatting and Wingdings font whilst removing gridlines arguably makes for a more aesthetic look:

	A	B	C	D	E	F	G	H	I	J
1	**Simple Balance Sheet Example**									
2										
3					2020	2021	2022	2023	2024	
4					$m	$m	$m	$m	$m	
5	Total Assets				100	100	100	140	185	
6	Total Liabilities				30	130	90	100	130	
7	**Net Assets**				70	(30)	10	40	55	
8										
9	Shareholders' Equity				50	70	(30)	10	40	
10	Retained Earnings				20	(100)	40	30	15	
11	**Total Equity**				70	(30)	10	40	55	
12										
13	Prima Facie Check:		☑		☑	☑	☑	☑	☑	
14	Balance Check:		☑		☑	☑	☑	☑	☑	
15	Insolvency Check:		☒		☑	☒	☑	☑	☑	
16	**Overall:**		☒							
17										

It will be a preference call, whether to include checks on a row by row basis or rather on an overall section basis (just be consistent), but these checks may then be summaries on an overall Error Check worksheet *viz.*

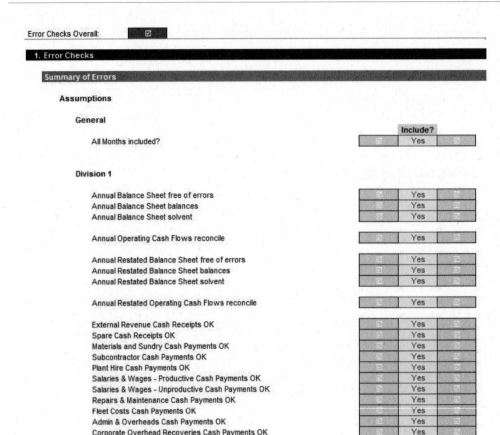

As mentioned previously, this screenshot is from a sanitised version of a real-life financial model. The first column of checks are merely links from checks built throughout the model – but hyperlinked, so that if the end user clicks on either this column or the second column of checks they will be taken back to the source. Do remember that the destination cell of a hyperlink should be given a range name, *e.g.* **HL_Check01**, in case the destination worksheet is renamed.

A Yes / No data validation list separates the two columns of checks, with a "No" making the check OK in all situations. This is fine during model development as construction can generate interim model errors (*e.g.* Balance Sheet does not balance), but all <u>error</u> checks should be switched on prior to a model being used operationally.

Finally, the summary check at the foot of the image is the overall check for the model. It is this one which is linked to the overall check at the top of each worksheet, just as I described when discussing the model layout. This should also be a hyperlink, so not only do you have a hyperlink to the Table of Contents for each worksheet, you also have immediate access to the Error Checks worksheet too.

To conclude this chapter, I have concentrated just on one section, suggestions for just *some* of the checks to consider for the Balance Sheet. This is not intended to be an exhaustive list. As you build a model, you will realise which checks you need to incorporate. If you forget one or two, it is likely they will come back to haunt you later when you are trying to diagnose an issue in your model!

Chapter 7: Model Template Example

If you are going to skip a chapter (and I am not suggesting you do), this would probably be the one to omit. Not that it isn't important, it's just that the actual template is included in the Excel files for your perusal.

This template is a **suggestion**. It will <u>not</u> work for everybody and that was never the intention in any case. Hopefully, it will give you several ideas whilst developing your own. And when I mean "your own", be careful: models should never be personalised. They are for business use (generally). "Template" means precisely that. Models built by colleagues should have a similar look and feel. If you think of models circulating in your office, are they all similar? Chances are that will not be the case. Using styles, spacing and hyperlinks should therefore be consistent. Opening a template will assist.

Difference Between a Template and a Reusable File

A **template file** is a file that has been created specifically to be a template (*i.e.* it is a base for building upon) and whilst the file is created in the usual way, it is saved as either a template or macro-enabled template, which it makes it (slightly) more difficult than a standard Excel file to overwrite.

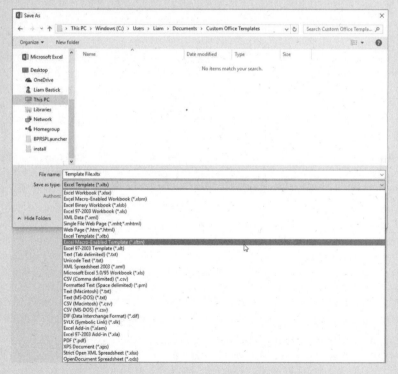

Reusable files can be more problematic, even if this is what many modellers often opt to use. A reusable file is akin to dusting off an "old favourite" and attempting to fit square pegs in round holes. Why? Because this is based on an existing model, not a foundation. The danger here is not only does the model not fit the purpose it is intended for, but irrelevant aspects are not fully deleted leading to potential errors in the model.

Unless scenario modelling where different versions of files need to be kept, always try to start with a template model whereby nothing needs to be deleted.

Let's take a guided tour of a suggested template for financial modelling. Where to start? How about on the front page? Imagine you had just opened up the file:

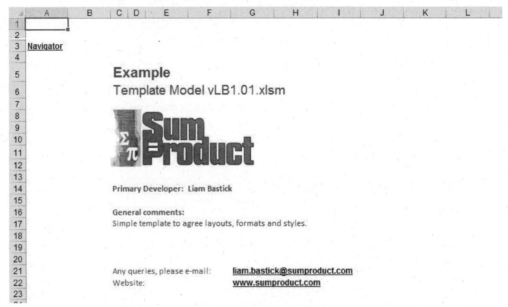

Do you see where the file opens up? I am situated in cell **A1** on the Cover sheet. Now you might be thinking, "wow, big deal", but reflect some more. Whenever you open up a Word of PowerPoint document it always opens in a similar location: the top of page 1. But what about Excel? Excel is the poor relation – it is the proverbial dog with no legs. Where would you find it? Wherever you left it (which reminds me, I used to have a dog with no legs – it was called Woodbine – I used to take it outside for a drag…).

Seriously, the problem with Excel is that people are not always good at tidying up after themselves. As mentioned when discussing how to construct a model layout, saving a workbook so that all sheets are repositioned back to cell **A1** and restoring the model back to the front worksheet are just examples of good manners.

This sheet does more than this though. It actually tells me who built it. No need to go to **File->Properties** (wherever that is this week) and finding out the model has been attributed to someone who actually passed away back in 1997. Moreover, this model actually provides contact details so that end users can get in touch with the author to ask questions where necessary. If you are a model developer, does that put the Fear of God into you? Well, perhaps it should. If we were all a little more accountable for the dross that is often referred to as a "financial model" then maybe we would take more pride in our Excel doodling and meanderings.

Aside from the shameless plug on the sheet (logo), did you notice the other key element on this worksheet? Cell **A3** contains a hyperlink that leads us on to our Table of Contents:

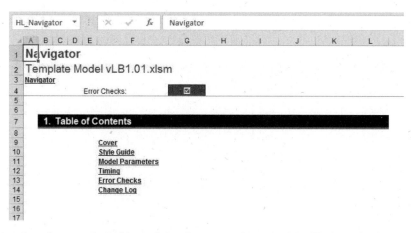

Clicking on the aforementioned hyperlink takes us to the top of the Table of Contents worksheet, our dedicated navigation page. Do note that the destination cell chosen has been given a range name (**HL_Navigator**). See? I have been following my own advice.

With the overall error check (another hyperlink) clearly visible in cell **G4**, the sheet title and workbook name clearly visible in accordance with my layout suggestions earlier, it is clear to an end user with no guidance whatsoever how to access other worksheets.

There are two other points to note on this worksheet. Firstly, the section heading, "Table of Contents" in row 7, has been given a section number. You may think this is unnecessary on this worksheet as it is the only section. That is true, but on other worksheets, there may be more sections. We want our worksheets all to have a similar look and feel. Other sheets may have more sections. In that case, section numbers would be useful (*e.g.* to make it easier to discuss a printout of the model with a third party over the telephone). Cell **B7** has not been hard coded. The number has been deduced by formula:

$$=MAX(\$B\$6:\$B6)+1$$

This will add one to the largest value located in column **B** prior to the row the formula is on. This way, if sections are reordered later, the numbering will update automatically (depending upon how you cut or copy the sections).

The second point concerns generating the Table of Contents itself. Contrary to many recipients' beliefs, this has not been created manually. Remember that I discussed macros earlier and argued that they were ideal for menial, repetitive tasks? Well, this is one such example.

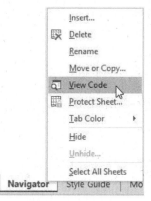

In this template, I have added a macro that creates the Table of Contents: it generates the worksheets in order and their associated hyperlinks. This is a macro that I would retain only whilst developing the model. Once all sheets have been constructed and the order has been finalised, there would no longer be a reason for this macro.

This macro was created as follows. On the Table of Contents worksheet, called 'Navigator' in the graphic *(below)*, right click on the sheet tab and select 'View code'.

This launches the Visual Basic Editor. Ensuring the right-hand pane is the code for 'Worksheet' and 'Activate', code may then be added to the right-hand pane which will run each time the worksheet is selected:

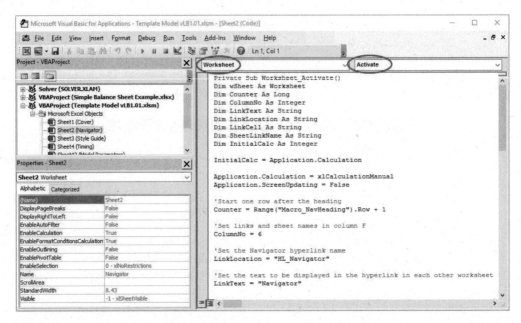

The actual code to use is reproduced below, including comments that explain how it works:

```
Private Sub Worksheet_Activate()
Dim wSheet As Worksheet
Dim Counter As Long
Dim ColumnNo As Integer
Dim LinkText As String
Dim LinkLocation As String
Dim LinkCell As String
Dim SheetLinkName As String
Dim InitialCalc As Integer

InitialCalc = Application.Calculation

Application.Calculation = xlCalculationManual
Application.ScreenUpdating = False

'Start one row after the heading
Counter = Range("Macro_NavHeading").Row + 1

'Set links and sheet names in column F
ColumnNo = 6

'Set the Navigator hyperlink name
LinkLocation = "HL_Navigator"

'Set the text to be displayed in the hyperlink in each other worksheet
LinkText = "Navigator"

'Set which cell in each other worksheet will contain the hyperlink
LinkCell = "A3"

'The following code clears column 6 (column F), types "Table of
Contents" in a pre-designated cell
```

```
'(named Macro_NavHeading) and adds a range name for cell A1 (1st row,
1st column)
'The destination of all hyperlinks are given range names (starting
with HL_)
'Range names allow the worksheet name to change without breaking the
hyperlink
'Me refers to the worksheet where this code is (currently the Navigator
worksheet)


With Me
    .Columns(ColumnNo).ClearContents
    .Range("Macro_NavHeading") = "Table of Contents"
    .Range("A1").Name = LinkLocation
End With

'The code looks for all other worksheets and adds a hyperlink in the
cell specified ("A3")
'The hyperlink is called "Navigator" (TextToDisplay), but this may be
changed (variable LinkText)
'Typically cell references are not entered in this way in VBA (reduced
flexibility)
'However, putting it in here anchors the hyperlink always to cell A3
and allows for transparency
'Changing the initial Counter value (above) and the column number (6,
above and in Me.Cells())
'moves the location of the Table of Contents list

For Each wSheet In Worksheets

    If wSheet.Name <> Me.Name Then

        'Increment the counter to shift to the next line in the
Navigator sheet
        Counter = Counter + 1

        SheetLinkName = "HL_" & wSheet.Index

        'Make changes to the target worksheet
        With wSheet
            .Range(LinkCell).Name = SheetLinkName
            .Hyperlinks.Add Anchor:=.Range(LinkCell), Address:="", _
            SubAddress:=LinkLocation, TextToDisplay:=LinkText
        End With

        'Add the hyperlink to the Navigator page
            Me.Hyperlinks.Add Anchor:=Me.Cells(Counter, ColumnNo),
Address:="", _
        SubAddress:=SheetLinkName, TextToDisplay:=wSheet.Name

    End If

Next wSheet

Application.Calculation = InitialCalc
Application.ScreenUpdating = True


End Sub
```

This book is not about Visual Basic for Applications, so if you wish to understand it more, feel free to read through the comments and experiment. No doubt some of you may just copy the code, set it and forget it (works for me)!

The next sheet in the template may surprise you. Many modellers will spend time setting up fancy colour schemes, complete with shading, conditional formatting and so on – and not explain their system of formatting anywhere. As a model auditor, I salute you. All that effort for nought. Together with an element of luck, a successful business thrives on three key components:

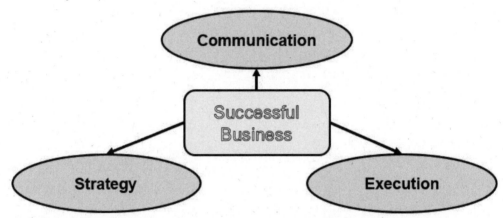

From a modeller's perspective, the key component here is **communication**. The aim of a financial model – aside from quantifying potential business critical decisions – is to communicate the business plan and understand variances so that remedial actions may be taken in a timely manner. If instead you have wonder formulae such as

```
=IF(ISERROR(IF(INDEX('TI"S & LC"s'!$K$31:$BN$31,MATCH('XYZ (BS)'!R$8,'TI"S
& LC"s'!$K$8:$BN$8))<0,0,INDEX('TI"S & LC"s'!$K$31:$BN$31,MATCH('XYZ
(BS)'!R$8,'TI"S & LC"s'!$K$8:$BN$8)))=TRUE),0,IF(INDEX('TI"S
& LC"s'!$K$31:$BN$31,MATCH('XYZ (BS)'!R$8,'TI"S &
LC"s'!$K$8:$BN$8))<0,0,INDEX('TI"S & LC"s'!$K$31:$BN$31,MATCH('XYZ
(BS)'!R$8,'TI"S & LC"s'!$K$8:$BN$8))))
```

you pretty much deserve all you get – and the same can be said for excluding a Styles Key:

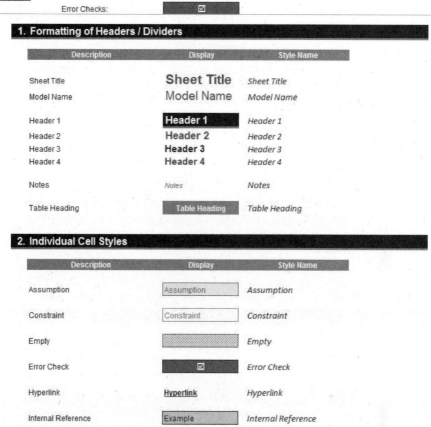

The above is an extract from the template model. There are actually more styles set up in this workbook than displayed above. I would imagine most people and / or organisations would probably not want our colour scheme. That is no problem. Changing an existing style is simple. Within the 'Styles' group of the 'Home' tab (**ALT + H + J**), right click on the style you wish to modify and click, er, 'Modify…':

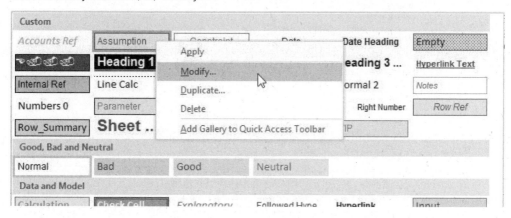

This gives rise to the 'Style' dialog box:

Clicking on the 'Format' button (in some versions of Excel this may be 'Modify') then allows you to revise the Style as discussed previously. Given the Style Guide worksheet has all styles displayed using their respective styles, so as you change a style, the style displayed on the worksheet will change accordingly.

Before a template goes "live", developers should agree on spacing, check methodologies and colour schemes. This makes it easier for one modeller to take over another's work and it also promotes brand identity / consistency.

The next sheet, Model Parameters, also explains to the end user key constants:

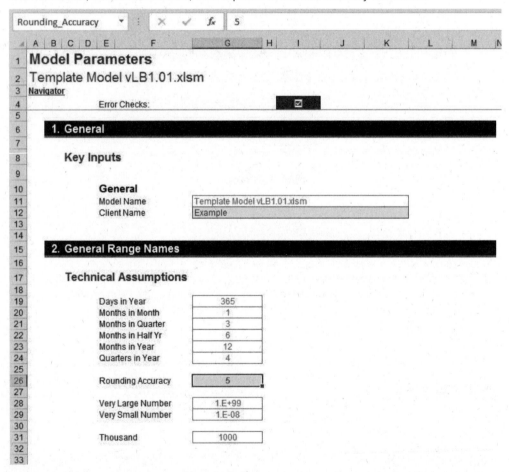

I have talked previously about the distinction between a variable and a constant (constants are sometimes referred to as constraints or parameters). Variables are just the standard inputs of a model, whereas constants are values that are entered to ensure *transparency* so that end users may understand certain constraints that the model is operating under. In this template, as previously suggested, these constants are not only labelled but are also assigned range names (note that the Name Box in the image above contains the range name **Rounding_Accuracy**).

Other types of parameters may be entered here. Our firm works in the professional services industry so we include a 'Client Name' input (row 12). That may not be relevant to you, but you might wish to include project name, team leader, category, *etc*.

The model name is just that wonderful name explained previously:

> =IFERROR(MID(CELL("filename",A1),FIND("[",CELL("filename",A1))+1,
> FIND("]",CELL("filename",A1))-FIND("[",CELL("filename",A1))-1),"")

PhD's available upon request.

The next worksheet is critical for any financial model: you need to get the time series correct. Too often in models, developers hard code the dates but this leads to a lack of flexibility in the model going forward. I have already explained the mechanics of a Timing worksheet:

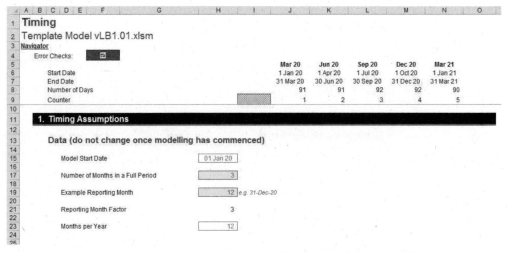

Relax, I am not planning to walk through all of this again. My intention here is simply to show you its application, but I will point out one interesting observation. Have you noticed the shaded cell in cell **I9** in the image above?

This is a "deliberately blank" cell. In an exam, you may have encountered a page such as

THIS PAGE HAS BEEN
LEFT BLANK INTENTIONALLY.

Actually, that has always irked me. By stating that, "This page has been left blank intentionally" the page *isn't* blank. Anyway, I digress. The shaded cell in **I9** *(above)* is analogous to this notion: the cell is <u>required</u> to be blank.

This is because the cells immediately to the right (cells **J9:N9**) are counters and add one to the value in the cell to its immediate left. If a number were to be entered in cell **I9** the counter values would be wrong; if text were to be entered instead, all cells would display *#VALUE!* errors.

By styling the cell as an **empty cell**, cell protection can prevent the cell being typed in and at the same time convey to the end user that this cell must remain blank. This point does not really have anything to do with time series modelling, but it is salient nonetheless.

The penultimate sheet in this template is the Error Checks summary sheet:

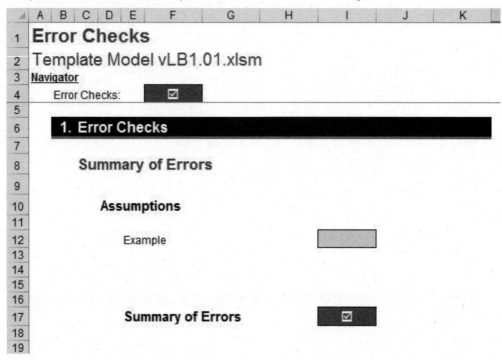

I discussed error checks and the importance of using a summary sheet in the last chapter. Cell **I17** sums the error checks above it in column **I**, with a dummy check set up in cell **I12** for illustrative purposes. Each reportable check should be linked to this sheet via a hyperlink. Then, the check in cell **F4** is simply equal to the summary check (cell **I17**), which it also hyperlinks to. Simple!

The final sheet in the template keeps the auditors happy:

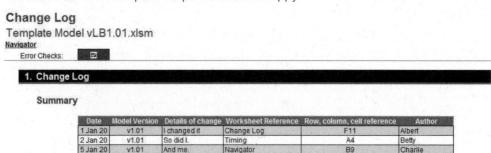

This is simply a worksheet that keeps track of *significant* changes. As a model auditor myself, it would be ludicrous to track *every* change. Can you imagine? You would have to note that you had noted a change and then note that you had noted that you had noted a change…

My general rule for detailing changes is when:

- there is a material change (say, 10% change in one of the key outputs);
- a milestone has been achieved; *or*
- the model is saved with a non-incremental new filename (*e.g.* to draw upon earlier discussions, upon saving when the filename changes from vLB1.19 to vLB2.01 rather than vLB1.20).

These are the main worksheets I would include in a template model. You and your colleagues may decide to add others, such as:

- blank time series sheet (for inputs, calculations and outputs)
- documentation worksheets
- depreciation schedules
- dashboard summary
- working capital adjustment worksheets
- taxation schedules.

That is all fine; create what works for you and try to never delete a worksheet from an existing template – it's better to add than subtract. If necessary, create more than one template (but this may cause version control issues).

Chapter 8: Financial Statement Theory

Are you all sleeping comfortably? Then I shall begin. At the risk of sending us all off to see the Sandman, I need to talk through the financial statements. Yes, I realise many of you will work in finance, be accountants or experienced analysts, but I need to ensure we are all on the same page. The reason is simple. I wish to propose a method of building up a financial model. I have discussed key Excel functions and functionalities, "Best Practice" methodology, layout tips, time series, error checks and even an example template. I want to put it all together to explain why you should build the model in a particular order, but I appreciate no one likes to learn by rote. I need to explain why. That is why I need to summarise the layout and purpose of each financial statement.

This book is not an accounting book. It is simply intended to provide a "jump start" into the world of financial modelling. I am not going to talk about Accounting Standards (such as the International Financial Reporting Standards, IFRS, or the US Generally Accepted Accounting Principles, US GAAP), but rather just explain generic principles. I appreciate things work differently in different parts of the world so I intend to be as general as I can be.

Nevertheless, most accounting regimens recognise the same three primary financial statements, so let's start with reviewing all of them.

Income Statement

Also known as the profit and loss account, revenue statement, statement of financial performance, earnings statement, operating statement or the statement of operations, this is the financial statement that shows the net operating profit of an entity for a given period of time. It works on an accruals basis, which whether you are an accountant or no, is probably how you think. Allow me to explain.

Most of you will be employees, presumably paid on a monthly basis. If you are such a reader, do you find you have too much month at the end of the money? Most try not to get into that situation; we **accrue**. The Income Statement is essentially the Net Operating Profit (accrued income less accrued expenditure) for a period of time after tax.

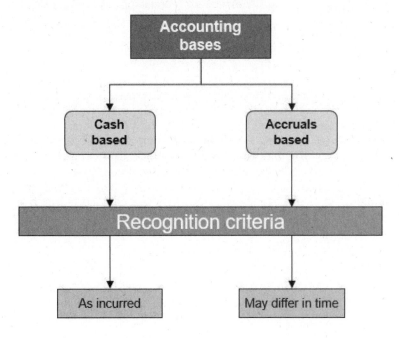

Income is recognised when products are delivered or services are provided, not when payment is received. Similarly, costs are attributed to the period they are incurred, not when they are necessarily paid. If our company sells one million widgets within the financial year at $1 each and incurs direct cost of 75c per widget, we would expect a gross profit of $250,000, *viz.*

Number of Widgets:	1,000,000
Unit Price:	$ 1.00
Unit Cost:	$ 0.75

The cash position could be radically different. We may have had to pay all of the costs and not yet received any monies. However, this is not how we think. We all attribute on an accruals basis, *i.e.* what pertains to the period in question.

	$
Sales	1,000,000
Cost of Goods Sold	(750,000)
Gross Profit	250,000

And there's more. If I asked, what would you model first, then second, then third, who here was thinking, revenue, costs of goods sold and then operating expenditure? Like it or not, we are walking talking income statements:

Revenue	X
COGS	(X)
Gross Profit	**X**
Operating Expenditure	(X)
EBITDA	**X**
Depreciation	(X)
EBIT	**X**
Interest Expense	(X)
Net Profit Before Tax (NPBT)	**X**
Tax Expense	(X)
Net Profit After Tax (NPAT)	**XX**

I love that accountants always put 'X' everywhere. I very much feel loved. Although I can't help feeling that if the Revenue is X and the Costs of Goods Sold is X and the Gross Profit is X, solving for X, X is zero and therefore I have proved all accounting examples are based on not-for-profit organisations... Maybe I need to get out more.

Now most of us are familiar with this income statement, but do you fully appreciate the majesty of its order? The order shouldn't just be learned by rote; it should be understood. For example, Revenue being first makes perfect sense for any company endeavouring to turn a profit. But why is Costs of Goods Sold (COGS) above Operating Expenditure?

Who here was thinking COGS is a variable cost whilst Operating Expenditure is a (stepped) fixed cost? That may be true up to a point, but that explains little. The point is that Costs of Goods Sold is defined as costs **directly** attributable to the sale. Direct costs may include raw material and some labour costs. Indirect costs, on the other hand, are legitimate costs of the business too, just not directly attributable to the sale. Typical examples include rent and utilities. Some could be argued either way (*e.g.* freight); the aim is to be consistent. Therefore, it makes sense that the direct costs are attributed first so that the gross profit (often referred to as **contribution**) can be assessed before the allocation of other costs, which in some instances may be rather arbitrary.

Clearly, Tax Expense is the final expense as it encapsulates all of the other incomes and expenses, but why does Depreciation Expense come before Interest Expense? This is perhaps not so clear cut and I offer two reasons, both of which can be argued with:

1. **Funding:** If you consider the income statement to contain the period's "fair share" of income and expenditure, one significant cost is Capital Expenditure. I am going to talk about this large cost in detail later, but essentially this is ascribed to the purchase of significant business assets to generate future profits for more than one year. It would be wrong to apportion all of this expenditure to one period if the benefit will extend over several / many years and depreciation is the allocation of that cost to the period in question. If financing, you often want to compare the funding – and its associated costs – against this allocated amount. Therefore, Depreciation Expense should be stated ahead of Interest Expense in the Profit and Loss account.

2. **Valuation:** It is hard to believe that Discounted Cash Flow (DCF) valuations and Net Present Value (NPV) analysis are still fairly recent valuation tools. Prior to the popularity of these approaches, the main method of choice was based on earnings multiples. For example, if companies A and B were similar in operation and profit margins, but B were twice the size of A, shouldn't B have a valuation approximately double A? It's difficult to argue with this logic. Capital structures (*i.e.* the mix of debt to equity) are irrelevant as if a company is purchased, the chances are the capital structure will be revised by the purchaser. Since depreciation is a relevant expense in the earnings multiple calculation, it should appear ahead of the debt expense (*i.e.* interest) so that the earnings figure to be used is readily visible.

Why have I made such a big deal of the order? Go and ask a non-accountant the order they would build a model in: the vast majority would build the income calculations first, the direct costs second and so on. The reason the Income Statement is always so popular is this is how people think. I am a great believer in "if it ain't broke, don't fix it" and this ideology very much applies here.

We should seriously consider building a model in the P&L order as this is most intuitive to modellers and users alike.

Balance Sheet

How would you explain the Balance Sheet to the financial *illiterati*? For those going, "it's the comparison for a moment in time of an entity's assets, liabilities and equity", please explain "assets", "liabilities" and "equity".

The Balance Sheet used to be known as the Net Worth statement; the Income Statement reports on financial performance, the Balance Sheet summarises the corresponding financial position. For a particular moment in time (the date stated) it displayed what a business was worth. It is a cumulative statement aggregating all of the factors that contribute to the value:

Non-Current Assets	
Property, plant and equipment	x
Other non-current assets	x
Total Non-Current Assets	*x*
Current Assets	
Cash	x
Account receivable	x
Other current assets	x
Total Current Assets	*x*
Total Assets	**x**
Current Liabilities	
Accounts payable	x
Other current liabilities	x
Total Current Liabilities	*x*
Non-Current Liabilities	
Debt	x
Other Non-Current Liabilities	x
Total Non-Current Liabilities	*x*
Total Liabilities	**x**
Net Assets	**x**
Equity	
Ordinary Equity	x
Net Profit After Tax (NPAT)	x
Retained Earnings	x
Total Equity	**x**

There are various ways of presenting the Balance Sheet. I am quite fond of this approach as it places Current Assets (items worth something to the business that will be held for less than or equal to one year) next to Current Liabilities (amounts owed that need to be paid within the next year). The ratio Current Assets divided by Current Liabilities assesses a business's ability to pay its bills and Current Assets less Current Liabilities shows the working capital of a business on the face of a primary financial statement.

The line items down to Net Assets are often colloquially known as the "top half" of the Balance Sheet (even if it is nearer 90% of all line items!) and the Total Equity section is known as the "bottom half". What is good about this presentation is the top half summarises what is controlled by a business whereas the bottom half communicates ownership.

This is why debt is not in the bottom half of the Balance Sheet. In the past, the Equity section was often headed "Financed by" and that always confused me as I did not understand why debt was not there. The reason it is not is because the shareholders of the business (the Equity) control the debt repayments and servicing. Yes, banks and other financial institutions may put contracts in place, but that is so they may go to court to force companies to pay if payment is not made voluntarily. Consequently, debt is "controlled", it usually is for a period of greater than one year and hence it is not in the bottom half but rather in the Long Term Liabilities section instead.

It may be clearer with another example. Ever bought a house? Did you buy it outright for cash? Chances are if you are lucky enough to be climbing the real estate ladder, in your first purchase you were not the principal stakeholder. So what about the risks and rewards? If the house goes up significantly in price will you be splitting the profits in proportion to the amount financed? Of course you wouldn't.

Similarly, imagine the house were to be damaged in a storm. Would you be on the phone the next day to get them to arrange someone to fix it? Good luck with that. "Do we know you?" may be the polite response, although more common replies may end in "off" instead.

The house would be a non-current (fixed) asset. The mortgage would be the linked non-current liability and – assuming the debt is less than the value of the house – the difference between you would be your equity stake. You control the house and the debt (top half), the equity goes in the bottom half. Easy.

Modellers tend to create Balance Sheets as a bit of an afterthought, but they are more important than that. Values may not be stated in the dollars of the day when purchased (this is known as **historical cost accounting**), which makes any summary meaningless as you are comparing apples with pears, but it is still better than nothing.

In fact, modellers *hate* Balance Sheets. They never seem to balance, reconcile or be understood. But this can all be circumvented with **control accounts** which I shall discuss in the next chapter. Balance Sheets are essential.

There is one other issue. Balance Sheets by their very nature are cumulative. They are stated at a point in time. They have to balance. So what if the Balance Sheet did not balance at the model start date? As a modeller, there is nothing you can do about this: this is an opening assumption (the Opening Balance Sheet). If this were to happen to you, reject the Opening Balance Sheet and wait until someone who knows what they are doing gives you a proper one.

All a modeller may ever be held accountable for is that the change in Net Assets equals the change in Total Equity.

Cash Flow Statement

The Cash Flow Statement never used to be one of the so-called primary financial statements. Originally, it was the reconciliatory note that demonstrated how the cash stated on the Balance Sheet had been derived. Changes in Balance Sheet and Income Statement numbers are often known as a "revision of accounting policies" and as long as the auditors and shareholders agree the changes everyone nods sagely and does not even bat an eyelid. If you start messing around with the Cash Flow Statement that's called fraud and you can go to jail. Recent high profile collapses and embezzlements have given greater prominence to this financial statement – even though it should have had equal standing from the beginning.

There are three sections to the Cash Flow Statement:

* Operating
* Investing
* Financing.

Can you think of an example of an Operating Cash Flow? Who said Revenue? That *isn't* one. Cash Receipts is the cash flow equivalent of Revenue. Be careful: it's making mistakes like this in modelling that cause Balance Sheets not to balance. Similarly, an example of Investing Activities might be Purchases of Non-Current Assets rather than "Capital Expenditure". Debt drawdowns and repayments would be two examples of Financing Activities.

Now, what about the other way around? Where does Interest Paid go? (You didn't realise you were taking a multiple choice exam?) The "proper" answer is Operating Activities, although I imagine you might be thinking Financing Activities. Three points:

1. As a company expands, sometimes its working capital (essentially cash and cash equivalents readily available after setting aside current bills) is insufficient to facilitate the growth required. Business owners may put more cash into their business (equity) or alternatively take out financing (debt). Should they choose the latter option, the mandatory servicing of that debt is an operational cost of the business – so Interest Paid should go in Operating Activities.

2. If all you read above was "blah blah blah… Operating Activities", I think you might not be alone. A simpler – although not quite correct – explanation is as follows. As detailed above, the Income Statement is essentially the Net Operating Profit after tax. Interest Expense is clearly an expense in the Profit and Loss Account. Therefore, it makes sense that the cash equivalent of Interest Expense – Interest Paid – is in the cash proxy for the P&L, namely the Cash Flows from Operating Activities section.

3. Some companies do indeed place Interest Paid in the Financing section of the Cash Flow Statement. This has been due to past practices (consistency) and case law precedent. So it can reside here, although it probably makes more sense to be in Operating Activities as explained above.

Hopefully, that makes sense. So what about Interest Received? Where should that be placed? Operating? Investing? Financing? Well, as Meat Loaf said, two out of three ain't bad:

- Banks and other financial institutions may place Interest Received in Operating Activities. This is because Interest Received may be their main source of income, e.g. from mortgages and unsecured loans.

- Other companies may place Interest Received in Investing Income. In this instance, interest has been earned and received from surplus cash on deposit.

Do you see in either scenario it would be incorrect to net off this amount with Interest Paid? The only time the two line items are in the same section (Operating Activities) is when Interest Received is essentially Cash Receipts and why would you want to combine this with debt servicing? This clearly highlights the accounting point of **no net off**. It is better if line items are shown gross so that end users may better understand their financials / forecasts.

One last one: let's consider Dividends Paid. This line item goes in Financing Activities. Some people do not understand why Interest Paid and Dividends Paid are (usually) placed in different sections of the Cash Flow Statement. Interest Paid is the *mandatory* servicing of debt; Dividends Paid is the *voluntary* servicing of equity. Hence it is a financing decision and therefore placed in the Financing Activities section.

I have concentrated on these elements as this is where many modellers make mistakes. Hopefully, this discussion makes things clearer and will prevent you from falling for some of the same traps your peers have repeated time and time again.

This all leads us nicely into the example Cash Flow Statement:

Operating Cash Flows

Cash Receipts	X
Cash Payments	X
Interest Paid	X
Tax Paid	X
Net Operating Cash Flows	**X**

Investing Cash Flows

Interest Received	X
Dividends Received	X
Purchase of Non-Current Assets	X
Net Investing Cash Flows	**X**

Financing Cash Flows

Debt Drawdowns	X
Debt Repayments	X
Ordinary Equity Issuance	X
Ordinary Equity Buybacks	X
Dividends Paid	X
Net Financing Cash Flows	**X**

Net Inc / (Dec) in Cash Held   **X**

The above is an example of what is known as a **direct** Cash Flow Statement. Pardon? What is one of those?

There are two forms to the Cash Flow Statements: direct and indirect. In many accounting jurisdictions it is stipulated that one variant must be displayed in the financial statements and the other should be the reconciliatory note to said accounts. It usually does not matter which way round this is done, as long as it is consistent from one period to the next.

Both variants affect the Net Operating Cash Flow section only of the Cash Flow Statement. They are defined as follows:

- **Direct:** This can reconcile Operating Cash Flows back to a large proportion of the bank statements. It is a summary of Cash Receipts, Cash Paid, Interest Paid and Tax Paid.

- **Indirect:** This starts with an element of the Income Statement and adds back non-cash items (deducting their cash equivalents) and adjusts for working capital movements.

A typical indirect Cash Flow Statement may compare to the direct version as follows:

Cash Flow Statement
Example

Go to Navigator							
Error Checks:	☑						
Period start			01-Jan-20	01-Jan-21	01-Jan-22	01-Jan-23	01-Jan-24
Period end			31-Dec-20	31-Dec-21	31-Dec-22	31-Dec-23	31-Dec-24
Counter			1	2	3	4	5
Operating Cash Flow (Direct)							
Cash Receipts	US$'000		384	440	485	526	555
Cash Payments	US$'000		(120)	(131)	(145)	(157)	(166)
Interest Paid	US$'000		(20)	(9)	(11)	(13)	(13)
Tax Paid	US$'000		(40)	-	-	-	(63)
Net Operating Cash Flow (Direct)	US$'000		204	300	330	356	313
Operating Cash Flow (Indirect)							
NPAT	US$'000		161	159	157	160	115
Add back:							
Depreciation Expense	US$'000		38	83	113	135	213
Interest Expense	US$'000		6	7	8	6	4
Tax Expense	US$'000		75	64	67	71	60
Movements in working capital:							
(Inc) / Dec in Current Assets	US$'000		(16)	(8)	(7)	(6)	(4)
Inc / (Dec) in Current Liabilities	US$'000		(0)	4	3	3	2
Deduct:							
Interest Paid	US$'000		(20)	(9)	(11)	(13)	(13)
Tax Paid	US$'000		(40)	-	-	-	(63)
Net Operating Cash Flow (Indirect)	US$'000		204	300	330	356	313

As explained above, the indirect version is calculated as follows:

- Start with a line item from the Income Statement (here, Net Profit After Tax)

- Add back non-cash items (Depreciation Expense, Interest Expense and Tax Expense)

- Adjust for working capital movements (increases and decreases in Current Assets and Current Liabilities)

- Deduct the cash equivalents of the non-cash items added back:

  ▸ Instead of Interest **Expense** deduct Interest **Paid**

  ▸ Instead of Tax **Expense** deduct Tax **Paid**

  ▸ Instead of Depreciation Expense *don't do anything*.

Que? Why is Depreciation Expense excluded altogether? Hands up those that said, "It's not a cash item". Well, Interest Expense and Tax Expense are not cash items either. That is an insufficient reason. What is the cash equivalent of Depreciation Expense? It's the Purchase of Non-Current Assets – and that is found in Investing Activities. The reason Depreciation Expense is excluded is for two reasons: (1) yes, it is a non-cash item, but (2) it is a double count.

So which one should you model? 87.4% of all modellers surveyed in my biased, made-up survey concluded that statistics were made up on the spot. It will not stop me from making my brash, unsubstantiated claim that the vast majority prefer the indirect version as it is easier to model: most will have modelled an Income Statement and (at least extracts from) the Balance Sheet, so it is easy.

Wrong. This is often what causes problems in Balance Sheet reconciliations. This facilitates the incorporation of control accounts and control accounts are a financial modeller's best friends. I will explain further in the next chapter. Use the direct method and calculate the indirect variant later, if required.

There is another important consideration for the Cash Flow Statement as well. Here is a sanitised version of a chart produced from a real-life model:

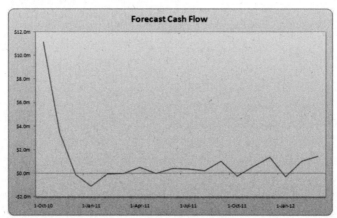

Picture yourself as the Board were back in 2010. Cash is tight and you are trying to determine precisely how much of a bank overdraft facility you require. What might you decide? About $1m? Look again.

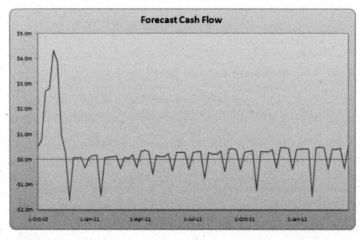

The first chart forecast cash flows on a monthly basis; the second displayed the same data weekly. Clearly, there is cyclicality in the cash flows and the troughs are deeper than the monthly output suggests. $1m would be insufficient according to the second chart. It may be even worse if modelling were undertaken on a daily basis.

The reason we prefer Income Statements to Cash Flow Statements is because the P&L frequently smooths out the inherent volatility in the latter. That is fine for understanding the trends in profitability and the overall financial performance of the business, but it may not be adequate to manage a business on a day-to-day basis. Determining the correct periodicity in a financial model is paramount in order to optimise the information available in financial forecasts.

Model Cash Flow Statements on a direct basis and use the periodicity required by the business to make effective business decisions.

Linking Financial Statements

You may have heard of the phrase "three-way integrated". It's not quite as kinky as it sounds. With regard to financial statements, "three-way" simply means incorporating all three financial statements and "integrated" means that if inputs in financial data were to change, the financials would update accordingly so that the Balance Sheet would still balance.

This requires linking up the financial statements. So how many do you need? One? Eight? 50? The correct answer, believe it or not, is **two**:

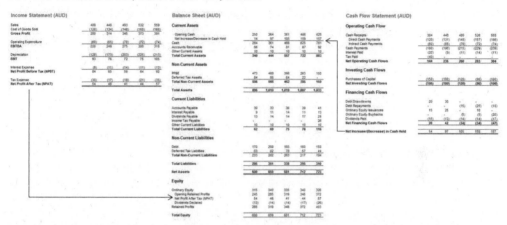

As long as the Net Profit After Tax links into the Retained Earnings section of the Balance Sheet and the Net Increase / Decrease in Cash Held from the Cash Flow Statement links into the Current Assets section of the Balance Sheet, you have all of the links you require to put a financial model together.

Appropriate Order of the Financial Statements

Right, it's time to invoke the Goldilocks Analogy. You are familiar with the tale of Baby Bear, Mummy Bear and Daddy Bear? Well, each of these is akin to one of our financial statements.

- **Income Statement:** This statement is "Baby Bear". I am neither talking about the magnitude of the numbers nor the number of line items within the financial statements. I am considering how small or large the Income Statement is conceptually compared with the other statements.

  The Income Statement considers the Net Operating Profit after tax. The Cash Flow Statement considers Operating Cash Flows, but it also considers Investing and Financial ones too. The Balance Sheet incorporates the summary (NPAT) of the Income Statements so must also be at least as large. Therefore, the Income Statement is the baby of the bunch.

- **Cash Flow Statement:** At the risk of sounding sexist (before you all send me hate mail, I am talking about size only, not importance), this one is "Mummy Bear". As discussed above, it considers more factors than the Income Statement (albeit from a different perspective), but since it is also summarised in the Balance Sheet (Cash), it is the 'middle' statement.

- **Balance Sheet:** So by a process of elimination, the Balance Sheet is "Daddy Bear". Not only does it summarise the other two financial statements, but it also details financials not captured elsewhere, e.g. movements between Non-Current and Current, and transfers in Reserves.

Now while you are all wondering what my drug of choice is, I had better explain why this is important. Earlier, I stated that when we start to build a model, in general we start to work our way down the Income Statement. That made sense and is commensurate with the magnitude of the concept of the financial statement. It also suggests that the Income Statement should be built second, which again makes sense, given the Balance Sheet includes a summary of the other two statements.

This gives us our conceptual order of constructing three-way integrated financial statement in a model:

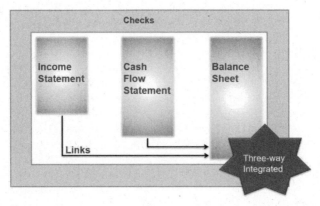

To summarise, we should:

- Develop the three financial statements, building up by line item and total

- Link the Income Statement and Cash Flow Statement into the Balance Sheet

- Add error checks to ensure no errors, that the Balance Sheet balances and is solvent (for example).

We have a plan…

Chapter 9: Control Accounts

I am going to let you in to one of the finance world's best kept secrets. I will explain what they are but I may have to kill you afterwards. I haven't decided yet.

They are easy to construct and even easier to understand. Consider the reconciliation of the line item Accounts Receivable (or Debtors):

	$
Accounts Receivable b/f	120,000
Sales	64,700
Cash Receipts	(82,750)
Accounts Receivable c/f	101,950

Chances are you have probably seen something similar to this before, maybe from accounting / finance studies. This reconciliation is known as a control account: it is a reconciliation of a Balance Sheet item from one period to the next ("b/f" means brought forward or last period and "c/f" means carried forward or current period).

Typically (although not always), the line items between the opening and closing balances come from the Income Statement and Cash Flow Statement. This is consistent with the idea that the Balance Sheet is stated at a point in time whereas the other two statements are for periods of time.

In the example above, if the opening balance of Accounts Receivable is $120,000 and we make further sales in the period of $64,700, assuming there are no bad debts (more on that later) and the cash received is $82,750, then the closing balance for Accounts Receivable has to be $101,950. In other words, assuming the opening balance was $120,000, entering:

- Sales of $64,700 in the Income Statement;

- Cash Receipts of $82,750 (as a positive number) in the Cash Flow Statement; and

- Closing Accounts Receivable of $101,950 in the Balance Sheet

means that the three-way integrated financial statements must balance. The end. Modelling financial statements really is that simple.

Control accounts tell you three key things:

1. **The number of calculations that need to be entered into the financial statement so that they balance:** This is always one less than the number of rows in the control account. The reason it is one less is because the opening balance is simply the closing balance calculated from the period before.

2. **The order to build the calculations into the financial statements:** This is always row 2 first, then row 3, then row 4 and so on. Think of it this way: assuming no opening balance (which there would not be in the beginning), if there were no sales, there could be no payments received. If there are no sales and no receipts, the difference between them (the amount owed, the Accounts Receivable) would also be zero. It is a logical order.

3. **It identifies the key driver:** Often you want to undertake sensitivity and scenario analysis in your models, but sometimes you may be unsure which variables should be included in the analysis. Line 2 of the control account is always the key driver. As above, if there were no sales, there could be no payments received. If there are no sales and no receipts, the difference between them (the amount owed, the Accounts Receivable) would also be zero. To make a point, I have repeated myself deliberately. To make a point, I have repeated myself deliberately. To make a point, I have repeated myself deliberately...

Therefore, in our example, we can conclude:

- In order to make the Balance Sheet balance we need to construct three calculations which need to be incorporated into the financial statements: Sales, Cash Receipts and closing Accounts Receivable.

- The order to calculate them should be Sales, Cash Receipts and finally closing Accounts Receivable.

- The key driver of Accounts Receivable is Sales.

The last two points do not appear to be too controversial, but have you reflected on the first point? If you have had any sort of accounting training whatsoever, you will have had double entry rammed down your throat (*you are not making any sort of joke at this point, Liam! – Ed.*).

The whole concept of double entry is you do one thing, then do another and *voila!* everything balances. Everything is performed in pairs. But I am telling you that you need to create **three** calculations. Does that go against everything you believe? Have I discussed debits and credits anywhere? (The answer is yes, in that last sentence.) Often in accounting, we talk about "reversing journals": this is code for "given we are forced into a double entry system, this is incorporated as a fiddle factor to make it work". In fact, in the example case study coming up shortly, not one control account contains an even number of calculation entries. So much for double entry.

From the last two chapters, I can now formulate an action plan regarding the order to construct a financial model:

Building a Financial Model

This approach remains moot on the order of calculation construction. This is how to build a hassle-free, three-way integrated financial model:

1. Create the forecast chart of accounts from either previous models, existing financials, ledgers, journals, trial balances, *etc*.

2. Add in the subtotals for each chart of account so that all totals flow through their respective financial statements

3. Add error and other checks to these outputs (*e.g.* balance checks, total cash flow in Cash Flow Statement equals cash movement on Balance Sheet) as necessary, updating the Error Checks worksheet as necessary

4. Create the Opening Balance Sheet, ensuring it uses the same format as the forecast Balance Sheet

5. Ensure the Opening Balance Sheet balances, else reject

6. Add checks as necessary

7. Link the financial statements together, adding any checks as necessary

8. Zero the Opening Balance Sheet

9. Ensure all checks are "OK"

10. Begin with the Income Statement, take the first line item in this account (e.g. Revenue)

11. Create calculations if not already computed

12. Construct control account

13. Add checks if necessary

14. Link control account to financial statements, ensuring checks are all OK (correct if necessary)

15. Move to the next line item in the financial statement not yet calculated

16. Return to Point 11

17. Once the Income Statement is completed, consider the first line item on the Cash Flow Statement not yet linked

18. Once the Cash Flow Statement is also completed, consider the first line item on the Balance Sheet not yet linked

19. Once the Balance Sheet has been completed, return to the Opening Balance Sheet and add back the original data

20. Correct any opening balance errors if necessary.

It seems a lot, but it really isn't as bad as it sounds. There is one controversial point in here though: *zero the Opening Balance Sheet*. That sounds "interesting" but don't worry, I will be explaining why when we link the financials in the case study.

That's a nice link. Bring on the case study!

Chapter 10: Example Model Build

Now before we all get carried away here, let me be clear: this is a simple model build. It wouldn't matter how complicated I made this model, it would never be exactly what you, dear reader, would want. So I am not even going to try. Too late for refunds though…

It is not possible to have an example that covers everything. If I could, I'd be much richer, trust me. Therefore, you may not find exactly what you want in this example. You could argue, where is inventory, provisions, foreign exchange, consolidations, indirect taxes and so on. Some cannot be covered in detail in a general book (*e.g.* indirect taxes vary from country to country and in many cases are ignored unless entities have cash flow difficulties), some are just extrapolations of what we are covering (*e.g.* inventory is often a linked combination of an account receivable and an account payable).

The intention of this case study is to demonstrate key concepts that come up time and time again, identify some of the traps and reinforce a process that should guide you each and every time through your model build, no matter how simple or complex. Don't worry about any specific formulae; ensure you get the concepts. **Concepts are key.**

The plan is simple. We are going to apply most of what we have done before in a contrived yet simple case study that will cover many of the key concepts of financial modelling. Some readers will want to model every last detail; others may use the accompanying material to review what has been built instead. That's up to you. All I ask is you work your way through this case study in the way that most benefits you.

> If you have trouble reading the formulae in the worksheets, you'll find a full list in the appendix on page 315.

So if there are no more questions, let's get going…

CHAPTER 10.1: INITIAL STRUCTURE

Do you really think I am going to advocate that you should build your financial model from scratch? Of course I'm not. Let's get someone else to do it instead. Oh no, wait, that's what *management* does.

This is precisely where the template from Chapter 7 comes in. I will make some "standard" assumptions about page set up, including:

- How many rows between headings in the same section (1)

- How many rows between sections (2)

- Width of columns that are blank (1). Remember, worksheets should be consistent, so deleting columns in particular can cause problems within links between worksheets and hiding columns may cause confusion. These are examples of *consistency* and *transparency* respectively

- Width of columns where text may be indented (3)

- The number of narrower columns at the left of the worksheet (5)

- The cell the Overall Error Check will be in for <u>most</u> worksheets (cell **G4**)

- The column for units (column **G**, depending upon width column has to be)

- The columns for time series forecasting (**J:N**)

The details in brackets are what I have chosen. This is not mandatory. You should just be *consistent*, not just within the model you are working, but all models you develop. This makes it easier for regular users to understand any new model you create.

We are going to start with the template model, with the above parameters incorporated. Before we add to it, let's make sure we are all on the same page regarding time series assumptions. This means creating the following inputs on the **Timing** worksheet:

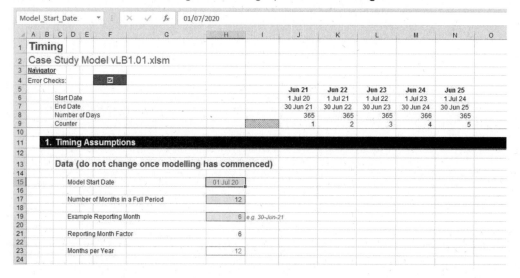

Cell **H15** is <u>not</u> an assumption cell. It is a constant and if the sheet were to be protected it would not be possible to change this date. In fact, once the model build has commenced this cell should not be revised (this is why the heading in cell **C13** reads "Data (do not change once modelling has commenced)". This is because if data is entered for a particular time period and then the dates were to change, input values may become associated with the wrong period and / or duration.

Cell **H15** is so important it is even given its own range name: **Model_Start_Date**. Even if output analysis were to change (*i.e.* the dates on an output sheet started with a later date), the calculations would work using a **LOOKUP** arrangement so that on input and calculation sheets the **Model_Start_Date** would always start in the first column reserved for time series (here, column **J**).

Cell **H17** (Number of Months in a Full Period) should be 12 and the Example Reporting Month (cell **H19**) should be set to the value 6 (*i.e.* June will be the period end). With five time periods, this will give us five full years from 1 July 2020 to 30 June 2025 inclusive:

	Jun 21	Jun 22	Jun 23	Jun 24	Jun 25
Start Date	1 Jul 20	1 Jul 21	1 Jul 22	1 Jul 23	1 Jul 24
End Date	30 Jun 21	30 Jun 22	30 Jun 23	30 Jun 24	30 Jun 25
Number of Days	365	365	365	366	365
Counter	1	2	3	4	5

Models will not always be a simple as this. Quite frequently, the first period may not be of equal duration (this is known as a **stub period**). For example, imagine you were forecasting annually but the first period was only for the last nine months of the financial year. If sales were $45,000 and the year-on-year growth rate was 10%, many models would calculate the Year 2 amount be $49,500, being $45,000 multiplied by 1 + 10%. This is wrong. The correct calculation is:

$$=\$45,000 \times 12 / 9 \times (1 + 10\%)$$

which is actually $66,000. The 12 / 9 factor scales up the stub period to an equivalent annual figure (it may need to be computed more accurately on a daily basis). Make sure you do not become a victim of this common error.

CHAPTER 10.2: ADDING SHEETS

The template is great as far as it goes, but we might need to add sheets. One way is to copy an existing worksheet, but Excel is unsure what to do with range names on the worksheet being copied. For each and every range name associated with the copied worksheet(s), you will have to decide whether to create a duplicate range name. If you have 10,000 range names, you have a fun day planned. There are no "Yes To All" or "No To All" options. Here's a tip: **don't**.

The problem with a copied range name, you may recall, is that it is worksheet specific rather than workbook specific which can cause problems. Therefore, try not to copy a worksheet containing range names, but if you have to, always decline creating a new range name definition for that worksheet. Always refer range names back to the original worksheet.

In this section I am not going to create a sheet copied from another: I will create one from anew. To do this, select the sheet tab to the left of where you want the worksheet to be and then click on the '+' button at the end of the tabs section:

This will create a new worksheet, *viz.*

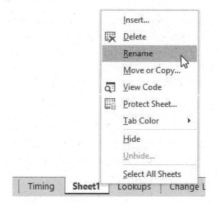

Right click or double-click on the tab to rename the sheet (let's call it "Calculations" here), and then as explained back in Chapter 4 (Layout Tips) I will narrow the first five columns (select the columns and right click) to a width of 3:

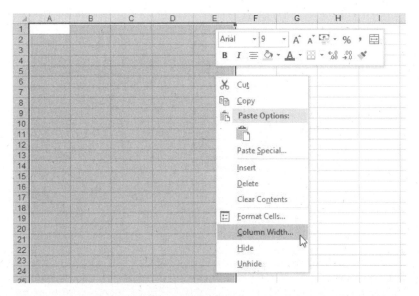

Next, I am going to return to the **Timing** worksheet and select cells **A1:O13** inclusive:

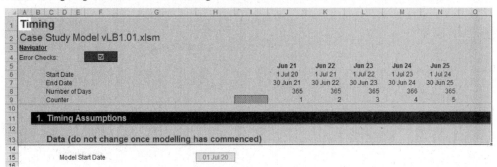

Once selected, this range is copied and pasted into cell **A1** of the newly-created **Calculations** worksheet:

	A	B	C	D	E	F	G	H	I	J	K	L	M	N	O
1	**Calculations**														
2	Case Study Model vLB1.01.xlsm														
3	**Navigator**														
4	Error Checks:				☑										
5										Jun 21	Jun 22	Jun 23	Jun 24	Jun 25	
6			Start Date							1 Jul 20	1 Jul 21	1 Jul 22	1 Jul 23	1 Jul 24	
7			End Date							30 Jun 21	30 Jun 22	30 Jun 23	30 Jun 24	30 Jun 25	
8			Number of Days							365	365	365	366	365	
9			Counter							1	2	3	4	5	
10															
11	**1. Timing Assumptions**														
12															
13		**Data (do not change once modelling has commenced)**													
14															
15															

Do you see that cell **A1** has updated to call itself "Calculations", *i.e.* the same as the sheet tab name? This was explained previously and is a nice shortcut. Adding a frozen pane into cell **A10** will ensure the top section is always visible on your worksheet and you have headings in rows 11 and 13 that may be revised as you start to create your new worksheet.

There is one other – optional – change you might elect to make. The time series data in rows 5:9 of the worksheet is fine as it is, but it can just simply link back to the **Timing** sheet. If you choose to do this, first link cell **C6** to its counterpart on the **Timing** sheet:

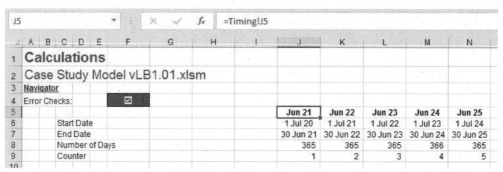

Do you see how consistency has made this formula easy to check? Cell **C6** points to cell **C6** in the **Timing** worksheet. A misreference will be identified quickly upon inspection. With cell **C6** modified, copy this cell down to cells **C7:C9**. Finally, click on cell **C6** once more and copy (**CTRL + C**) and select cells **J5:N9** and Paste Special as Formulas (**ALT + E + S + F + ENTER**). All of these cells will now point to the **Timing** worksheet and the 'Empty Cell' style applied in cell **I9** may be removed.

J5				f_x	=Timing!J5					
	A B C D E	F	G	H	I	J	K	L	M	N
1	**Calculations**									
2	Case Study Model vLB1.01.xlsm									
3	Navigator									
4	Error Checks:									
5						**Jun 21**	**Jun 22**	**Jun 23**	**Jun 24**	**Jun 25**
6	Start Date					1 Jul 20	1 Jul 21	1 Jul 22	1 Jul 23	1 Jul 24
7	End Date					30 Jun 21	30 Jun 22	30 Jun 23	30 Jun 24	30 Jun 25
8	Number of Days					365	365	365	366	365
9	Counter					1	2	3	4	5
10										

With practice, a worksheet may be added into the model within 30 seconds, if not even more quickly. Alternatively, you could create a template sheet to copy as you wish.

CHAPTER 10.3: CREATING THE FINANCIAL STATEMENTS

Building a Financial Model

1. Create the forecast chart of accounts from either previous models, existing financials, ledgers, journals, trial balances, *etc*.

Now that we know how to add in a new worksheet, we need to add four sheets in:

- Opening Balance Sheet

- Income Statement

- Balance Sheet

- Cash Flow Statement

If you are wondering why the Opening Balance Sheet and the Balance Sheet worksheets are distinct, think of the Opening Balance Sheet as an input sheet, which is what it is essentially.

The aim is to create skeleton financial statements, *i.e.* what the line items will be in each statement, together with all subtotals, so that once calculations are linked in, numbers will flow through the financial statements correctly. The line items (often referred to *en masse* as a **chart of accounts**) will need to be researched. This may come from existing financial statements, a previous model, the General Ledger, *etc*.

Also, the Balance Sheet and Opening Balance Sheet should be consistent: not only should the line entries coincide, it would work well if the entries were in exactly the same cells on the two worksheets.

Before we add in these sheets, let us ensure that the model parameters will be as intended, for we will start using some of these constraints and constants shortly. This sheet was part of the template, although it has been slightly modified. The first part is relatively straightforward:

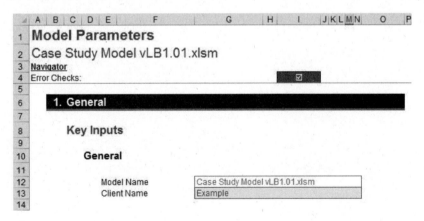

The model name is still generated by the formula (using the filename convention suggested previously) and the Client Name (Project Name) here is simply 'Example'. However, the second part needs to be replicated carefully:

	A	B	C	D	E	F	G	H	I	J K L M N	O	P
1	**Model Parameters**											
2	Case Study Model vLB1.01.xlsm											
3	Navigator											
4	Error Checks:						☑					

2. General Range Names

Technical Assumptions

Days in Year	365	Days_in_Year
Months in Month	1	Months_in_Month
Months in Quarter	3	Months_in_Qtr
Months in Half Yr	6	Months_in_Half_Yr
Months in Year	12	Months_in_Year
Quarters in Year	4	Quarters_in_Year
Rounding Accuracy	5	Rounding_Accuracy
Very Large Number	1.E+99	Very_Large_Number
Very Small Number	1.E-08	Very_Small_Number
Thousand	1000	Thousand

3. Technical assumptions

Model Information

Start Date	01/07/2020	

Units

Unit	#	Unit
Currency	US$'000	Currency
Boolean	[1,0]	Boolean
Percentage	%	Percentage
No of Days	# Days	No_of_Days
Year	Year	Year
No of Years	# Year(s)	No_of_Years
Multiplier	x	Multiplier

Financial Statement Abbreviations

Income Statement	IS	Income_Statement
Balance Sheet	BS	Balance_Sheet
Cash Flow Statement	CFS	Cash_Flow_Statement

I have modified the layout slightly and I have decided to use a currency (cell **G45** of US$'000). Feel free to choose any currency you wish. I don't even live in the United States, but my publisher will sulk if I don't use the unit of currency they will be reporting this book's losses in.

All but the Start Date (cell **G39**) have been given range names. The reason this cell hasn't is because this links to the **Model_Start_Date** constant already entered on the **Timing** worksheet. Column **I** contains the range name names, so that an end user may understand this worksheet is printed out (*transparency*). In other models, you may have to add other parameters as you require them.

Let me now turn my attention back to the four new worksheets to be added. The line items will need to be agreed from a previous model, management reports, financial statements, a management information system or something similar. It needs to be consistent period to period.

When constructing, remember the first three incorporate the time series headings as discussed above. First, let's consider the Income Statement:

	A B C	D	E F	G	H I	J	K	L	M	N	O	P
1	**Income Statement**											
2	Case Study Model vLB1.01.xlsm											
3	Navigator											
4	Error Checks:			☑								
5						Jun 21	Jun 22	Jun 23	Jun 24	Jun 25		
6	Start Date					1 Jul 20	1 Jul 21	1 Jul 22	1 Jul 23	1 Jul 24		
7	End Date					30 Jun 21	30 Jun 22	30 Jun 23	30 Jun 24	30 Jun 25		
8	Number of Days					365	365	365	366	365		
9	Counter					1	2	3	4	5		
10												
11	**1. Income Statement**											=A1
12												
13	Revenue		US$'000									
14	COGS		US$'000									
15	**Gross Profit**		US$'000			-	-	-	-	-		=SUM(J13:J14)
16												
17	Operating Expenditure		US$'000									
18	**EBITDA**		US$'000			-	-	-	-	-		=SUM(J15,J17)
19												
20	Depreciation		US$'000									
21	**EBIT**		US$'000			-	-	-	-	-		=SUM(J18,J20)
22												
23	Interest Expense		US$'000									
24	**NPBT**		US$'000			-	-	-	-	-		=SUM(J21,J23)
25												
26	Tax Expense		US$'000									
27	**NPAT**		US$'000			-	-	-	-	-		=SUM(J24,J26)
28												

In case you are wondering why, the **Model Parameters** worksheet does not have grid lines switched on (**ALT + W + VG**) because it is fairly easy to see which cells contain which entry and even if you do get it wrong, because all parameters contain range names, it will not matter anyway. In final models, I always switch gridlines off because I think it looks neater. However, for the screenshots for the model we build, I am going to leave them on so it makes it easier to see what goes where.

It also makes it clearer how I have modified column widths. If untampered, the default width of an Excel column is 8.43. I am unsure what the units are, I presume it is light years. Column **A** and other columns where indenting of headings may occur all have a width of 3 in my example and unused columns are neither hidden nor deleted: they are given a width of 1 instead. Again, you do not need to follow this protocol. Please choose your own system, just be *consistent*.

The formulae in column **P** relate to the formulae in column J of that row, apart from cell **P11**, which refers to the formula in cell **C11**. Several things to note:

- Especially in output worksheets, such as the Income Statement, do not create summations which include blank rows. End users often add percentages (e.g. Gross Margin) which may inadvertently be added, causing the Balance Sheet not to balance.

- The units in column **G** have all been generated by the formula **=Currency**. This makes it easy to change the units in the model quickly if necessary.

- You may think the formula in cell **C11** seems like overkill. Where possible, try never to type the same thing into a model twice. This is obvious for inputs, but for text this makes changes easier to implement (*flexibility*) and leads to fewer typographical errors (*robustness*).

- Obviously, do not include the entries in column **P**!

When entering *anything* into a cell, always consider the following:

- **Check the spelling of anything typed:** Users become very wary of typos in a models. If they see spelling errors, users cannot help but think that formulae will be similarly erroneous. I am always reminded of one applicant for a model auditing job who stated one of her strengths was "…a meticulous attention to *detali*…".

- **Never type cell references in, always click on cells to ensure the correct references:** It is always tempting to do this as a shortcut, but it is amazing how often this leads to the wrong cell being referenced.

- **Add absolute referencing as required:** You are never as close to the formula as you are when you are creating it. Adding in anchoring (the **$** signs) may save time later if you need to copy a set of calculations elsewhere.

- **Style the cell:** Have I taught you nothing!? It just makes your life easier – especially if managers are fussy and keep changing their mind with regard to the look and feel of a model. This promotes brand recognition too.

- **Copy the cell down and across there and then:** Modellers get a great deal of satisfaction in creating several formulae in a section and then copying them across the columns all at the same time. They feel they are being more efficient. I beg to differ. If there is an error in one of the earlier formulae, the flaw in any logic may be replicated in later formulae, which means more calculations need to be revised. For the sake of saving a few seconds per day, I recommend copying each formula across and ensure you inspect the results in later periods to confirm the calculation is working as intended.

This last point brings me to another issue. In this model case study, I only have five periods, but most models have considerably more. If I am asking you to copy across a row each time, some of you may realise that for models with a great number of periods, this may lead to a legal claim for Repetitive Strain Injury if you are copying across by dragging the mouse. There is an easier way. Unless these cells are already non-blank keyboard shortcuts such as **CTRL + SHIFT + Right Arrow** appear useless. However, all is not lost. The following trick can be used on many occasions.

Imagine you needed to copy formulae across columns **J** to **XZ** (say):

- Select the column TWO columns to the right of the last column required (here, this would be column **YB**)

- A quick way to get there would be to press the **F5** function key and then type **YB1** + **ENTER** to go to cell **YB1** and then press **CTRL + SPACEBAR** to select the column **YB**

- Next, highlight all columns to the right (assuming these are all blank) using **CTRL + SHIFT + Right Arrow**

- Right click on the mouse and select 'Hide' (this will hide columns **YB** to the end)

- Now return to where the formula will start (say, cell **J9**)

- Type the formula in and press **ENTER**

- Select the cell again and then use the keystroke **CTRL + SHIFT + Right Arrow** which will highlight cells **J9:YA9** inclusive

- Having removed all fingers from the keyboard press **SHIFT + Left Arrow** which will reduce the range to cells **J9:XZ9** inclusive

- Having removed all fingers from the keyboard once more, press **CTRL + R** to fill the formulae into all cells simultaneously.

Practice will make this second nature! There are four points to note:

1. On first glance, there appears to be no reason to retain a blank column. However, if column **XZ** is the final column, **CTRL + SHIFT + Right Arrow** will take you straight to column **XZ**. However, if you click and drag past this point, all of the hidden columns will have formulae copied into them too, leading to potential model errors and needless file size bloating.

2. Some modellers will hide or group columns instead of using the above technique. The problem with this approach is that whilst these columns are hidden, errors may occur in these columns which are only picked up when the fields are made visible once more. This can lead to tremendous re-work which could have been avoided if the developer had inspected ranges periodically instead.

3. **CTRL + R** will not always retain all cell details (e.g. comments). If this is important, copy the formula (**CTRL + C**) before highlighting the whole range and then paste in the usual way (**CTRL + V**) instead.

4. Once you have copied one formula across a row, you do not necessarily need to copy the rest of the formulae on that worksheet the same way. Ensuring you have the row copied across in the active cell of your selection, **CTRL + SHIFT + Right Arrow** will take you to the end of that row rather than the edge of the sheet. This emphasises the need for ensuring all formulae are *consistent* across each and every row.

Returning to our Income Statement example, do make sure you have incorporated all of the above points. The aim is that as formulae are entered into the rows, the numbers will flow down correctly to the Net Profit After Tax (NPAT) line.

Next up is the Cash Flow Statement:

	F	G	H	I	J	K	L	M	N	O	P
1	**Cash Flow Statement**										
2	Case Study Model vLB1.01 .xlsm										
3	Navigator										
4	Error Checks:										
5					Jun 21	Jun 22	Jun 23	Jun 24	Jun 25		
6	Start Date				1 Jul 20	1 Jul 21	1 Jul 22	1 Jul 23	1 Jul 24		
7	End Date				30 Jun 21	30 Jun 22	30 Jun 23	30 Jun 24	30 Jun 25		
8	Number of Days				365	365	365	366	365		
9	Counter				1	2	3	4	5		
10											
11	**1. Cash Flow Statement**										=A1
12											
13	**Direct Cash Flow Statement**										
14											
15	**Operating Cash Flow**										
16	Cash Receipts	US$'000									
17	Direct Cash Payments	US$'000									
18	Indirect Cash Payments	US$'000									
19	Cash Payments	US$'000			-	-	-	-	-		=SUM(J17:J18)
20	Interest Paid	US$'000									
21	Tax Paid	US$'000									
22	**Net Operating Cash Flow**	US$'000			-	-	-	-	-		=SUM(J16,J19:J21)
23											
24	**Investing Cash Flows**										
25	Interest Received	US$'000									
26	Purchases of Non-Current Assets	US$'000									
27	**Net Investing Cash Flows**	US$'000			-	-	-	-	-		=SUM(J25:J26)
28											
29	**Financing Cash Flows**										
30	Debt Drawdowns	US$'000									
31	Debt Repayments	US$'000									
32	Ordinary Equity Issuances	US$'000									
33	Ordinary Equity Buybacks	US$'000									
34	Dividends Paid	US$'000									
35	**Net Financing Cash Flows**	US$'000			-	-	-	-	-		=SUM(J30:J34)
36											
37	**Net Increase / (Decrease) in Cash Held**	US$'000			-	-	-	-	-		=J22+J27+J35

Having rambled on and on about the Income Statement I don't think I need to spend as much time on this worksheet. Column I is not narrowed as I am going to need to put something in here later. That's great for a case study where I already know what I am going to do, but in reality, you may not have this foresight. It is no big deal if you have to re-widen a column later!

Moving on to the Balance Sheet:

					Jun 21	Jun 22	Jun 23	Jun 24	Jun 25	
1	**Balance Sheet**									
2	Case Study Model vLB1.0.xlsm									
3	Navigator									
4	Error Checks:		☑							
5					Jun 21	Jun 22	Jun 23	Jun 24	Jun 25	
6	Start Date				1 Jul 20	1 Jul 21	1 Jul 22	1 Jul 23	1 Jul 24	
7	End Date				30 Jun 21	30 Jun 22	30 Jun 23	30 Jun 24	30 Jun 25	
8	Number of Days				365	365	365	366	365	
9	Counter				1	2	3	4	5	
10										
11	1. Balance Sheet									=A1
12										
13	**Current Assets**									
14	Cash		US$'000							
15	Accounts Receivable		US$'000							
16	Other Current Assets		US$'000							
17	**Total Current Assets**		US$'000		-	-	-	-	-	=SUM(J14:J16)
18										
19	**Non-Current Assets**									
20	PP&E		US$'000							
21	Deferred Tax Assets		US$'000							
22	**Total Non-Current Assets**		US$'000		-	-	-	-	-	=SUM(J20:J21)
23										
24	**Total Assets**		US$'000		-	-	-	-	-	=J17+J22
25										
26	**Current Liabilities**									
27	Accounts Payable		US$'000							
28	Interest Payable		US$'000							
29	Dividends Payable		US$'000							
30	Tax Payable		US$'000							
31	Other Current Liabilities		US$'000							
32	**Total Current Liabilities**		US$'000		-	-	-	-	-	=SUM(J27:J31)
33										
34	**Non-Current Liabilities**									
35	Debt		US$'000							
36	Deferred Tax Liabilities		US$'000							
37	**Total Non-Current Liabilities**		US$'000		-	-	-	-	-	=SUM(J35:J36)
38										
39	**Total Liabilities**		US$'000		-	-	-	-	-	=J32+J37
40										
41	**Net Assets**		US$'000		-	-	-	-	-	=J24-J39
42										
43										
44	**Equity**									
45	Ordinary Equity		US$'000							
46	Opening Profits		US$'000							
47	NPAT		US$'000							
48	Dividends Declared		US$'000							
49	Retained Profits		US$'000		-	-	-	-	-	=SUM(J46:J48)
50	**Total Equity**		US$'000		-	-	-	-	-	=J45+J49
51										

It is already starting to look like a financial model! Again, the currency in column **G** links to the range name **=Currency**, but otherwise this is simple to set up. There is one other thing to add at this stage: error checks. If you recall Chapter 6, I have already explained suitable checks for the Balance Sheet, so I am now going to add them in:

Cells **I55**, **I56** and **I57** are then given the range names **HL_BS_Errors**, **HL_BS_Balance** and **HL_BS_Insolvency** respectively, as these will be the names of the destinations of three range names. These can then be added as hyperlinks to the **Error Checks** worksheet as discussed generally earlier.

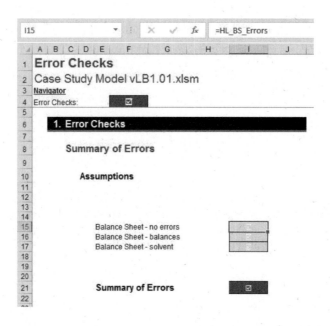

In a real life modelling situation, you will probably not have rows 12:14 blank, but in a case study, it's amazing what you know is going to happen. Note: in this model I am not bothering with having the ability to switch the check on or off, but it is not much more work to add this functionality.

This brings us to the fourth of our financial statements: the Opening Balance Sheet:

	A	B	C	D	E	F	G	H	I	J	K
1	**Opening Balance Sheet**										
2	Case Study Model vLB1.02.xlsm										
3	Navigator										
4	Error Checks:						☑		**Jun 20**		=Model_Start_Date-1
5											
6											
7											
8											
9											
10											
11		**1. Opening Balance Sheet**									=A1
12											
13			**Current Assets**								
14				Cash			US$'000		250		
15				Accounts Receivable			US$'000		50		
16				Other Current Assets			US$'000		10		
17				**Total Current Assets**			US$'000		**310**		=SUM(I14:I16)
18											
19			**Non-Current Assets**								
20				PP&E			US$'000		450		
21				Deferred Tax Assets			US$'000		75		
22				Total Non-Current Assets			US$'000		**525**		=SUM(I20:I21)
23											
24			**Total Assets**				US$'000		**835**		=I17+I22
25											
26			**Current Liabilities**								
27				Accounts Payable			US$'000		30		
28				Interest Payable			US$'000		20		
29				Dividends Payable			US$'000		15		
30				Tax Payable			US$'000		40		
31				Other Current Liabilities			US$'000		10		
32				**Total Current Liabilities**			US$'000		**115**		=SUM(I27:I31)
33											
34			**Non-Current Liabilities**								
35				Debt			US$'000		150		
36				Deferred Tax Liabilities			US$'000		25		
37				**Total Non-Current Liabilities**			US$'000		**175**		=SUM(I35:I36)
38											
39			**Total Liabilities**				US$'000		**290**		=I32+I37
40											
41			**Net Assets**				US$'000		**545**		=I24-I39
42											
43											
44			**Equity**								
45				Ordinary Equity			US$'000		300		
46											
47				NPAT			US$'000		-		
48				Dividends Declared			US$'000		-		
49				Retained Profits			US$'000		245		=I41-I45-I47-I48
50			**Total Equity**				US$'000		**545**		=SUM(I45,I47:I49)
51											

I have entered the opening inputs. These are in column I, and note that they are styled as Assumptions (the yellow background and blue text). Remember, we use this to highlight cells that we are letting users change.

Remember the Opening Balance Sheet must balance, so in this model cell **I49** is the "balancing cell": **=I41-I45-I47-I48**. This is the only "balancing cell" we will have in our entire model. It is okay to do this here. Our Opening Balance Sheet is basically a set of inputs which <u>must</u> balance. This forces it to balance.

Do you see that rows 5:10 of the above figure are blank? Do you see that the lines line up precisely with the Balance Sheet cell references? This is so we can link one worksheet to the other and have our two Balance Sheets exactly the same. There's one other thing: I haven't chosen the column for the Opening Balance Sheet at random. It is column **I**, *i.e.* the column before the time series starts on the other worksheets (column **J**). It just makes it easier to reference cells correctly.

Also, the date in cell **I4** is **=Model_Start_Date-1**. There is no need to type hard coded dates anywhere: everything is driven from the **Timing** worksheet to ensure *consistency*, *flexibility* and *transparency*. And talking of these three of the four key qualities of Best Practice Model let me add in *robustness* too:

	HL_Open_BS_Errors			× ✓ ƒx	=IF(ISERROR(I41-I50),1,0)					
⊿	A	B	C D	E	F	G	H	I	J	K
1	**Opening Balance Sheet**									
2	Case Study Model vLB1.02.xlsm									
3	**Navigator**									
4	Error Checks:					☑		Jun 20		=Model_Start_Date-1
40										
41			Net Assets		US$'000			545		=I24-I39
42										
43										
44			Equity							
45			Ordinary Equity		US$'000			300		
46										
47			NPAT		US$'000			-		
48			Dividends Declared		US$'000			-		
49			Retained Profits		US$'000			245		=I41-I45-I47-I48
50			Total Equity		US$'000			545		=SUM(I45,I47:I49)
51										
52										
53			Checks							
54										
55			PF Error Check		[1,0]			☑		=IF(ISERROR(I41-I50),1,0)
56			Balance Check		[1,0]			☑		=IF(I55<>0,0,(ROUND(I41-I50,Rounding_Accuracy)<>0)*1)
57			Insolvency Check		[1,0]			☑		=IF(AND(I55=0,I56=0),(I41<0)*1,0)
58										

Similar to the **Balance** Sheet, cells **I55**, **I56** and **I57** are then given the range names **HL_Open_BS_Errors**, **HL_Open_BS_Balance** and **HL_Open_BS_Insolvency** respectively, as these will be the names of the destinations of three range names. These can then be added as hyperlinks to the **Error Checks** worksheet as discussed generally earlier.

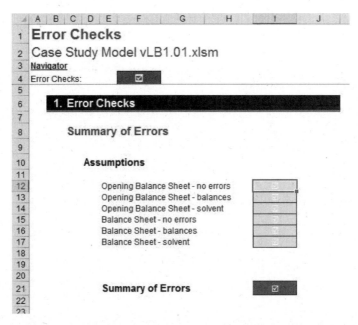

Now we can see why I kept rows 12:14 blank – maybe there's something for rows 18:19 too? Later – in fact, *much* later. As far as error check modelling goes, this is where the case study and a real model will part company. In reality, you would just keep adding checks as you realise you need one. Here, I am going to be a little more *laissez-faire*.

Now we have our four financial statements incorporated into the model.

Building a Financial Model

1. Create the forecast chart of accounts from either previous models, existing financials, ledgers, journals, trial balances, etc.

In fact, we have done more than that:

Building a Financial Model

2. Add in the subtotals for each chart of account so that all totals flow through their respective financial statements

3. Add error and other checks to these outputs (*e.g.* balance checks, total cash flow in the Cash Flow Statement equals cash movement on Balance Sheet) as necessary, updating the Error Checks worksheet as necessary

4. Create the Opening Balance Sheet, ensuring it uses the same format as the forecast Balance Sheet

5. Ensure the Opening Balance Sheet balances, else reject

6. Add checks as necessary

Our financial statements are three-way but they are not yet integrated...

CHAPTER 10.4: LINKING THE FINANCIAL STATEMENT WORKSHEETS

Building a Financial Model

7. Link the financial statements together, adding any checks as necessary

To integrate our financial statements, we need to link them together. Remember, there aren't 6,000 links here, just the two:

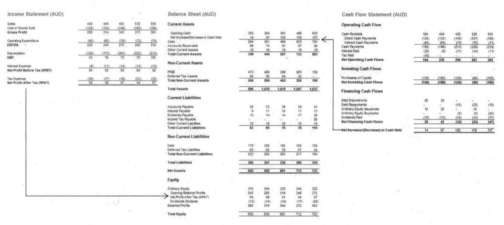

All we must do is link the Net Profit After Tax into the Retained Earnings section of the Balance Sheet and then link the Net Increase / Decrease in Cash Held from the Cash Flow Statement into the Current Assets section of the Balance Sheet. There are two common methods of doing this. In a real-life situation, I would model the two links similarly (*consistency*), but here I will show both so that you know them, can recognise them and even build them.

Firstly, I am going to link in the Income Statement. On the Balance Sheet add the following formulae:

J46						f_x	=IF(J$9=1,'Opening Balance Sheet'!$I$49,I49)						
A B C D	E	F G H I	J	K	L	M	N	O	P

	A B C D	E	J	K	L	M	N	P
1	**Balance Sheet**							
2	Case Study Model vLB1.01.xlsm							
3	**Navigator**							
4	Error Checks:	☒						
5			Jun 21	Jun 22	Jun 23	Jun 24	Jun 25	
6	Start Date		1 Jul 20	1 Jul 21	1 Jul 22	1 Jul 23	1 Jul 24	
7	End Date		30 Jun 21	30 Jun 22	30 Jun 23	30 Jun 24	30 Jun 25	
8	Number of Days		365	365	365	366	365	
9	Counter		1	2	3	4	5	
40								
41	**Net Assets**	US$'000	-	-	-	-	-	=J24-J39
42								
43								
44	**Equity**							
45	Ordinary Equity	US$'000						
46	Opening Profits	US$'000	245	245	245	245	245	=IF(J$9=1,'Opening Balance Sheet'!$I$49,I49)
47	NPAT	US$'000	-	-	-	-	-	='Income Statement'!J27
48 w	Dividends Declared	US$'000						
49	Retained Profits	US$'000	245	245	245	245	245	=SUM(J46:J48)
50	**Total Equity**	US$'000	245	245	245	245	245	=J45+J49
51								
52								
53	**Checks**							
54								
55	PF Error Check	[1,0]	☒					
56	Balance Check	[1,0]	☒	☒	☒	☒	☒	☒
57	Insolvency Check	[1,0]	☒					
58								

Let me go through these formulae. If you had linked to the cells rather than just type the formula in – as I asked you to – you would actually have created a slightly different formula in cell **J46**:

> **=IF(J$9=1,'Opening Balance Sheet'!$I$49,'Balance Sheet'!I49)**

This formula is taking the opening balance from the Opening Balance Sheet (**'Opening Balance Sheet'!$I$49**), which is why this cell is anchored when it is the first period. **J$9** determines whether it is the first period and is anchored to row 9 so that if the formula is copied elsewhere it will always link to row 9, the counter. The last argument of the formula as it stands though, **'Balance Sheet'!I49**, could be perceived to be a little dangerous from a modelling viewpoint.

Note that this formula occurs on the **Balance Sheet** worksheet. Therefore, we only require the reference **I49** – the worksheet reference **'Balance Sheet'!** is superfluous. Therefore, I have deleted it in the model:

> **=IF(J$9=1,'Opening Balance Sheet'!$I$49,I49)**

Not only is this easier to read, it is "safer". The worksheet reference comes up whenever you have previously linked to another worksheet or workbook in this formula. Up until this point Excel will refer only to the cell reference on the worksheet and not the worksheet as well, after an external reference all bets are off.

If you do not remove the worksheet reference from the formula as I have, should you copy the worksheet (depending upon how it is copied), the reference will link to the original worksheet rather than the copied worksheet. This may cause inadvertent errors which are easy to miss and may lead to creating an incorrect model. To remove the possibility of this occurring, do become disciplined in removing these superfluous references as soon as they arise.

The formula in row 47 is much less controversial: it is simply linking to the closing Net Profit After Tax (NPAT) for the relevant period. I don't have anything else to say about that really.

Now row 48 is interesting. I have absolutely no idea how to calculate Dividends Declared presently, but I know these must be deducted from profits as Retained Earnings is the cumulative sum of profits retained and dividends are the profits distributed.

Therefore, I have formatted these cells with the WIP (Work In Progress) style:

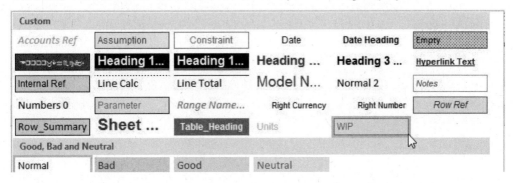

It is gaudy so you cannot help but notice it – deliberately. In fact, I have based the colour on my last urine sample, but hey, enough about my personal problems. Did you also note the letter "w" placed in cell **A48**? This is to highlight the issue. You may recall from my Layout discussions that column **A** is used to help us notice aspects of the model that are not yet completed as they will be identified when resetting worksheets and saving the file.

Row 49 is thus the closing balance for Retained Earnings and is the value used in the Balance Sheet. It is important to realise this. Remember, the Balance Sheet displays amounts for a point in time and therefore represents cumulative figures. However, NPAT and Dividends Declared will be based on amounts for a particular period of time and therefore need to be aggregated. This is exactly what Row 49 is.

We cannot carry on yet. We may not continue until the Balance Sheet balances. No exceptions. Did you see the error checks have gone ballistic? Row 56 highlights that Net Assets (row 41) no longer equal Total Equity (row 50). The Overall Error Check (cell **G4** on this worksheet) ensures you will notice this as soon as you have coded the section – which is what you want – no matter what worksheet you are on. Strike 1 for the Error Checks system.

So how do we amend the issue? First of all, what is causing the issue? There is only one non-zero number in the section we have added (245) and that emanates from Retained Earnings (**'Opening Balance Sheet'!$I$49**) on the Opening Balance Sheet. I cannot carry on until I find the balancing figure for Retained Earnings. What's that? Essentially, it's *everything else*. This causes us a little conundrum as what we should do next. There are essentially three alternatives:

1. **Add all the other opening balances to the Balance Sheet:** This will make the Balance Sheet balance as we are basically inserting the Opening Balance Sheet into the model and we know that balances. However, this causes a problem as we won't know which rows of the **Balance Sheet** worksheet have completed formulae and which ones are work in progress. This could lead to errors of omission or even double-counting. This risk is unacceptable and therefore this option is **rejected**.

2. **Don't do anything:** We know what has caused the Balance Sheet not to balance. Let's just keep building the model and hope that when we have finished the Balance Sheet balances. This is a very common approach for modellers. If you are one of those who has taken this Road to Hell, how did it work out for you? What is your record for finding the 33 Balance Sheet errors that also arose that you didn't realise? This option is also **rejected**.

3. **Cheat:** Now if I know my modellers, I think ears will have suddenly pricked up. Let's do this.

So what does Option 3 involve? It isn't really a cheat. I know what has caused the error: I have added one opening balance number in without bringing in the others. I have already rejected the notion of bringing all of the others in so what about the contrapositive? How about I remove that opening balance instead? You may recall earlier I argued that a modeller may only be held to ensuring that changes in Net Assets must equal changes in Total Equity. This works for me.

How do I do this? It is easy. Head back to the **Opening Balance Sheet** and highlight cells **I14:I50**, then copy (**CTRL + C**) these cells. Paste these cells into the range **K14:K50** (**CTRL + V**); you only need to select cell **K14** to do this. Now, re-select cells **I14:I50** and then press the 'Delete' key on your keyboard to clear the contents of these cells. Feeling a little uncomfortable?

	A	B	C	D	E	F	G	H	I	J	K	L
1	**Opening Balance Sheet**											
2	Case Study Model vLB1.01.xlsm											
3	Navigator											
4	Error Checks:						☑		Jun 20			
10												
11		**1. Opening Balance Sheet**										
12												
13			**Current Assets**									
14				Cash		US$'000					250	
15				Accounts Receivable		US$'000					50	
16				Other Current Assets		US$'000					10	
17				**Total Current Assets**		US$'000					310	
18												
19			**Non-Current Assets**									
20				PP&E		US$'000					450	
21				Deferred Tax Assets		US$'000					75	
22				**Total Non-Current Assets**		US$'000					525	
23												
24			**Total Assets**			US$'000					835	
25												
26			**Current Liabilities**									
27				Accounts Payable		US$'000					30	
28				Interest Payable		US$'000					20	
29				Dividends Payable		US$'000					15	
30				Tax Payable		US$'000					40	
31				Other Current liabilities		US$'000					10	
32				**Total Current liabilities**		US$'000					115	
33												
34			**Non-Current Liabilities**									
35				Debt		US$'000					150	
36				Deferred Tax Liabilities		US$'000					25	
37				**Total Non-Current Liabilities**		US$'000					175	
38												
39			**Total Liabilities**			US$'000					290	
40												
41			**Net Assets**			US$'000					545	
42												
43												
44			**Equity**									
45				Ordinary Equity		US$'000					300	
46												
47				NPAT		US$'000					-	
48				Dividends Declared		US$'000					-	
49				Retained Profits		US$'000					245	
50			**Total Equity**			US$'000					545	
51												
52												

Do you see that the error check in cell **G4** is now showing that all is well? There is no longer a misbalance in the **Balance Sheet** worksheet:

	A	B	C	D	E	F	G	H	I	J	K	L	M	N
1	**Balance Sheet**													
2	Case Study Model vLB1.01.xlsm													
3	Navigator													
4	Error Checks:						☑							
5									Jun 21	Jun 22	Jun 23	Jun 24	Jun 25	
6			Start Date						1 Jul 20	1 Jul 21	1 Jul 22	1 Jul 23	1 Jul 24	
7			End Date						30 Jun 21	30 Jun 22	30 Jun 23	30 Jun 24	30 Jun 25	
8			Number of Days						365	365	365	366	365	
9			Counter						1	2	3	4	5	
43														
44			Equity											
45				Ordinary Equity		US$'000								
46				Opening Profits		US$'000			-	-	-	-	-	
47				NPAT		US$'000			-	-	-	-	-	
48	w			Dividends Declared		US$'000								
49				Retained Profits		US$'000			-	-	-	-	-	
50			**Total Equity**			US$'000			-	-	-	-	-	
51														
52														
53			Checks											
54														
55				PF Error Check		[1,0]		☑						
56				Balance Check		[1,0]		☑						
57				Insolvency Check		[1,0]		☑						
58														

The Income Statement is now linked to the Balance Sheet. The Opening Balance Sheet has been set to zero, but it is easy to resurrect as we will just copy the data from column **K** on the **Opening Balance Sheet** back to column **I**. Effectively, we have just completed the following steps (for the Income Statement at least):

Great. We can move on. Rows 46:49 on the **Balance Sheet** represent a control account on the face of the Balance Sheet: opening Retained Earnings plus NPAT for the period less Dividends Declared equals the closing Retained Earnings. It is very *transparent* making the modeller simpler for users to understand.

There is another method. This other method basically constructs the control account all in one cell. Let me explain using the other item that needs to be linked: cash.

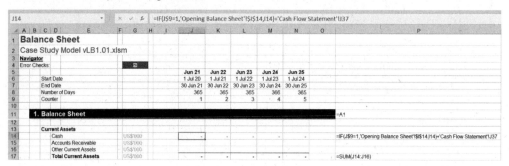

The formula in cell **J14** of the **Balance Sheet** worksheet is

=IF(J$9=1,'Opening Balance Sheet'!$I$14,I14)+'Cash Flow Statement'!J37

Again, the first part of the formula checks if the calculation is for the first period. The great thing about creating a template is that some calculation arguments become instantly recognisable; for this model, **=IF(J$9=1,…** is the formula for "if it is the first period". Modelling will very soon become second nature.

If it is the first period, the formula references the Opening Balance Sheet. Remember, this is the cell in column **I** of the **Opening Balance Sheet** <u>not</u> column **K** – otherwise you will have another misbalance before you can say

Taumatawhakatangihangakoauauotamateaturipukakapikimaungahoronukupokaiwhenuakita-natahu (look it up).

Now that I have annoyed the typesetters, let me continue. If it is not the first period, the formula simply refers to the cell to the left, *i.e.* the previous period's cash balance. However the last period balance is derived, the formula then adds the incremental cash generated in the period (**'Cash Flow Statement'!J37**). This is simply a control account, just all in one cell.

These two methods show alternative display methods rather than calculation approaches. Personally, I would use the first method which displays the control account on the face of the Balance Sheet. The more transparent you make a model, the less likely errors will creep in.

Now that linking is completed and error checks have all been added, we now have our three-way integrated structure set up. We're good to go.

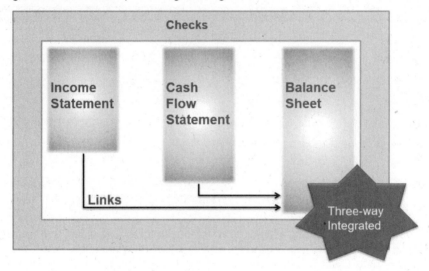

CHAPTER 10.5: REVENUE

Building a Financial Model

11. Begin with the Income Statement, take the first line item in this account (*e.g.* Revenue)

12. Create calculations if not already computed

13. Construct control account

14. Add checks if necessary

15. Link control account to financial statements, ensuring checks are all OK (correct if necessary)

And so we begin. You may recall my discussion from earlier where I said we simply work our way down the Income Statement. In this case, our Income Statement looks like this:

1. Income Statement

Revenue	US$'000					
COGS	US$'000					
Gross Profit	US$'000	-	-	-	-	-
Operating Expenditure	US$'000					
EBITDA	US$'000	-	-	-	-	-
Depreciation	US$'000					
EBIT	US$'000	-	-	-	-	-
Interest Expense	US$'000					
NPBT	US$'000	-	-	-	-	-
Tax Expense	US$'000					
NPAT	US$'000	-	-	-	-	-

The first line item to be modelled is therefore **Revenue**. To do this, we shall need to construct some assumptions. Creating assumptions requires a new worksheet to be added:

	A	B	C	D	E	F	G	H	I	J	K	L	M	N	O
1	**General Assumptions**														
2	Case Study Model vLB1.01.xlsm														
3	Navigator														
4	Error Checks						☑								
5										Jun 21	Jun 22	Jun 23	Jun 24	Jun 25	
6		Start Date								1 Jul 20	1 Jul 21	1 Jul 22	1 Jul 23	1 Jul 24	
7		End Date								30 Jun 21	30 Jun 22	30 Jun 23	30 Jun 24	30 Jun 25	
8		Number of Days								365	365	365	366	365	
9		Counter								1	2	3	4	5	
10															
11	**1. General Assumptions**														
12															
13		**Revenue and Related**													
14															
15			**Revenue**												
16															
17			Revenue First Year			US$'000				400					
18			Revenue Growth Rate			%					12%	10%	8%	5%	
19															
20			**Working Capital**												
21															
22			Days Receivable			# Days				60	60	60	60	60	
23															
24															

This worksheet has been created in exactly the manner I described earlier and then I have created a new section (General Assumptions), where the first section is entitled 'Revenue and Related'. This covers the assumptions for calculating Revenue and how to calculated Cash Receipts thereon.

I appreciate these assumptions are very simple. There is no point in constructing a really complex Revenue calculation since no matter how detailed I make it, I know it will not be relevant or appropriate as far as 99% of you will be concerned (that will be both my readers).

I do want to comment on these input methodologies though. No matter how complex a model's calculations may become, inputs may only be entered into a model in one of four ways.

The Four Methods of Entering Inputs into a Model

There are only four ways to enter data into a financial model. The actual method may incorporate combinations of the following:

1. **Amounts:** Data is entered in as numerical (absolute) values. It may be in units, thousands, millions, GWh and so on, but ultimately it is a number. This is an ideal entry method where data is copied from elsewhere or may eventually be linked to another model (say).

2. **Percentages:** Data is typed in as a percentage or ratio of another value, be it input or calculated. This is often the approach employed for variable costs, for example.

3. **Amount and growth rates:** Data is entered in two forms, an amount in at least the first period and then a percentage thereafter. This is often the method used for sky blue forecasting and sometimes leads to what the modelling connoisseur may describe as "hockey stick projections".

4. **Combination:** Usually perceived as a more sophisticated version of the **amount and growth rates** approach, this method combines two or more input methodologies. The combination may be selected by use of a switch (manual input) or a trigger (calculation). This is often used for reforecasting or replacing forecast with actuals, *etc*. **IF** and **CHOOSE** are functions often associated with this methodology.

We have two inputs in this 'Revenue and Related' section:

- Revenue uses the **amount and growth rates** methodology. Do note that I put the amount (400) in on row (row 17) and the amount in the row below (row 18). This ensures units are not mixed up and will be treated correctly in calculations, as well as understood as intended by end users.

- The Days Receivable assumptions are **amounts**. This may be based on guesstimates or historical / trend data for the business from the past.

It is beneficial to recognise which approach is being used as developers need to be wary of the common mistakes that are associated with the different types of data input.

Working Capital Adjustments

Before creating the calculations, I want to explain the working capital assumption and how it works. If money is owed, the people who owe it are **Debtors** and, assuming no write-offs of sales made, the amounts owed are known as **Accounts Receivable** or simply **Receivables**. This amount owed is viewed as an asset of the business. It isn't cash but it should convert to cash *soon*. Cynical businesses may quite rightly think if only it were that simple, but it is for the purposes of this case study.

Consider the following example:

Control Account

Opening Debtors	–	Prior BS
Sales in Period	1,000	IS
Cash Receipts	(753)	CFS
Closing Debtors	247	Current BS

Imagine a company has just started off in business *(i.e.* has no amounts due) and generates sales of $1,000 in the period. At the end of the period, assuming no bad debts, $753 has been paid, leaving a closing debtor balance of $247. This difference is what I refer to as the **working capital adjustment**. If we had modelled the sales of $1,000 in the period, how might we generate the cash receipts forecast such that if the assumptions changed, the receipts would calculate appropriately?

Clearly, if I am given the closing debtor balances, the problem becomes trivial, so I will assume that this is not so. Therefore, I am going to consider an alternative approach and some of the associated underlying issues that need to be considered when modelling. Let me first derive an alternative method.

I will assume that the sales accrue evenly over the period of time and for the sake of this example, that period is one year (365 days). Presuming (i) all sales are made on credit terms, (ii) all customers pay their invoices on the day the amounts fall due and (iii) no bad debts are incurred, this can be reflected graphically as follows:

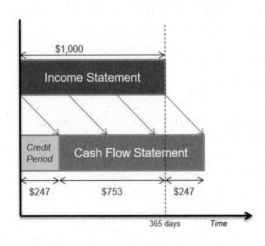

Clearly, the credit period is the "gap" at the beginning of the time period, i.e. 247/1000 x 365 days = 90 days. This can be represented formulaically as:

Days Receivable = (Closing Debtors x Days in Period) / Sales in Period

Rearranging, this becomes:

Closing Debtors = (Sales in Period x Days Receivable) / Days in Period,

e.g. in our example: 247 = (1000 x 90) / 365.

Therefore, in modelling, we often set the number of days receivable (and days payable) as key assumptions for cash flow forecasting. However, it is not always as simple as that. Let me explain. Consider we are planning to build a monthly model (assuming 30 days in a month) and sales for the month are again $1,000. Debtor days remain at 90 days.

Based on these calculations, we would generate the following control account:

Control Account

Opening Debtors	–	Prior BS
Sales in Period	1,000	IS
Cash Receipts	2,000	CFS
Closing Debtors	**3,000**	Current BS

Erm, that's right: make sales of $1,000 and have $3,000 (= 90/30 x 365) owing to you by the end of the month. Also, the company pays $2,000 to customers – a reclaimable $2 for each $1 spent. That's nonsense – and yet, as an experienced model auditor I have seen this erroneous calculation crop up on a regular basis. The problem is, in this current economic climate most businesses want to prepare monthly – sometimes weekly and even daily – cash flow projections. Clearly, if the days receivable or days payable assumption exceeds the number of days in each forecast period this approach is inappropriate and will lead to calculation errors. This is an example of where we ought to employ error checks to ensure that our inputs do not breach this key assumption.

There are alternatives. If payments are made exactly one month or two months or three months later (and so on), the resolution is simple: the receipts can be calculated using a simple **OFFSET** (displacement) formula.

Rather than consider that situation, let me complicate the scenario slightly. Imagine we are building a monthly forecast model, but that the days receivable are 75. For the purposes of keeping this section reasonably brief, I will simplify the problem by assuming an average number of days in a month (say, 30). Using this simplifying assumption, this will mean that payments are made on average 2.5 (2.5 = 75 / 30) months after the sale has been made.

That 2.5 months figure is important. The integer part (2) denotes how many complete months (including the current month) have sales payments outstanding. The residual (0.5 or 50%) shows the proportion of the month preceding these complete months that is also outstanding. With this borne in mind, the **OFFSET** function can now come to the rescue, viz.

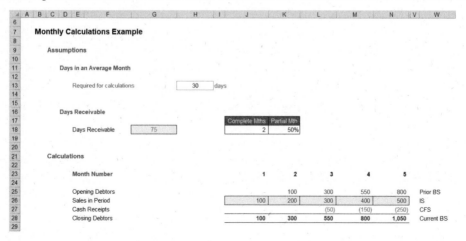

In this illustration (above), cells **J18** and **K18** break the number of days receivable (cell **G18**) into the number of whole months and residual proportion respectively, assuming that each month has 30 days (cell **H13**).

The key formula here is the calculation for Closing Debtors (Cash Receipts is simply the balancing figure). For example, the formula in cell **J28** (above) is:

=IF($J$18,SUM(OFFSET(J26,,,1,-MIN($J$18,J$23))),)
+IF(J$23-$J$18<=0,,OFFSET(J26,,-$J$18)*$K$18)

It may seem a little complex upon first inspection, but it's not as bad as it seems. Essentially, there are two parts to this formula identified by the two added **IF** statements:

1. **IF($J$18,SUM(OFFSET(J26,,,1,-MIN($J$18,J$23))),)** considers the completed number of months where sales remain outstanding and adds up the sales for these periods.

   In essence, this part of the formula checks that the number of completed months is not zero (in this case the amount is just zero), and assuming this is not the case, it sums the sales for the relevant number of completed months (i.e. starts with the current month and then considers the sales in previous months, working from right to left in the spreadsheet). The MIN formula is required to ensure that the model does not try to include periods prior to the beginning of the forecast period).

2. **IF(J$23-$J$18<=0,,OFFSET(J26,,-$J$18)*$K$18)** considers the residual (remaining) amount for the month before the earliest completed month. For example, if the credit period is 2.5 months and the current month is April, then March and April will be "whole months" where no payment has been received, with half of February's monies still outstanding too.

   The reason for the **IF** statement here is to prevent calculations considering periods before the beginning of the forecast period.

To clarify, consider the Closing Debtor figure of $1,050 in Period 5 (above, cell **N28** in the illustration). This is calculated as the sales for Periods 4 and 5 (400 + 500 respectively), plus half of the Period 3 sales (300 x 0.5 = 150), i.e. 400 + 500 + 150 = 1,050.

Working capital adjustments may become even more complicated. What if payments are not made evenly? Or that some sales are written off as payments are never made (i.e. bad debts)?

More Sophisticated Monthly Example

Assumptions

Month Number		1	2	3	4	5	6	7	8	9	10	11	12
Forecast Sales Revenue		100	200	300	400	500	600	700	800	900	1,000	1,100	1,200
Cash Receipt Profile		40%	25%	15%	10%	5%							
Bad Debt	5%													
Month Written Off	6													
Amount Written Off		-	-	-	-	-	5	10	15	20	25	30	35

Calculations

Simple Grid Method

Month Number		1	2	3	4	5	6	7	8	9	10	11	12
Sales: Period 1	100	40	25	15	10	5							
Sales: Period 2	200		80	50	30	20	10						
Sales: Period 3	300			120	75	45	30	15					
Sales: Period 4	400				160	100	60	40	20				
Sales: Period 5	500					200	125	75	50	25			
Sales: Period 6	600						240	150	90	60	30		
Sales: Period 7	700							280	175	105	70	35	
Sales: Period 8	800								320	200	120	80	40
Sales: Period 9	900									360	225	135	90
Sales: Period 10	1,000										400	250	150
Sales: Period 11	1,100											440	275
Sales: Period 12	1,200												480
Cash Receipts		40	105	185	275	370	465	560	655	750	845	940	1,035

Control Account

Month Number	1	2	3	4	5	6	7	8	9	10	11	12	
Opening Debtors	-	60	155	270	395	525	655	785	915	1,045	1,175	1,305	BS
Sales in Period	100	200	300	400	500	600	700	800	900	1,000	1,100	1,200	IS
Bad Debts Written Off	-	-	-	-	-	(5)	(10)	(15)	(20)	(25)	(30)	(35)	IS
Cash Receipts	(40)	(105)	(185)	(275)	(370)	(465)	(560)	(655)	(750)	(845)	(940)	(1,035)	CFS
Closing Debtors	60	155	270	395	525	655	785	915	1,045	1,175	1,305	1,435	BS

Some of you realise this looks like a depreciation grid. I shall discuss this concept more later. For the meantime, in this illustration it is worth noting that the Cash Receipt Profile percentages do not add up to 100%. This is deliberate – the missing 5% is the assumed bad debt here.

There is one other method. Large infrastructure projects may simply have cash payments input rather than calculated, triggered by certain milestone payments. This goes to show you that bigger does not always mean more complex.

Revenue Calculations

Now that I have put working capital adjustments in context, let me return to the calculations in hand, which will adopt the first approach described above. At the beginning of the case study, I showed how to add a worksheet and this sheet was called **Calculations**. It looks like a good time to use that worksheet now.

					Jun 21	Jun 22	Jun 23	Jun 24	Jun 25		
1	**Calculations**										
2	Case Study Model vLB1.01.xlsm										
3	Navigator										
4	Error Checks:		☑								
5											
6	Start Date				1 Jul 20	1 Jul 21	1 Jul 22	1 Jul 23	1 Jul 24		
7	End Date				30 Jun 21	30 Jun 22	30 Jun 23	30 Jun 24	30 Jun 25		
8	Number of Days				365	365	365	366	365		
9	Counter				1	2	3	4	5		
10											
11	**1. Calculations**									=A1	
12											
13	**Revenue and Related**										
14											
15	**Revenue**										
16											
17	Revenue First Year	US$'000			400					='General Assumptions'!J17	
18	Revenue Growth Rate	%				12%	10%	8%	5%	Cell K18: ='General Assumptions'!K18	
19	**Revenue**	US$'000			400	448	493	532	559	=IF(J$9=1,$J17,I19*(1+J18))	
20											
21	**Working Capital**										
22											
23	Days Receivable	# Days			60	60	60	60	60	='General Assumptions'!J22	
24											
25	Days in Period	# Days			365	365	365	366	365	=J$8	
26											
27	Closing Receivables	US$'000			66	74	81	87	92	=J23/J25*J19	
28											
29	**Control Account**										
30											
31	Opening Receivables	US$'000			-	66	74	81	87 BS	=I34	
32	Revenue	US$'000			400	448	493	532	559 IS	=J19	
33	Cash Receipts	US$'000			(334)	(440)	(485)	(526)	(554) CFS	=J34-SUM(J31:J32)	
34	Closing Receivables	US$'000			66	74	81	87	92 BS	=J27	
35											

One of the first things that surprises many when they first see this example is that rows 13:23 effectively replicate what is on the **General Assumptions** worksheet. The majority of these cells simply link back and are formatted as off-sheet references (Internal_Ref). This is so the calculation may be followed on a piece of paper without access to the formula bar. Take a look for yourself: it is possible to understand this section from the screenshot without even glancing at the explanatory formulae in column **P**.

Take care with row 19. There is a common mistake modellers make with the **amounts and growth rates** method. Some modellers create this incorrect formula instead:

J19			f_x	=IF(J$9=1,$J17,I19*(1+K18))							
A B C D	E	F G H	I	J	K	L	M	N			
1 **Calculations**											
2 Case Study Model vLB1.01.xlsm											
3 Navigator											
4 Error Checks:		☑									
5				Jun 21	Jun 22	Jun 23	Jun 24	Jun 25			
6 Start Date				1 Jul 20	1 Jul 21	1 Jul 22	1 Jul 23	1 Jul 24			
7 End Date				30 Jun 21	30 Jun 22	30 Jun 23	30 Jun 24	30 Jun 25			
8 Number of Days				365	365	365	366	365			
9 Counter				1	2	3	4	5			
10											
11 **1. Calculations**											
12											
13 **Revenue and Related**											
14											
15 **Revenue**											
16											
17 Revenue First Year		US$000		400							
18 Revenue Growth Rate		%			12%	10%	8%	5%			
19 **Revenue**		US$000		400	440	475	499	499			
20											

This above example is <u>wrong</u>. The formula in cell **J19** in this instance is

$$=IF(J\$9=1,\$J17,I19*(1+\underline{K}18))$$

instead of

$$=IF(J\$9=1,\$J17,I19*(1+\underline{J}18))$$

I think modellers get it into their head that the formula, which takes a value in the first period otherwise grows the last period by a factor of (1 + growth rate), are looking for a growth rate in the first period. Given the first period (cell J18) is an empty cell, they therefore select the next cell, K18. Unfortunately, this is for the next period. This method could easily give rise to circular references later in the modelling as well as growing Revenue by an incorrect growth rate for that period.

There is an easy way to identify this particular mistake. If each period is actually taking the growth rate in the next period, then the final period will actually be referring to a blank cell. Since Excel will consider a blank cell to have a value of zero in a formula, the erroneous calculation will take the previous period's number and simply multiply it by one. This will be easy to spot: Revenue in the final two periods will be identical, as in the illustration above (499 in the last two periods). Keep an eye out for this.

With the income calculated correctly, row 27 works out the Closing Receivable using the formula

Closing Receivables = Sales in Period x Days Receivable / Days in Period

(the brackets in the early formula are not actually required). Note that the Days in Period (row 25) simply refers to the Number of Days in row 8, with the formula anchored on row 8. This is again to make it easier for the end user to follow.

The control account is then simple to construct:

- Cell **I34** references Accounts Receivable in the Opening Balance Sheet (cell **I15** of **Opening Balance Sheet**), making sure this links to the blank column, not the figures that were moved to column **K**.

- Opening Receivables simply equals the previous period's closing balance.

- Closing Receivables simply equals the figure calculated in row 27.

- Cash Receipts is therefore the balancing figure, so for cell **J33** this will be equal to **=J34-SUM(J31:J32)**.

We have our first control account. In column **O**, I have actually stipulated which financial statement each line item is to go in. That is for the case study. In a real life model, this may be problematic as columns may need to be extended for further forecasting analysis.

This control account provides us with three things:

1. **Number of calculations that need to be entered into the financial statement so that they balance:** This is always one less than the number of rows in the control account. In this instance it will be four minus one, which is **three**.

2. **The order to build the calculations into the financial statements:** This is always row 2 first, then row 3, then row 4 and so on. In this instance, this will be Revenue (Income Statement), Cash Receipts (which will be a positive number in the Cash Flow Statement) and Closing Receivables (Balance Sheet).

3. **It identifies the key driver:** Line 2 of the control account is always the key driver, so in this case it will be Revenue. If there was never any Revenue, there would be no Cash Receipts and without either of these items, Accounts Receivable would always be zero.

Modellers are used to do something and then do something else for the Balance Sheet to balance (*i.e.* double entry). Here, I have identified it will take three calculations, so I must not fret when I have included the first two calculations into the financial statements and still note that the Balance Sheet does not balance.

Firstly, let me insert Revenue into the Income Statement:

J13			× ✓ f_x	=Calculations!J32							
	A	B	C	D	E F	G	H I	J	K	L	M	N
1	**Income Statement**											
2	Case Study Model vLB1.01.xlsm											
3	Navigator											
4	Error Checks:						🔲					
5								**Jun 21**	**Jun 22**	**Jun 23**	**Jun 24**	**Jun 25**
6		Start Date						1 Jul 20	1 Jul 21	1 Jul 22	1 Jul 23	1 Jul 24
7		End Date						30 Jun 21	30 Jun 22	30 Jun 23	30 Jun 24	30 Jun 25
8		Number of Days						365	365	365	366	365
9		Counter						1	2	3	4	5
10												
11		**1. Income Statement**										
12												
13		Revenue			US$'000			400	448	493	532	559
14		COGS			US$'000							
15		**Gross Profit**			US$'000			400	448	493	532	559
16												

There are two things to note here:

1. Revenue should be referenced from the control account (row 32 of the **Calculations** worksheet), not from row 19 of the same sheet where it was originally calculated. This is to help you track down Balance Sheet errors. If the Balance Sheet does not balance, you simply need to go back to each control account and see what has not been linked or what has been linked incorrectly.

2. The error check in cell **G4** has been triggered. This is to be expected and I would be more concerned if it hadn't been, as this would indicate Revenue was not flowing through the model correctly. This is where we use the error checks "the wrong way round" in that we need to ensure that the error checks actually alert us of issues whilst we put in all but the final entry of a control account.

Secondly, working our way down the control account, Cash Receipts needs to go in as a <u>positive</u> number in the Cash Flow Statement. This means negating the cell reference:

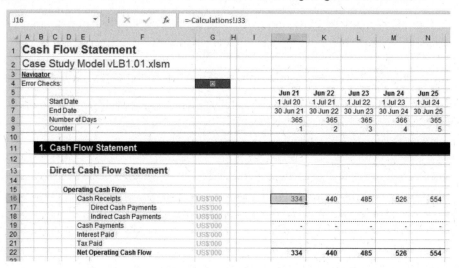

It is at this stage that some inexperienced modellers may become concerned that the Balance Sheet still does not balance (again, check cell **G4**). However, this is about to be remedied.

Thirdly and finally, reference the Closing Receivable to the Balance Sheet:

J15				×	✓	*fx*	=Calculations!J34				

	A	B	C	D	E	F	G	H	I	J	K	L	M	N
1	**Balance Sheet**													
2	Case Study Model vLB1.01.xlsm													
3	Navigator													
4	Error Checks:						☑							
5										Jun 21	Jun 22	Jun 23	Jun 24	Jun 25
6		Start Date								1 Jul 20	1 Jul 21	1 Jul 22	1 Jul 23	1 Jul 24
7		End Date								30 Jun 21	30 Jun 22	30 Jun 23	30 Jun 24	30 Jun 25
8		Number of Days								365	365	365	366	365
9		Counter								1	2	3	4	5
10														
11		**1. Balance Sheet**												
12														
13		Current Assets												
14		Cash			US$'000					334	774	1,260	1,786	2,340
15		Accounts Receivable			US$'000					66	74	81	87	92
16		Other Current Assets			US$'000									
17		**Total Current Assets**			US$'000					400	848	1,341	1,873	2,432

Note that this formula also references the control account for the reasons stipulated above. Now you will notice that the Balance Sheet balanced and all is well in the world again. This might be a good time to save the model: if you make a huge mistake later, you can always close without saving and re-open to this "restore point".

It's time to move on.

CHAPTER 10.6: COSTS OF GOODS SOLD

Building a Financial Model

10. Move to the next item in the financial statement not yet calculated

11. Return to Point 11

Our Income Statement looks like this:

1. Income Statement

Revenue	US$'000	400	448	493	532	559
COGS	US$'000					
Gross Profit	US$'000	400	448	493	532	559
Operating Expenditure	US$'000					
EBITDA	US$'000	400	448	493	532	559
Depreciation	US$'000					
EBIT	US$'000	400	448	493	532	559
Interest Expense	US$'000					
NPBT	US$'000	400	448	493	532	559
Tax Expense	US$'000					
NPAT	US$'000	400	448	493	532	559

The next line item is COGS (Costs Of Goods Sold). This calls for more assumptions on the **General Assumptions** worksheet:

	A	B	C	D	E	F	G	H	I	J	K	L	M	N
1	**General Assumptions**													
2	Case Study Model vLB1.01.xlsm													
3	Navigator													
4	Error Checks:					☑								
5										Jun 21	Jun 22	Jun 23	Jun 24	Jun 25
6			Start Date							1 Jul 20	1 Jul 21	1 Jul 22	1 Jul 23	1 Jul 24
7			End Date							30 Jun 21	30 Jun 22	30 Jun 23	30 Jun 24	30 Jun 25
8			Number of Days							365	365	365	366	365
9			Counter							1	2	3	4	5
24														
25			**COGS and Related**											
26														
27			**COGS**											
28														
29				Gross Margin		%				70%	70%	70%	70%	70%
30														
31			**Working Capital**											
32														
33				Days Payable		# Days				90	90	90	90	90
34														
35														

You may recall I mentioned in the previous section there are four ways of entering data. To recap:

The Four Methods of Entering Inputs into a Model

There are only four ways to enter data into a financial model. The actual method may incorporate combinations of the following:

1. **Amounts:** Data is entered in as numerical (absolute) values. It may be in units, thousands, millions, GWh and so on, but ultimately it is a number. This is an ideal entry method where data is copied from elsewhere or may eventually be linked to another model (say).

2. **Percentages:** Data is typed in as a percentage or ratio of another value, be it input or calculated. This is often the approach employed for variable costs, for example.

3. **Amount and growth rates:** Data is entered in two forms, an amount in at least the first period and then a percentage thereafter. This is often the method used for sky blue forecasting and sometimes leads to what the modelling connoisseur may describe as "hockey stick projections".

4. **Combination:** Usually perceived as a more sophisticated version of the **amount and growth rates** approach, this method combines two or more input methodologies. The combination may be selected by use of a switch (manual input) or a trigger (calculation). This is often used for reforecasting or replacing forecast with actuals, *etc.* **IF** and **CHOOSE** are functions often associated with this methodology.

We have two inputs in this 'COGS and Related' section:

*   Gross Margin uses the **percentages** methodology. This will be based on Revenue. This percentage will not calculate COGS *per se*, but once Gross Margin has been computed, COGS will be a simple deduction.

*   The Days Payable assumptions are **amounts**. This may be based on guesstimates or historical / trend data for the business from the past. The method of making the working capital adjustments will be very similar to the approach adopted for Days Receivable earlier.

These need to be incorporated into the **Calculations** worksheet:

	E	F	G	H	I	J	K	L	M	N	O	P
1	**Calculations**											
2	Case Study Model vLB1.01.xlsm											
3	Navigator											
4	Error Checks:		☑									
5						Jun 21	Jun 22	Jun 23	Jun 24	Jun 25		
6	Start Date					1 Jul 20	1 Jul 21	1 Jul 22	1 Jul 23	1 Jul 24		
7	End Date					30 Jun 21	30 Jun 22	30 Jun 23	30 Jun 24	30 Jun 25		
8	Number of Days					365	365	365	366	365		
9	Counter					1	2	3	4	5		
37	**COGS and Related**											
39	**COGS**											
41	Revenue	US$'000				400	448	493	532	559	=J19	
42	Gross Margin	%				70%	70%	70%	70%	70%	='General Assumptions'!J29	
43	Gross Profit	US$'000				280	314	345	373	391	=J41*J42	
45	**COGS**	US$'000				120	134	148	160	168	=J41-J43	
47	**Working Capital**											
49	Days Payable	# Days				90	90	90	90	90	='General Assumptions'!J33	
51	Days in Period	# Days										
53	Closing Payables	US$'000										
55	**Control Account**											
57	Opening Payables	US$'000										
58	COGS	US$'000										
59	Cash Payments	US$'000										
60	Closing Payables	US$'000										

COGS has been stepped out so it may be readily followed on a piece of paper. This gives us our Income Statement figure. Now, as before, I have to calculate the working capital adjustments and hence the control account. To this end, I reference the Accounts Payable figure from the **Opening Balance Sheet** worksheet (cell **I27**).

I have been *very* careful how I have set out the worksheet. I have droned on and on previously about *consistent* spacing and so forth. Well, now it's time for the payback. Do you recall our Revenue calculation from earlier? I am going to select cells **J25:O34** and then copy them.

	E	F	G	H	I	J	K	L	M	N	O
1	**Calculations**										
2	Case Study Model vLB1.01.xlsm										
3	Navigator										
4	Error Checks:		☑								
5						Jun 21	Jun 22	Jun 23	Jun 24	Jun 25	
6	Start Date					1 Jul 20	1 Jul 21	1 Jul 22	1 Jul 23	1 Jul 24	
7	End Date					30 Jun 21	30 Jun 22	30 Jun 23	30 Jun 24	30 Jun 25	
8	Number of Days					365	365	365	366	365	
9	Counter					1	2	3	4	5	
11	**1. Calculations**										
13	**Revenue and Related**										
15	**Revenue**										
17	Revenue First Year	US$'000				400					
18	Revenue Growth Rate	%					12%	10%	8%	5%	
19	Revenue	US$'000				400	448	493	532	559	
21	**Working Capital**										
23	Days Receivable	# Days				60	60	60	60	60	
25	Days in Period	# Days				365	365	365	366	365	
27	Closing Receivables	US$'000				66	74	81	87	92	
29	**Control Account**										
31	Opening Receivables	US$'000				-	66	74	81	87	BS
32	Revenue	US$'000				400	448	493	532	559	IS
33	Cash Receipts	US$'000				(334)	(440)	(485)	(526)	(554)	CFS
34	Closing Receivables	US$'000				-	66	74	81	87	92	BS

This range will then be pasted (**CTRL + V**) into cells **J51:O60**.

A B C D	E	F G	H	I	J	K	L	M	N	O	P
1 **Calculations**											
2 Case Study Model vLB1.01.xlsm											
3 **Navigator**		☑									
4 Error Checks:											
5					Jun 21	Jun 22	Jun 23	Jun 24	Jun 25		
6 Start Date					1 Jul 20	1 Jul 21	1 Jul 22	1 Jul 23	1 Jul 24		
7 End Date					30 Jun 21	30 Jun 22	30 Jun 23	30 Jun 24	30 Jun 25		
8 Number of Days					365	365	365	366	365		
9 Counter					1	2	3	4	5		
36											
37 **COGS and Related**											
38											
39 **COGS**											
40											
41 Revenue	US$'000				400	448	493	532	559		=J19
42 Gross Margin	%				70%	70%	70%	70%	70%		='General Assumptions'!J29
43 Gross Profit	US$'000				280	314	345	373	391		=J41*J42
44											
45 **COGS**	US$'000				120	134	148	160	168		=J41-J43
46											
47 **Working Capital**											
48											
49 Days Payable	# Days				90	90	90	90	90		='General Assumptions'!J33
50											
51 Days in Period	# Days				365	365	365	366	365		=J$8
52											
53 Closing Payables	US$'000				30	33	36	39	41		=J49/J51*J45
54											
55 **Control Account**											
56											
57 Opening Payables	US$'000				-	30	33	36	39 BS	=I60
58 COGS	US$'000				120	134	148	160	168 IS	=J45
59 Cash Payments	US$'000				(90)	(131)	(145)	(157)	(166) CFS	=J60-SUM(J57:J58)
60 Closing Payables	US$'000				30	33	36	39	41 BS	=J53

How hard was that? This is why it is so important to be consistent with your model layout. It makes your life easier. Further, if sections are regularly copied without error, this also suggests that the robustness of the model is high. It is a cheap victory for checking your model without getting a second pair of eyes; you get a second (or subsequent) section instead.

We are almost there; as before, using the control account we can identify:

1. **Number of calculations that need to be entered into the financial statement so that they balance:** This is always one less than the number of rows in the control account. In this instance it will be four minus one again, which is **three**.

2. **The order to build the calculations into the financial statements:** This is always row 2 first, then row 3, then row 4 and so on. In this instance, this will be COGS (which will be a <u>negative</u> number in the Income Statement), Cash Payments (Cash Flow Statement) and Closing Payables (Balance Sheet).

3. **It identifies the key driver:** Line 2 of the control account is always the key driver, so in this case it will be COGS. If there were never any COGS, there would be no need to make Cash Payments and without either of these items, Accounts Payable would always be zero.

Time to insert. As with Revenue, the first financial statement for COGS is the Income Statement, but I am taking care to ensure that the link is brought in as a negative number:

						Jun 21	Jun 22	Jun 23	Jun 24	Jun 25
1	**Income Statement**									
2	Case Study Model vLB1.01.xlsm									
3	Navigator									
4	Error Checks:									
5						Jun 21	Jun 22	Jun 23	Jun 24	Jun 25
6		Start Date				1 Jul 20	1 Jul 21	1 Jul 22	1 Jul 23	1 Jul 24
7		End Date				30 Jun 21	30 Jun 22	30 Jun 23	30 Jun 24	30 Jun 25
8		Number of Days				365	365	365	366	365
9		Counter				1	2	3	4	5
10										
11		1. Income Statement								
12										
13		Revenue	US$'000			400	448	493	532	559
14		COGS	US$'000			(120)	(134)	(148)	(160)	(168)
15		Gross Profit	US$'000			280	314	345	373	391
16										
17		Operating Expenditure	US$'000							
18		EBITDA	US$'000			280	314	345	373	391
19										
20		Depreciation	US$'000							
21		EBIT	US$'000			280	314	345	373	391
22										
23		Interest Expense	US$'000							
24		NPBT	US$'000			280	314	345	373	391
25										
26		Tax Expense	US$'000							
27		NPAT	US$'000			280	314	345	373	391

I note that COGS (row 14) flows down the Income Statement as intended and that the error check is triggered once more. I can deduce COGS is linking correctly. Once I am satisfied with this addition, I can turn my attention to the Cash Flow Statement:

J17 f_x =Calculations!J59

				Jun 21	Jun 22	Jun 23	Jun 24	Jun 25
1	**Cash Flow Statement**							
2	Case Study Model vLB1.01.xlsm							
3	Navigator							
4	Error Checks:							
5				Jun 21	Jun 22	Jun 23	Jun 24	Jun 25
6	Start Date			1 Jul 20	1 Jul 21	1 Jul 22	1 Jul 23	1 Jul 24
7	End Date			30 Jun 21	30 Jun 22	30 Jun 23	30 Jun 24	30 Jun 25
8	Number of Days			365	365	365	366	365
9	Counter			1	2	3	4	5
10								
11	1. Cash Flow Statement							
12								
13	Direct Cash Flow Statement							
14								
15	Operating Cash Flow							
16	Cash Receipts	US$'000		334	440	485	526	554
17	Direct Cash Payments	US$'000		(90)	(131)	(145)	(157)	(166)
18	Indirect Cash Payments	US$'000						
19	Cash Payments	US$'000		(90)	(131)	(145)	(157)	(166)
20	Interest Paid	US$'000						
21	Tax Paid	US$'000						
22	Net Operating Cash Flow	US$'000		244	309	341	369	389

As discussed earlier, COGS is a **direct** cost, so it is linked to row 17, the Direct Cash Payments. These amounts flow correctly but the Balance Sheet still does not balance. Now the **Balance Sheet** worksheet may be modified:

J27			✕	✓	*fx*	=Calculations!J60				

	A B C D	E	F G H I	J	K	L	M	N
1	**Balance Sheet**							
2	Case Study Model vLB1.01.xlsm							
3	Navigator							
4	Error Checks:		☑					
5				**Jun 21**	**Jun 22**	**Jun 23**	**Jun 24**	**Jun 25**
6	Start Date			1 Jul 20	1 Jul 21	1 Jul 22	1 Jul 23	1 Jul 24
7	End Date			30 Jun 21	30 Jun 22	30 Jun 23	30 Jun 24	30 Jun 25
8	Number of Days			365	365	365	366	365
9	Counter			1	2	3	4	5
25								
26	**Current Liabilities**							
27	Accounts Payable	US$'000		30	33	36	39	41
28	Interest Payable	US$'000						
29	Dividends Payable	US$'000						
30	Tax Payable	US$'000						
31	Other Current liabilities	US$'000						
32	**Total Current liabilities**	US$'000		30	33	36	39	41

Once more, the Balance Sheet is balanced. It is probably time to save the model once more before we turn our attention to the next line item.

CHAPTER 10.7: OPERATING EXPENDITURE

Building a Financial Model

15. Move to the next item in the financial statement not yet calculated

16. Return to Point 11

The Income Statement has been updated as follows:

1. Income Statement

Revenue	US$'000	400	448	493	532	559
COGS	US$'000	(120)	(134)	(148)	(160)	(168)
Gross Profit	US$'000	280	314	345	373	391
Operating Expenditure	US$'000					
EBITDA	US$'000	280	314	345	373	391
Depreciation	US$'000					
EBIT	US$'000	280	314	345	373	391
Interest Expense	US$'000					
NPBT	US$'000	280	314	345	373	391
Tax Expense	US$'000					
NPAT	US$'000	280	314	345	373	391

The next line item is Operating Expenditure, *i.e.* the **indirect** costs associated with the business being modelled. This calls for another section on the **General Assumptions** worksheet:

	A	B	C	D	E	F	G	H	I	J	K	L	M	N
1	**General Assumptions**													
2	Case Study Model vLB1.01.xlsm													
3	Navigator													
4	Error Checks:					☑								
5										Jun 21	Jun 22	Jun 23	Jun 24	Jun 25
6		Start Date								1 Jul 20	1 Jul 21	1 Jul 22	1 Jul 23	1 Jul 24
7		End Date								30 Jun 21	30 Jun 22	30 Jun 23	30 Jun 24	30 Jun 25
8		Number of Days								365	365	365	366	365
9		Counter								1	2	3	4	5
35														
36		**Opex and Cash Payments**												
37		All expenses are assumed to be paid as they are incurred.												
38														
39			**Opex**											
40														
41			Growth Rates Used From		Year			30-Jun-23						
42			Amounts		US$'000					60	65	70	75	80
43			Growth Rates		%						5%	4%	3%	2%

So far, I have introduced three of the four input types (**amounts, percentages** and **amount and growth rates**); Operating Expenditure (Opex) is modelled as an example of the final method, **combination**.

This method combines two or more input methodologies. The combination may be selected by use of a switch (manual input) or a trigger (calculation). In this instance, the switch is located in cell **I41**, *i.e.* it is a manual input:

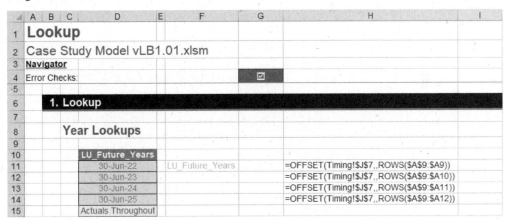

This dropdown box in cell **I41** has been created by a **Data Validation -> List (ALT + D + L)**. This was explained previously, including the Best Practice idea of having the list on a different worksheet and given a range name. To this end, I have created a **Lookup** worksheet for the range name as follows:

⬚	A	B	C	D	E	F	G	H	I
1	**Lookup**								
2	Case Study Model vLB1.01.xlsm								
3	**Navigator**								
4	Error Checks:						☑		
5									
6		**1. Lookup**							
7									
8		**Year Lookups**							
9									
10			LU_Future_Years						
11			30-Jun-22		LU_Future_Years		=OFFSET(Timing!$J$7,,ROWS($A$9:$A9))		
12			30-Jun-23				=OFFSET(Timing!$J$7,,ROWS($A$9:$A10))		
13			30-Jun-24				=OFFSET(Timing!$J$7,,ROWS($A$9:$A11))		
14			30-Jun-25				=OFFSET(Timing!$J$7,,ROWS($A$9:$A12))		
15			Actuals Throughout						

Cells **D11:D15** have been named **LU_Future_Years** for easy reference in the Data Validation dialog box.

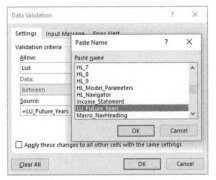

As described when extolling the virtues of **OFFSET** previously, I have used this function to transpose dates from the **Timing** worksheet, so that if the **Model_Start_Date** were to change, this lookup table would update automatically. With conditional formatting prevalent, I will be using the growth rates from the date specified. Obviously, the first period must be an amount.

Before I turn attention to the **Calculations** worksheet, there is one other thing to note in this **General Assumptions** section. Did you note the text in cell **C37**? It states, "All expenses are assumed to be paid as they are incurred". This means no cash timing difference. That will have an impact upon our control account.

There is a lot going on in the **Calculations** worksheet regarding Operating Expenditure:

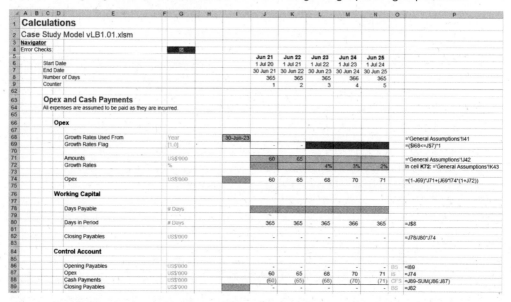

							Jun 21	Jun 22	Jun 23	Jun 24	Jun 25		
1	Calculations												
2	Case Study Model vLB1.01.xlsm												
3	Navigator												
4	Error Checks				☑									
5								Jun 21	Jun 22	Jun 23	Jun 24	Jun 25		
6	Start Date						1 Jul 20	1 Jul 21	1 Jul 22	1 Jul 23	1 Jul 24		
7	End Date						30 Jun 21	30 Jun 22	30 Jun 23	30 Jun 24	30 Jun 25		
8	Number of Days						365	365	365	366	365		
9	Counter						1	2	3	4	5		
62													
63	Opex and Cash Payments												
64	All expenses are assumed to be paid as they are incurred.												
65													
66	Opex												
67													
68	Growth Rates Used From	Year		30-Jun-23								='General Assumptions'!I41	
69	Growth Rates Flag	[1,0]				-	-					=($I68<=J$7)*1	
70													
71	Amounts	US$'000				60	65					='General Assumptions'!J42	
72	Growth Rates	%						4%	3%	2%	In cell K72: ='General Assumptions'!K43	
73													
74	Opex	US$'000				60	65	68	70	71	=(1-J69)*J71+(J69*I74*(1+J72))	
75													
76	Working Capital												
77													
78	Days Payable	# Days											
79													
80	Days in Period	# Days				365	365	365	366	365	=J$8	
81													
82	Closing Payables	US$'000			-	-	-	-	-	=J78/J80*J74	
83													
84	Control Account												
85													
86	Opening Payables	US$'000			-	-	-	-	-	BS	=I89	
87	Opex	US$'000			60	65	68	70	71	IS	=J74	
88	Cash Payments	US$'000			(60)	(65)	(68)	(70)	(71)	CFS	=J89-SUM(J86:J87)	
89	Closing Payables	US$'000			-	-	-	-	-	BS	=J82	

The first thing to note is the Growth Rates Flag in row 79. The formula in cell **J69** produces a Boolean result of 1 or 0:

$$=(\$I68<=J\$7)*1$$

This will give a value of 1 if the date growth rates are to be used from (cell **I68**) is less than or equal to the end date of the period (row 7). This effectively provides a marker of when to use the growth rates from and also drives the conditional formatting (**CTRL + O + D**) employed in rows 71 and 72, *e.g.*

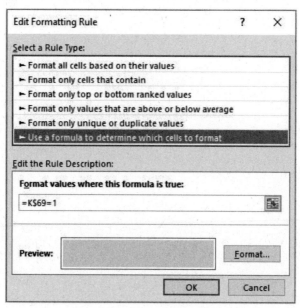

This flag formula has been used to write an alternative formula for when to use values and when to use the growth rates. The "traditional" approach in cell **J74** might be

$$=IF(J69=1,I74*(1+J72),J71)$$

whereas I have used

$$=(1-J69)*J71+(J69*I74*(1+J72))$$

Admittedly, it is slightly longer but I wanted to take the opportunity of showing a relatively common variant of the **IF** formula. They achieve precisely the same effect: if the flag equals 1, grow the previous period by (1 + growth rate) else use the input value. Do note also the importance of cells **J72** and **I74** being blank, hence the required style formatting.

Talking of deliberately blank cells, **J78:N78** and **I89** are also blank intentionally. The Days Payable line (row 78) is blank because payments are made as and when they fall due. The initial Closing Payables is blank for another reason: this has already been referenced in the COGS control account and to include it again here would be a double count which would lead to the Balance Sheet not balancing. With this borne in mind, cells **J80:O89** can just be copied in using the same approach employed for COGS.

Remember to follow my guidance on how utilise control accounts:

1. **Number of calculations that need to be entered into the financial statement so that they balance:** This is always one less than the number of rows in the control account. In this instance it will be four minus one yet again, which is **three**. It is <u>not</u> two. You <u>must</u> include Closing Payables even if it will always be zero. This is in case Days Payable comes into play later when someone changes their mind on how realistic all bills will be paid as they fall due might be.

2. **The order to build the calculations into the financial statements:** This is always row 2 first, then row 3, then row 4 and so on. In this instance, this will be Operating Expenditure (which will be a <u>negative</u> number in the Income Statement), Cash Payments (Cash Flow Statement) and Closing Payables (Balance Sheet).

3. **It identifies the key driver:** Line 2 of the control account is always the key driver, so in this case it will be Operating Expenditure. If there were never any Operating Expenditure, there would be no need to make Cash Payments and without either of these items, Accounts Payable would always be zero.

Is this all starting to sound familiar? Good. That's the plan. Financial modelling isn't that complicated. The main problem with most modellers is that they tend to be great problem solvers. Now usually that is a fantastic skill to have, but the problem is that they exhibit a natural tendency to try and take shortcuts in putting the financial statements together. This is what causes the Balance Sheet errors. Leva your brain at the door, follow the guidelines laid out in this book and you will find a financial model comes together relatively simply. Yes, you will still have to create more complex calculations than the ones used as illustrations here, but with skill and experience that will come together.

Right, let me get off my soapbox and onto the **Income Statement** worksheet:

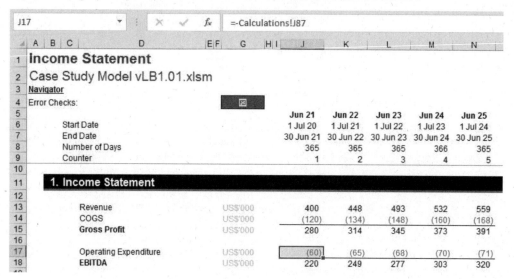

Like COGS, the reference to Operating Expenditure must be negated and must link to the control account. As usual, the error check alerts us that the model no longer balances – which is correct.

			Jun 21	Jun 22	Jun 23	Jun 24	Jun 25
Start Date			1 Jul 20	1 Jul 21	1 Jul 22	1 Jul 23	1 Jul 24
End Date			30 Jun 21	30 Jun 22	30 Jun 23	30 Jun 24	30 Jun 25
Number of Days			365	365	365	366	365
Counter			1	2	3	4	5

1. Cash Flow Statement

Direct Cash Flow Statement

			Jun 21	Jun 22	Jun 23	Jun 24	Jun 25
Operating Cash Flow							
Cash Receipts	US$'000		334	440	485	526	554
Direct Cash Payments	US$'000		(90)	(131)	(145)	(157)	(166)
Indirect Cash Payments	US$'000		(60)	(65)	(68)	(70)	(71)
Cash Payments	US$'000		(150)	(196)	(212)	(226)	(237)
Interest Paid	US$'000						
Tax Paid	US$'000						
Net Operating Cash Flow	US$'000		184	244	273	299	318

Watch out after adding in the Indirect Cash Payments (row 18, above). The error check in cell **G4** now seems to suggest that the model is now working correctly. However, the Accounts Payable calculation – albeit with zero impact – has not yet been added. This must be included in case of a change of assumptions in the model later.

| J27 | | | | | ▾ | : | × | ✓ | *fx* | =Calculations!J60+Calculations!J89 | | | | |

▲	A	B	C	D	E		F	G	H	I	J	K	L	M	N
1	**Balance Sheet**														
2	Case Study Model vLB1.01.xlsm														
3	Navigator														
4	Error Checks:							☑							
5											Jun 21	Jun 22	Jun 23	Jun 24	Jun 25
6			Start Date								1 Jul 20	1 Jul 21	1 Jul 22	1 Jul 23	1 Jul 24
7			End Date								30 Jun 21	30 Jun 22	30 Jun 23	30 Jun 24	30 Jun 25
8			Number of Days								365	365	365	366	365
9			Counter								1	2	3	4	5
25															
26			**Current Liabilities**												
27				Accounts Payable				US$'000			30	33	36	39	41
28				Interest Payable				US$'000							
29				Dividends Payable				US$'000							
30				Tax Payable				US$'000							
31				Other Current liabilities				US$'000							
32				**Total Current liabilities**				US$'000			30	33	36	39	41

The formula in the **Balance Sheet** worksheet has now been amended to

=Calculations!J60+Calculations!J89

This effectively adds zero, but is essential for a *flexible* model going forward.

CHAPTER 10.8: CAPITAL EXPENDITURE

Building a Financial Model

15. Move to the next item in the financial statement not yet calculated

16. Return to Point 11

The Income Statement is starting to take shape. We are now able to calculate up to **EBITDA** (Earnings Before Interest, Tax, Depreciation and Amortisation):

1. Income Statement

Revenue	US$'000	400	448	493	532	559
COGS	US$'000	(120)	(134)	(148)	(160)	(168)
Gross Profit	US$'000	280	314	345	373	391
Operating Expenditure	US$'000	(60)	(65)	(68)	(70)	(71)
EBITDA	US$'000	220	249	277	303	320
Depreciation	US$'000					
EBIT	US$'000	220	249	277	303	320
Interest Expense	US$'000					
NPBT	US$'000	220	249	277	303	320
Tax Expense	US$'000					
NPAT	US$'000	220	249	277	303	320

The next line item required is Depreciation, but to calculate this we need to understand the concept of capital expenditure first. **Capital expenditure** is the cost to procure any asset that meets the following criteria:

- The asset must have an economic life of greater than one year when purchased

- It is held for continuing use in the business

- The asset must generate an accounting profit / economic return

- The value of the asset when purchased must exceed a de minimis limit which varies from geographic region / accounting jurisdiction.

The idea is that capital expenditure tends to be expensive (*e.g.* acquiring a building, purchasing a fleet of cars) and expensing all of these costs in any one period would lead to an horrific loss and go against the accruals concept. The intention is to match the costs over the life of the profits they generate (hence the test for profitability).

There are four common methods of depreciation. They are based on the **depreciable amount**, which is defined as the original price of the asset less its estimated resale price (**residual** or **salvage value**):

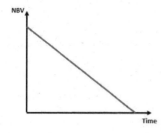

1. **Straight Line:** By far the most common method, this approach linearly apportions the depreciable amount evenly over the remaining number of periods. Favoured by accountants and statutory reporting, for many industries and sectors it is the simplest and least contentious approach. This gets its name as plotting time against an asset's remaining value (known as **Net Book Value**) will generate a straight line on a chart.

2. **Diminishing Value or Declining Balance:** This approach calculates a proportion of the remaining value to depreciate each year, based on the initial purchase price, not the depreciable amount. The rate is usually a function of the economic life and a multiplier.

	$
	1,000.00
Depn: P1	(500.00)
	500.00
Depn: P2	(250.00)
	250.00
Depn: P3	(125.00)
	125.00
Depn: P4	(62.50)
	62.50

For example, consider an asset purchased for $1,000 that has a depreciable amount of $1,000 also. The asset has a four year life and a multiplier of 2.0x (this is known as **Double Declining Balance**). This would give a depreciation rate of 2.0 / 4 = 50% on the remaining balance:

This method is frequently used in many jurisdictions / territories for tax computations.

3. **Sum Of Digits (SOD):** This method considers the economic life but apportions on an increasing or decreasing proportion each year. For example, a four year economic life might depreciate the depreciable amount by 1/10 in Year 1, 2/10 in Year 2, 3/10 in Year 3 and 4/10 in Year 4, where the common denominator 10 = 1 + 2 + 3 + 4. (This can be decreasing as well as increasing.) This approach is becoming less and less common.

4. **Usage Basis:** This amortises the depreciable amount based on what proportion of the asset is estimated to have been used in a particular year. This is quite common in the mining and resources industries.

Typically, 21st century modelling tends to assume no residual value so that generally the depreciable amount is the initial purchase price.

Excel has several functions that calculate depreciation:

- **SLN(Cost,Residual_Value,Economic_Life)** calculates the depreciable amount each year. This is simply **=(Cost – Residual_Value) / Economic_Life**.

- **DB(Cost,Residual_Value,Economic_Life,Year_Number,[Months_Left_in_1st_Year])** calculates the depreciation on a declining balance basis. The fixed rate is calculated as **1 - ((Residual_Value / Cost) ^ (1 / Economic_Life))**. This is good for finding the depreciation in later years quickly. Note that **Months_Left_in_1st_Year** allows you to calculate depreciation for part-year acquisitions; left blank, it assumes the first year is a full year.

- **DDB(Cost,Residual_Value,Economic_Life,Year_Number,[Factor])** calculates the Double Declining Balance, *i.e.* **2 / Economic_Life** for a particular **Year_Number**. If **Factor** is specified, the formula uses the **Factor** rather than 2, *e.g.* a **Factor** of 3 would effectively be "triple declining balance".

- **VDB(Cost,Residual_Value,Economic_Life,Starting_Year_Number,Ending_Year_Number,[Factor],[No_Switch])** calculates the Variable Declining Balance, similar in operation to the **DDB** function. It ensures that the **Residual_Value** is achieved at the end of the **Economic_Life** by switching to straight line depreciation when this becomes higher than the declining balance amount. If you do not want this switch to occur set **No_Switch** to FALSE (the default value if unspecified is TRUE). **Factor** works similarly to the same argument in the **DDB** function.

- **SYD(Cost,Residual_Value,Economic_Life,Year_Number)** calculates the depreciation on a Sum Of <u>Years</u> Digits basis on a declining basis (*i.e.* depreciation is front-loaded).

Got it? Me neither. Do you know I have *never* used <u>any</u> of these functions? That is why I don't provide copious examples for each and the fact they were not described earlier as I talked through various key functions in Excel. If you use any of these function you are trusting Microsoft has got its sums right and is performing the calculation *exactly* as you want. It is opaque and end users do not tend to be very trusting of numbers that appear to come out of thin air. Besides, these functions only consider the capital expenditure for a particular period. What happens when you have to work it out for multiple periods? First principles work well.

In fact, it is worth starting with first principles because depreciation is by far the area of financial modelling most frequently modelled incorrectly. Let me show you. Consider the following example:

	A	B	C	D	E	F	G	H	I	J	K	L	M	N	O
1															
2		Capex:		1,000											
3		Economic Life:		10.0											
4															
5		Period No.		1	2	3	4	5	6	7	8	9	10		
6		Opening NBV		1,000	1,000	1,000	1,000	1,000	1,000	1,000	1,000	1,000	1,000		=IF(D$5=1,$D$2,C8)
7		Depreciation													
8		**Closing NBV**		1,000	1,000	1,000	1,000	1,000	1,000	1,000	1,000	1,000	1,000		=SUM(D6:D7)
9															

Have a go at this. Create the above spreadsheet. Imagine depreciation is to be calculated on a straight line basis with an initial amount of $1,000 (cell **D2**) and an economic life of 10 years (cell **D3**). Just put one formula in cell **D7** to be copied across so that the depreciation is calculated correctly. This is not as easy as you may think.

Once you think you have a solution, change the Capex to $2,000 in cell **D2**:

	A	B	C	D	E	F	G	H	I	J	K	L	M	N	O
1															
2		Capex:		2,000											
3		Economic Life:		10.0											
4															
5		Period No.		1	2	3	4	5	6	7	8	9	10		
6		Opening NBV		2,000	1,800	1,600	1,400	1,200	1,000	800	600	400	200		=IF(D$5=1,$D$2,C8)
7		Depreciation		(200)	(200)	(200)	(200)	(200)	(200)	(200)	(200)	(200)	(200)		
8		**Closing NBV**		1,800	1,600	1,400	1,200	1,000	800	600	400	200	-		=SUM(D6:D7)
9															

So far so good? Now try changing the economic life to 20 years in cell **D3**:

	A	B	C	D	E	F	G	H	I	J	K	L	M	N	O
1															
2		Capex:		2,000											
3		Economic Life:		20.0											
4															
5		Period No.		1	2	3	4	5	6	7	8	9	10		
6		Opening NBV		2,000	1,900	1,800	1,700	1,600	1,500	1,400	1,300	1,200	1,100		=IF(D$5=1,$D$2,C8)
7		Depreciation		(100)	(100)	(100)	(100)	(100)	(100)	(100)	(100)	(100)	(100)		
8		**Closing NBV**		1,900	1,800	1,700	1,600	1,500	1,400	1,300	1,200	1,100	1,000		=SUM(D6:D7)
9															

Still a walk in a park? Don't get too confident just yet. Now change the economic life to 8 years:

	A	B	C	D	E	F	G	H	I	J	K	L	M	N	O
1															
2		Capex:		2,000											
3		Economic Life:		8.0											
4															
5		Period No.		1	2	3	4	5	6	7	8	9	10		
6		Opening NBV		2,000	1,750	1,500	1,250	1,000	750	500	250	-	-		=IF(D$5=1,$D$2,C8)
7		Depreciation		(250)	(250)	(250)	(250)	(250)	(250)	(250)	(250)	-	-		
8		**Closing NBV**		1,750	1,500	1,250	1,000	750	500	250	-	-	-		=SUM(D6:D7)
9															

Have you over-depreciated? I reckon some of you will have. If you have negative numbers in row 8 that is **wrong** and I will have to send the auditors round.

This is a common mistake that is not always as easy as this to spot. Here, we have no additional capital expenditure, all we are doing is depreciating the opening amount. If capital expenditure keeps going up, it may be very easy not to notice that over-depreciation is occurring.

For those still with me and thinking, "Try harder Liam", okay, I shall. I am going to change the economic life to 6.8 years:

	A	B	C	D	E	F	G	H	I	J	K	L	M	N	O
1															
2		Capex:		2,000											
3		Economic Life:		6.8											
4															
5		Period No.		1	2	3	4	5	6	7	8	9	10		
6		Opening NBV		2,000	1,706	1,412	1,118	824	529	235	-	-	-		=IF(D$5=1,$D$2,C8)
7		Depreciation		(294)	(294)	(294)	(294)	(294)	(294)	(235)	-	-	-		
8		**Closing NBV**		1,706	1,412	1,118	824	529	235	-	-	-	-		=SUM(D6:D7)
9															

If you are still with me, you are doing very well, but I am not finished yet. Try changing the economic life to 0.8 years:

	A	B	C	D	E	F	G	H	I	J	K	L	M	N	O
1															
2		Capex:		2,000											
3		Economic Life:		0.8											
4															
5		Period No.		1	2	3	4	5	6	7	8	9	10		
6		Opening NBV		2,000	-	-	-	-	-	-	-	-	-		=IF(D$5=1,$D$2,C8)
7		Depreciation		(2,000)	-	-	-	-	-	-	-	-	-		
8		**Closing NBV**		-	-	-	-	-	-	-	-	-	-		=SUM(D6:D7)
9															

Technically, this isn't capital expenditure as the economic life is less than one year, so it should be fully expensed. However, to get it out of Closing NBV I have fully amortised the amount.

Still with me? Last one: make Capex $(1,000) and the Economic Life two years:

	A	B	C	D	E	F	G	H	I	J	K	L	M	N	O
1															
2		Capex:		(1,000)											
3		Economic Life:		2.0											
4															
5		Period No.		1	2	3	4	5	6	7	8	9	10		
6		Opening NBV		(1,000)	(1,000)	(1,000)	(1,000)	(1,000)	(1,000)	(1,000)	(1,000)	(1,000)	(1,000)		=IF(D$5=1,$D$2,C8)
7		Depreciation		-	-	-	-	-	-	-	-	-	-		
8		**Closing NBV**		(1,000)	(1,000)	(1,000)	(1,000)	(1,000)	(1,000)	(1,000)	(1,000)	(1,000)	(1,000)		=SUM(D6:D7)
9															

Again, this shouldn't be capital expenditure, but there is absolutely no way I am adding depreciation back.

Did you make it to the end? If you did, I suggest you be a brilliant modeller or you may have peeked ahead. Here is the formula I used:

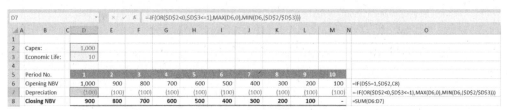

	A	B	C	D	E	F	G	H	I	J	K	L	M	N	O
1															
2		Capex:		1,000											
3		Economic Life:		10											
4															
5		Period No.		1	2	3	4	5	6	7	8	9	10		
6		Opening NBV		1,000	900	800	700	600	500	400	300	200	100		=IF(D$5=1,$D$2,C8)
7		Depreciation		(100)	(100)	(100)	(100)	(100)	(100)	(100)	(100)	(100)	(100)		=-IF(OR($D$2<0,$D$3<=1),MAX(D6,0),MIN(D6,($D$2/$D$3)))
8		Closing NBV		900	800	700	600	500	400	300	200	100	-		=SUM(D6:D7)

D7 = -IF(OR($D$2<0,$D$3<=1),MAX(D6,0),MIN(D6,($D$2/$D$3)))

I have no real plans to go through the formula in cell **D7**,

$$\text{=-IF(OR(\$D\$2<0,\$D\$3<=1),MAX(D6,0),MIN(D6,(\$D\$2/\$D\$3)))}$$

because it is <u>wrong</u> also. It may allow for negative Capex, Economic Life of less than or equal to one year and ensure no over-depreciation, but it will not cope with part-period acquisitions / disposals, revaluations, changes in economic life, *etc.*

If you had tried to use the **SLN** function how did you do? That wouldn't have been a great deal of use either. This is what I mean about going back to first principles. Depreciation is awkward, no matter what method you choose.

But it gets worse. What happens if you have multiple periods of capital expenditure? Let me create another example.

E7 = IF(E$4<$B7,,MIN($C7-SUM($D7:D7),$C7/$C$2))

	A	B	C	D	E	F	G	H	I	J	K
1											
2		Economic Life:	4								
3											
4		Period Number:			1	2	3	4	5	6	
5		Capex:			1,000	2,000	3,000	4,000	5,000	6,000	
6											
7		Depn - Yr 1	1,000		250	250	250	250	-	-	
8		Depn - Yr 2	2,000		-	500	500	500	500	-	
9		Depn - Yr 3	3,000		-	-	750	750	750	750	
10		Depn - Yr 4	4,000		-	-	-	1,000	1,000	1,000	
11		Depn - Yr 5	5,000		-	-	-	-	1,250	1,250	
12		Depn - Yr 6	6,000		-	-	-	-	-	1,500	
13					250	750	1,500	2,500	3,500	4,500	
14											

The above is known as a **depreciation grid**. Cells **C7:C12** transpose the values in cells **E5:J5** using the **OFFSET** function as I explained previously (*e.g.* the formula in cell **C7** is =OFFSET($D$5,,$B7), given the contents of cells **B7:B12** are simply numbers made to look like text using number formatting). The formula in the grid (*e.g.* cell **E7**),

=IF(E$4<$B7,,MIN($C7-SUM($D7:D7),$C7/$C$2))

calculates the depreciation amount assuming the period is a period where depreciation should be calculated. The grid is great for explaining how depreciation works. Users understand the logic without looking at the formula – which is probably just as well given what lurks beneath. There is a major disadvantage with this method though. A few years back, I had to construct several hundred depreciation calculations where users required monthly calculations for a 20-year period. That means each grid had 240 columns and 240 rows, *i.e.* 57,600 calculations per grid. Yuck!

There is a shorter method, using the **SUM(OFFSET)** method discussed back in the Excel functions section. Look at the following alternative calculation:

	E20				f_x =SUM(OFFSET(E19,,,,-E17))						
	A	B	C	D	E	F	G	H	I	J	K	L
1												
2	Economic Life:		4									
3												
4	Period Number:				1	2	3	4	5	6		
5	Capex:				1,000	2,000	3,000	4,000	5,000	6,000		
6												
7	Depn - Yr 1	1,000			250	250	250	250	-	-		
8	Depn - Yr 2	2,000			-	500	500	500	500	-		
9	Depn - Yr 3	3,000			-	-	750	750	750	750		
10	Depn - Yr 4	4,000			-	-	-	1,000	1,000	1,000		
11	Depn - Yr 5	5,000			-	-	-	-	1,250	1,250		
12	Depn - Yr 6	6,000			-	-	-	-	-	1,500		
13	**Total Depn**				**250**	**750**	**1,500**	**2,500**	**3,500**	**4,500**		
14												
15												
16	Period Number:				1	2	3	4	5	6		
17	Depreciation Width:				1	2	3	4	4	4	=MIN(E$16,$C$2)	
18	Capex:				1,000	2,000	3,000	4,000	5,000	6,000	=E5	
19	Depreciation:				250	500	750	1,000	1,250	1,500	=E18/$C$2	
20	**Total Depn**				**250**	**750**	**1,500**	**2,500**	**3,500**	**4,500**	=SUM(OFFSET(E19,,,,-E17))	

It may not look intuitive to begin with, but allow me to talk you through it.

- Row 17 takes the minimum of the period counter and the economic life. This formula is used to determine how many periods need to be considered. The maximum number of periods is 4 here, so that no year's capital expenditure may be over-depreciated.

- Row 18 simply restates the capital expenditure from row 5.

- Row 19 is another simple formula: it simply takes the capital expenditure figure and divides it by the economic life (I have simplified this formula here as really we to need ensure that the economic life is a positive integer).

- Row 20 simply uses the SUM(OFFSET) approach to add up amounts. The formula in cell E20,

=SUM(OFFSET(E19,,,,-E17))

- starts with the Depreciation in cell **E19** and does not move any rows or columns. Given the **Height** parameter is unspecified it is assumed to be 1 (*i.e.* just row 19) but the **Width** parameter is -1. A **Width** of 1 or -1 simply means the column you are in so for the first period, the amount is simply **=SUM(250)** which equals 250.

  For **F20**, the **OFFSET** function starts in cell **F19**, does not move anywhere, has a **Height** of 1 and a width of -2, which is column **F** and the column to the immediate left (**E**). The formula evaluates to **=SUM(500+250)** which equals 750.

  Moving on, cell **I20** (Period 5) takes the sum of the value in cell **I19** and the three cells to the left. This formula evaluates to **=SUM(1250+ 1000+750+500)** which equals 3,500.

This method is shorter, but perhaps not quite so transparent. This is where judgment is required. Sometimes with Best Practice Modelling you need to make a call when two or more of the four qualities conflict. Here, I am having to decide which I require more: *transparency* (using the grid) versus *robustness* (using the **SUM(OFFSET)** method). In our case study – that's right, I haven't completely forgotten about it – I have chosen the **SUM(OFFSET)** approach.

Before I wrap this section up, I need to extend the **SUM(OFFSET)** idea for depreciation. This works fine if the rate remains constant, but what happens if it can change each period (*i.e.* you are using just about any other depreciation method)?

Reverse Depreciation Rates Method

This is the "universal" formula but is conceptually even more complex than **SUM(OFFSET)**. This uses **SUMPRODUCT(OFFSET,OFFSET)**. Feel free to skip this section if you are thinking of getting the razor blades out!

For those who aren't busy washing their hair, consider the following example:

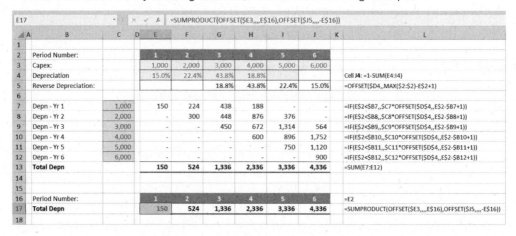

In this example, I have made the depreciation methodology the "Liam Random Method" where I have put arbitrary percentages in cells **E4:I4**, with **J4** the balancing figure. Ignoring row 5 for a moment, the depreciation grid in rows 7:13 calculates the depreciation on a period by period basis using the formula

```
=IF(E$2<$B7,,$C7*OFFSET($D$4,,E$2-$B7+1))
```

in cell **E7** for instance. This formula may look terrible, but the first argument determines whether depreciation should be calculated as in my previous example and the **OFFSET** calculation simply ensures the right percentage is used in each period as the percentages 'move' depending upon which row you are in. You will admit though it is not the world's simplest calculation even though it is still fairly easy to understand if the calculation were simply printed out.

We can get a lot smarter though.

- Consider the Total Depreciation in cell **E13**. This is simply 1,000 x 15%, which is **=E3*E4** or **=SUMPRODUCT(E3,J5)** (even if this does look like over the top).

- Now examine the Total Depreciation in cell **F13**. This is (1,000 x 22.4%) + (2,000 x 15%) or **=SUMPRODUCT(E3:F3,I5:J5)**.

- I shall keep going. Look at the Total Depreciation in cell **G13**. This is (1,000 x 43.8%) + (2,000 x 22.4%) + (3,000 x 15%) or **=SUMPRODUCT(E3:G3,H5:J5)**.

Do you see where I am going? By reversing the depreciation rates in row formula using the formula

$$\text{=OFFSET(\$D4,,MAX(\$2:\$2)-E\$2+1)}$$

in cell **E5** for instance, I have a row vector that I can cross-multiply with the Capex in row 3 using the **SUMPRODUCT** function. The final argument in the formula above merely moves the reference **MAX($2:$2)-E$2+1** columns to the right. This effectively moves Period 1 to Period 6, Period 2 to Period 5 and so on.

I may get more and more product formulae depending upon the number of periods, but the **SUMPRODUCT** formula remains fairly simple, once someone has explained it. The formula in cell **E17** is actually not that bad:

$$\text{=SUMPRODUCT(OFFSET(\$E3,,,,E\$16),OFFSET(\$J5,,,,-E\$16))}$$

It may look horrible to start off with, but it's not that bad when considered systematically. All the two **OFFSET** functions do is keep expanding the two row vectors, the first further right and the second further left. It won't actually be long before this formula is simpler than its long hand equivalent which will not even be a consistent formula period to period.

Back to the Case Study

Still awake? Let me get back to the model. I need to add more inputs to the **General Assumptions** worksheet:

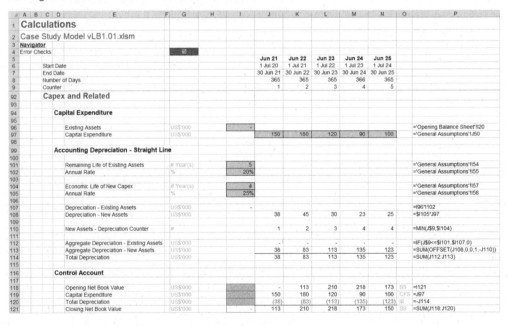

	Jun 21	Jun 22	Jun 23	Jun 24	Jun 25
General Assumptions					
Case Study Model vLB1.01.xlsm					
Navigator					
Error Checks:					
Start Date	1 Jul 20	1 Jul 21	1 Jul 22	1 Jul 23	1 Jul 24
End Date	30 Jun 21	30 Jun 22	30 Jun 23	30 Jun 24	30 Jun 25
Number of Days	365	365	365	366	365
Counter	1	2	3	4	5
Capex and Related					
Capital Expenditure					
Capital Expenditure US$'000	150	180	120	90	100
Accounting Depreciation - Straight Line					
Remaining Life of Existing Assets # Year(s) 5 Year(s)					
Annual Rate % 20%					
Economic Life of New Capex # Year(s) 4 Year(s)					
Annual Rate % 25%					

This 'Capex and Related' section uses more **amounts** to get the data in. In our simple illustration, there are only two asset classes: the existing capital expenditure all with one economic life and new capital expenditure with another economic life. In reality, there may be many asset classes, but it will just be the same formulae copied again and again.

Turning our attention to the **Calculations** worksheet:

	Jun 21	Jun 22	Jun 23	Jun 24	Jun 25	
Calculations						
Case Study Model vLB1.01.xlsm						
Navigator						
Error Checks:						
Start Date	1 Jul 20	1 Jul 21	1 Jul 22	1 Jul 23	1 Jul 24	
End Date	30 Jun 21	30 Jun 22	30 Jun 23	30 Jun 24	30 Jun 25	
Number of Days	365	365	365	366	365	
Counter	1	2	3	4	5	
Capex and Related						
Capital Expenditure						
Existing Assets US$'000	-					='Opening Balance Sheet'!I20
Capital Expenditure US$'000	150	180	120	90	100	='General Assumptions'!J50
Accounting Depreciation - Straight Line						
Remaining Life of Existing Assets # Year(s)	5					='General Assumptions'!I54
Annual Rate %	20%					='General Assumptions'!I55
Economic Life of New Capex # Year(s)	4					='General Assumptions'!I57
Annual Rate %	25%					='General Assumptions'!I58
Depreciation - Existing Assets US$'000	-					=I96*I102
Depreciation - New Assets US$'000	38	45	30	23	25	=$I105*J97
New Assets - Depreciation Counter #	1	2	3	4	4	=MIN(J$9,$I104)
Aggregate Depreciation - Existing Assets US$'000	-	-	-	-	-	=IF(J$9<=$I101,$I107,0)
Aggregate Depreciation - New Assets US$'000	38	83	113	135	123	=SUM(OFFSET(J108,0,0,1,-J110))
Total Depreciation US$'000	38	83	113	135	123	=SUM(J112:J113)
Control Account						
Opening Net Book Value US$'000	-	113	210	218	173 BS	=I121
Capital Expenditure US$'000	150	180	120	90	100 CFS	=J97
Total Depreciation US$'000	(38)	(83)	(113)	(135)	(123) IS	=-J114
Closing Net Book Value US$'000	113	210	218	173	150 BS	=SUM(J118:J120)

Rows 92:105 simply link the data in from the **General Assumptions** worksheet. If you have followed through the worked **SUM(OFFSET)** example from earlier, the formulae in rows 107:114 will look very familiar:

- Cell **I107** simply calculates the depreciation for existing assets, which is the Opening Net Book Value multiplied by the depreciation rate. This is zero presently as the Opening Balance Sheet numbers were all removed.

- For the new assets, cells **J108:N108** are the product of the Capital Expenditure (row 97) and the Annual Rate of depreciation (cell **I105**).

- Row 110 contains the adjusted counter which is used to calculate the **Width** for the **SUM(OFFSET)** function so that assets do not over-depreciate. It is the minimum of the Counter (row 9) and the Economic Life of New Capex (cell **I104**).

- Rows 112:114 then calculate the total depreciation. Row 112 computes this for existing assets using the formula **=IF(J$9<=$I101,$I107,0)**, *i.e.* it brings the depreciation calculated in cell **I107** only for the first **X** years where **X** is the Remaining Life of Existing Assets (cell **I101**).

  Row 113 calculates the depreciation for new assets using the **SUM(OFFSET)** function demonstrated earlier and row 114 simply adds the two calculations together. The Capital Expenditure and Total Depreciation then simply flow into the control account (rows 118:121 below).

So we are back to the control accounts where again we can determine:

1. **Number of calculations that need to be entered into the financial statement so that they balance:** This is always one less than the number of rows in the control account. In this instance it will be four minus one again, which is **three**. This is getting boring, but needs to be done each time as not all control accounts have four line items.

2. **The order to build the calculations into the financial statements:** This is always row 2 first, then row 3, then row 4 and so on. In this instance, this will be Capital Expenditure (which will be a <u>negative</u> number in the Cash Flow Statement), Total Depreciation (Income Statement) and PP&E (Property, Plant and Equipment in the Balance Sheet).

3. **It identifies the key driver:** Line 2 of the control account is always the key driver, so in this case it will be Capital Expenditure. If there were never any Capital Expenditure, there would be no depreciation and without either of these items, the Net Book Value of PP&E would always be zero.

This time, even though we have been working our way down the Income Statement, our first entry is not for the Profit & Loss Account, but the Cash Flow Statement instead:

| J26 | | | f_x | =-Calculations!J119 | | | | | | | |

	A B C D E	F	G H	I	J	K	L	M	N
1	**Cash Flow Statement**								
2	Case Study Model vLB1.01.xlsm								
3	Navigator								
4	Error Checks:		☒						
5					Jun 21	Jun 22	Jun 23	Jun 24	Jun 25
6	Start Date				1 Jul 20	1 Jul 21	1 Jul 22	1 Jul 23	1 Jul 24
7	End Date				30 Jun 21	30 Jun 22	30 Jun 23	30 Jun 24	30 Jun 25
8	Number of Days				365	365	365	366	365
9	Counter				1	2	3	4	5
23									
24	**Investing Cash Flows**								
25	Interest Received	US$'000							
26	Purchases of Non-Current Assets	US$'000			(150)	(180)	(120)	(90)	(100)
27	**Net Investing Cash Flows**	US$'000			(150)	(180)	(120)	(90)	(100)
28									

Remember, this has to be added as a <u>negative</u> number in the Cash Flow Statement. As always, this first entry causes an error in our overall error check. However, two more links should rectify this issue, the first being in the Income Statement:

Income Statement
Case Study Model vLB1.01.xlsm

Navigator

Error Checks:

			Jun 21	Jun 22	Jun 23	Jun 24	Jun 25
Start Date			1 Jul 20	1 Jul 21	1 Jul 22	1 Jul 23	1 Jul 24
End Date			30 Jun 21	30 Jun 22	30 Jun 23	30 Jun 24	30 Jun 25
Number of Days			365	365	365	366	365
Counter			1	2	3	4	5

1. Income Statement

			Jun 21	Jun 22	Jun 23	Jun 24	Jun 25
Revenue	US$'000		400	448	493	532	559
COGS	US$'000		(120)	(134)	(148)	(160)	(168)
Gross Profit	US$'000		280	314	345	373	391
Operating Expenditure	US$'000		(60)	(65)	(68)	(70)	(71)
EBITDA	US$'000		220	249	277	303	320
Depreciation	US$'000		(38)	(83)	(113)	(135)	(123)
EBIT	US$'000		183	166	165	168	198
Interest Expense	US$'000						
NPBT	US$'000		183	166	165	168	198
Tax Expense	US$'000						
NPAT	US$'000		183	166	165	168	198

Finally, the PP&E numbers should be linked in the Balance Sheet:

Balance Sheet
Case Study Model vLB1.01.xlsm

Navigator

Error Checks:

			Jun 21	Jun 22	Jun 23	Jun 24	Jun 25
Start Date			1 Jul 20	1 Jul 21	1 Jul 22	1 Jul 23	1 Jul 24
End Date			30 Jun 21	30 Jun 22	30 Jun 23	30 Jun 24	30 Jun 25
Number of Days			365	365	365	366	365
Counter			1	2	3	4	5
Non-Current Assets							
PP&E	US$'000		113	210	218	173	150
Deferred Tax Assets	US$'000						
Total Non-Current Assets	US$'000		113	210	218	173	150
Total Assets	US$'000		212	382	550	721	920

Now the error check in cell **G4** is showing the Balance Sheet once again balances. Now is probably a good time to save as we continue our progress down the Income Statement.

CHAPTER 10.9: DEBT

Building a Financial Model

15. Move to the next item in the financial statement not yet calculated

16. Return to Point 11

Now to talk about something I have over 25 years' experience of, none of it professionally: debt. Our Income Statement presently looks like this:

1. Income Statement

Revenue	US$'000	400	448	493	532	559
COGS	US$'000	(120)	(134)	(148)	(160)	(168)
Gross Profit	US$'000	280	314	345	373	391
Operating Expenditure	US$'000	(60)	(65)	(68)	(70)	(71)
EBITDA	US$'000	220	249	277	303	320
Depreciation	US$'000	(38)	(83)	(113)	(135)	(123)
EBIT	US$'000	183	166	165	168	198
Interest Expense	US$'000					
NPBT	US$'000	183	166	165	168	198
Tax Expense	US$'000					
NPAT	US$'000	**183**	**166**	**165**	**168**	**198**

The next line item is Interest Expense. However, I cannot calculate this until I consider debt.

Over the years, I have seen various forms of business and project financing, including equity, shareholder loans, senior debt, mezzanine finance, hire purchase, bonds, convertibles, warrants and so on. *Prima facie*, this myriad of financial instruments can obfuscate the uninitiated, but like this last phrase, the jargon can be simplified.

No matter what the financial instrument, the mechanics essentially boil down to two key elements:

- **Return on finance:** the yield to investors or the costs of capital to the recipient of capital (e.g. interest, dividends); *and*

- **Return of finance:** repayments (or conversion) of original capital issued / drawn down.

And it really is as simple as that. The logic behind how the calculations may vary, such as when capital and returns are paid or rolled up, what order it is paid in and so on, but the computations may be summarised by two control accounts (*i.e.* summaries that show / reconcile how the Balance Sheet varies from one period to the next):

Returns of Finance

Opening Balance (e.g. Debt / Equity) b/f	XX	*Previous period Balance Sheet item*
Additions (e.g. drawdowns / issuances / conversions)	X	*Typically in Cash Flow Statement*
Returns on finance rolled up (e.g. "interest capitalised")	X	*Usually a Balance Sheet movement*
Deductions (e.g. repayments / buybacks / conversions)	(X)	*Typically in Cash Flow Statement*
Closing Balance (e.g. Debt / Equity) c/f	**XX**	*Current period Balance Sheet item*

Returns on Finance

Opening Return Payable (e.g. Interest Payable) b/f	XX	*Previous period Balance Sheet item*
Return Accrued (e.g. Interest Expense)	X	*Income Statement or Balance Sheet movement*
Return Paid (e.g. Interest Paid)	(X)	*Cash Flow Statement*
Closing Return Payable (e.g. Interest Payable) c/f	**XX**	*Current period Balance Sheet item*

The 3 R's of Debt Modelling

When both businesses and lenders consider debt they look at two key aspects: risk and return. These are important for credit risk modelling / portfolio analysis, etc. However, when undertaking financial modelling, it is the third 'R' that is often the most important.

In a financial model, risk and return are usually modelled via simple inputs and occasional what-if analysis. Ranking, on the other hand, affects the entire financial structure of the model:

1. Debt Cascade

	Date 1	Date 2	Date 3	Date 4	Date 5	Date 6	Date 7	Date 8	Date 9	Date 10	Date 11	Date 12
Cashflow Before Funding	(16.0)	(0.2)	(0.5)	(0.5)	(0.5)	4.3	6.7	6.8	6.8	7.1	7.3	7.4
Funding	16.0	-	-	-	-	-	-	-	-	-	-	-
Cashflow After Funding	-	(0.2)	(0.5)	(0.5)	(0.5)	4.3	6.7	6.8	6.8	7.1	7.3	7.4
Tax	-	-	-	-	-	-	-	-	-	-	-	-
Cashflow Available before WC Funding	-	(0.2)	(0.5)	(0.5)	(0.5)	4.3	6.7	6.8	6.8	7.1	7.3	7.4
Working Capital Facility Funding	-	0.2	0.5	0.5	0.5	-	-	-	-	-	-	-
Cash Flow Available for Debt Service (CFADS)	-	-	-	-	-	4.3	6.7	6.8	6.8	7.1	7.3	7.4
Senior Debt Service	-	(0.4)	(0.4)	(0.4)	(0.4)	(1.7)	(1.7)	(1.7)	(1.7)	(1.7)	(1.7)	(1.7)
Cashflow Available for Debt Service Reserve Account	-	(0.4)	(0.4)	(0.4)	(0.4)	2.6	5.0	5.1	5.1	5.4	5.6	5.7
Debt Service Reserve Account	-	4.0	0.0	-	-	(2.6)	(0.8)	0.0	0.0	(0.0)	(0.0)	0.0
Cashflow Available for Mezzanine	-	3.6	(0.4)	(0.4)	(0.4)	-	4.2	5.1	5.1	5.4	5.6	5.7
Mezzanine Debt Service	-	(2.7)	-	-	-	-	(3.1)	(3.8)	(3.8)	(4.1)	(4.2)	(4.3)
Cashflow Available for WC Facility	-	0.9	(0.4)	(0.4)	(0.4)	-	1.0	1.3	1.3	1.4	1.4	1.4
Working Capital Facility	-	(0.2)	(0.0)	(0.0)	(0.0)	-	(1.0)	(0.5)	-	-	-	-
Cashflow Available for Equity	-	0.7	(0.4)	(0.4)	(0.5)	-	-	0.7	1.3	1.4	1.4	1.4
Dividends	-	5.3	5.2	5.2	5.3	(2.0)	(2.0)	(2.2)	(2.3)	(3.0)	(3.1)	(3.4)
Net Cashflow	-	5.9	4.7	4.8	4.8	(2.0)	(2.0)	(1.4)	(1.0)	(1.6)	(1.7)	(1.9)
Cash Balance B/f	-	-	5.9	10.7	15.4	20.2	18.3	16.2	14.8	13.8	12.1	10.4
Cash Balance C/f	-	5.9	10.7	15.4	20.2	18.3	16.2	14.8	13.8	12.1	10.4	8.4

As the above graphic shows, if the order of service repaying capital changes, the entire logic will change. This may affect interest / debt service cover ratios (see below). It is important in scoping any such model that the order is understood and how it will be affected by such factors as:

- Breach of covenants
- Conversion of financial instruments
- Breach of covenants or other ratios
- Liquidation / insolvency.

It is not correct to assume that the order of financing will never change.

Capitalised vs. Rolled Up

There is confusion between the jargon used by the banking industry and accountants when considering debt mechanics:

Scenario	Banking term	Accounting term
Interest is not paid (either by agreement or due to insufficient funds) and is added to the outstanding principal for future interest calculations	Interest capitalised	Interest rolled-up
Interest is not added to the balance but is paid (although there may be a slight timing issue)	Interest amortised (principal is amortised similarly)	**When accrued:** interest expense **When paid:** interest paid
Regardless of whether paid or not in reality, interest meets the criteria specified in the relevant accounting standards to be held in the Balance Sheet	n/a	Interest capitalised
When capitalised under accounting rules, the interest charge is released to the P&L over the life of a project on some agreed equitable basis	n/a	Interest amortised

When holding conversations with financiers, be sure you are on the same page before building interest into a financial model. Debt term sheets can be difficult enough to understand without unnecessarily adding to the complexity.

Avoiding Circularity

When a formula refers back to its own cell, either directly or indirectly, it is called a circular reference. Microsoft Excel cannot automatically calculate all open workbooks when one or more of them contains a circular reference and usually will put zero as the default value in the cell(s) instead.

You can remove a circular reference, or you can have Excel calculate each cell involved in the circular reference using the 'calculate iterations' feature. This requires you enabling iterations:

* Go to Excel Options (**ALT + T + O**)

* Choose 'Formulas' from the list in the left hand column

* In the first section, 'Calculation options', ensure the check box 'Enable iterative calculation' is checked

* Amend the Maximum Number of Iterations (maximum is still 32,767) as required

* Amend the Maximum Change as required (the smaller the number, the longer it will take for Excel to calculate the answer)

* Click 'OK'.

Various problems may arise with circular references:

- Many users will agree that circular arguments can cause the Excel file to become unstable and even crash;

- When solved, Excel may give one solution when there may be several, only one of which is correct in the given circumstances. If the problem is not fully understood, the danger is an incorrect solution may be accepted;

- If Excel stops calculating after a given number of iterations / when the difference between iterations becomes miniscule, users expect the resulting values to be a solution when it may not be (you must always verify that the value reported provides the result required).

Therefore, circular arguments are not recommended, although it is conceded on occasion there may be no alternative viable solution. Try to calculate interest wherever possible on opening balances rather than average or closing balances. This will remove the need to consider circularity.

Calculating Interest without Circularity

In a financial model, it is commonplace to have to calculate interest. For this illustration, let's assume we are calculating interest received (rather than paid, but is conceptually equivalent) on the business's average cash balance for certain periods of time (it could just as simply be interest paid on a debt balance, etc.). This gives rise to a perceived circular logic:

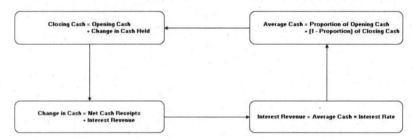

This problem can be solved algebraically in, er, a relatively straightforward manner without creating circularities – and is therefore our recommended approach.

I apologise for the following mathematical assault (for those not interested in the derivation, simply skip to the end) – unfortunately, Excel modelling sometimes boils down to solving simultaneous equations!

Let:

OB = opening cash balance for the period

CB = closing cash balance for the period

M = non-interest cash movement for the period (including tax)

I = interest cash movement for the period (excluding tax)

r = interest rate

t = tax rate (it is assumed this cannot equal 100%)

x = proportion into the period that the non-interest cash movements are assumed to occur, e.g.

- If x = 0%, this means the movement occurred at the start of the period
- If x = 100%, this means that the movement occurred at the end of the period
- If x = 50%, this means that the movement occurred midway through the period

So, $$CB = OB + M + I(1-t) \quad \text{and}$$
$$I(1-t) = (x.OB + (1-x).CB).r.(1-t) \quad \text{so (as } t \neq 100\%)$$
$$I = (x.OB + (1-x).CB).r$$
$$= (x.OB + (1-x).(OB + M + I(1-t))).r$$
$$= OB.r + (1-x).M.r + (1-x).I.(1-t).r$$

Therefore,

$$I.(1-(1-x).(1-t).r) = OB.r + (1-x).M.r$$

$$\Leftrightarrow I = \frac{(OB + (1-x).M).r}{(1-(1-x).(1-t).r)}$$

Hence, we can calculate interest from this final equation and have no circular references or need to use Goal Seek, *e.g.*

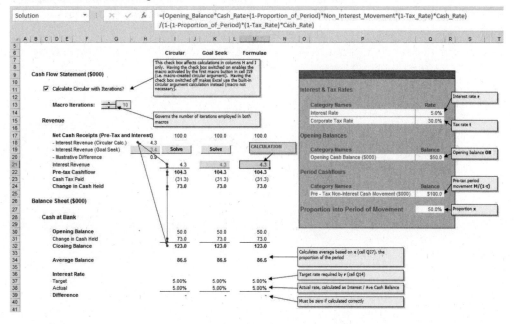

Back to the Case Study

How do I follow that? Would you believe I posted a variation of the above simultaneous equation solution on our company website and for several years it was the most popular webpage (thanks Mum)? Here, I shall assume only one debt instrument (violin?) and that interest is calculated on the opening balance, but I will use the above derivation for the interest receivable calculation.

I need to add more inputs to the **General Assumptions** worksheet:

				E	F	G	H	I	J	K	L	M	N
1	**General Assumptions**												
2	Case Study Model vLB1.01.xlsm												
3	Navigator												
4	Error Checks:						☑							
5										Jun 21	Jun 22	Jun 23	Jun 24	Jun 25
6		Start Date								1 Jul 20	1 Jul 21	1 Jul 22	1 Jul 23	1 Jul 24
7		End Date								30 Jun 21	30 Jun 22	30 Jun 23	30 Jun 24	30 Jun 25
8		Number of Days								365	365	365	366	365
9		Counter								1	2	3	4	5
60														
61		**Debt and Related**												
62		Movements are assumed to occur ar the end of each period.												
63		Interest is assumed to be paid in the following period.												
64														
65			**Debt**											
66														
67				Debt Drawdowns	US$'000					20	20	-	-	-
68				Debt Repayments	US$'000					-	-	15	25	10
69														
70			**Interest**											
71														
72				Interest Rate	%					6%	7%	7%	8%	8%
73														
74			**Interest Receivable**	%										
75														
76				Interest Receivable Rate	%					1%	1%	1%	1%	1%
77														
78				Proportion into Period of Movement	%		50%							

On this occasion, Debt Drawdowns and Debt Repayments are hard coded inputs (**amounts**), but in a more complex model, these formulae may be based on the forecast cash position of the company (*i.e.* they may need to be calculated).

Similarly, the interest assumptions all use the **percentage** method of input. These may be more sophisticated in real life too as swap rates, base rates, hedging instruments *etc.* may all come into play.

Turning our attention to the **Calculations** worksheet, let me first look at the Debt section:

	A B C D	E	F G	H	I	J	K	L	M	N	O	P
1	**Calculations**											
2	Case Study Model vLB1.01.xlsm											
3	**Navigator**											
4	Error Checks:		☑									
5						Jun 21	Jun 22	Jun 23	Jun 24	Jun 25		
6	Start Date					1 Jul 20	1 Jul 21	1 Jul 22	1 Jul 23	1 Jul 24		
7	End Date					30 Jun 21	30 Jun 22	30 Jun 23	30 Jun 24	30 Jun 25		
8	Number of Days					365	365	365	366	365		
9	Counter					1	2	3	4	5		
123												
124	**Debt and Related**											
125	Movements are assumed to occur ar the end of each period.											
126	Interest is assumed to be paid in the following period.											
127												
128	**Debt**											
129												
130	Debt Drawdowns	US$'000				20	20	-	-	-		='General Assumptions'!J67
131	Debt Repayments	US$'000				-	-	15	25	10		='General Assumptions'!J68
132												
133	**Control Account**											
134												
135	Opening Debt	US$'000				-	20	40	25	-	BS	=I138
136	Debt Drawdowns	US$'000				20	20	-	-	-	CFS	=J130
137	Debt Repayments	US$'000				-	-	(15)	(25)	(10)	CFS	=-J131
138	Closing Debt	US$'000				20	40	25	-	(10)	BS	=SUM(J135:J137)
139												
140	**Interest**											
141												
142	Interest Rate	%				6%	7%	7%	8%	8%		='General Assumptions'!J72
143												
144	Opening Debt	US$'000				-	20	40	25	-		=J135
145												
146	Days in Period	#				365	365	365	366	365		=J$8
147	Days in Standard Year	#				365	365	365	365	365		=Days_in_Yr
148	Proportion of Year	%				100%	100%	100%	100%	100%		=MIN(J146/J147,1)
149												
150	Interest	US$'000				-	1	3	2	-		=J144*J142*J148
151												
152	**Control Account**											
153												
154	Opening Interest Payable	US$'000				-	-	1	3	2	BS	=I157
155	Interest Expense	US$'000				-	1	3	2	-	IS	=J150
156	Interest Paid	US$'000				-	-	(1)	(3)	(2)	CFS	=-J154
157	Closing Interest Payable	US$'000				-	1	3	2	-	BS	=SUM(J154:J156)

In the comments section of 'Debt and Related' (either rows 62 and 63 of the **General Assumptions** worksheet or rows 125 and 126 of the **Calculations** worksheet), it states that movements in debt are assumed to occur at the end of each period. This means that interest should be calculated wholly on the opening balances. Further, interest is assumed to be paid in the next period – and that gives me the opportunity to show you a neat trick for the control account there too. Gosh, you might actually consider I put some thought into this case study...

Has there ever been an easier control account than the Return **of** Finance control account here (rows 135 to 138)? Debt Drawdowns and Debt Repayments have been linked through in rows 1030 and 131, and then all that is required for the Debt Repayments in the control account (row 137) is to negate this calculation. Once the Opening Debt (cell I138) has been linked in from the **Opening Balance Sheet**, the control account runs itself.

The reason for this is that creating a Debt control account is easy. In practice, calculating the drawdowns and repayments is the hard part. Often, debt may only be borrowed if there is borrower capacity and then it is subject to various stipulated financial ratios not being breached. It can be quite complex – but I could write a book just on Debt alone. The intention of this text is to provide an introduction to the world of financial modelling.

Therefore, returning to our Debt control account, we may deduce:

1. **Number of calculations that need to be entered into the financial statement so that they balance:** This is always one less than the number of rows in the control account. In this instance it will be four minus one just for a change, which is **three**. Blah, blah, blah.

2. **The order to build the calculations into the financial statements:** This is always row 2 first, then row 3, then row 4 and so on. In this instance, this will be Debt Drawdowns

(Cash Flow Statement), Debt Repayments (also Cash Flow Statement) and Debt (Non-Current Liability in the Balance Sheet). Do you see that even though we have been using the Income Statement to "drive" us through the model, I have finally come to a control account that does not impact upon the Income Statement at all?

3. **It identifies the key driver:** Line 2 of the control account is always the key driver, so in this case it will be Debt Drawdowns. If there were never any debt borrowed, there would be no repayments and therefore, no debt balance.

Therefore, our first two entries are entered into the Cash Flow Statement:

	J30			×	✓	fx		=Calculations!J136				

	A	B	C	D	E	F	G	H	I	J	K	L	M	N
1	**Cash Flow Statement**													
2	Case Study Model vLB1.01.xlsm													
3	Navigator													
4	Error Checks:						☒							
5										Jun 21	Jun 22	Jun 23	Jun 24	Jun 25
6		Start Date								1 Jul 20	1 Jul 21	1 Jul 22	1 Jul 23	1 Jul 24
7		End Date								30 Jun 21	30 Jun 22	30 Jun 23	30 Jun 24	30 Jun 25
8		Number of Days								365	365	365	366	365
9		Counter								1	2	3	4	5
28														
29		**Financing Cash Flows**												
30		Debt Drawdowns				US$'000				20	20	-	-	-
31		Debt Repayments				US$'000				-	-	(15)	(25)	(10)
32		Ordinary Equity Issuances				US$'000								
33		Ordinary Equity Buybacks				US$'000								
34		Dividends Paid				US$'000								
35		**Net Financing Cash Flows**				US$'000				20	20	(15)	(25)	(10)
36														
37		**Net Increase / (Decrease) in Cash Held**				US$'000				54	84	138	184	208

Debt Drawdowns and Debt Repayments are easily linked into rows 30:31. This represents two calculations, but we need to enter the final (third) one for the error check (cell **G4**) to reset. This requires a link to the **Balance Sheet** worksheet:

	J35			×	✓	fx		=Calculations!J138				

	A	B	C	D	E	F	G	H	I	J	K	L	M	N
1	**Balance Sheet**													
2	Case Study Model vLB1.01.xlsm													
3	Navigator													
4	Error Checks:						☑							
5										Jun 21	Jun 22	Jun 23	Jun 24	Jun 25
6		Start Date								1 Jul 20	1 Jul 21	1 Jul 22	1 Jul 23	1 Jul 24
7		End Date								30 Jun 21	30 Jun 22	30 Jun 23	30 Jun 24	30 Jun 25
8		Number of Days								365	365	365	366	365
9		Counter								1	2	3	4	5
33														
34		**Non-Current Liabilities**												
35		Debt				US$'000				20	40	25	-	(10)
36		Deferred Tax Liabilities				US$'000								
37		**Total Non-Current Liabilities**				US$'000				20	40	25	-	(10)
38														
39		**Total Liabilities**				US$'000				50	73	61	39	31
40														
41		**Net Assets**				US$'000				183	349	513	681	879

Once Debt is linked in here, the Balance Sheet balances once more.

Now, before I return my attention to the Return on Capital control account, I wish to take a closer inspection of the control account we have just created:

	Control Account								
133	Control Account								
134									
135	Opening Debt	US$'000			-	20	40	25	- BS
136	Debt Drawdowns	US$'000			20	20	-	-	- CFS
137	Debt Repayments	US$'000			-	-	(15)	(25)	(10) CFS
138	Closing Debt	US$'000		-	20	40	25	-	(10) BS

Observant readers may have noticed that the Closing Debt in the final period is negative, *i.e.* we have overpaid. In a real model we would have put in a check to ensure the model alerts us if this were the case, but there's no harm done as I have noticed it anyway in this instance. We need to take care of overpayments. Banks charge us enough without us offering up Christmas presents.

Be careful. The initial opening balance is zero in this control account as we made the Opening Balance Sheet zero earlier. The truth is,

	A	B	C	D	E	F	G	H	I	J	K
1	**Opening Balance Sheet**										
2	Case Study Model vLB1.01.xlsm										
3	Navigator										
4	Error Checks:						☑		Jun 20		
10											
11	**1. Opening Balance Sheet**										
12											
13			Current Assets								
14				Cash		US$'000					250
15				Accounts Receivable		US$'000					50
16				Other Current Assets		US$'000					10
17				Total Current Assets		US$'000					310
18											
19			Non-Current Assets								
20				PP&E		US$'000					450
21				Deferred Tax Assets		US$'000					75
22				Total Non-Current Assets		US$'000					525
23											
24			Total Assets			US$'000					835
25											
26			Current Liabilities								
27				Accounts Payable		US$'000					30
28				Interest Payable		US$'000					20
29				Dividends Payable		US$'000					15
30				Tax Payable		US$'000					40
31				Other Current liabilities		US$'000					10
32				Total Current liabilities		US$'000					115
33											
34			Non-Current Liabilities								
35				Debt		US$'000					150
36				Deferred Tax Liabilities		US$'000					25
37				Total Non-Current Liabilities		US$'000					175
38											
39			Total Liabilities			US$'000					290
40											
41			Net Assets			US$'000					545
42											
43											
44			Equity								
45				Ordinary Equity		US$'000					300
46											
47				NPAT		US$'000					-
48				Dividends Declared		US$'000					-
49				Retained Profits		US$'000					245
50			Total Equity			US$'000					545
51											

the real opening balance is $150,000 (see cell **K35**) once the opening balances are restored.

All we have done in our control account is repay $10,000 of this amount over five years.

One control account down, two to go. Next up is calculating Interest Expense:

					Jun 21	Jun 22	Jun 23	Jun 24	Jun 25	
1	**Calculations**									
2	Case Study Model vLB1.01.xlsm									
3	Navigator									
4	Error Checks		☑							
5					Jun 21	Jun 22	Jun 23	Jun 24	Jun 25	
6	Start Date				1 Jul 20	1 Jul 21	1 Jul 22	1 Jul 23	1 Jul 24	
7	End Date				30 Jun 21	30 Jun 22	30 Jun 23	30 Jun 24	30 Jun 25	
8	Number of Days				365	365	365	366	365	
9	Counter				1	2	3	4	5	
140	**Interest**									
141										
142	Interest Rate	%			6%	7%	7%	8%	8%	='General Assumptions'!J72
143										
144	Opening Debt	US$'000			-	20	40	25	-	=J135
145										
146	Days in Period	#			365	365	365	366	365	=J$8
147	Days in Standard Year	#			365	365	365	365	365	=Days_in_Yr
148	Proportion of Year	%			100%	100%	100%	100%	100%	=MIN(J146/J147,1)
149										
150	Interest	US$'000			-	1	3	2	-	=J144*J142*J148
151										
152	**Control Account**									
153										
154	Opening Interest Payable	US$'000			-	-	1	3	2 BS	=I157
155	Interest Expense	US$'000			-	1	3	2	- IS	=J150
156	Interest Paid	US$'000			-	-	(1)	(3)	(2) CFS	=-J154
157	Closing Interest Payable	US$'000	-		-	1	3	2	- BS	=SUM(J154:J156)

I am showing this extract again, so that you don't have to keep flicking pages. The Interest Rate reference and the Opening Debt balances are straightforward enough, but rows 146:148 are worth a second look.

In many territories / debt agreements, interest is calculated on a pro-rated daily basis. Interest may be calculated on a simple basis (*i.e.* only considering the principal or opening debt balance for the period) or on a compounding basis (*i.e.* including past unpaid interest in future interest calculations). Either way, the proportion of a period is required. Row 146 references the number of days in the period (from row 8), whilst row 147 shows the number of days in a non-leap year, regardless of whether the year is a leap year (this is standard practice in financial modelling). Row 148 calculates the proportion of the year by dividing the number of days in the period by the number of days in a "standard" year, restricting the quotient so that the ratio may never exceed one.

To calculate the interest rate for the period, it then depends upon the basis:

- **Simple: = Interest Rate p.a. x Proportion of Year**
- **Compounding: = (1 + Interest Rate)$^{\text{Proportion of Year}}$ – 1**

In our example, I am using the **simple** basis in row 150.

This brings me nicely to the control account. With the opening balance coming from the **Opening Balance Sheet** worksheet and Interest Expense from row 150, the only sophistication is Interest Paid in row 156. With a one period delay, I could use the following formula:

$$\text{=-IF(J\$9=1,'Opening Balance Sheet'!\$I\$28,I155)}$$

where **'Opening Balance Sheet'!$I$28** is the reference to the Opening Balance Sheet (Interest Payable). However, there is a much simpler option when the delay is one period:

$$\text{=-J154}$$

Yes, that's all it is. By referencing the opening balance, I bring in everything but the current period's Interest Expense, which will get paid in the next period, *i.e.* there will be a one period delay. Simple.

So now we are in a position to inspect our second of three control accounts:

1. **Number of calculations that need to be entered into the financial statement so that they balance:** Three.

2. **The order to build the calculations into the financial statements:** This is always row 2 first, then row 3, then row 4 and so on. In this instance, this will be Interest Expense (finally, we return to the Income Statement but remember this will be a <u>negative</u> number), Interest Paid (Cash Flow Statement) and Interest Payable (Balance Sheet).

3. **It identifies the key driver:** Line 2 of the control account is always the key driver, so in this case it will be Interest Expense.

Therefore, our first entry is for the Income Statement:

J23			fx	=Calculations!J155					
	A B C	D	E F	G H I	J	K	L	M	N
1	**Income Statement**								
2	Case Study Model vLB1.01.xlsm								
3	Navigator								
4	Error Checks:								
5					Jun 21	Jun 22	Jun 23	Jun 24	Jun 25
6	Start Date				1 Jul 20	1 Jul 21	1 Jul 22	1 Jul 23	1 Jul 24
7	End Date				30 Jun 21	30 Jun 22	30 Jun 23	30 Jun 24	30 Jun 25
8	Number of Days				365	365	365	366	365
9	Counter				1	2	3	4	5
10									
11	**1. Income Statement**								
12									
13	Revenue		US$'000		400	448	493	532	559
14	COGS		US$'000		(120)	(134)	(148)	(160)	(168)
15	**Gross Profit**		US$'000		280	314	345	373	391
16									
17	Operating Expenditure		US$'000		(60)	(65)	(68)	(70)	(71)
18	**EBITDA**		US$'000		220	249	277	303	320
19									
20	Depreciation		US$'000		(38)	(83)	(113)	(135)	(123)
21	**EBIT**		US$'000		183	166	165	168	198
22									
23	Interest Expense		US$'000		-	(1)	(3)	(2)	-
24	**NPBT**		US$'000		183	165	162	166	198
25									
26	Tax Expense		US$'000						
27	**NPAT**		US$'000		**183**	**165**	**162**	**166**	**198**
28									

Do note that the reference to the control account is negative and that the error check has triggered. Then I will turn my attention to the Cash Flow Statement:

Cash Flow Statement

Case Study Model vLB1.01.xlsm

			Jun 21	Jun 22	Jun 23	Jun 24	Jun 25
Navigator							
Error Checks:		☒					
			Jun 21	Jun 22	Jun 23	Jun 24	Jun 25
Start Date			1 Jul 20	1 Jul 21	1 Jul 22	1 Jul 23	1 Jul 24
End Date			30 Jun 21	30 Jun 22	30 Jun 23	30 Jun 24	30 Jun 25
Number of Days			365	365	365	366	365
Counter			1	2	3	4	5
Operating Cash Flow							
Cash Receipts	US$'000		334	440	485	526	554
Direct Cash Payments	US$'000		(90)	(131)	(145)	(157)	(166)
Indirect Cash Payments	US$'000		(60)	(65)	(68)	(70)	(71)
Cash Payments	US$'000		(150)	(196)	(212)	(226)	(237)
Interest Paid	US$'000		-	-	(1)	(3)	(2)
Tax Paid	US$'000						
Net Operating Cash Flow	US$'000		184	244	272	297	316

This leaves me with just the Balance Sheet:

Balance Sheet

Case Study Model vLB1.01.xlsm

			Jun 21	Jun 22	Jun 23	Jun 24	Jun 25
Navigator							
Error Checks:		☑					
			Jun 21	Jun 22	Jun 23	Jun 24	Jun 25
Start Date			1 Jul 20	1 Jul 21	1 Jul 22	1 Jul 23	1 Jul 24
End Date			30 Jun 21	30 Jun 22	30 Jun 23	30 Jun 24	30 Jun 25
Number of Days			365	365	365	366	365
Counter			1	2	3	4	5
Current Liabilities							
Accounts Payable	US$'000		30	33	36	39	41
Interest Payable	US$'000		-	1	3	2	-
Dividends Payable	US$'000						
Tax Payable	US$'000						
Other Current liabilities	US$'000						
Total Current liabilities	US$'000		30	34	39	41	41

That is actually Debt completed, but we had Interest Receivable in the same section:

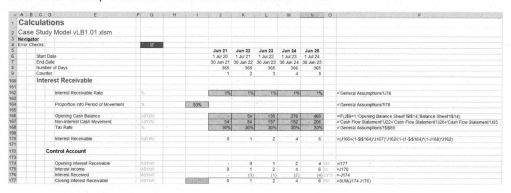

	A	B	C	D	E	F	G	H	I	J	K	L	M	N
1	**General Assumptions**													
2	Case Study Model vLB1.01.xlsm													
3	<u>Navigator</u>													
4	Error Checks:						☑							
5										Jun 21	Jun 22	Jun 23	Jun 24	Jun 25
6		Start Date								1 Jul 20	1 Jul 21	1 Jul 22	1 Jul 23	1 Jul 24
7		End Date								30 Jun 21	30 Jun 22	30 Jun 23	30 Jun 24	30 Jun 25
8		Number of Days								365	365	365	366	365
9		Counter								1	2	3	4	5
73														
74		**Interest Receivable**				%								
75														
76			Interest Receivable Rate			%				1%	1%	1%	1%	1%
77														
78			Proportion into Period of Movement			%		50%						
79														
80														

I think we ought to finish this section off by completing this as well.

It may be giving you nightmares, but you will recall earlier in this section that

$$ I = \frac{(OB + (1-x).M).r}{(1-(1-x).(1-t).r)} $$

So time for a deep breath as we visit the calculations:

	A	B	C	D	E	F	G	H	I	J	K	L	M	N	O	P
1	**Calculations**															
2	Case Study Model vLB1.01.xlsm															
3	Navigator															
4	Error Checks:						☑									
5										Jun 21	Jun 22	Jun 23	Jun 24	Jun 25		
6		Start Date								1 Jul 20	1 Jul 21	1 Jul 22	1 Jul 23	1 Jul 24		
7		End Date								30 Jun 21	30 Jun 22	30 Jun 23	30 Jun 24	30 Jun 25		
8		Number of Days								365	365	365	366	365		
9		Counter								1	2	3	4	5		
160		**Interest Receivable**														
161																
162			Interest Receivable Rate			%				1%	1%	1%	1%	1%		='General Assumptions'!J76
163																
164			Proportion into Period of Movement			%		50%								='General Assumptions'!I78
165																
166			Opening Cash Balance			A$'000				-	54	138	276	460		=IF(J$9=1,'Opening Balance Sheet'!$I$14,'Balance Sheet'!I$14)
167			Non-Interest Cash Movement			A$'000				54	84	137	182	206		='Cash Flow Statement'!J22+'Cash Flow Statement'!J26+'Cash Flow Statement'!J35
168			Tax Rate			%				30%	30%	30%	30%	30%		='General Assumptions'!I$85
169																
170			Interest Receivable			A$'000				0	1	2	4	6		=(J166+(1-$I$164)*J167)*J162/(1-(1-$I$164)*(1-J168)*J162)
171																
172		**Control Account**														
173																
174			Opening Interest Receivable			A$'000				-	0	1	2	4	BS	=I177
175			Interest Income			A$'000				0	1	2	4	6	IS	=J170
176			Interest Received			A$'000				-	(0)	(1)	(2)	(4)	CFS	=-J174
177			Closing Interest Receivable			A$'000				0	1	2	4	6	BS	=SUM(J174:J176)

Bringing in the Interest Receivable Rate and the Proportion into Period of Movement references (cells **J162:N162** and **I164** respectively) are simple enough. The Opening Cash Balance in row 166 is simply a variation on the linked cash item in the **Balance Sheet** worksheet. For example, the formula in cell **J166** of the **Calculations** worksheet is

=IF(J$9=1,'Opening Balance Sheet'!$I$14,'Balance Sheet'!I$14)

which takes the Opening Balance Sheet number in the first period or simply the Cash figure in the Balance Sheet for the last period otherwise.

The Non-Interest Cash Movement (including tax) is not particularly difficult, you just have to be careful how you reference, given Interest Received will form part of the Cash Flow Statement. We just need everything else. The formula in cell **J167** is

='Cash Flow Statement'!J22+'Cash Flow Statement'!J26+'Cash Flow Statement'!J35

which equates to = **Net Operating Cash Flows + Purchases of Non-Current Assets + Net Financing Cash Flows**. With the Tax Rate a linked cell, this leaves us with the following horror for Interest Receivable, using the first period as (cell **J170**) as our illustration:

$$=(J166+(1-\$I\$164)^*J167)^*J162/(1-(1-\$I\$164)^*(1-J168)^*J162)$$

However, if you follow the cell references you will immediately realise it is the algebraic solution derived above.

The control account is then plain sailing, being extremely similar to the last one for Interest Expense. Since Interest Receivable is simply the opposite of Interest Payable, there is no opening balance: it has already been used in the Interest Payable and if it were referenced again, this would form a double count. Interest Income is derived from the formula above and Interest Received (being one period later) links to the opening balance as explained in the trick above.

This control account thus conveys the following information:

1. **Number of calculations that need to be entered into the financial statement so that they balance:** Three (yawn!).

2. **The order to build the calculations into the financial statements:** This is always row 2 first, then row 3, then row 4 and so on. In this instance, this will be Interest Income (Income Statement), Interest Received (as a <u>positive</u> number in the Cash Flow Statement) and Interest Payable (Balance Sheet). All will be netted off – unusually – against their Interest Expense counterparts.

3. **It identifies the key driver:** Line 2 of the control account is always the key driver, so in this case it will be Interest Income.

Therefore, our first entry is for the Income Statement once more:

J23					f_x	=-Calculations!J155+Calculations!J175				

	A B C	D	E F	G	H I	J	K	L	M	N
1	**Income Statement**									
2	Case Study Model vLB1.01.xlsm									
3	Navigator									
4	Error Checks:									
5						Jun 21	Jun 22	Jun 23	Jun 24	Jun 25
6	Start Date					1 Jul 20	1 Jul 21	1 Jul 22	1 Jul 23	1 Jul 24
7	End Date					30 Jun 21	30 Jun 22	30 Jun 23	30 Jun 24	30 Jun 25
8	Number of Days					365	365	365	366	365
9	Counter					1	2	3	4	5
10										
11	**1. Income Statement**									
12										
13	Revenue		US$'000			400	448	493	532	559
14	COGS		US$'000			(120)	(134)	(148)	(160)	(168)
15	**Gross Profit**		US$'000			280	314	345	373	391
16										
17	Operating Expenditure		US$'000			(60)	(65)	(68)	(70)	(71)
18	**EBITDA**		US$'000			220	249	277	303	320
19										
20	Depreciation		US$'000			(38)	(83)	(113)	(135)	(123)
21	**EBIT**		US$'000			183	166	165	168	198
22										
23	Interest Expense		US$'000			0	(0)	(1)	2	6
24	**NPBT**		US$'000			183	166	164	170	203
25										
26	Tax Expense		US$'000							
27	**NPAT**		US$'000			183	166	164	170	203
28										

Noting that the error check has triggered, as you can see this has been <u>added</u> to the reference already included for Interest Expense. Sometimes, this entry will actually be included as its own line item (Interest Income) before EBITDA. The second entry is for the Cash Flow Statement:

J25				× ✓	fx	=-Calculations!J176					

	A B C D E	F	G H I	J	K	L	M	N
1	**Cash Flow Statement**							
2	Case Study Model vLB1.01.xlsm							
3	Navigator							
4	Error Checks:		☒					
5				Jun 21	Jun 22	Jun 23	Jun 24	Jun 25
6	Start Date			1 Jul 20	1 Jul 21	1 Jul 22	1 Jul 23	1 Jul 24
7	End Date			30 Jun 21	30 Jun 22	30 Jun 23	30 Jun 24	30 Jun 25
8	Number of Days			365	365	365	366	365
9	Counter			1	2	3	4	5
23								
24	**Investing Cash Flows**							
25	Interest Received	US$'000		-	0	1	2	4
26	Purchases of Non-Current Assets	US$'000		(150)	(180)	(120)	(90)	(100)
27	**Net Investing Cash Flows**	US$'000		(150)	(180)	(119)	(88)	(96)

Adding Interest Received into the Cash Flow Statement completes the Net Investing Cash Flows section. With the error check still reporting an issue, let me fix this by adding in the final entry to the Balance Sheet:

J28				× ✓	fx	=Calculations!J157-Calculations!J177				

	A B C D	E	F G H I	J	K	L	M	N
1	**Balance Sheet**							
2	Case Study Model vLB1.01.xlsm							
3	Navigator							
4	Error Checks:		☑					
5				Jun 21	Jun 22	Jun 23	Jun 24	Jun 25
6	Start Date			1 Jul 20	1 Jul 21	1 Jul 22	1 Jul 23	1 Jul 24
7	End Date			30 Jun 21	30 Jun 22	30 Jun 23	30 Jun 24	30 Jun 25
8	Number of Days			365	365	365	366	365
9	Counter			1	2	3	4	5
25								
26	**Current Liabilities**							
27	Accounts Payable	US$'000		30	33	36	39	41
28	Interest Payable	US$'000		(0)	0	1	(2)	(6)
29	Dividends Payable	US$'000						
30	Tax Payable	US$'000						
31	Other Current Liabilities	US$'000						
32	**Total Current Liabilities**	US$'000		29	33	37	37	36

Interest Receivable has been <u>deducted</u> from Interest Payable. This final link has made the Balance Sheet balance again. Some modellers may not net off in this way:

- Given three of these five figures are negative, they may appear instead (sign reversed) as Interest Receivable in the Current Assets section.

- Interest Receivable may be displayed separately in the Current Assets section.

- The net figure will be shown as a positive number as Net Interest Receivable (Current Assets) when Interest Receivable is greater than or equal to Interest Payable and as a positive number as Net Interest Payable (Current Liabilities) otherwise.

Well, that was a big section and I really only scraped the surface. I feel like another book may be in the offing. In the meantime, what's next? Now that's a taxing question...

CHAPTER 10.10: TAXATION

Building a Financial Model

15. Move to the next item in the financial statement not yet calculated

16. Return to Point 11

The Income Statement is nearly complete:

1. Income Statement						
Revenue	US$'000	400	448	493	532	559
COGS	US$'000	(120)	(134)	(148)	(160)	(168)
Gross Profit	US$'000	280	314	345	373	391
Operating Expenditure	US$'000	(60)	(65)	(68)	(70)	(71)
EBITDA	US$'000	220	249	277	303	320
Depreciation	US$'000	(38)	(83)	(113)	(135)	(123)
EBIT	US$'000	183	166	165	168	198
Interest Expense	US$'000	0	(0)	(1)	2	6
NPBT	US$'000	183	166	164	170	203
Tax Expense	US$'000					
NPAT	US$'000	183	166	164	170	203

They say there's only two things certain in life: death and taxes. I can't help but wonder, what happens if the taxman dies..?

This book is only going to cover company (income) tax. Indirect taxes such as Goods and Services Tax (GST) or Value Added Tax (VAT) vary too much from territory to territory and are not usually included in a model as essentially the company is collecting taxes on behalf of the State. Similarly, state and federal taxes, capital gains taxes, mining resources tax, "need a new tax" tax *etc.* are to be ignored as the rules for how they are calculated varies under different circumstances. For the purposes of simplification, I am going to assume a very simple income tax with a flat tax rate of 30%.

Now this tax may be a simple or a complex calculation. Consider the following Interest Expense control account:

This all makes sense, now let me change it to Tax:

Opening Interest Payable	10	Opening Tax Payable	10
Interest Expense	20	Tax Expense	20
Interest Paid	(10)	Tax Paid	(10)
Closing Interest Payable	20	Closing Tax Payable	97

Pardon? What happened there? Welcome to the wonderful world of **Accounting v. Taxation**. Accounting is all about producing a true and fair view of the world (although the terms "true" and "fair" are never actually defined anywhere), whereas you could say that the Tax authorities do not give two figs for true and fair. *You* could say that. I won't. I might get taxed.

To be "fair", there are many more accounting auditors than their tax counterparts. It is important for shareholders and stakeholders to have a true and fair view of a company's accounts in order to form a view for the basis of making future decisions. Tax authorities, by and large, tend to look for a simple prescriptive rule book, *e.g.* if companies A and B both make the same profit from the same sources with similar cost and financing structures, they should pay a similar level of tax. Therefore, there tend to be simplifying rules.

Accounting works on an accruals basis, dealing with revenue and cost recognition which may differ from tax. This will give rise to **timing differences**, often referred to as **temporary differences**. But there are other types of difference too. If I choose not to pay tax, get taken to court and I am fined, that would be a legitimate expense to me and would have to be shown in my Income Statement. However, I can't claim this as a tax deduction – how cool would that be..?

This would be an example of a **permanent difference**, that is, an amount that will never reconcile between accounting and taxation. Any income or expenditure derived from breaking the law is usually excluded from a tax calculation. Other examples may be costs or income assessable to a different type of tax, and so on.

It is not always bad news. It usually is though. You might wish to consider **Liam's Law of Tax**:

Liam's Law of Tax

Often in tax legislation, rules may be ambiguous. If this occurs, calculate the tax to be paid under the different possibilities. Whichever is the worst for you is the one that was meant.

I have yet to find an exception to this rule and remember:

All rules have exceptions, except this one.

It's best not to think about that too much.

Most of the time, expenses are disallowed, but sometimes revenue is non-assessable. For example, if you are creating a forecast of worldwide revenues for all subsidiaries of a group of companies, all external income must be included for accounting purposes. That may not be the case for tax: Tax treaties, double taxation relief and other rulings may be in place that permanently exclude some income from the tax calculation.

Permanent differences need to be recognised in a model as these must be adjusted for in calculating the Tax Expense. For example,

	$	$
Net Profit Before Tax		1,000
Adjustments:		
Deduct: Non-Assessable Revenue	(100)	
Add Back: Disallowable Expenses	200	
Accounting Taxable Profit	1,100	
Tax Expense (@ 30%)		(330)
Net Profit After Tax		670

The permanent differences are adjusted for to derive an **Accounting Taxable Profit** of $1,100. The tax rate of 30% is applied to this to generate a Tax Expense of $330, leaving a Net Profit After Tax (NPAT) of $670. The effective tax rate here is 33%, being 330 / 1,000.

Timing differences on the other hand lead to **deferred tax** issues instead as these differences will eventually reconcile. The most common cause of a timing difference is depreciation, *e.g.*

Assumptions

Economic Life	4 years
Tax Life	4 years

	Accounting	Tax	Difference	Tax Effect
Multiplier	n/a	2.0x		
Depreciation Rate	25%	50%		
	$	$	$	$
Capex	1,000	1,000		
Depn: Yr 1	(250)	(500)	250	75
	750	500		
Depn: Yr 2	(250)	(250)	-	-
	500	250		
Depn: Yr 3	(250)	(125)	(125)	(38)
	250	125		
Depn: Yr 4	(250)	(125)	(125)	(38)
	-	-	-	-

In this example, the $1,000 non-current asset in question has both an economic life and a tax life of four years. There is absolutely no reason why these values should coincide, but I am keeping it simple for this example.

No residual value is assumed. For accounting purposes, depreciation is calculated on a straight line basis of 25% p.a. For tax purposes, I am assuming a double declining balance method, which would be 50% of the remaining balance. Assuming the asset is disposed of at the end of four years, the final year's tax balance is written down to zero.

Let me compare the differences (the first of the two shaded columns in the figure above). In the first year, more depreciation may be claimed for the tax calculation than under the comparable accounting calculation. This will lead to a lower taxable profit, meaning less tax to pay. This is usually what happens in the early years of tax depreciation: companies benefit from these **accelerated capital allowances**, sometimes referred to as **ACAs**.

In our example, the profit in the first period would be $250 higher. With a tax rate of 30%, this would mean the tax to pay would be $75 less. This is real money. Whilst it all balances out in the end (*i.e.* the total differences for the actual amount and the tax effected amounts sum to zero), taking into account the time value of money, this would be of benefit to a company.

Why would a Tax authority do this? Remember, Tax authorities work for the government of the territory to which they pertain and they want to encourage economic investment. By providing beneficial capital allowances, companies may be encouraged to spend more in a territory, providing more jobs, economic growth and ultimately more taxable income.

The tax effect shows what the benefit is worth – measurements of worth are shown in the Balance Sheet at their tax effected (*i.e.* after tax) amounts. If we receive a benefit of $75 now and the differences eventually sum to zero, in the future we will have to pay $75 more than accounting forecasts will show. Since it is in the future, this will be a **tax deferred liability**.

This all ties up with the patented *Liam Theory of Smiley Faces*:

Who would have equated tax with smiley faces? Only a madman, I suspect. A deferred tax liability provides a benefit now, but will cause a greater cost later. Deferred tax assets create bad news now, but good news later.

The most common cause of a deferred tax asset occurs when losses are made. If I make a $1m loss this year, will the Tax authority send me flowers, provide counselling and kiss it all better? Will they reimburse me 30%? Careful, these are trick questions. Depending upon how you answer, you may be sectioned in your nearest Mental Health facility.

No. In most jurisdictions (if not all), the Tax authority will not provide any sort of "refund". However, most territories will allow you to memorialise the loss to use against future profits. Some countries may allow you to use the loss to offset profits in earlier periods. Some may restrict their use (so they may only be carried forward several years and / or against similar activities that caused the loss and / or assume the majority of owners remain the same). This is not a book on the intricacies of taxation. I will be keeping it very simple.

If you make a loss of $1m, the Tax Credit for the period (assuming a 30% tax rate) would be 30%. That is correct as it is associated with the period. However, you will not receive any cash back. Assume you make $3m profit the following year. Normally, you would have to pay $900,000 tax on this. However, in many territories you can offset the loss against this profit and pay tax on only $2m, *i.e.* $600,000. The loss is worth $300,000 as this is the amount it has saved. This could have been calculated in the first instance as $1m x 30%, which is the tax effected amount. Even though there is pain now, you could recognise this as a **deferred tax asset** on the Balance Sheet – as long as it may be assumed you will make a profit in future years / before the tax credit expires, if applicable.

Accounting regulations suggest you discount this amount to take into account the time value of money, but nowhere can you find guidance on how this might be calculated. It doesn't really matter though. For financial modelling and management accounts, deferred tax assets are calculated, but you will seldom see one in statutory accounts.

The reason for this is that auditors have to sign off on statutory accounts. If they acknowledge a deferred tax asset on the face of the Balance Sheet, they are signing off that the company that has just made a loss will make a profit again in the future. Would you be prepared to bet everything you own that this would be the case? No? Neither would auditors. There have been case law precedents where investors have successfully sued auditors for displaying deferred tax assets on a company that subsequently went into liquidation. The investors argued that they could infer auditors were signing off that the company would be profitable again in the future and relied upon this inference in making their investment decisions. Courts have agreed. Hence deferred tax assets are as likely to be seen on the face of statutory accounts as white is likely to be the new black (if that happens, be extra careful on zebra crossings).

Deferred tax is a definite Friday afternoon accounting rule. I say this because:

- Deferred tax assets and deferred tax liabilities are always non-current even if they will crystallise three nano-seconds from now.

- They should be netted off in the accounts (why would you net depreciation differences against tax losses?).

There are other causes of deferred tax, such as revaluations, but that is for another book. I think we have more than enough to go on with. I can now revisit the tax control account from earlier:

Opening Tax Payable	10
Tax Expense	20
Tax Paid	(10)
Movement in Deferred Tax Assets	(15)
Movement in Deferred Tax Liabilities	92
Closing Tax Payable	97

The reason the control account didn't balance was because we hadn't completed it. There were line items missing, namely the **Movement** in Deferred Tax Assets and the **Movement** in Deferred Tax Liabilities. I have stressed **Movement** because Deferred Tax Assets and Deferred Tax Liabilities are to be found in the Balance Sheet and amounts in this financial statement must be shown cumulatively. We will need to keep a running total (*i.e.* more control accounts) of these balances.

I think we are good to go!

Back to the Case Study

I think it is time to construct some inputs for the **General Assumptions** worksheet:

						Jun 21	Jun 22	Jun 23	Jun 24	Jun 25
1	**General Assumptions**									
2	Case Study Model vLB1.01.xlsm									
3	Navigator									
4	Error Checks:		☑							
5						Jun 21	Jun 22	Jun 23	Jun 24	Jun 25
6	Start Date					1 Jul 20	1 Jul 21	1 Jul 22	1 Jul 23	1 Jul 24
7	End Date					30 Jun 21	30 Jun 22	30 Jun 23	30 Jun 24	30 Jun 25
8	Number of Days					365	365	365	366	365
9	Counter					1	2	3	4	5
80										
81	**Taxation**									
82										
83	**Tax Rate**									
84										
85	Tax Rate	%		30%						
86										
87	**Permanent Differences**									
88										
89	Non-Assessable Revenue	US$'000				25	25	25	25	25
90	Disallowable Expenses	US$'000				40	16	25	30	50
91										
92	**Tax Depreciation (Declining Balance)**									
93										
94	Declining Balance Multiplier	x		2.00						
95										
96	Remaining Life of Tax Assets	# Year(s)		5 Year(s)						
97	Annual Rate	%		40%						
98										
99	Tax Asset Life of New Capex	# Year(s)		4 Year(s)						
100	Annual Rate	%		50%						
101										
102	**DTA**									
103	DTAs are assumed to arise through losses carried forward.									
104										
105	DTA	US$'000		-						
106										
107	**DTL**									
108	DTLs are assumed to arise through depreciation timing differences.									
109										
110	DTL	US$'000		-						
111										
112	**Tax Payable and Paid**									
113										
114	Payment Delay	# Year(s)		1 Year(s)						
115										

There is nothing particularly controversial with regard to these assumptions, now I have put them in context. In reality, Non-Assessable Revenue and Disallowable Expenses (rows 89 band 90) may need to be provided by a tax expert and may need the construction of a linked or separate financial model.

Do note also that the Deferred Tax Assets and Deferred Tax Liabilities (cells **I105** and **I110** respectively) are not inputs. These are linked from the figures supplied in the **Opening Balance Sheet**.

The **Calculations** sheet is involved, but nevertheless understandable now that I have explained the rudiments of taxation. I shall break it up into bite-sized chunks:

						Jun 21	Jun 22	Jun 23	Jun 24	Jun 25	
1	**Calculations**										
2	Case Study Model vLB1.01.xlsm										
3	Navigator										
4	Error Checks			☑							
5						Jun 21	Jun 22	Jun 23	Jun 24	Jun 25	
6	Start Date					1 Jul 20	1 Jul 21	1 Jul 22	1 Jul 23	1 Jul 24	
7	End Date					30 Jun 21	30 Jun 22	30 Jun 23	30 Jun 24	30 Jun 25	
8	Number of Days					365	365	365	366	365	
9	Counter					1	2	3	4	5	
180	**Taxation**										
182	**Permanent Differences**										
184	Non-Assessable Revenue	US$'000			25	25	25	25	25	='General Assumptions'!J89
185	Disallowable Expenses	US$'000			40	16	25	30	50	='General Assumptions'!J90
187	**Accounting Taxable Profit**										
189	NPBT	US$'000			183	166	164	170	203	='Income Statement'!J24
190	Deduct: Non-Assessable Revenue	US$'000			(25)	(25)	(25)	(25)	(25)	=-J184
191	Add: Disallowable Expenses	US$'000			40	16	25	30	50	=J185
192	**Accounting Taxable Profit**	US$'000			198	157	164	175	228	=SUM(J189:J191)
194	Tax Rate	%			30%	30%	30%	30%	30%	='General Assumptions'!$I$85
196	**Tax Expense / (Credit)**	US$'000			59	47	49	52	68	=J194*J192

As usual, the calculations start with a link through of the assumptions and Net Profit Before Tax. Non-Assessable Revenue is deducted and Disallowable Expenses are added back, giving rise to Accounting Taxable as before. Multiplying this by the prevailing tax rate gives rise to the Tax Expense or, if negative, Tax Credit.

This last point is important. Some modellers make the mistake of restricting the Tax Expense to a non-negative figure. This is incorrect. Tax Expense is displayed in the Income Statement. This is calculated on an accruals basis. If a loss has been made, the associated Tax Credit should be displayed for that period as that is the period to which it relates.

Continuing our journey down the **Calculations** worksheet:

							Jun 21	Jun 22	Jun 23	Jun 24	Jun 25	
1	**Calculations**											
2	Case Study Model vLB1.01.xlsm											
3	Navigator											
4	Error Checks			☑								
5							Jun 21	Jun 22	Jun 23	Jun 24	Jun 25	
6	Start Date						1 Jul 20	1 Jul 21	1 Jul 22	1 Jul 23	1 Jul 24	
7	End Date						30 Jun 21	30 Jun 22	30 Jun 23	30 Jun 24	30 Jun 25	
8	Number of Days						365	365	365	366	365	
9	Counter						1	2	3	4	5	
198	**Tax Depreciation (Declining Balance)**											
200	**Capital Expenditure**											
201	Existing Assets	US$'000			-						
202	Capital Expenditure	US$'000			150	180	120	90	100	=J97
204	Declining Balance Multiplier	x	2.00x								='General Assumptions'!I94
206	Remaining Life of Tax Assets	# Year(s)	5								='General Assumptions'!I96
207	Annual Rate	%	40%								='General Assumptions'!I97
209	Tax Asset Life of New Capex	# Year(s)	4								='General Assumptions'!I99
210	Annual Rate	%	50%								='General Assumptions'!I100
212	Depreciation - Existing Assets	US$'000			-	-	-	-	-	=($H212-SUM($I212:I212))*IF(J$9=$I206,1,$I207)
213	Depreciation - New Capex: Year 1	US$'000	150		75	38	19	19	-	=IF(J$9>=$E213,($H213-SUM($I213:I213))*IF(J$9=$I$209+$E213-1,1,$I$210),0)
214	Depreciation - New Capex: Year 2	US$'000	180		-	90	45	23	23	=IF(J$9>=$E214,($H214-SUM($I214:I214))*IF(J$9=$I$209+$E214-1,1,$I$210),0)
215	Depreciation - New Capex: Year 3	US$'000	120		-	-	60	30	15	=IF(J$9>=$E215,($H215-SUM($I215:I215))*IF(J$9=$I$209+$E215-1,1,$I$210),0)
216	Depreciation - New Capex: Year 4	US$'000	90		-	-	-	45	23	=IF(J$9>=$E216,($H216-SUM($I216:I216))*IF(J$9=$I$209+$E216-1,1,$I$210),0)
217	Depreciation - New Capex: Year 5	US$'000	100		-	-	-	-	50	=IF(J$9>=$E217,($H217-SUM($I217:I217))*IF(J$9=$I$209+$E217-1,1,$I$210),0)
218	Tax Depreciation	US$'000	640	553	75	128	124	116	110	=SUM(J212:J217)
220	**Accounting Depreciation**										
222	Accounting Depreciation	US$'000		490	38	83	113	135	123	=J114
224	**Depreciation Timing Difference**										
226	Accounting Depreciation	US$'000			38	83	113	135	123	=J222
227	Tax Depreciation	US$'000			(75)	(128)	(124)	(116)	(110)	=-J218
228	Depreciation Timing Difference	US$'000			(38)	(45)	(11)	19	13	=SUM(J226:J227)
230	Tax Rate	%			30%	30%	30%	30%	30%	='General Assumptions'!$I$85
232	Movement in DTLs	US$'000			11	14	3	(6)	(4)	=-J230*J228
234	Opening DTLs	US$'000			-	11	25	28	23	=I236
235	Movement in DTLs	US$'000			11	14	3	(6)	(4)	=J232
236	Closing DTLs	US$'000			11	25	28	23	19 BS	=SUM(J234:J235)

The first section of this screenshot calculates the Tax Depreciation on a declining balance basis, from first principles rather than using one of the Excel formulae from previously. I have no plans to go through this in detail as I discussed depreciation previously.

I do wish to draw your attention to the styled empty cells in cells **I212:I217**. These cells must be blank for the formula in the depreciation grid to work. For example, the formula in cell **J213**,

> **=IF(J$9>=$E213,($H213-SUM($I213:I213))*IF(J$9=$I$209+$E213-1,1,$I$210),0)**

checks that depreciation is only calculated for periods after the asset has been purchased. It then takes the amount not yet depreciated (**$H213-SUM($I213:I213)**) and multiplies it by the depreciation rate unless it is the final period of the tax life, when the remainder is amortised. If cell **I213** were populated, this formula would not work correctly: it has to be blank to calculate the depreciation correctly for the first period.

This Tax Depreciation is then compared to the Accounting Depreciation previously calculated in row 114 and the difference between the two is then multiplied by the tax rate to determine the movement in the Deferred Tax Liability for that period. The movement will be used in the overall control account at the end of the section, but rows 234:236 keep a running total of the closing balance so that the corresponding amount can be included in the Balance Sheet:

Movement in DTLs	US$'000			11	14	3	(6)	(4)
Opening DTLs	US$'000			-	11	25	28	23
Movement in DTLs	US$'000			11	14	3	(6)	(4)
Closing DTLs	US$'000		-	11	25	28	23	19 BS

We need to remember this when incorporating the figures into the financial statements at the end of this Tax computation. Moving forward:

	A B C D	E	F G	H	I	J	K	L	M	N	O	P
1	Calculations											
2	Case Study Model vLB1.01.xlsm											
3	Navigator											
4	Error Checks:		☑									
5						Jun 21	Jun 22	Jun 23	Jun 24	Jun 25		
6	Start Date					1 Jul 20	1 Jul 21	1 Jul 22	1 Jul 23	1 Jul 24		
7	End Date					30 Jun 21	30 Jun 22	30 Jun 23	30 Jun 24	30 Jun 25		
8	Number of Days					365	365	365	366	365		
9	Counter					1	2	3	4	5		
238	Tax Payable and Paid	US$'000										
239												
240	Accounting Taxable Profit	US$'000				198	157	164	175	228		=J192
241	Depreciation Timing Difference	US$'000				(38)	(45)	(11)	19	13		=J228
242	Taxable Profit / (Loss) Before Losses	US$'000				160	112	153	193	241		=SUM(J240:J241)
243	Tax Losses Used	US$'000				-	-	-	-	-		=J263
244	Taxable Profit / (Loss) after Losses	US$'000				160	112	153	193	241		=SUM(J242:J243)
245	Tax Rate	%				30%	30%	30%	30%	30%		=J230
246	Tax Payable for Period	US$'000				48	34	46	58	72		=MAX(J244*J245,0)
247												
248	Payment Delay	# Year(s)		1 Year(s)								='General Assumptions'!I114
249												
250	Opening Tax Payable	US$'000				-	48	34	46	58		=I253
251	Tax Payable for Period	US$'000				48	34	46	58	72		=J246
252	Tax Paid	US$'000				-	(48)	(34)	(46)	(58)		=-IF(J$9-$I248<0,0,OFFSET(J251,0,-$I248))
253	Closing Tax Payable	US$'000		-		48	34	46	58	72		=SUM(J250:J252)
254												
255	Tax Losses Memorandum											
256												
257	DTA	US$'000		-								='General Assumptions'!I105
258	Tax Rate	%		30%								='General Assumptions'!I85
259	Opening Tax Losses	US$'000		-								
260												
261	Opening Tax Losses	US$'000				-	-	-	-	-		=I264
262	Tax Losses Created During the Period	US$'000				-	-	-	-	-		=-MIN(J242,0)
263	Tax Losses Used	US$'000				-	-	-	-	-		=IF(J242>0,-MAX(MIN(J242,J261),0),0)
264	Closing Tax Losses	US$'000				-	-	-	-	-		=SUM(J261:J263)
265												
266	Movement in Tax Losses	US$'000				-	-	-	-	-		=SUM(J262:J263)
267												
268	Tax Rate	%				30%	30%	30%	30%	30%		=J230
269												
270	Movement in DTAs	US$'000				-	-	-	-	-		=J268*J266
271												
272	Opening DTAs	US$'000				-	-	-	-	-		=I274
273	Movement in DTAs	US$'000				-	-	-	-	-		=J270
274	Closing DTAs	US$'000		-		-	-	-	-	-	BS	=SUM(J272:J273)

The Tax Payable and Paid section now summarises the above. It restates the Accounting Taxable Profit, makes an adjustment for the difference between accounting and tax depreciation as computed to generate the Taxable Profit / (Loss) Before Losses.

In this calculation, I assume that tax losses may be carried forward indefinitely against all taxable income. This may not always be the case. You need to consult a tax professional in your territory to work out the tax rules which will apply in your model. As always, this is about concepts, not formulae.

The Tax Losses have been memorialised in rows 255:266. The Deferred Tax Asset (DTA) referenced in cell **I257** comes indirectly from the **Opening Balance Sheet** and it is assumed that the entire DTA here is attributed to prior tax losses carried forward. Therefore, dividing this number by the prevailing tax rate (30% here) converts the tax effected amount back to the opening tax loss. Losses made in the period are then added to this balance and any profits in the period may be netted off against any remaining losses.

Given we have made our Opening Balance Sheet zero, there will be no opening losses as the DTA will also be zero. Since this company is profitable in all periods, the Tax Losses Memorandum will have a zero value control account, which causes problems for checking the formula. It is often worthwhile at this point to modify numbers to create an opening loss and a loss in at least one period to confirm that this account is working as intended.

The Movement in Tax Losses is then multiplied by the tax rate to generate the Movement in Deferred Tax Assets. As with Deferred Tax Liabilities, the movement will be used in the overall control account at the end of the section, but rows 272:274 keep a running total of the closing balance so that the corresponding amount can be included in the Balance Sheet:

Movement in DTAs	US$'000			-	-	-	-	-
Opening DTAs	US$'000			-	-	-	-	-
Movement in DTAs	US$'000			-	-	-	-	-
Closing DTAs	US$'000		-	-	-	-	-	- BS

Apologies this graphic is not very informative in this instance!

Once satisfied with these calculations, any losses can be used in row 243 to reduce the Taxable Profit / (Loss). This final figure is then multiplied by the tax rate to derive the Tax Payable for Period. This number <u>cannot</u> be negative. The Tax authorities will not give a company money for making a loss.

The control account in rows 250:253 summarises the Tax Payable. The opening and closing balances must reconcile to the corresponding balances in the overall control account at the end of the section. Tax Payable is referenced from row 246 and the Tax Paid allows for the delay specified in cell **I248** by implementing an **OFFSET** function.

All that is now needed is to summarise the above in the overall control account:

					Jun 21	Jun 22	Jun 23	Jun 24	Jun 25		
Calculations											
Case Study Model vLB1.01 pg263.xlsm											
Navigator											
Error Checks:		☑									
					Jun 21	Jun 22	Jun 23	Jun 24	Jun 25		
	Start Date				1 Jul 20	1 Jul 21	1 Jul 22	1 Jul 23	1 Jul 24		
	End Date				30 Jun 21	30 Jun 22	30 Jun 23	30 Jun 24	30 Jun 25		
	Number of Days				365	365	365	366	365		
	Counter				1	2	3	4	5		
	Control Account										
	Opening Tax Payable		US$'000		-	48	34	46	58	BS	=I283
	Tax Expense / (Credit)		US$'000		59	47	49	52	68	IS	=J196
	Tax Paid		US$'000		-	(48)	(34)	(46)	(58)	CFS	=J252
	Movement in DTAs		US$'000		-	-	-	-	-		=J270
	Movement in DTLs		US$'000		(11)	(14)	(3)	6	4		=J232
	Closing Tax Payable		US$'000	-	48	34	46	58	72	BS	=SUM(J278:J282)

The entries of this control account are just references to the line items calculated earlier. Do note that the Movement in Deferred Tax Liabilities (row 282) should be negated and that rows 281 and 282 are not to be referenced to the Balance Sheet (their cumulative counterparts in rows 274 and 236 should be used instead). Again, a real model would also check the opening balances of the Tax Payable and Paid control account against the overall one. Given this is a simple case study, I have not added these checks in. So sue me.

Let me evaluate this control account:

1. **Number of calculations that need to be entered into the financial statement so that they balance:** Something different! There are six lines in this control account, so ignoring the top line, this means there are five calculations in this instance. We may have a different number, but it is still an odd number: so much for double entry.

2. **The order to build the calculations into the financial statements:** This is always row 2 first, then row 3, then row 4 and so on. In this instance, this will be Tax Expense (our final visit to the Income Statement ensuring this is a <u>negative</u> number), Tax Paid (Cash Flow Statement), Closing DTAs rather than the Movement in DTAs (Balance Sheet), Closing DTLs rather than the Movement in DTLs (Balance Sheet) and Tax Payable (Balance Sheet).

3. **It identifies the key driver:** Line 2 of the control account is always the key driver, so in this case it will be Tax Expense.

Therefore, our first entry is for the Income Statement once more, remembering to negate the Tax Expense reference:

| J26 | | | ▼ | : | ✕ | ✓ | *fx* | =Calculations!J279 | | | | |

Income Statement (cell reference bar)

	A	B	C	D	E	F	G	H	I	J	K	L	M	N	O
1	**Income Statement**														
2	Case Study Model vLB1.01.xlsm														
3	Navigator														
4	Error Checks:						☒								
5										Jun 21	Jun 22	Jun 23	Jun 24	Jun 25	
6		Start Date								1 Jul 20	1 Jul 21	1 Jul 22	1 Jul 23	1 Jul 24	
7		End Date								30 Jun 21	30 Jun 22	30 Jun 23	30 Jun 24	30 Jun 25	
8		Number of Days								365	365	365	366	365	
9		Counter								1	2	3	4	5	
10															
11		**1. Income Statement**													
12															
13		Revenue			US$'000					400	448	493	532	559	
14		COGS			US$'000					(120)	(134)	(148)	(160)	(168)	
15		**Gross Profit**			US$'000					280	314	345	373	391	
16															
17		Operating Expenditure			US$'000					(60)	(65)	(68)	(70)	(71)	
18		**EBITDA**			US$'000					220	249	277	303	320	
19															
20		Depreciation			US$'000					(38)	(83)	(113)	(135)	(123)	
21		**EBIT**			US$'000					183	166	165	168	198	
22															
23		Interest Expense			US$'000					0	(0)	(1)	2	6	
24		**NPBT**			US$'000					183	166	164	170	203	
25															
26		Tax Expense			US$'000					(59)	(47)	(49)	(52)	(68)	
27		**NPAT**			US$'000					123	119	115	117	135	

Tax Paid will then complete the Net Operating Cash Flow section of the Cash Flow Statement:

| J21 | | | ▼ | : | ✕ | ✓ | *fx* | =Calculations!J280 | | | | |

	A	B	C	D	E	F	G	H	I	J	K	L	M	N
1	**Cash Flow Statement**													
2	Case Study Model vLB1.01.xlsm													
3	Navigator													
4	Error Checks:						☒							
5										Jun 21	Jun 22	Jun 23	Jun 24	Jun 25
6		Start Date								1 Jul 20	1 Jul 21	1 Jul 22	1 Jul 23	1 Jul 24
7		End Date								30 Jun 21	30 Jun 22	30 Jun 23	30 Jun 24	30 Jun 25
8		Number of Days								365	365	365	366	365
9		Counter								1	2	3	4	5
10														
11		**1. Cash Flow Statement**												
12														
13		**Direct Cash Flow Statement**												
14														
15		**Operating Cash Flow**												
16			Cash Receipts			US$'000				334	440	485	526	554
17			Direct Cash Payments			US$'000				(90)	(131)	(145)	(157)	(166)
18			Indirect Cash Payments			US$'000				(60)	(65)	(68)	(70)	(71)
19			Cash Payments			US$'000				(150)	(196)	(212)	(226)	(237)
20			Interest Paid			US$'000				-	-	(1)	(3)	(2)
21			Tax Paid			US$'000				-	(48)	(33)	(46)	(58)
22			**Net Operating Cash Flow**			US$'000				184	196	239	251	258

The remaining three line items are all for the Balance Sheet. Firstly, we require the Closing DTA from row 274 of the **Calculations** worksheet:

J21				✕	✓	*fx*	=Calculations!J274				

	A	B	C	D	E	F	G	H	I	J	K	L	M	N
1	**Balance Sheet**													
2	Case Study Model vLB1.01.xlsm													
3	Navigator													
4	Error Checks:						☒							
5										Jun 21	Jun 22	Jun 23	Jun 24	Jun 25
6		Start Date								1 Jul 20	1 Jul 21	1 Jul 22	1 Jul 23	1 Jul 24
7		End Date								30 Jun 21	30 Jun 22	30 Jun 23	30 Jun 24	30 Jun 25
8		Number of Days								365	365	365	366	365
9		Counter								1	2	3	4	5
10														
11	**1. Balance Sheet**													
12														
13		**Current Assets**												
14		Cash				US$'000				54	90	195	332	483
15		Accounts Receivable				US$'000				66	74	81	87	92
16		Other Current Assets				US$'000								
17		**Total Current Assets**				US$'000				120	164	276	419	575
18														
19		**Non-Current Assets**												
20		PP&E				US$'000				113	210	218	173	150
21		Deferred Tax Assets				US$'000				-	-	-	-	-
22		**Total Non-Current Assets**				US$'000				113	210	218	173	150
23														
24		**Total Assets**				US$'000				232	374	493	592	725
25														

Secondly, the Closing DTL from row 236 of the **Calculations** worksheet is added into Non-Current Liabilities:

	A	B	C	D	E	F	G	H	I	J	K	L	M	N
1	**Balance Sheet**													
2	Case Study Model vLB1.01.xlsm													
3	Navigator													
4	Error Checks:						☒							
5										Jun 21	Jun 22	Jun 23	Jun 24	Jun 25
6		Start Date								1 Jul 20	1 Jul 21	1 Jul 22	1 Jul 23	1 Jul 24
7		End Date								30 Jun 21	30 Jun 22	30 Jun 23	30 Jun 24	30 Jun 25
8		Number of Days								365	365	365	366	365
9		Counter								1	2	3	4	5
33														
34		**Non-Current Liabilities**												
35		Debt				US$'000				20	40	25	-	(10)
36		Deferred Tax Liabilities				US$'000				11	25	28	23	19
37		**Total Non-Current Liabilities**				US$'000				31	65	53	23	9
38														
39		**Total Liabilities**				US$'000				61	98	91	61	46
40														
41		**Net Assets**				US$'000				172	275	402	531	679

Still the error check in cell **G4** remains active. Our final entry, Tax Payable in Current Liabilities will make the Balance Sheet balance once more:

J30			× ✓	f_x	=Calculations!J283				

	A B C D	E	F G H I	J	K	L	M	N
1	**Balance Sheet**							
2	Case Study Model vLB1.01.xlsm							
3	Navigator							
4	Error Checks:		☑					
5				**Jun 21**	**Jun 22**	**Jun 23**	**Jun 24**	**Jun 25**
6	Start Date			1 Jul 20	1 Jul 21	1 Jul 22	1 Jul 23	1 Jul 24
7	End Date			30 Jun 21	30 Jun 22	30 Jun 23	30 Jun 24	30 Jun 25
8	Number of Days			365	365	365	366	365
9	Counter			1	2	3	4	5
25								
26	**Current Liabilities**							
27	Accounts Payable	US$'000		30	33	36	39	41
28	Interest Payable	US$'000		(0)	1	1	(1)	(4)
29	Dividends Payable	US$'000						
30	Tax Payable	US$'000		48	33	46	58	72
31	Other Current Liabilities	US$'000						
32	**Total Current Liabilities**	US$'000		77	67	83	96	109

Was that all a bit taxing? Well fear not, the Income Statement is now complete:

1. Income Statement

Revenue	US$'000	400	448	493	532	559
COGS	US$'000	(120)	(134)	(148)	(160)	(168)
Gross Profit	US$'000	280	314	345	373	391
Operating Expenditure	US$'000	(60)	(65)	(68)	(70)	(71)
EBITDA	US$'000	220	249	277	303	320
Depreciation	US$'000	(38)	(83)	(113)	(135)	(123)
EBIT	US$'000	183	166	165	168	198
Interest Expense	US$'000	0	(1)	(1)	1	4
NPBT	US$'000	183	166	163	169	202
Tax Expense	US$'000	(59)	(47)	(49)	(52)	(68)
NPAT	US$'000	123	119	114	117	134

It is now time to turn our attention to the next financial statement…

CHAPTER 10.11: EQUITY

Building a Financial Model

1. Once the Income Statement is completed, consider the first line item on the Cash Flow Statement not yet linked.

I have just shown that the Income Statement is complete. With corresponding line items already entered on other financial statements, I need only fill in the blanks. To revert to my Goldilocks analogy from earlier, Baby Bear is dead (it's a violent re-telling of the story), so we move on to Mummy Bear – the Cash Flow Statement:

1. Cash Flow Statement

Direct Cash Flow Statement

Operating Cash Flow						
Cash Receipts	US$'000	334	440	485	526	554
Direct Cash Payments	US$'000	(90)	(131)	(145)	(157)	(166)
Indirect Cash Payments	US$'000	(60)	(65)	(68)	(70)	(71)
Cash Payments	US$'000	(150)	(196)	(212)	(226)	(237)
Interest Paid	US$'000	-	-	(1)	(3)	(2)
Tax Paid	US$'000	-	(48)	(33)	(46)	(58)
Net Operating Cash Flow	US$'000	**184**	**196**	**239**	**251**	**258**
Investing Cash Flows						
Interest Received	US$'000	-	0	1	1	3
Purchases of Non-Current Assets	US$'000	(150)	(180)	(120)	(90)	(100)
Net Investing Cash Flows	US$'000	**(150)**	**(180)**	**(119)**	**(89)**	**(97)**
Financing Cash Flows						
Debt Drawdowns	US$'000	20	20	-	-	-
Debt Repayments	US$'000	-	-	(15)	(25)	(10)
Ordinary Equity Issuances	US$'000					
Ordinary Equity Buybacks	US$'000					
Dividends Paid	US$'000					
Net Financing Cash Flows	US$'000	**20**	**20**	**(15)**	**(25)**	**(10)**
Net Increase / (Decrease) in Cash Held	US$'000	**54**	**36**	**104**	**137**	**151**

The Cash Flow Statement is almost complete. There are only three lines left and they all relate to Equity, *i.e.* owner's funds.

Discussing financing general earlier, you may recall I stated that no matter what the financial instrument, the mechanics essentially boil down to two key elements:

- **Return on finance:** the yield to investors or the costs of capital to the recipient of capital (e.g. interest, dividends); *and*

- **Return of finance:** repayments (or conversion) of original capital issued / drawn down.

The aim is to create the two appropriate control accounts:

Returns of Finance

Opening Balance (e.g. Debt / Equity) b/f	XX	*Previous period Balance Sheet item*
Additions (e.g. drawdowns / issuances / conversions)	X	*Typically in Cash Flow Statement*
Returns on finance rolled up (e.g. "interest capitalised")	X	*Usually a Balance Sheet movement*
Deductions (e.g. repayments / buybacks / conversions)	(X)	*Typically in Cash Flow Statement*
Closing Balance (e.g. Debt / Equity) c/f	**XX**	*Current period Balance Sheet item*

Returns on Finance

Opening Return Payable (e.g. Interest Payable) b/f	XX	*Previous period Balance Sheet item*
Return Accrued (e.g. Interest Expense)	X	*Income Statement or Balance Sheet movement*
Return Paid (e.g. Interest Paid)	(X)	*Cash Flow Statement*
Closing Return Payable (e.g. Interest Payable) c/f	**XX**	*Current period Balance Sheet item*

For Equity, the Return **of** Equity is Equity Buybacks (the drawdown is Equity Issuance); the Return **on** Equity is the Dividends Received and, where quoted the gain on the price of any shares (Share Capital). Equity is the most basic form of capital. At the end of the day, somebody must own the company.

For the purposes of our case study, the final inputs on the **General Assumptions** worksheet are as follows:

	A	B	C	D	E	F	G	H	I	J	K	L	M	N
1	**General Assumptions**													
2	Case Study Model vLB1.01.xlsm													
3	Navigator													
4	Error Checks:						☑							
5										Jun 21	Jun 22	Jun 23	Jun 24	Jun 25
6				Start Date						1 Jul 20	1 Jul 21	1 Jul 22	1 Jul 23	1 Jul 24
7				End Date						30 Jun 21	30 Jun 22	30 Jun 23	30 Jun 24	30 Jun 25
8				Number of Days						365	365	365	366	365
9				Counter						1	2	3	4	5
116														
117			**Ordinary Equity and Related**											
118														
119				**Ordinary Equity**										
120														
121					Equity Issuances	US$'000				15	25	-	10	-
122					Equity Buybacks	US$'000				-	-	5	5	20
123														
124				**Dividends**										
125				Dividends are assumed to be paid in the period after they are declared.										
126														
127					Dividend Payout Ratio	%				25%	30%	35%	40%	45%

There are two control accounts to formulate here. The first is the Closing Equity control account. After bringing in the linked cells,

	A	B	C	D	E	F	G	H	I	J	K	L	M	N	O	
1	**Calculations**															
2	Case Study Model vLB1.01.xlsm															
3	**Navigator**															
4	Error Checks:					☑										
5										Jun 21	Jun 22	Jun 23	Jun 24	Jun 25		
6		Start Date								1 Jul 20	1 Jul 21	1 Jul 22	1 Jul 23	1 Jul 24		
7		End Date								30 Jun 21	30 Jun 22	30 Jun 23	30 Jun 24	30 Jun 25		
8		Number of Days								365	365	365	366	365		
9		Counter								1	2	3	4	5		
285																
286		**Ordinary Equity and Related**														
287																
288			**Ordinary Equity**													
289																
290				Equity Issuances		US$'000				15	25	-	10	-		='General Assumptions'!J121
291				Equity Buybacks		US$'000				-	-	5	5	20		='General Assumptions'!J122
292																
293			**Control Account**													
294																
295				Opening Equity		US$'000									BS	
296				Equity Issuances		US$'000									CFS	
297				Equity Buybacks		US$'000									CFS	
298				Closing Equity		US$'000			-						BS	='Opening Balance Sheet'!I45

it becomes easy. Do you see that this section is very similar to the Debt control account created earlier?

	A	B	C	D	E	F	G	H	I	J	K	L	M	N	O	
1	**Calculations**															
2	Case Study Model vLB1.01.xlsm															
3	**Navigator**															
4	Error Checks					☑										
5										Jun 21	Jun 22	Jun 23	Jun 24	Jun 25		
6		Start Date								1 Jul 20	1 Jul 21	1 Jul 22	1 Jul 23	1 Jul 24		
7		End Date								30 Jun 21	30 Jun 22	30 Jun 23	30 Jun 24	30 Jun 25		
8		Number of Days								365	365	365	366	365		
9		Counter								1	2	3	4	5		
123																
124		**Debt and Related**														
125		Movements are assumed to occur ar the end of each period.														
126		Interest is assumed to be paid in the following period.														
127																
128			**Debt**													
129																
130				Debt Drawdowns		US$'000				20	20	-	-	-		
131				Debt Repayments		US$'000				-	-	15	25	10		
132																
133			**Control Account**													
134																
135				Opening Debt		US$'000				-	20	40	25	-	BS	
136				Debt Drawdowns		US$'000				20	20	-	-	-	CFS	
137				Debt Repayments		US$'000				-	-	(15)	(25)	(10)	CFS	
138				Closing Debt		US$'000			-	20	40	25	-	(10)	BS	

In fact, to finish the Closing Equity control account, all that you need to do is highlight cells **J135:O138**, copy and paste into cell **J295**:

	A	B	C	D	E	F	G	H	I	J	K	L	M	N	O	
1	**Calculations**															
2	Case Study Model vLB1.01.xlsm															
3	**Navigator**															
4	Error Checks:					☑										
5										Jun 21	Jun 22	Jun 23	Jun 24	Jun 25		
6		Start Date								1 Jul 20	1 Jul 21	1 Jul 22	1 Jul 23	1 Jul 24		
7		End Date								30 Jun 21	30 Jun 22	30 Jun 23	30 Jun 24	30 Jun 25		
8		Number of Days								365	365	365	366	365		
9		Counter								1	2	3	4	5		
267																
288			**Ordinary Equity**													
289																
290				Equity Issuances		US$'000				15	25	-	10	-		='General Assumptions'!J121
291				Equity Buybacks		US$'000				-	-	5	5	20		='General Assumptions'!J122
292																
293			**Control Account**													
294																
295				Opening Equity		US$'000				-	15	40	35	40	BS	
296				Equity Issuances		US$'000				15	25	-	10	-	CFS	
297				Equity Buybacks		US$'000				-	-	(5)	(5)	(20)	CFS	
298				Closing Equity		US$'000			-	15	40	35	40	20	BS	='Opening Balance Sheet'!I45

It took seconds: yet another advantage of *consistency*. Now that we have our control account, I can confirm:

1. **Number of calculations that need to be entered into the financial statement so that they balance:** It is back to three.

2. **The order to build the calculations into the financial statements:** This is always row 2 first, then row 3, then row 4 and so on. In this instance, this will be Equity Issuances (Cash Flow Statement), Equity Buybacks (also Cash Flow Statement) and Ordinary Equity (Total Equity section of the Balance Sheet).

3. **It identifies the key driver:** Line 2 of the control account is always the key driver, so in this case it will be Equity Issuances. If there were never any equity, there would be no buybacks, no closing equity and in fact no company.

Therefore, our first two entries are entered into the Cash Flow Statement:

J32							fx	=Calculations!J296				

	A B C D E	F	G H	I	J	K	L	M	N
1	**Cash Flow Statement**								
2	Case Study Model vLB1.01.xlsm								
3	Navigator								
4	Error Checks:		☒						
5					Jun 21	Jun 22	Jun 23	Jun 24	Jun 25
6	Start Date				1 Jul 20	1 Jul 21	1 Jul 22	1 Jul 23	1 Jul 24
7	End Date				30 Jun 21	30 Jun 22	30 Jun 23	30 Jun 24	30 Jun 25
8	Number of Days				365	365	365	366	365
9	Counter				1	2	3	4	5
28									
29	Financing Cash Flows								
30	Debt Drawdowns	US$'000			20	20	-	-	-
31	Debt Repayments	US$'000			-	-	(15)	(25)	(10)
32	Ordinary Equity Issuances	US$'000			15	25	-	10	-
33	Ordinary Equity Buybacks	US$'000			-	-	(5)	(5)	(20)
34	Dividends Paid	US$'000							
35	Net Financing Cash Flows	US$'000			35	45	(20)	(20)	(30)
36									
37	Net Increase / (Decrease) in Cash Held	US$'000			69	62	99	143	131
38									

With two of the three line items added, the error check remains triggered. This alert is cancelled once Ordinary Equity is added to the **Balance Sheet** worksheet:

J45			▼	:	×	✓	*fx*	=Calculations!J298				

	A	B	C	D	E	F	G	H	I	J	K	L	M	N
1	**Balance Sheet**													
2	Case Study Model vLB1.01.xlsm													
3	Navigator													
4	Error Checks:						☑							
5										Jun 21	Jun 22	Jun 23	Jun 24	Jun 25
6			Start Date							1 Jul 20	1 Jul 21	1 Jul 22	1 Jul 23	1 Jul 24
7			End Date							30 Jun 21	30 Jun 22	30 Jun 23	30 Jun 24	30 Jun 25
8			Number of Days							365	365	365	366	365
9			Counter							1	2	3	4	5
43														
44			Equity											
45				Ordinary Equity		US$'000				15	40	35	40	20
46				Opening Profits		US$'000				-	123	242	357	474
47				NPAT		US$'000				123	119	115	117	134
48	w			Dividends Declared		US$'000								
49				Retained Profits		US$'000				123	242	357	474	608
50			**Total Equity**			US$'000				138	282	392	514	628
51														
52														
53			Checks											
54														
55				PF Error Check		[1.0]		☑						
56				Balance Check		[1.0]		☑						
57				Insolvency Check		[1.0]		☑						
58														

This leaves us with the dividends calculation. Dividends may only be paid out of what are known as distributable reserves (this is a bit of an oxymoron as dividends are also known as **distributions**). Revaluation reserves, share premium accounts, capital redemption reserves are all non-distributable. Essentially, dividends may only be paid out of the current year's Net Profit After Tax (NPAT) and the aggregation of all previous year's profits after past distributions, Retained Earnings. Dividends may not make the Balance Sheet's Total Equity become negative. This shows insolvency and this sort of distribution is illegal in most territories. Given non-distributable reserves may not become negative and that I already have a Balance Sheet check in place for this, I will be concentrating on NPAT and Retained Earnings here.

In this case study, the dividends are going to be a proportion of NPAT. This method is known as the **dividend payout ratio method**. However, I need to check what the maximum dividend is I can use before I calculate this relatively straightforward metric.

To derive the maximum dividend, let me consider some scenarios. Let's imagine the following scenario:

It isn't rocket science that if Retained Earnings and NPAT are both positive, then the maximum dividend allowed is the sum of the two.

Retained Earnings	100
NPAT	40
Maximum Dividend	140

Retained Earnings	100
NPAT	(40)
Maximum Dividend	60

If NPAT is negative, but Retained Earnings are positive and exceed the NPAT figure, then the maximum dividend allowed is the net of the two figures. Should the net be negative, no dividend is allowed.

Retained Earnings	(100)
NPAT	40
Maximum Dividend	40

Here is the one that surprises people. If Retained Earnings is negative but NPAT is positive, regardless of whether the net is positive or negative, the maximum dividend allowed is the NPAT amount. This may seem incomprehensible upon first thought, but it is dependent upon two conditions:

- The company's auditors must sign off on it. This is to ensure the company is still seen to be a going concern (*i.e.* it can still continue to operate and trade its way out of any short-term difficulties).

- The shareholders must vote for it. Almost as hilarious as when Members of Parliament solemnly vote for their 50% pay rise each year.

If you think about it some more, this makes sense. Remember, dividends cannot be paid if the company is insolvent. The auditors check to see whether the company can "afford" it for other reasons. But if you don't allow this scenario how would anyone ever attract share capital for a start-up company? A new company may have to provide for certain factors which may never come to fruition. A large non-current asset may have to be written off as not fit for purpose if a company's strategy changes without any cash consequence. Is it acceptable that shareholders have to wait 10 years for the Retained Earnings losses to be covered even if the business is hugely profitable in the meantime? No, and this is precisely why this is the rule.

The next scenario is more obvious:

Retained Earnings	(100)
NPAT	(40)
Maximum Dividend	-

With both a negative NPAT and Retained Earnings, there is no leeway now. These scenarios seem to suggest the following formula:

=MAX(NPAT + Retained Earnings, NPAT, 0)

This allows for the above scenarios. The check to ensure that the value is non-negative (*i.e.* the inclusion of zero in the **MAX** formula) is so that shareholders do not get asked to pay a dividend to the company. I can't imagine that would go down too well.

We are not done yet though. Let's go back to the penultimate scenario but now consider the cash position as well:

Retained Earnings	(100)
NPAT	40
Cash Available	30
Maximum Dividend	30

Here, the Cash Available is the total amount of cash available to pay the dividend. Technically, this includes any cash reserves built up over time, but many companies only consider the cash position for the period the dividend relates to (this is the scenario I shall be modelling in the case study shortly). This seems to suggest the formula:

=MIN(MAX(NPAT + Retained Earnings, NPAT, 0), Cash Available)

Let me just check with slightly revised numbers:

Retained Earnings		(100)
NPAT		40
Cash Available		(30)
		_____
Maximum Dividend		(30)

In this scenario, the company is overdrawn. Oops. Here, this company is going to be asking for money again from its shareholders. Not a good idea. This leads to the slightly revised – and finally correct – formula:

> **Maximum Dividend = MAX(MIN(MAX(NPAT + Retained Earnings, NPAT), Cash Available), 0)**

Ah yes, the wonderful **MAX(MIN(MAX))** formula. It may not be the prettiest formula in the world, but the point is, it gives the right number. I can now return to the **Calculations** worksheet for the Dividends control account derivation.

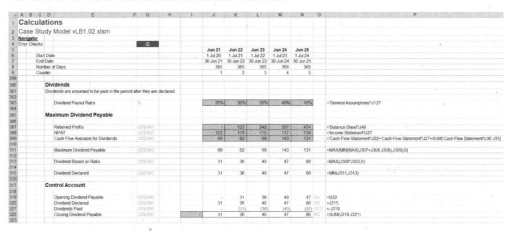

This calculation block should make sense in light of the above reasoning. The Dividend Payout Ratio, Retained Profits and NPAT are all linked through. The Cash Flow Available for Dividends (row 309) formula may look awful, but it is just the way of getting all of the cash from the Cash Flow Statement for the period excluding Dividends Paid without creating a circular argument.

The Maximum Dividend Payable formula in cell **J311** (say),

> **=MAX(MIN(MAX(J307+J308,J308),J309),0)**

is just the equivalent **MAX(MIN(MAX))** formula created above.

A little care is needed for the Dividend Based on Ratio (row 313). This has to equal **MAX(NPAT x Dividend Payout Ratio, 0)**, *i.e.* the amount cannot be negative as again, I am not looking for angry shareholders.

The Dividends Declared is then simply the minimum of the maximum allowed and the amount based on the ratio. No further restriction is required as neither calculation may be negative. The control account is then simple, with the Dividends Paid in the following period, using the trick of linking to the opening balance as used in previous control account calculations.

That leads us to analysing our control account as always:

1. **Number of calculations that need to be entered into the financial statement so that they balance:** Surprise, surprise, it's three.

2. **The order to build the calculations into the financial statements:** This is always row 2 first, then row 3, then row 4 and so on. In this instance, this will be Dividends Declared (Balance Sheet as a <u>negative</u> number), Dividends Paid (Cash Flow Statement) and Dividends Payable (Balance Sheet).

3. **It identifies the key driver:** Line 2 of the control account is always the key driver, so in this case it will be Dividends Declared. If there is nothing to declare, there cannot be any amounts paid or owed.

This control differs from the Tax control account in how it deals with the movement in a Balance Sheet item. The key driver here is Dividends Declared, which resides on the Balance Sheet. Since this relates to a period of time, normally I would have to calculate the cumulative sum before it could be referenced on the Balance Sheet, but this is not the case here. This is because Dividends Declared has a special place on the Balance Sheet: it is part of the Income Statement link and forms part of the internal working of the Retained Earnings control account:

J48				f_x	=-Calculations!J320				

	A B C D	E	F G H I	J	K	L	M	N
1	**Balance Sheet**							
2	Case Study Model vLB1.01.xlsm							
3	Navigator							
4	Error Checks:		☒					
5				Jun 21	Jun 22	Jun 23	Jun 24	Jun 25
6	Start Date			1 Jul 20	1 Jul 21	1 Jul 22	1 Jul 23	1 Jul 24
7	End Date			30 Jun 21	30 Jun 22	30 Jun 23	30 Jun 24	30 Jun 25
8	Number of Days			365	365	365	366	365
9	Counter			1	2	3	4	5
40								
41	Net Assets	US$'000		138	282	392	514	628
42								
43								
44	Equity							
45	Ordinary Equity	US$'000		15	40	35	40	20
46	Opening Profits	US$'000		-	93	176	250	320
47	NPAT	US$'000		123	119	115	117	134
48	Dividends Declared	US$'000		(31)	(36)	(40)	(47)	(60)
49	Retained Profits	US$'000		93	176	250	320	394
50	Total Equity	US$'000		108	216	285	360	414
51								
52								
53	Checks							
54								
55	PF Error Check	[1.0]	☑	☒	☒	☒	☒	☒
56	Balance Check	[1.0]	☒	☒	☒	☒	☒	☒
57	Insolvency Check	[1.0]	☑					

As you can see from the screenshot, I have finally cleared the Work In Progress I have been carrying ever since I linked the Income Statement to the Balance Sheet. The letter "w" has been removed from cell **A48**. The movement is referenced here (as a negative amount) as it is within the Income Statement / Retained Earnings link control account. Row 49 effectively sums the effect of all dividends declared over time up to the Balance Sheet period forecast.

The Balance Sheet clearly does not balance, as we still have two more line items to add. The next one is Dividends Paid in the Cash Flow Statement:

J34			f_x	=Calculations!J321					

	A B C D E	F	G H I	J	K	L	M	N
1	**Cash Flow Statement**							
2	Case Study Model vLB1.01.xlsm							
3	Navigator							
4	Error Checks:		☒					
5				Jun 21	Jun 22	Jun 23	Jun 24	Jun 25
6	Start Date			1 Jul 20	1 Jul 21	1 Jul 22	1 Jul 23	1 Jul 24
7	End Date			30 Jun 21	30 Jun 22	30 Jun 23	30 Jun 24	30 Jun 25
8	Number of Days			365	365	365	366	365
9	Counter			1	2	3	4	5
28								
29	**Financing Cash Flows**							
30	Debt Drawdowns	US$'000		20	20	-	-	-
31	Debt Repayments	US$'000		-	-	(15)	(25)	(10)
32	Ordinary Equity Issuances	US$'000		15	25	-	10	-
33	Ordinary Equity Buybacks	US$'000		-	-	(5)	(5)	(20)
34	Dividends Paid	US$'000		-	(31)	(36)	(40)	(46)
35	**Net Financing Cash Flows**	US$'000		35	14	(56)	(60)	(76)
36								
37	**Net Increase / (Decrease) in Cash Held**	US$'000		69	31	64	102	84

Finally, Dividends Payable is referenced in the Balance Sheet:

J29			f_x	=Calculations!J322					

	A B C D	E	F G H I	J	K	L	M	N
1	**Balance Sheet**							
2	Case Study Model vLB1.01.xlsm							
3	Navigator							
4	Error Checks:		☑					
5				Jun 21	Jun 22	Jun 23	Jun 24	Jun 25
6	Start Date			1 Jul 20	1 Jul 21	1 Jul 22	1 Jul 23	1 Jul 24
7	End Date			30 Jun 21	30 Jun 22	30 Jun 23	30 Jun 24	30 Jun 25
8	Number of Days			365	365	365	366	365
9	Counter			1	2	3	4	5
25								
26	**Current Liabilities**							
27	Accounts Payable	US$'000		30	33	36	39	41
28	Interest Payable	US$'000		(0)	0	1	(0)	(3)
29	Dividends Payable	US$'000		31	36	40	46	60
30	Tax Payable	US$'000		48	33	46	58	71
31	Other Current Liabilities	US$'000						
32	**Total Current Liabilities**	US$'000		108	103	124	143	170

With this addition, the Balance Sheet balances again and indeed, the Cash Flow Statement has now been completed too.

1. Cash Flow Statement

Direct Cash Flow Statement

Operating Cash Flow						
Cash Receipts	US$'000	334	440	485	526	554
Direct Cash Payments	US$'000	(90)	(131)	(145)	(157)	(166)
Indirect Cash Payments	US$'000	(60)	(65)	(68)	(70)	(71)
Cash Payments	US$'000	(150)	(196)	(212)	(226)	(237)
Interest Paid	US$'000	-	-	(1)	(3)	(2)
Tax Paid	US$'000	-	(48)	(33)	(46)	(58)
Net Operating Cash Flow	US$'000	**184**	**196**	**239**	**251**	**258**
Investing Cash Flows						
Interest Received	US$'000	-	0	1	1	2
Purchases of Non-Current Assets	US$'000	(150)	(180)	(120)	(90)	(100)
Net Investing Cash Flows	US$'000	**(150)**	**(180)**	**(119)**	**(89)**	**(98)**
Financing Cash Flows						
Debt Drawdowns	US$'000	20	20	-	-	-
Debt Repayments	US$'000	-	-	(15)	(25)	(10)
Ordinary Equity Issuances	US$'000	15	25	-	10	-
Ordinary Equity Buybacks	US$'000	-	-	(5)	(5)	(20)
Dividends Paid	US$'000	-	(31)	(36)	(40)	(46)
Net Financing Cash Flows	US$'000	**35**	**14**	**(56)**	**(60)**	**(76)**
Net Increase / (Decrease) in Cash Held	US$'000	69	31	64	102	84

Two down, one to go. It is time to complete the Balance Sheet.

CHAPTER 10.12: SINGLE ENTRY ACCOUNTING

Building a Financial Model

1. Once the Income Statement is completed, consider the first line item on the Balance Sheet not yet linked.

I have just shown that the Cash Flow Statement is complete, to go with the finished Income Statement. With corresponding line items already entered elsewhere, there are very few links outstanding for Daddy Bear, the Balance Sheet:

1. Balance Sheet

Current Assets						
Cash	US$'000	69	99	163	266	349
Accounts Receivable	US$'000	66	74	81	87	92
Other Current Assets	US$'000					
Total Current Assets	US$'000	135	173	244	353	441
Non-Current Assets						
PP&E	US$'000	113	210	218	173	150
Deferred Tax Assets	US$'000	-	-	-	-	-
Total Non-Current Assets	US$'000	113	210	218	173	150
Total Assets	US$'000	247	383	462	525	591
Current Liabilities						
Accounts Payable	US$'000	30	33	36	39	41
Interest Payable	US$'000	(0)	0	1	(0)	(3)
Dividends Payable	US$'000	31	36	40	46	60
Tax Payable	US$'000	48	33	46	58	71
Other Current Liabilities	US$'000					
Total Current Liabilities	US$'000	108	103	124	143	170
Non-Current Liabilities						
Debt	US$'000	20	40	25	-	(10)
Deferred Tax Liabilities	US$'000	11	25	28	23	19
Total Non-Current Liabilities	US$'000	31	65	53	23	9
Total Liabilities	US$'000	139	167	177	166	178
Net Assets	US$'000	108	216	285	360	413
Equity						
Ordinary Equity	US$'000	15	40	35	40	20
Opening Profits	US$'000	-	93	176	250	320
NPAT	US$'000	123	119	114	116	133
Dividends Declared	US$'000	(31)	(36)	(40)	(46)	(60)
Retained Profits	US$'000	93	176	250	320	393
Total Equity	US$'000	108	216	285	360	413

There are just two line items left: Other Current Assets and Other Current Liabilities. There are no more assumptions for the **General Assumptions** worksheet, so I conclude there are no movements to model for these line items.

Alright, so if there are no movements to model, this poses a conundrum: if I place the balances from the Opening Balance Sheet on the Balance Sheet, what are the balancing items *without exception*?

The answer is surprising: *nothing*. Welcome to the dark world of single entry accounting. Your finance teachers have lied to you. I have built an entire case study without once creating a control account with an even number of line items to add to the financial statements. Do the letters F, T and W come to mind (not necessarily in that order)?

Think about it. The Opening Balance Sheet already balanced. I also said that a modeller is only responsible for the movement in Net Assets equalling the movement in Total Equity. There are no movements for these two line items so we are off the hook.

I could just link these two line items directly from the Opening Balance Sheet, but I advise against this on the grounds of *consistency*. In a few moments, we will be adding back the opening balances from the **Opening Balance Sheet** worksheet. If this causes an error, we have linked an opening balance incorrectly to one of the control accounts, by either misreferencing, double counting or omitting. All I will need to do to fix that is go through each and every control account on the **Calculations** worksheet and check the opening balances are linked correctly, both back to the **Opening Balance Sheet** worksheet and through to the **Balance Sheet** worksheet too. If some line items (such as Other Current Assets and Other Current Liabilities) are not here, they may be missed and the check may be pointless. Therefore, I am going to add the two most boring control accounts of all time to the **Calculations** sheet:

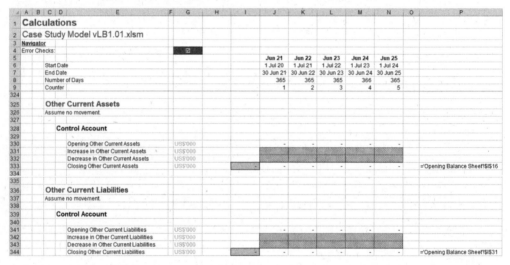

Wow. That was exciting. As I have mentioned before, make financial modelling (and in particular getting the financial statements to work) easy – just leave your brain at the door. All we have to do is link these closing balances into the Balance Sheet, here:

J16		× ✓ *fx*	=Calculations!J333			

Balance Sheet with formula bar showing =Calculations!J333

								Jun 21	Jun 22	Jun 23	Jun 24	Jun 25
1	**Balance Sheet**											
2	Case Study Model vLB1.01.xlsm											
3	Navigator											
4	Error Checks:				☑							
5								Jun 21	Jun 22	Jun 23	Jun 24	Jun 25
6	Start Date							1 Jul 20	1 Jul 21	1 Jul 22	1 Jul 23	1 Jul 24
7	End Date							30 Jun 21	30 Jun 22	30 Jun 23	30 Jun 24	30 Jun 25
8	Number of Days							365	365	365	366	365
9	Counter							1	2	3	4	5
10												
11	**1. Balance Sheet**											
12												
13	Current Assets											
14	Cash			US$'000				69	99	163	266	349
15	Accounts Receivable			US$'000				66	74	81	87	92
16	Other Current Assets			US$'000				-	-	-	-	-
17	**Total Current Assets**			US$'000				135	173	244	353	441

and there:

| J31 | | | | : | × | ✓ | fx | =Calculations!J344 | | | | |

	A	B	C	D	E	F	G	H	I	J	K	L	M	N
1	**Balance Sheet**													
2	Case Study Model vLB1.01.xlsm													
3	Navigator													
4	Error Checks:						☑							
5										Jun 21	Jun 22	Jun 23	Jun 24	Jun 25
6		Start Date								1 Jul 20	1 Jul 21	1 Jul 22	1 Jul 23	1 Jul 24
7		End Date								30 Jun 21	30 Jun 22	30 Jun 23	30 Jun 24	30 Jun 25
8		Number of Days								365	365	365	366	365
9		Counter								1	2	3	4	5
25														
26		**Current Liabilities**												
27		Accounts Payable				US$'000				30	33	36	39	41
28		Interest Payable				US$'000				(0)	0	1	(0)	(3)
29		Dividends Payable				US$'000				31	36	40	46	60
30		Tax Payable				US$'000				48	33	46	58	71
31		Other Current Liabilities				US$'000				-	-	-	-	-
32		**Total Current Liabilities**				US$'000				108	103	124	143	170
33														

That concludes the Balance Sheet too.

1. Balance Sheet

Current Assets						
Cash	US$'000	69	99	163	266	349
Accounts Receivable	US$'000	66	74	81	87	92
Other Current Assets	US$'000	-	-	-	-	-
Total Current Assets	US$'000	135	173	244	353	441
Non-Current Assets						
PP&E	US$'000	113	210	218	173	150
Deferred Tax Assets	US$'000	-	-	-	-	-
Total Non-Current Assets	US$'000	113	210	218	173	150
Total Assets	US$'000	247	383	462	525	591
Current Liabilities						
Accounts Payable	US$'000	30	33	36	39	41
Interest Payable	US$'000	(0)	0	1	(0)	(3)
Dividends Payable	US$'000	31	36	40	46	60
Tax Payable	US$'000	48	33	46	58	71
Other Current Liabilities	US$'000	-	-	-	-	-
Total Current Liabilities	US$'000	108	103	124	143	170
Non-Current Liabilities						
Debt	US$'000	20	40	25	-	(10)
Deferred Tax Liabilities	US$'000	11	25	28	23	19
Total Non-Current Liabilities	US$'000	31	65	53	23	9
Total Liabilities	US$'000	139	167	177	166	178
Net Assets	US$'000	108	216	285	360	413
Equity						
Ordinary Equity	US$'000	15	40	35	40	20
Opening Profits	US$'000	-	93	176	250	320
NPAT	US$'000	123	119	114	116	133
Dividends Declared	US$'000	(31)	(36)	(40)	(46)	(60)
Retained Profits	US$'000	93	176	250	320	393
Total Equity	US$'000	108	216	285	360	413

There appears to be one last thing to do.

CHAPTER 10.13: OPENING BALANCE SHEET REVISITED

Building a Financial Model

1. Once the Balance Sheet has been completed, return to the Opening Balance Sheet and add back the original data.

2. Correct any opening balances if necessary.

Now the three main financial statements have been completed and all checks are satisfied, it is time to turn my attention back to the **Opening Balance Sheet** worksheet.

	A	B	C	D	E	F	G	H	I	J	K	L
1	**Opening Balance Sheet**											
2	Case Study Model vLB1.01.xlsm											
3	Navigator											
4	Error Checks:					☑			Jun 20			
10												
11	**1. Opening Balance Sheet**											
12												
13			Current Assets									
14				Cash		US$'000					250	
15				Accounts Receivable		US$'000					50	
16				Other Current Assets		US$'000					10	
17				Total Current Assets		US$'000					310	
18												
19			Non-Current Assets									
20				PP&E		US$'000					450	
21				Deferred Tax Assets		US$'000					75	
22				Total Non-Current Assets		US$'000					525	
23												
24			Total Assets			US$'000					835	
25												
26			Current Liabilities									
27				Accounts Payable		US$'000					30	
28				Interest Payable		US$'000					20	
29				Dividends Payable		US$'000					15	
30				Tax Payable		US$'000					40	
31				Other Current Liabilities		US$'000					10	
32				Total Current Liabilities		US$'000					115	
33												
34			Non-Current Liabilities									
35				Debt		US$'000					150	
36				Deferred Tax Liabilities		US$'000					25	
37				Total Non-Current Liabilities		US$'000					175	
38												
39			Total Liabilities			US$'000					290	
40												
41			Net Assets			US$'000					545	
42												
43												
44			Equity									
45				Ordinary Equity		US$'000					300	
46												
47				NPAT		US$'000					-	
48				Dividends Declared		US$'000					-	
49				Retained Profits		US$'000					245	
50			Total Equity			US$'000					545	
51												
52												

You may recall earlier that I removed all of the data from the Opening Balance Sheet (column

I) in order to have the checks work as I wanted. Yes, it was a bit of a cheat, but as I have stated several times modellers are only responsible for the movements in Total Equity and Net Assets, not the cumulative amounts. Therefore, if I made the base position zero, it would have only one impact on my modelling – it would make it easier.

All I have to do is remember to put it back at the end of the exercise. Let's do that now. I am going to copy (**CTRL + C**) cells **K14:K50** and paste them back into cells **I14:I50**. They must neither be dragged back using the mouse nor cut and paste back into position (the latter can give rise to some rather lovely #*REF!* errors). Assuming there is no error upon pasting, I can then delete column **K**:

	A	B	C	D	E	F	G	H	I	J
1	**Opening Balance Sheet**									
2	Case Study Model vLB1.01.xlsm									
3	Navigator									
4	Error Checks:						☑		Jun 20	
10										
11		**1. Opening Balance Sheet**								
12										
13		**Current Assets**								
14			Cash				US$'000		250	
15			Accounts Receivable				US$'000		50	
16			Other Current Assets				US$'000		10	
17			**Total Current Assets**				US$'000		310	
18										
19		**Non-Current Assets**								
20			PP&E				US$'000		450	
21			Deferred Tax Assets				US$'000		75	
22			Total Non-Current Assets				US$'000		525	
23										
24		**Total Assets**					US$'000		835	
25										
26		**Current Liabilities**								
27			Accounts Payable				US$'000		30	
28			Interest Payable				US$'000		20	
29			Dividends Payable				US$'000		15	
30			Tax Payable				US$'000		40	
31			Other Current Liabilities				US$'000		10	
32			**Total Current Liabilities**				US$'000		115	
33										
34		**Non-Current Liabilities**								
35			Debt				US$'000		150	
36			Deferred Tax Liabilities				US$'000		25	
37			**Total Non-Current Liabilities**				US$'000		175	
38										
39		**Total Liabilities**					US$'000		290	
40										
41		**Net Assets**					US$'000		545	
42										
43										
44		**Equity**								
45			Ordinary Equity				US$'000		300	
46										
47				NPAT			US$'000		-	
48				Dividends Declared			US$'000		-	
49				Retained Profits			US$'000		245	
50		**Total Equity**					US$'000		545	
51										

All is well and the exercise is complete. The final Income Statement:

1. Income Statement

Revenue	US$'000	400	448	493	532	559
COGS	US$'000	(120)	(134)	(148)	(160)	(168)
Gross Profit	US$'000	280	314	345	373	391
Operating Expenditure	US$'000	(60)	(65)	(68)	(70)	(71)
EBITDA	US$'000	220	249	277	303	320
Depreciation	US$'000	(128)	(173)	(203)	(225)	(213)
EBIT	US$'000	93	76	75	78	108
Interest Expense	US$'000	(6)	(8)	(9)	(8)	(5)
NPBT	US$'000	86	68	66	70	103
Tax Expense	US$'000	(30)	(18)	(20)	(23)	(38)
NPAT	US$'000	56	50	46	48	64

The final Cash Flow Statement:

1. Cash Flow Statement

Direct Cash Flow Statement

Operating Cash Flow						
Cash Receipts	US$'000	384	440	485	526	554
Direct Cash Payments	US$'000	(120)	(131)	(145)	(157)	(166)
Indirect Cash Payments	US$'000	(60)	(65)	(68)	(70)	(71)
Cash Payments	US$'000	(180)	(196)	(212)	(226)	(237)
Interest Paid	US$'000	(20)	(9)	(11)	(13)	(13)
Tax Paid	US$'000	(40)	-	-	-	-
Net Operating Cash Flow	US$'000	144	235	262	286	305
Investing Cash Flows						
Interest Received	US$'000	-	3	3	4	5
Purchases of Non-Current Assets	US$'000	(150)	(180)	(120)	(90)	(100)
Net Investing Cash Flows	US$'000	(150)	(177)	(117)	(86)	(95)
Financing Cash Flows						
Debt Drawdowns	US$'000	20	20	-	-	-
Debt Repayments	US$'000	-	-	(15)	(25)	(10)
Ordinary Equity Issuances	US$'000	15	25	-	10	-
Ordinary Equity Buybacks	US$'000	-	-	(5)	(5)	(20)
Dividends Paid	US$'000	(15)	(14)	(15)	(16)	(19)
Net Financing Cash Flows	US$'000	20	31	(35)	(36)	(49)
Net Increase / (Decrease) in Cash Held	US$'000	14	89	110	164	161

The final Balance Sheet:

1. Balance Sheet

Current Assets						
Cash	US$'000	264	353	463	627	788
Accounts Receivable	US$'000	66	74	81	87	92
Other Current Assets	US$'000	10	10	10	10	10
Total Current Assets	US$'000	340	436	554	724	890
Non-Current Assets						
PP&E	US$'000	473	480	398	263	150
Deferred Tax Assets	US$'000	83	84	60	17	-
Total Non-Current Assets	US$'000	555	564	458	279	150
Total Assets	US$'000	895	1,000	1,012	1,004	1,040
Current Liabilities						
Accounts Payable	US$'000	30	33	36	39	41
Interest Payable	US$'000	6	8	9	8	5
Dividends Payable	US$'000	14	15	16	19	29
Tax Payable	US$'000	-	-	-	-	35
Other Current Liabilities	US$'000	10	10	10	10	10
Total Current Liabilities	US$'000	60	66	72	76	120
Non-Current Liabilities						
Debt	US$'000	170	190	175	150	140
Deferred Tax Liabilities	US$'000	63	82	78	57	44
Total Non-Current Liabilities	US$'000	233	272	253	207	184
Total Liabilities	US$'000	293	338	325	283	304
Net Assets	US$'000	602	662	687	721	736
Equity						
Ordinary Equity	US$'000	315	340	335	340	320
Opening Profits	US$'000	245	287	322	352	381
NPAT	US$'000	56	50	46	48	64
Dividends Declared	US$'000	(14)	(15)	(16)	(19)	(29)
Retained Profits	US$'000	287	322	352	381	416
Total Equity	US$'000	602	662	687	721	736

There you go. All finished. Except we're not…

CHAPTER 10.14: INDIRECT CASH FLOW EXTRACT

Before I finish this case study, there is one more set of calculations to perform. As I explained earlier there are two forms to the Cash Flow Statements: **direct** and **indirect**:

- **Direct:** This can reconcile Operating Cash Flows back to a large proportion of the bank statements. It is a summary of Cash Receipts, Cash Paid, Interest Paid and Tax Paid.

- **Indirect:** This starts with an element of the Income Statement and adds back non-cash items (deducting their cash equivalents) and adjusts for working capital movements.

A typical indirect Cash Flow Statement – which may look surprisingly like our case study – may compare to the direct version as follows:

1. Cash Flow Statement

Direct Cash Flow Statement

Operating Cash Flow						
Cash Receipts	US$'000	384	440	485	526	554
Direct Cash Payments	US$'000	(120)	(131)	(145)	(157)	(166)
Indirect Cash Payments	US$'000	(60)	(65)	(68)	(70)	(71)
Cash Payments	US$'000	(180)	(196)	(212)	(226)	(237)
Interest Paid	US$'000	(20)	(9)	(11)	(13)	(13)
Tax Paid	US$'000	(40)	-	-	-	-
Net Operating Cash Flow	US$'000	**144**	**235**	**262**	**286**	**305**

Indirect Extract

	US$'000					
Operating Cash Flow						
NPAT	US$'000	56	50	46	48	64
Add Back:	US$'000					
Depreciation	US$'000	128	173	203	225	213
Interest Expense	US$'000	6	8	9	8	5
Tax Expense	US$'000	30	18	20	23	38
Movements in Working Capital:						
(Inc) / Dec in Current Assets	US$'000	(16)	(8)	(7)	(6)	(5)
Inc / (Dec) in Current Liabilities	US$'000	(0)	4	3	3	2
Deduct:						
Interest Paid	US$'000	(20)	(9)	(11)	(13)	(13)
Tax Paid	US$'000	(40)	-	-	-	-
Net Operating Cash Flow	US$'000	**144**	**235**	**262**	**286**	**305**

As explained above, the indirect version is calculated as follows:

- Start with a line item from the Income Statement (here, Net Profit After Tax)

- Add back non-cash items (Depreciation Expense, Interest Expense and Tax Expense)

- Adjust for working capital movements (increases and decreases in Current Assets and Current Liabilities)

- Deduct the cash equivalents of the non-cash items added back:

  - Instead of Interest **Expense** deduct Interest **Paid**

  - Instead of Tax **Expense** deduct Tax **Paid**

  - Instead of Depreciation Expense *don't do anything*. It's a double count.

Most will have modelled an Income Statement and therefore used the Income Statement to work back to the Cash Flow Statement. We have made *transparent* assumptions instead using control accounts and that has necessitated using the direct method. Control accounts are a financial modeller's best friends. Now, should it be required, the Indirect Extract is easy to compute:

	F	G H I	J	K	L	M	N O	P
1	**Cash Flow Statement**							
2	Case Study Model vLB1.02.xlsm							
3	Navigator							
4	Error Checks:							
5			Jun 21	Jun 22	Jun 23	Jun 24	Jun 25	
6	Start Date		1 Jul 20	1 Jul 21	1 Jul 22	1 Jul 23	1 Jul 24	
7	End Date		30 Jun 21	30 Jun 22	30 Jun 23	30 Jun 24	30 Jun 25	
8	Number of Days		365	365	365	366	365	
9	Counter		1	2	3	4	5	
10								
11	**1. Cash Flow Statement**							
12								
13	**Direct Cash Flow Statement**							
14								
15	**Operating Cash Flow**							
16	Cash Receipts	US$'000	384	440	485	528	554	
17	Direct Cash Payments	US$'000	(120)	(131)	(145)	(157)	(168)	
18	Indirect Cash Payments	US$'000	(80)	(65)	(68)	(70)	(71)	
19	Cash Payments	US$'000	(180)	(196)	(212)	(226)	(237)	
20	Interest Paid	US$'000	(20)	(9)	(11)	(13)	(13)	
21	Tax Paid	US$'000	(40)	-	-	-	-	
22	Net Operating Cash Flow	US$'000	144	235	262	286	305	
23								
24	**Investing Cash Flows**							
25	Interest Received	US$'000	-	3	3	4	5	
26	Purchases of Non-Current Assets	US$'000	(150)	(180)	(120)	(90)	(100)	
27	Net Investing Cash Flows	US$'000	(150)	(177)	(117)	(86)	(95)	
28								
29	**Financing Cash Flows**							
30	Debt Drawdowns	US$'000	20	20	-	-	-	
31	Debt Repayments	US$'000	-	-	(15)	(25)	(10)	
32	Ordinary Equity Issuances	US$'000	15	25	-	10	-	
33	Ordinary Equity Buybacks	US$'000	-	-	(5)	(5)	(20)	
34	Dividends Paid	US$'000	(15)	(14)	(15)	(16)	(19)	
35	Net Financing Cash Flows	US$'000	20	31	(35)	(36)	(49)	
36								
37	Net Increase / (Decrease) in Cash Held	US$'000	14	89	110	164	161	
38								
39								
40	**Indirect Extract**	US$'000						
41								
42	**Operating Cash Flow**							
43	NPAT	US$'000	56	50	46	48	64	='Income Statement'!J27
44	Add Back:	US$'000						
45	Depreciation	US$'000	128	173	203	225	213	='Income Statement'!J20
46	Interest Expense	US$'000	6	8	9	8	5	='Income Statement'!J23
47	Tax Expense	US$'000	30	18	20	23	38	='Income Statement'!J26
48	Movements in Working Capital:							
49	(Inc) / Dec in Current Assets	US$'000	(18)	(8)	(7)	(6)	(5)	=-SUM(Calculations!J32:J33,Calculations!J331:J332)
50	Inc / (Dec) in Current Liabilities	US$'000	(0)	4	3	3	2	=SUM(Calculations!J58:J59,Calculations!J87:J88,Calculations!J342:J343)
51	Deduct:							
52	Interest Paid	US$'000	(20)	(9)	(11)	(13)	(13)	=J20
53	Tax Paid	US$'000	(40)	-	-	-	-	=J21
54	Net Operating Cash Flow	US$'000	144	235	262	286	305	=SUM(J43,J45:J47,J49:J50,J52:J53)
55								

NPAT, Depreciation, Interest Expense and Tax Expense are all linked in from the Income Statement (negating all of the costs as they are added back). The movements in working capital do not require me to have to create convoluted formulae using Balance Sheet movements, I can simply link to the movements in the Revenue, Costs Of Goods Sold (COGS) and Operating Expenditure control accounts, plus the presently "blank" control accounts for Other Current Assets and Other Current Liabilities. However, it should be noted that:

- An increase in a non-cash Current Asset is a bad thing from a cash perspective as it is tying up the cash; decreases release cash.

- An increase in Current Liabilities means payments are piling up. This may be good from a cash flow perspective but it is a questionable tactic for supplier relations and the ongoing credibility of the firm.

Finally, Interest Paid and Tax Paid just link to rows 20 and 21 of the Operating Cash Flow (direct method) in the same worksheet. Once this has been completed. Checks may be put in place to ensure model integrity is assured:

	C D E F	G H I	J	K	L	M	N	O	P
13	**Direct Cash Flow Statement**								
14									
15	**Operating Cash Flow**								
16	Cash Receipts	US$'000	384	440	485	526	554		
17	Direct Cash Payments	US$'000	(120)	(131)	(145)	(157)	(166)		
18	Indirect Cash Payments	US$'000	(60)	(65)	(68)	(70)	(71)		
19	Cash Payments	US$'000	(180)	(196)	(212)	(226)	(237)		
20	Interest Paid	US$'000	(20)	(9)	(11)	(13)	(13)		
21	Tax Paid	US$'000	(40)	-	-	-	-		
22	**Net Operating Cash Flow**	US$'000	**144**	**235**	**262**	**286**	**305**		
23									
39									
40	**Indirect Extract**	US$'000							
41									
42	**Operating Cash Flow**								
43	NPAT	US$'000	56	50	46	48	64		='Income Statement'!J27
44	Add Back:	US$'000							
45	Depreciation	US$'000	128	173	203	225	213		='Income Statement'!J20
46	Interest Expense	US$'000	6	8	9	8	5		='Income Statement'!J23
47	Tax Expense	US$'000	30	18	20	23	38		='Income Statement'!J26
48	Movements in Working Capital:								
49	(Inc) / Dec in Current Assets	US$'000	(16)	(8)	(7)	(6)	(5)		=-SUM(Calculations!J32:J33)
50	Inc / (Dec) in Current Liabilities	US$'000	(0)	4	3	3	2		=SUM(Calculations!J58:J59,Calculations!J87:J88)
51	Deduct:								
52	Interest Paid	US$'000	(20)	(9)	(11)	(13)	(13)		=J20
53	Tax Paid	US$'000	(40)	-	-	-	-		=J21
54	**Net Operating Cash Flow**	US$'000	**144**	**235**	**262**	**286**	**305**		=SUM(J43,J45:J47,J49:J50,J52:J53)
55									
56									
57	PF Error Check	[1,0]							=IF(ISERROR(J37+J54),1,)
58	Reconciliation Check:	[1,0]							=IF(J57<>0,0,(ROUND(J22-J54,Rounding_Accuracy)<>0)*1)

The first check here checks for *prima facie* errors (similar to the checks in the Balance Sheets), whereas the second check then confirms that the two methods of constructing the Net Operating Cash Flow coincide. These checks can then be added to the **Error Checks** worksheet:

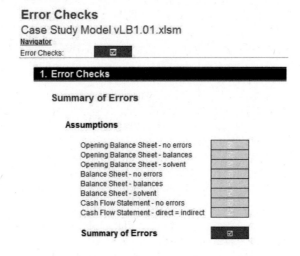

Error Checks
Case Study Model vLB1.01.xlsm
Navigator
Error Checks:

1. Error Checks

Summary of Errors

Assumptions

Opening Balance Sheet - no errors	
Opening Balance Sheet - balances	
Opening Balance Sheet - solvent	
Balance Sheet - no errors	
Balance Sheet - balances	
Balance Sheet - solvent	
Cash Flow Statement - no errors	
Cash Flow Statement - direct = indirect	

Summary of Errors

Now we are done, even if a real model would have had many more checks by this stage.

CHAPTER 10.15: CASE STUDY WRAP-UP

This isn't intended to be a long section, I just wanted to conclude as this is the main example in the book. Model development can be very daunting for the uninitiated and the inexperienced, but it is something that can be learnt. You need a methodology. That is what I have spent a long time developing.

- You need to be acquainted with the key functions in model construction. Several come up time and time again and I discussed these earlier.

- Be comfortable with the functionalities of Excel. Number formatting is useful. Use Styles. Consider hyperlinks, conditional formatting and data validation amongst other functionalities.

- Create a good template and *use it*.

- Make your models <u>C</u>onsistent, <u>R</u>obust, <u>F</u>lexible and <u>T</u>ransparent – **CRaFT**.

- Use control accounts. They are your friends and make your life easy.

- Learn from your mistakes. Don't be afraid to make them as long as they are different each time. I am a firm believer that you only learn from what comes back to bite you.

- Use the modelling process explained earlier, viz.

Hopefully, this process has made sense, hangs together and provides you with the confidence to go and build much more complex models. This case study has concentrated solely on the mechanics, discussing key concepts as we went. Real life models are larger and more complex but the principles remain the same.

Good luck and enjoy it!

Chapter 11: Self Review

In our day to day work, my colleagues and I see time and time again poor decisions made by management based on mistakes held to be true in financial models. Companies are loathe to pay for specialists to come in and check their models, seemingly happier to pay a greater price through lost sales, higher costs and reduced market share instead. It is important to understand why a self-review or an audit is so cost-effective and necessary.

"Best Practice Modelling"

I am going to go over this again. It needs emphasising. Spreadsheeting is often seen as a core skill for accountants, many of whom are reasonably conversant with Excel. However, many would-be modellers frequently forget that the key customers of a spreadsheet model (*i.e.* the decision makers) are not necessarily sophisticated Excel users and often only see the final output on a printed page, *e.g.* as an appendix to a Word document or as part of a set of PowerPoint slides.

With this borne in mind, it becomes easier to understand why there have been numerous high profile examples of material spreadsheet errors. I am not saying that well-structured models will ensure no mistakes, but in theory it should *reduce* both the number and the magnitude of these errors.

Modellers should strive to build "Best Practice" models. Here, we want to avoid the semantics of what constitutes 'best' in "Best Practice". There is no set of rules that is applicable for each and every situation. A quick scan of the web will find you various rules such as *Best Practice Spreadsheet Modelling Standards*, *FAST*, *SMART* and *TransparencEY* amongst others. Each requires modellers to read a large set of rules to learn by heart. Who does this? When was the last time *you* read documentation or instructions? Instead, let me revisit one final time to consider the term as a proper noun and reflect upon the idea that a good model has four key attributes (**CRaFT**):

- **Consistency**: Formulae should be copied uniformly across ranges, to make it easy to add / remove periods or categories as necessary. Sheet titles and hyperlinks should be consistently positioned to aid navigation and provide details about the content and purpose of the particular worksheet. For forecast spreadsheets incorporating dates, the dates should be consistently positioned (*i.e.* first period should always be in one particular column), the number of periods should be consistent where possible and the periodicity should be uniform (the model should endeavour to show all sheets monthly or quarterly, *etc.*). If periodicities must change, they should be in clearly delineated sections of the model.

- **Robustness:** Models should be materially free from error, mathematically accurate and readily auditable. Key output sheets should ensure that error messages such as *#DIV/0!*, *#VALUE!*, *#REF! etc.* cannot occur (ideally, these error messages should not occur anywhere).

- **Flexibility:** When building a model, the user should consider what inputs should be variable and how they should be able to vary. This may force the model builder to consider how assumptions should be entered.

- **Transparency:** Most Excel users are familiar with keeping inputs / assumptions away from calculations away from outputs. However, this concept can be extended: if most decision-makers see models printed out or on slides, the spreadsheets should be understandable without sight of the formula bar.

If your model adheres to these four standards, you are most likely in possession of a "Best Practice" model.

Formats and Styles

One way to make your spreadsheets appear more consistent is to employ styles in your models. The terms 'format' and 'style' are often used interchangeably but they are not the same thing. To see this, select any cell in Excel and apply the shortcut keystroke CTRL + 1. This shortcut brings up the Format Cells dialog box:

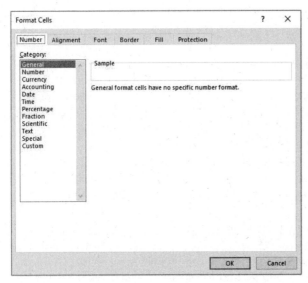

Excel has six format properties: Number, Alignment, Font, Border, Patterns and Protection. A style is simply a pre-defined set of these various formats. With a little forethought, these styles can be set up and applied to a worksheet cell or range very easily.

In all versions of Excel, styles may be accessed via the keyboard shortcut **ALT + O + S**:

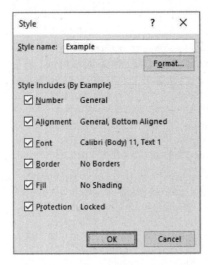

Depending upon your version of Excel, the dialog box may look slightly different to the image above. The dropdown box (highlighted above) can be edited so that new styles may be created. If you click the 'Modify' button (Excel 2003 and earlier) or the 'Format' button (Excel 2007 and later) the 'Format Cells' dialog box appear again and formats may be created in the usual way, clicking on 'OK' or 'Add' to complete the process.

Now that this style has been added, in Excel 2007 and later you simply select the range and then click on the style in the Styles gallery on the Home tab:

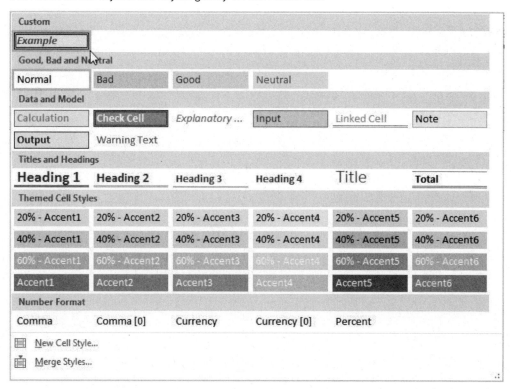

The difference between Formats and Styles becomes obvious when you realise you want to change (update) a style. Just select one of the cells that the style is attached to and call up the Style dialog box in the usual way, modifying the style as required. Click 'OK' when finished. Note that every cell in the open workbook that uses this style has automatically updated.

Inconsistent Formulae

Consider the following block of data:

	A	B	C	D	E	F	G	H	I	J	K	L
1	16	80	79	80	17	12	46	20	63	67	28	
2	64	58	72	39	63	90	73	15	29	36	45	
3	94	79	30	21	1	49	63	66	85	49	97	
4	87	73	36	88	44	27	59	0	1	21	19	
5	88	74	87	16	78	39	56	98	40	84	21	
6	96	98	15	63	59	89	70	36	99	25	50	
7	6	65	10	27	12	4	55	32	71	74	72	
8	64	0	51	1	14	34	18	81	46	62	94	
9	18	67	18	89	23	8	52	51	17	48	0	
10	7	47	57	31	24	38	30	5	90	75	37	
11	60	1	67	62	89	41	10	99	10	36	72	
12	12	53	3	0	53	58	29	95	28	7	65	
13	99	70	28	81	10	25	14	31	47	7	25	
14	42	82	51	46	18	79	33	63	9	53	20	
15	49	63	47	95	95	25	82	49	76	1	58	
16	55	88	77	95	73	60	25	37	20	87	48	
17	59	97	20	68	12	82	3	23	90	69	78	
18												

Let's assume this data is supposed to refer to a similar block of data elsewhere. How can we tell if the formula has been copied across and down correctly? Inspection by eye achieves nothing here.

One option is to use the keyboard shortcut **CTRL + `** (the character is the key to the left of the 1 on a standard QWERTY keyboard):

	A	B	C	D	E	F	G	H	I	J	K	L
1	=A23	=B23	=C23	=D23	=E23	=F23	=G23	=H23	=I23	=J23	=K23	
2	=A24	=B24	=C24	=D24	=E24	=F24	=G24	=H24	=I24	=J24	=K24	
3	=A25	=B25	=C25	=D25	=E25	=F25	=G25	=H25	=I25	=J25	=K25	
4	=A26	=B26	=C26	=D26	=E26	=F26	=G26	=H26	=I26	=J26	=K26	
5	=A27	=B27	=C27	=D27	=E27	=F27	=G27	=H27	=I27	=J27	=K27	
6	=A28	=B28	=C28	=D28	=E28	=F28	=G28	=H28	=I28	=J28	=K28	
7	=A29	=B29	=C29	=D29	=E29	=F29	=G29	=H29	=I29	=J29	=K29	
8	=A30	=B30	=C30	=D30	=E30	=F30	=G30	=H30	=I30	=J30	=K30	
9	=A31	=B31	=C31	=D31	=E31	=F31	=G31	=H31	=I31	=J31	=K31	
10	=A32	=B32	=C32	=D32	=E32	=F32	=G32	=H32	=I32	=J32	=K32	
11	=A33	=B33	=C33	=D33	=E33	=F33	=F42	=H33	=I33	=J33	=K33	
12	=A34	=B34	=C34	=D34	=E34	=F34	=F43	=H34	=I34	=J34	=K34	
13	=A35	=B35	=C35	=D35	=E35	=F35	=F44	=H35	=I35	=J35	=K35	
14	=A36	=B36	=C36	=D36	=E36	=F36	=F45	=H36	=I36	=J36	=K36	
15	=A37	=B37	=C37	=D37	=E37	=F37	=F46	=H37	=I37	=J37	=K37	
16	=A38	=B38	=C38	=D38	=E38	=F38	=F47	=H38	=I38	=J38	=K38	
17	=A39	=B39	=C39	=D39	=E39	=F39	=F48	=H39	=I39	=J39	=K39	
18												

This shortcut toggles cell values with their content (*i.e.* formulae). This will show formulae which have not been copied across properly, but this is still fraught with user error (can you spot the relevant cells?) and would be cumbersome with vast arrays of data.

Instead, there is a simpler, automatic approach. Select all of the data (click anywhere in the range and press **CTRL + ***). Then use the keyboard shortcut **CTRL + ** *viz.*

	A	B	C	D	E	F	G	H	I	J	K	L
1	16	80	79	80	17	12	46	20	63	67	28	
2	64	58	72	39	63	90	73	15	29	36	45	
3	94	79	30	21	1	49	63	66	85	49	97	
4	87	73	36	88	44	27	59	0	1	21	19	
5	88	74	87	16	78	39	56	98	40	84	21	
6	96	98	15	63	59	89	70	36	99	25	50	
7	6	65	10	27	12	4	55	32	71	74	72	
8	64	0	51	1	14	34	18	81	46	62	94	
9	18	67	18	89	23	8	52	51	17	48	0	
10	7	47	57	31	24	38	30	5	90	75	37	
11	60	1	67	62	89	41	10	99	10	36	72	
12	12	53	3	0	53	58	29	95	28	7	65	
13	99	70	28	81	10	25	14	31	47	7	25	
14	42	82	51	46	18	79	33	63	9	53	20	
15	49	63	47	95	95	25	82	49	76	1	58	
16	55	88	77	95	73	60	25	37	20	87	48	
17	59	97	20	68	12	82	3	23	90	69	78	
18												

This automatically selects all of the cells whose contents are different from the comparison cell in each row (for each row, the comparison cell is in the same column as the active cell).

**CTRL + SHIFT + ** selects all cells whose contents are different from the comparison cell in each column (for each column, the comparison cell is in the same row as the active cell). In this example, where a formula is supposed to be copied across and down, there will be no difference.

These cells can now be highlighted and reviewed at leisure.

Self-Review Checklist: The Quick and Dirty Dozen

Whilst nothing replaces the peace of mind in obtaining a third party model audit (see later), I often get asked to provide an initial list of checks model builders can perform on their own models. Assuming modellers do not have access to specialist auditing software, this list is not intended to be exhaustive (I can't give away all of my secrets!), but it's a good starting point:

1. **Use Excel's Background Error Checking** – Strictly speaking, this should be instigated during the model development phase as it can assist the modeller throughout construction.

   To enable this functionality, go to Excel's Options (**ALT + T + O**) and in the 'Formulas' section, ensure that the 'Enable background error checking' tick box is checked. Once activated, the user can select which error checking rules should be catered for by inspecting the 'Error checking rules' section directly beneath this check box.

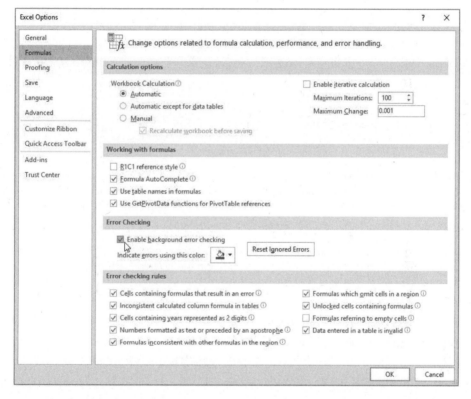

This functionality does not prevent errors from occurring, but potentially erroneous cells are highlighted by Excel in a fashion similar to cells that include comments, *viz.*

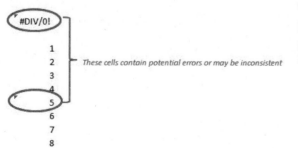

These cells contain potential errors or may be inconsistent

The problem with this approach is it is easy to miss this annotation, but it is better than nothing.

2. **Use Excel's Formula Auditing tools** – In the 'Formulas' tab of the Ribbon, use the tools in the 'Formula Auditing' section of the toolbar. In particular, 'Error Checking' is useful (although it may only be applied to one worksheet at a time) as it highlights a lot of issues Excel is programmed to consider as "dubious" (*e.g.* inconsistent formulae, #DIV/0! errors).

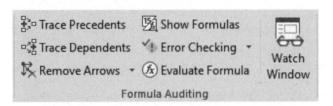

For those lucky enough to have the Professional Plus version of Excel 2013 or later, Spreadsheet Inquire adds to Excel's in-built functionalities to allow users to analyse the links between workbooks, worksheets and / or individual cells:

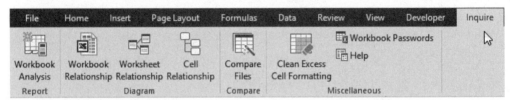

3. **Find *Prima Facie* Errors** – There are glitches in Excel and occasionally, a *prima facie* error may slip through. These obvious errors are particularly embarrassing to miss, as these are usually identified by end users picoseconds after a model has been handed over.

   There is a simple sure-fire check: **CTRL + F** (Excel's 'Find' functionality).

   Simply type '#' in 'Find what' (the obvious errors all begin with '#'), but then click on the 'Options' button to display the options and change the 'Within' setting to 'Workbook" and then look at 'Formulas', 'Values' and 'Comments' in turn using the 'Find All' button to correct any issues identified.

4. **Review inconsistencies in formulae** – as discussed earlier.

5. **Look for errors in unintentional links in range names** – The Name Manager in Excel (**CTRL + F3**) can be used to both identify links and range names containing errors.

6. **Locate unintentional links** – How often does the following dialog box send shivers down your spine?

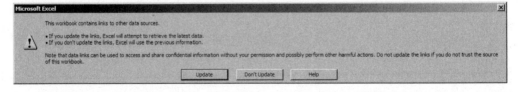

So-called "phantom links" (*i.e.* links that seem to appear from nowhere) should be located and eradicated.

7. **Perform high level analysis** – Depending upon the purpose and scope of the model built, you can create a check list of items to review for each model (*e.g.* does your Balance Sheet balance? Does the cash in the Cash Flow Statement reconcile to the amount in the Balance Sheet? What is the forecast days receivable?). Using accounting ratios focusing on profitability, liquidity and gearing may be beneficial too. More of that in the next – and final – chapter.

8. **Create "quick" charts** – For key outputs, you can graph the data momentarily. Simply highlight the data and press the **F11** function key, *viz.*

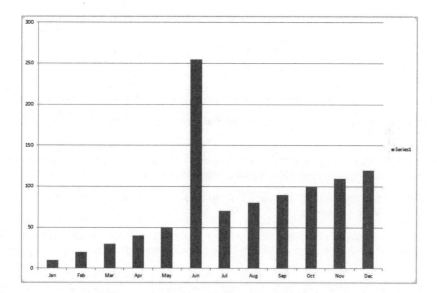

Do the charts make sense? Are there unseemly 'blips' or inconsistent trends? Can dramatic changes be readily explained? These rough and ready charts can highlight calculation mistakes in an instant on occasion.

9. **Close and re-open** – Do you get unexpected error messages upon opening? This is a frequent oversight made by modellers. Are calculations set to 'Automatic'? Are there any unexpected links, circular arguments or other error messages (e.g. "Not enough memory to display")? It is better that you discover these issues before your customers do.

10. **Spell check** – Nothing looks less professional than opening a Dashboard Summary to look at the "Selas Turnover" or items labelled incorrectly. There is really no excuse for not spell checking a model ('Review' tab of the Ribbon has a spelling check or simply hit 'F7').

11. **Printing and viewing** – Not strictly speaking an error, how many times have you decided to print out a model sent to you only to find it print over several reams of paper that even Tolstoy would have been proud of? It is worth taking time to set up print margins and included headers and footers. Also, each page should be reset (**CTRL + HOME**) and saved on the front page so that models are not opened with the end user finding themselves in cell **GG494** of a sheet called "ID_Rev_MR". Been there, done that, bought the consequences.

12. **Protection** – If as a modeller you have invested sleepless nights in getting a model to work, you do not really want an end user typing "17" over a sophisticated formula that has taken hours to get precisely right. These unowned hard codes often come back to haunt the modeller – unfairly – and cast doubt over the credibility of an otherwise robust model. Take the time to protect cells, worksheets and the workbook as required to avoid these issues.

Third Party Audit

A self-review is a cheap way of checking a model. Sometimes you need more than that. There are professional model audit firms out there that specialise in reviewing models (such as ourselves – quick advertising plug). They will incorporate a rigorous analysis of a model incorporating one or both of the following processes:

- Line-by-line (detailed) review; *and*

- Analytical (high level) review.

The line-by-line review tests each unique formula in the model to be checked using specialist model auditing software such as Spreadsheet Advantage, Spreadsheet Detective or Spreadsheet Professional in the base case scenario. Other scenarios may be reviewed depending upon the scope of the work. After careful analysis, auditors will provide recipients with a report, called the Model Review Findings, detailing any errors identified. These Model Review Findings will be categorised as to severity. We using the following definitions:

- **Category 1:** Affects the calculations in versions of the model within the scope of the review;

- **Category 2:** May affect the calculations under assumptions outside the scope of the current review;

- **Category 3:** Unclear or bad practice. This may affect the user's interpretation of the results, but does not necessarily affect the calculations; and

- **Queries:** Questions asked to increase understanding of the calculations with the express intention of identifying errors.

Before a final report can be provided, all Queries and Category 1 issues have to be resolved. Category 2 and 3 issues do not necessarily have to be corrected for the review, but may represent a risk to model users under other scenarios.

Once these errors have been corrected, if applicable, the audit will undertake a high-level analytical review of the model and its key outputs. Once completed, usually the model auditors will provide a report describing whether:

- The calculations in the model are in all material respects internally consistent and mathematically correct, with respect to whatever scope was agreed; and

- The model allows agreed selected changes in assumptions to correctly flow through to the results.

Given a model audit is a highly formal review made by a third party, auditing firms will generally not be responsible for performing any of the following tasks:

- Commenting on the completeness or reasonableness of the assumptions, including accounting, tax and regulatory-related assumptions;

- Commenting on the probability of the projections being achieved;

- Considering the cash flows or other balances from the perspective of specific shareholders and lenders, other than to the extent that they are explicitly represented in the model;

- Reviewing links to files outside the model;

- Assessing whether the financial statements are presented in a format suitable for public financial or tax reporting;

- Reviewing commentary embedded within cell notes; and

- Commenting on the model's compliance with generally accepted accounting principles or tax legislation.

This is often an expensive exercise, but when business decisions will prove very costly if model outputs are wrong, this is often a better option when much is riding on the logic of the model. Audits do not usually comment on the assumptions. I would recommend undertaking a self-review first before submitting a model to a formal audit. It saves time and money and leads to a more collaborative exercise.

Chapter 12: Ratio Analysis

I want to end this book on one key area of financial statement analysis, which is **ratio analysis**. This is typically used to review published statutory accounts after taking into account certain details, typically found in the Notes to the Accounts. However, it is just as pertinent to the world of financial model development. I would strongly recommend reviewing draft models to see if things look odd or inconsistent with previous assumptions or historical data. Seldom do model developers perform this review. I highly recommend it.

Not only is the data required readily available in most models, using ratios rather than absolute calculations allows comparison between previous years, previous models and with peers in a similar industry at a similar stage in their business lifecycle. Errors may be identified and once corrected, trends can be derived to identify improvements / deficiencies and assess the underlying story of the business evaluated.

There are limitations to ratio analysis. Most ratios are derived from accounting data and these line items are dependent upon the accounting policies of the firm and the accounting standards of the jurisdiction. As more companies convert to report by International Financial Reporting Standards (IFRS), comparisons between companies in similar sectors but different geographical locales will become easier. However, due to the accounting policies adopted, ratios should always be considered over the longer term in conjunction with other methods of financial analysis (*e.g.* discounted cash flow).

Ratios are often separated into various categories, *e.g.* profitability, liquidity, asset management, debt (gearing), equity and market value. However, there is no universal agreement as to either how these ratios should be calculated or categorised. It is possible to discover that different texts use slightly different formulae for the computation of many ratios. Therefore, when comparing a calculated ratio with a published ratio or an industry average, make sure that the formula used in the calculation is consistent with the published ratio.

Profitability Ratios

Profitability ratios measure a company's operating efficiency, including its ability to generate income and cash flow. Cash flow affects the company's ability to obtain debt and equity financing and therefore ensure the company's long-term viability and ultimately profitability.

$$\text{Gross Profit Margin} = \frac{\text{Gross Profit}}{\text{Sales}}$$

This is the calculation that shows the ratio of contribution divided by sales. This ratio considers the profit of direct costs. In essence, the gross profit ratio is essentially the percentage mark-up on merchandise from its cost. This ratio is essential in understanding break-even analysis.

It is best used when the splits of direct costs and sales revenue by category can be determined.

$$\text{Net Profit Margin} = \frac{\text{Net Profit}}{\text{Sales}}$$

Sometimes known as the EBITDA margin, this ratio differs from the Gross Profit Margin in that it includes the indirect costs in the calculation also.

This demonstrates company profitability before capital expenditure requirements, financing and taxation and is often seen as an operating cashflow ratio proxy.

$$\text{EBIT Margin} = \frac{\text{Earnings Before Interest and Taxation}}{\text{Sales}}$$

Similar to Net Profit (EBITDA) Margin, this considers profitability including capital expenditure but excluding financing and taxation considerations.

$$\text{Net Income Margin} = \frac{\text{Net Income}}{\text{Sales}}$$

This provides the ultimate profitability as a proportion of sales allowing for easy comparison to other companies.

It can be argued this ratio is too high level as it is unclear how the profitability is derived between direct costs, indirect costs, capital expenditure attribution (i.e. depreciation), financing and taxation.

$$\text{Return on Assets} = \frac{\text{Net Income}}{\text{Average Total Assets}}$$

The return on assets ratio, often called the return on total assets, is a profitability ratio that measures the net income produced by total assets during a period by comparing net income to the average total assets, i.e. it measures how efficiently a company can manage its assets to produce profits during a period.

That is, this ratio measures how profitable a company's assets are.

$$\text{Return on Net Assets} = \frac{\text{Net Income}}{\text{Average Net Assets}}$$

The return on net assets depicts how much the balance sheet "sweats" profitability.

Net Assets equals Total Assets less Total Liabilities and is therefore equal to Total Equity. Therefore, depending upon how equity is defined, this ratio is often the equivalent of Return On Equity.

$$\text{Return on Capital Employed} = \frac{\text{Earnings Before Interest and Taxation}}{\text{Average Total Assets -}\ \text{Average Current Liabilities}}$$

Capital Employed is defined as Total Assets less Current Liabilities, which is effectively Total Debt + Total Equity.

This is effectively an accounting return proxy for the return on weighted capital.

ROCE is a long-term profitability ratio because it shows how effectively assets are performing while taking into consideration long-term financing. This is why ROCE is considered a more useful ratio than Return On Equity to evaluate the longevity of a company.

$$\text{Return on Equity} = \frac{\text{Net Income}}{\text{Average Total Owners' Equity}}$$

The return on equity ratio or ROE is a profitability ratio that measures the ability of a firm to generate profits from its shareholders' investments in the company.

ROE is also an indicator of how effective management is at using equity financing to fund operations and grow the company.

$$\text{Return on Shareholders' Equity} = \frac{\text{Net Income}}{\text{Average Common Stock}}$$

Similar to Return On Equity, this specifically looks at the return on the average Common Stock (Share Capital).

Liquidity Ratios

These ratios analyse the ability of a company to pay off both its current liabilities as they become due as well as their long-term liabilities as they become current. These ratios frequently consider the ability to turn other assets into cash to pay off liabilities and other current obligations.

It should be emphasised that liquidity is not only a measure of how much cash a business has. It is also a measure of how easy it will be for the company to raise enough cash or convert assets into cash.

$$\text{Current Ratio} = \frac{\text{Current Assets}}{\text{Current Liabilities}}$$

The current ratio is a liquidity ratio that measures a firm's ability to pay off its short-term liabilities with its current assets.

This means that a company has a limited amount of time in order to raise the funds to pay for these liabilities, due within one year. Current assets like cash, cash equivalents, and marketable securities can easily be converted into cash in the short term.

Companies with larger amounts of current assets will find it easier to pay off current liabilities when they become due without having to sell off key long-term, revenue generating assets.

$$\text{Quick Ratio} = \frac{\text{Current Assets - Inventory}}{\text{Current Liabilities}}$$

The quick ratio (alternatively known as the acid test ratio) is a liquidity ratio that measures the ability of a company to pay its current liabilities when they come due with only quick assets.

Quick assets are current assets that can be converted to cash within the short-term (typically 90 days).

Cash, cash equivalents, short-term investments or marketable securities, and current accounts receivable are considered quick assets.

Short-term investments or marketable securities include trading securities and available for sale securities that can easily be converted into cash within the next 90 days. Marketable securities are traded on an open market with a known price and readily available buyers. Inventory is specifically excluded.

$$\text{Cash Ratio} = \frac{\text{Cash and Cash Equivalents}}{\text{Current Liabilities}}$$

This is the ratio of a company's total cash and cash equivalents to its current liabilities.

A highly restrictive liquidity ratio, the cash ratio is most commonly used as a measure of company liquidity. It can therefore determine if, and how quickly, the company can repay its short-term debt. A strong cash ratio is useful to creditors when deciding how much debt, if any, they would be willing to extend to the asking party.

$$\textbf{Net Working Capital Ratio} \; = \; \frac{\textbf{Current Assets - Current Liabilities}}{\textbf{Total Assets}}$$

Not to be confused with the Working Capital Ratio (another name for the Current Ratio), this ratio notes the level of surplus / deficit in working capital as a proportion of total assets.

This can provide a reader of the proportion of capital used in operations as a proportion of the total assets utilised.

Asset Management Ratios

Profitability ratios measure a company's operating efficiency, including its ability to generate income and cash flow. Cash flow affects the company's ability to obtain debt and equity financing and therefore ensure the company's long-term viability and ultimately profitability.

Many of these ratios in particular are based on using year-end balances (either in averages or in closing balances). Reporting companies are aware of this and this can lead to Balance Sheet manipulation. Auditors cannot remedy this situation: their role is merely to report that amounts are true and fair as at the reporting date.

$$\text{Receivables Turnover} = \frac{\text{Net Credit Sales}}{\text{Average Accounts Receivable}}$$

This ratio should actually be net credit sales, but this figure is not always readily available and sales are often used as a proxy in practice, even if this is technically incorrect.

This measures the level of turnover within one year: the lower this figure, the more it demonstrates the inefficiency of the Accounts Receivable team to collect owed monies.

$$\text{Days Receivable} = \frac{\text{Average Accounts Receivable}}{\text{Net Credit Sales}} \times 365$$

This alternative ratio is easier to understand for many: essentially, this divides the last ratio into 365 (the number of days in a year) to derive how long it takes to recover credit sales.

$$\text{Inventory Turnover} = \frac{\text{Cost of Goods Sold}}{\text{Average Inventory}}$$

This ratio measures the level of inventory turnover within one year: this figure needs to be compared against previous years and industry averages to have any real meaning.

$$\text{Days Inventory} = \frac{\text{Average Inventory}}{\text{Cost of Goods Sold}} \times 365$$

This alternative ratio is easier to understand for many: essentially, this divides the last ratio into 365 (the number of days in a year) to derive how long cash is tied up in inventory.

$$\text{Payables Turnover} = \frac{\text{Cost of Goods Sold} + \text{Operating Expenditure}}{\text{Average Accounts Payable}}$$

This ratio measures the level of turnover within one year: the lower this figure, the longer it takes the company to make its payments to creditors which may suggest cash flow difficulties, for example.

$$\text{Days Payable} \; = \; \frac{\text{Average Accounts Payable}}{\text{Cost of Goods Sold + Operating Expenditure}} \times 365$$

This alternative ratio is easier to understand for many: essentially, this divides the last ratio into 365 (the number of days in a year) to derive how long is taken on average before creditors are paid.

Working Capital Cycle = Days Receivable + Days Inventory - Days Payable

Not strictly a ratio, this calculation computes how long working capital is tied up in the company's business. If this extends over time or is greater than the industry average this may suggest a company may soon suffer cash flow problems (if not already).

$$\text{Working Capital Turnover} \; = \; \frac{365}{\text{Working Capital Cycle}}$$

This alternative ratio is perhaps not as easy to understand. Essentially, this divides the last ratio into 365 (the number of days in a year) to derive how frequently the working capital is turned over in one year.

$$\text{Fixed Assets Turnover} \; = \; \frac{\text{Sales}}{\text{Average Fixed Assets}}$$

This measures the level of fixed assets turnover within one year. This ratio is an efficiency measure to see how productive its fixed assets are in generating sales.

$$\text{Total Assets Turnover} \; = \; \frac{\text{Sales}}{\text{Average Total Assets}}$$

Similar to the previous ratio, the asset turnover ratio is an efficiency ratio that measures a company's ability to generate sales from its assets by comparing net sales with average total assets.

Debt (Gearing) Ratios

Sometimes referred to as solvency ratios, this looks at longer-term concerns affected by debt rather than shorter-term issues derived from operations. These ratios consider the level of debt carried by the business, how this financial leverage affects the business and its ability to service its financing obligations.

$$\text{(Total) Debt Ratio} = \frac{\text{Current and Long-Term Liabilities}}{\text{Total Liabilities and Owners' Equity}}$$

This ratio measures the level of total liabilities as a proportion of the total liabilities and equity added together.

The idea behind this ratio is that all forms of liability are financing the business in some shape or form (e.g. not paying a tax creditor means that the cash may be used elsewhere in the short term).

$$\text{(Total) Debt to (Total) Equity Ratio} = \frac{\text{Current and Long-Term Liabilities}}{\text{Owners' Equity}}$$

Similar to the above ratio, this ratio measures the level of total liabilities as a proportion – this time of just owners' equity.

This can be useful as an accounting proxy for determining ungearing and re-gearing betas for valuation purposes.

$$\text{Total Equity Multiplier} = \frac{\text{Total Liabilities and Owners' Equity}}{\text{Owners' Equity}}$$

This financial leverage ratio measures the amount of a firm's assets that are financed by its shareholders by comparing total assets with total shareholder's equity.

Like all liquidity ratios and financial leverage ratios, the equity multiplier is an indication of company risk to creditors. Companies that rely too heavily on debt financing will have high debt service costs and will have to raise more cash flows in order to pay for their operations and obligations.

$$\text{Long Term Debt Ratio} = \frac{\text{Long-Term Debt}}{\text{Total Liabilities and Owners' Equity}}$$

Similar to the Total Debt ratio, this measures more specific debt as a proportion of the total liabilities and equity added together.

$$\text{Long Term Debt to Shareholders' Equity} = \frac{\text{Long-Term Debt}}{\text{Common Stock}}$$

This ratio tightens the focus even more, specifically looking at Debt to Equity.

$$\text{Times Interest Earned} = \frac{\text{Earnings before Interest and Taxation}}{\text{Interest Expense}}$$

The times interest earned ratio, sometimes called the P&L interest coverage ratio, is a coverage ratio that measures the proportionate amount of income that can be used to cover interest expenses in the future.

In some respects the times interest ratio is considered a solvency ratio because it measures a firm's ability to make interest and debt service payments. Since these interest payments are usually made on a long-term basis, they are often treated as an ongoing, fixed expense. As with most fixed expenses, if the company can't make the payments, it could go bankrupt and cease to exist. Thus, this ratio could be considered a solvency ratio.

In practice, the cash versions of this metric are more commonplace as accounting figures may be manipulated.

$$\text{Debt Service Coverage Ratio} = \frac{\text{Cash Flow available for Debt Servicing}}{\text{Principal and Interest Paid}}$$

This is an extremely important ratio for financing. Cash Flow Available for Debt Servicing (CFADS) is defined as operating and investing income excluding interest paid and (usually) debt drawdowns and equity issuances. More often than not this only considers the cash generated in the period and excludes any opening cash balance.

This measures the company's ability to meet all of its debt obligations (i.e. principal and interest).

Financiers prefer this value to be between 1.20 and 1.50 (too low can trigger a default, too high may trigger a cash sweep).

$$\text{Interest Coverage Ratio} = \frac{\text{Cash Flow available for Debt Servicing}}{\text{Interest Paid}}$$

Similar to the DSCR, this ratio is used to confirm interest obligations may be met (often used when principal is not yet due).

Equity Ratios

Equity ratios are measures shareholders will pay particular interest in. They need to understand how the market values the business compared to book values and what the price / performance equates to on a per share basis.

$$\text{Earnings per Share} = \frac{\text{Net Income}}{\text{Average Number of Shares}}$$

Earnings per share (EPS), also called net income per share, is a market prospect ratio that measures the amount of net income earned per share of average stock outstanding for the period in question.

Earnings per share is also a calculation that shows how profitable a company is on a shareholder basis. Therefore, a larger company's profits per share can be compared to smaller company's profits per share, but this will mean they need to make more profit. Size is sometimes "normalised" in this metric.

This is still meaningful if negative.

$$\text{Dividend per Share} = \frac{\text{Dividend Declared}}{\text{Average Number of Shares}}$$

Similar to EPS, this measure is useful for minority shareholders who cannot necessarily access the earnings attributed to them.

This cannot be negative.

$$\text{Book Value per Share} = \frac{\text{Owners' Equity}}{\text{Closing Number of Shares}}$$

This measures the Owners' Equity (or Net Assets) ascribed to each share. Note that this should be undertaken on a closing balance, rather than an average balance, basis.

$$\text{Dividend Payout Ratio} = \frac{\text{Dividends Paid}}{\text{Net Income}}$$

This reports how much of the current period's profit is paid out. Depending upon the law where the company resides and its retained earnings, this figure can be greater than 100%.

$$\text{Retention Ratio} = \frac{\text{Net Income - Dividends Paid}}{\text{Net Income}}$$

This ratio reports how much of the current period's profit is retained and hence reinvested. Dividend Payout Ratio plus Retention Ratio should equal 100%.

$$\text{Financial Leverage Ratio} = \frac{\text{Total Liabilities and Owners' Equity}}{\text{Total Owners' Equity}}$$

Some may consider this metric better positioned in another category, but the financial leverage ratio measures the value of equity in a company by analysing its overall debt picture.

These ratios either compare debt or equity to assets as well as shares outstanding to measure the true value of the equity in a business.

When shareholders own a majority of the assets, the company is said to be less leveraged. When creditors own a majority of the assets, the company is considered highly leveraged. All of these measurements are important for investors to understand how risky the capital structure of a company and if it is worth investing in.

$$\text{Return on Equity} = \frac{\text{Net Income}}{\text{Average Total Owners' Equity}}$$

Also situated in profitability, the return on equity ratio or ROE is a profitability ratio that measures the ability of a firm to generate profits from its shareholders' investments in the company.

ROE is also an indicator of how effective management is at using equity financing to fund operations and grow the company.

Sometimes this is calculated on the Du Pont basis, where it is calculated as the Net Income Margin multiplied by Total Assets Turnover multiplied by the Financial Leverage Ratio. Whichever method is adopted, the results should equate (the Du Pont method provides more information).

Market Value Ratios

A subset of equity ratios, these measures shareholders specifically address market value. These ratios pre-suppose the company is marketable and a valuation is readily available.

$$\text{Price Earnings Ratio} = \frac{\text{Price per Share}}{\text{Earnings per Share}}$$

The price earnings ratio, often called the P/E ratio, is a market prospect ratio that calculates the market value of a stock relative to its earnings by comparing the market price per share by the earnings per share.

Investors often use this ratio to evaluate what a stock's fair market value should be by predicting future earnings per share.

The PE ratio helps investors analyse how much they should pay for a stock based on its current earnings. This is why the price to earnings ratio is often called a price multiple or earnings multiple.

This ratio is not calculated when EPS is negative.

$$\text{Market to Book Ratio} = \frac{\text{Price per Share}}{\text{Book Value per Share}}$$

Similar to the P/E ratio, this measure shows the market uplift to show whether investors have valued the company's performance at a premium or a discount.

Example

Ratios Example

Income Statement

	2015
Sales	1,200
Cost of Goods Sold	900
Administrative Expenses	300
Depreciation	129
Earnings Before Interest and Taxes	- 129
Interest Expense	20
Taxable Income	- 149
Taxes	- 34
Net Income	- 115
Dividends	50
Addition to Retained Earnings	- 165

Other Information

No. of Shares Outstanding (Millions)	400
Price Per Share	4.63

Cash Flow Statement

	2015
Operating Cash Flows	
Cash Receipts	1,200
Cash Payments	- 1,200
Interest Paid	- 20
Tax Paid	34
Net Operating Cash Flows	14
Investing Cash Flows	
Net Capex (Payments) / Proceeds	-
Interest Received	-
Net Investing Cash Flows	-
Financing Cashflows	
Debt Drawdowns	-
Debt Repayments	-
Equity Issuances	-
Equity Buybacks	-
Dividends Paid	- 50
Net Financing Cashflows	- 50
Cash Movement for 2015	- 36

Balance Sheet

ASSETS	2015	2014
Current Assets		
Cash	564	600
Accounts Receivable	600	600
Inventory	1,100	1,100
Total Current Assets	2,264	2,300
Fixed Assets		
Non-Current Assets	1,000	1,000
less: Accumulated Depreciation	- 1,029	- 900
Total Fixed Assets	- 29	100
TOTAL ASSETS	2,235	2,400

LIABILITIES AND OWNERS' EQUITY	2015	2014
Current Liabilities		
Bank Overdraft	-	-
Accounts Payable	800	800
Interest Payable	-	-
Dividends Payable	-	-
Tax Payable	-	-
Total Current Liabilities	800	800
Long-Term Liabilities		
Long-Term Debt	200	200
Other Long-Term Liabilities	-	-
Total Long-Term Liabilities	200	200
Owners' Equity		
Common Stock	400	400
Capital Surplus	500	500
Retained Earnings	335	500
Total Owners' Equity	1,235	1,400
TOTAL LIABILITIES AND OWNERS' EQUITY	2,235	2,400

Ratios

Profitability

Gross Profit Margin	25.00%
Net Profit Margin	-
EBIT Margin	- 10.75%
Net Income Margin	- 9.58%
Return On Assets	- 4.96%
Return On Net Assets	- 8.73%
Return On Capital Employed	- 8.50%
Return On Equity	- 8.73%
Return On Shareholders' Equity	- 28.75%

Asset Management

Receivables Turnover	2.00x
Days Receivable	182.50
Inventory Turnover	0.82x
Days Inventory	446.11
Payables Turnover	1.50
Days Payable	243.33
Working Capital Turnover	0.95x
Working Capital Cycle (Days)	385.28
Fixed Assets Turnover	33.80x
Total Assets Turnover	0.52x

Market Value Ratios

Price / Earnings Ratio	-
Market to Book Ratio	1.50

Liquidity

Current Ratio	2.83x
Quick Ratio	1.46x
Cash Ratio	0.75x
Net Working Capital Ratio	0.66x

Debt / Gearing

Total Debt Ratio	0.45x
Total Debt to Total Equity Ratio	0.81x
Total Equity Multiplier	1.81x
Long-Term Debt Ratio	0.09x
Long-Term Debt to Shareholders' Equity	0.50x
Times Interest Earned	- 6.45x
Debt Service Coverage Ratio	1.70x
Interest Coverage Ratio	1.70x

Equity

Earnings Per Share	- 0.29
Dividend Per Share	0.13
Book Value Per Share	3.09
Dividend Payout Ratio	- 43.48%
Retention Ratio	143.48%
Dividend Yield	2.70%
Financial Leverage Ratio	1.76x
Return On Equity (Du Point Method)	- 8.73%

Appendix

There have been a number of different examples and files that have been created as part of the materials in this book. Where possible, we have tried to provide clear screenshots so that you, our readers, can reproduce these. In some instances, it may be easier to go straight to the file itself. With that in mind, we have set up a page on our website for further reference, where we will provide files containing examples that we have used throughout this book, as well as any supplementary materials that we think may be useful. You find this at www.sumproduct.com/book-resources.

Also, if you are interested in further learning material, a number of the examples in the book have been inspired by previous articles that we have produced over the years. You can find these, and many more, at www.sumproduct.com/thought.

Calculations Worksheet

Description	Cell	Formula
Error Checks	G4	=Overall_Error_Check
Months	J5	=Timing!J5
Start Date	C6	=Timing!C6
Revenue First Year	J17	='General Assumptions'!J17
Revenue Growth Rate	K18	='General Assumptions'!K18
Revenue	J19	=IF(J$9=1,$J$17,I19*(1+J18))
Days Receivable	J23	='General Assumptions'!J22
Days in Period	J25	=J$8
Closing Receivables	J27	=J23/J25*J19
Opening Receivables	J31	=I34
Revenue	J32	=J19
Cash Receipts	J33	=J34-SUM(J31:J32)
Closing Receivables	I34	='Opening Balance Sheet'!$I$15
Closing Receivables	J34	=J27
Revenue	J41	=J19
Gross Margin	J42	='General Assumptions'!J29
Gross Profit	J43	=J41*J42
COGS	J45	=J41-J43
Days Payable	J49	='General Assumptions'!J33
Days in Period	J51	=J$8
Closing Payables	J53	=J49/J51*J45
Opening Payables	J57	=I60
COGS	J58	=J45
Cash Payments	J59	=J60-SUM(J57:J58)
Closing Payables	I60	='Opening Balance Sheet'!I27
Closing Payables	J60	=J53
Growth Rates Used From	I68	='General Assumptions'!I41
Growth Rates Flag	J69	=($I68<=J$7)*1
Amounts	J71	='General Assumptions'!J42
Growth Rates	K72	='General Assumptions'!K43
Opex	J74	=(1-J69)*J71+(J69*I74*(1+J72))
Days in Period	J80	=J$8
Closing Payables	J82	=J78/J80*J74
Opening Payables	J86	=I89
Opex	J87	=J74
Cash Payments	J88	=J89-SUM(J86:J87)
Closing Payables	J89	=J82
Existing Assets	I96	='Opening Balance Sheet'!I20
Capital Expenditure	J97	='General Assumptions'!J50
Remaining Life of Existing Assets	I101	='General Assumptions'!I54
Annual Rate	I102	='General Assumptions'!I55
Economic Life of New Capex	I104	='General Assumptions'!I57
Annual Rate	I105	='General Assumptions'!I58
Depreciation - Existing Assets	I107	=I96*I102
Depreciation - New Assets	J108	=$I105*J97

Description	Cell	Formula
New Assets - Depreciation Counter	J110	=MIN(J$9,$I104)
Aggregate Depreciation - Existing Assets	J112	=IF(J$9<=$I101,$I107,0)
Aggregate Depreciation - New Assets	J113	=SUM(OFFSET(J108,0,0,1,-J110))
Total Depreciation	J114	=SUM(J112:J113)
Opening Net Book Value	J118	=I121
Capital Expenditure	J119	=J97
Total Depreciation	J120	=-J114
Closing Net Book Value	I121	=I96
Closing Net Book Value	J121	=SUM(J118:J120)
Debt Drawdowns	J130	='General Assumptions'!J67
Debt Repayments	J131	='General Assumptions'!J68
Opening Debt	J135	=I138
Debt Drawdowns	J136	=J130
Debt Repayments	J137	=-J131
Closing Debt	I138	='Opening Balance Sheet'!I35
Closing Debt	J138	=SUM(J135:J137)
Interest Rate	J142	='General Assumptions'!J72
Opening Debt	J144	=J135
Days in Period	J146	=J$8
Days in Standard Year	J147	=Days_in_Yr
Proportion of Year	J148	=MIN(J146/J147,1)
Interest	J150	=J144*J142*J148
Opening Interest Payable	J154	=I157
Interest Expense	J155	=J150
Interest Paid	J156	=-J154
Closing Interest Payable	I157	='Opening Balance Sheet'!I28
Closing Interest Payable	J157	=SUM(J154:J156)
Interest Receivable Rate	J162	='General Assumptions'!J76
Proportion into Period of Movement	I164	='General Assumptions'!I78
Opening Cash Balance	J166	=IF(J$9=1,'Opening Balance Sheet'!$I$14,'Balance Sheet'!I$14)
Non-Interest Cash Movement	J167	='Cash Flow Statement'!J22+'Cash Flow Statement'!J26+'Cash Flow Statement'!J35
Tax Rate	J168	='General Assumptions'!$I$85
Interest Receivable	J170	=(J166+(1-$I$164)*J167)*J162/(1-(1-$I$164)*(1-J168)*J162)
Opening Interest Receivable	J174	=I177
Interest Income	J175	=J170
Interest Received	J176	=-J174
Closing Interest Receivable	J177	=SUM(J174:J176)
Non-Assessable Revenue	J184	='General Assumptions'!J89
Disallowable Expenses	J185	='General Assumptions'!J90
NPBT	J189	='Income Statement'!J24
Deduct: Non-Assessable Revenue	J190	=-J184
Add: Disallowable Expenses	J191	=J185

Description	Cell	Formula
Accounting Taxable Profit	J192	=SUM(J189:J191)
Tax Rate	J194	='General Assumptions'!$I$85
Tax Expense / (Credit)	J196	=J194*J192
Existing Assets	I201	=I96
Capital Expenditure	J202	=J97
Declining Balance Multiplier	I204	='General Assumptions'!I94
Remaining Life of Tax Assets	I206	='General Assumptions'!I96
Annual Rate	I207	='General Assumptions'!I97
Tax Asset Life of New Capex	I209	='General Assumptions'!I99
Annual Rate	I210	='General Assumptions'!I100
Depreciation - Existing Assets	H212	=I201
Depreciation - Existing Assets	J212	=($H212-SUM($I212:I212))*IF(J$9=$I206,1,$I207)
Depreciation - New Capex: Year 1	H213	=OFFSET($I$202,0,$E213)
Depreciation - New Capex: Year 1	J213	=IF(J$9>=$E213,($H213-SUM($I213:I213))*IF(J$9=$I$209+$E213-1,1,$I$210),0)
Tax Depreciation	H218	=SUM(H212:H217)
Tax Depreciation	I218	=SUM(J218:N218)
Tax Depreciation	J218	=SUM(J212:J217)
Accounting Depreciation	I222	=SUM(J222:N222)
Accounting Depreciation	J222	=J114
Accounting Depreciation	J226	=J222
Tax Depreciation	J227	=-J218
Depreciation Timing Difference	J228	=SUM(J226:J227)
Tax Rate	J230	='General Assumptions'!$I$85
Movement in DTLs	J232	=-J230*J228
Opening DTLs	J234	=I236
Movement in DTLs	J235	=J232
Closing DTLs	I236	='Opening Balance Sheet'!I36
Closing DTLs	J236	=SUM(J234:J235)
Accounting Taxable Profit	J240	=J192
Depreciation Timing Difference	J241	=J228
Taxable Profit / (Loss) Before Losses	J242	=SUM(J240:J241)
Tax Losses Used	J243	=J263
Taxable Profit / (Loss) after Losses	J244	=SUM(J242:J243)
Tax Rate	J245	=J230
Tax Payable for Period	J246	=MAX(J244*J245,0)
Payment Delay	I248	='General Assumptions'!I114
Opening Tax Payable	J250	=I253
Tax Payable for Period	I251	=I253
Tax Payable for Period	J251	=J246
Tax Paid	J252	=-IF(J$9-$I248<0,0,OFFSET(J251,0,-$I248))
Closing Tax Payable	I253	='Opening Balance Sheet'!I30
Closing Tax Payable	J253	=SUM(J250:J252)
DTA	I257	='General Assumptions'!I105
Tax Rate	I258	='General Assumptions'!I85
Opening Tax Losses	I259	=IF(I258<=0,0,I257/I258)

Description	Cell	Formula
Opening Tax Losses	J261	=I264
Tax Losses Created During the Period	J262	=-MIN(J242,0)
Tax Losses Used	J263	=IF(J242>0,-MAX(MIN(J242,J261),0),0)
Closing Tax Losses	I264	=I259
Closing Tax Losses	J264	=SUM(J261:J263)
Movement in Tax Losses	J266	=SUM(J262:J263)
Tax Rate	J268	=J230
Movement in DTAs	J270	=J268*J266
Opening DTAs	J272	=I274
Movement in DTAs	J273	=J270
Closing DTAs	I274	=I257
Closing DTAs	J274	=SUM(J272:J273)
Opening Tax Payable	J278	=I283
Tax Expense / (Credit)	J279	=J196
Tax Paid	J280	=J252
Movement in DTAs	J281	=J270
Movement in DTLs	J282	=-J232
Closing Tax Payable	I283	=I253
Closing Tax Payable	J283	=SUM(J278:J282)
Equity Issuances	J290	='General Assumptions'!J121
Equity Buybacks	J291	='General Assumptions'!J122
Opening Equity	J295	=I298
Equity Issuances	J296	=J290
Equity Buybacks	J297	=-J291
Closing Equity	I298	='Opening Balance Sheet'!I45
Closing Equity	J298	=SUM(J295:J297)
Dividend Payout Ratio	J303	='General Assumptions'!J127
Retained Profits	J307	='Balance Sheet'!J46
NPAT	J308	='Income Statement'!J27
Cash Flow Available for Dividends	J309	='Cash Flow Statement'!J22+'Cash Flow Statement'!J27+SUM('Cash Flow Statement'!J30:J33)
Maximum Dividend Payable	J311	=MAX(MIN(MAX(J307+J308,J308),J309),0)
Dividend Based on Ratio	J313	=MAX(J308*J303,0)
Dividend Declared	J315	=MIN(J311,J313)
Opening Dividend Payable	J319	=I322
Dividend Declared	J320	=J315
Dividends Paid	J321	=-J319
Closing Dividend Payable	I322	='Opening Balance Sheet'!$I$29
Closing Dividend Payable	J322	=SUM(J319:J321)
Opening Other Current Assets	J330	=I333
Closing Other Current Assets	I333	='Opening Balance Sheet'!$I$16
Closing Other Current Assets	J333	=SUM(J330:J332)
Opening Other Current Liabilities	J341	=I344
Closing Other Current Liabilities	I344	='Opening Balance Sheet'!$I$31
Closing Other Current Liabilities	J344	=SUM(J341:J343)

Opening Balance Sheet

Description	Cell	Formula
Error Checks	G4	=Overall_Error_Check
Total Current Assets	I17	=SUM(I14:I16)
Total Non-Current Assets	I22	=SUM(I20:I21)
Total Assets	I24	=I17+I22
Total Current Liabilities	I32	=SUM(I27:I31)
Total Non-Current Liabilities	I37	=SUM(I35:I36)
Total Liabilities	I39	=I32+I37
Net Assets	I41	=I24-I39
Retained Profits	I49	=I41-I45-I47-I48
Total Equity	I50	=SUM(I45,I47:I49)
PF Error Check	I55	=IF(ISERROR(I41-I50),1,0)
Balance Check	I56	=IF(I55<>0,0,(ROUND(I41-I50,Rounding_Accuracy)<>0)*1)
Insolvency Check	I57	=IF(AND(I55=0,I56=0),(I41<0)*1,0)

Income Statement Worksheet

Description	Cell	Formula
Error Checks	G4	=Overall_Error_Check
Months	J5	=Timing!J5
Start Date	C6	=Timing!C6
Revenue	J13	=Calculations!J32
COGS	J14	=-Calculations!J58
Gross Profit	J15	=SUM(J13:J14)
Operating Expenditure	J17	=-Calculations!J87
EBITDA	J18	=J15+J17
Depreciation	J20	=Calculations!J120
EBIT	J21	=J18+J20
Interest Expense	J23	=-Calculations!J155+Calculations!J175
NPBT	J24	=J21+J23
Tax Expense	J26	=-Calculations!J279
NPAT	J27	=J24+J26

Error Checks Worksheet

Description	Cell	Formula
Opening Balance Sheet - no errors	F4	=Overall_Error_Check
Opening Balance Sheet - balances	I12	='Opening Balance Sheet'!I55
Opening Balance Sheet - solvent	I13	='Opening Balance Sheet'!I56
Balance Sheet - no errors	I14	='Opening Balance Sheet'!I57
Balance Sheet - balances	I15	='Balance Sheet'!I55
Balance Sheet - solvent	I16	='Balance Sheet'!I56
Cash Flow Statement - no errors	I17	='Balance Sheet'!I57
Cash Flow Statement - direct = indirect	I18	='Cash Flow Statement'!I57
Summary of Errors	I21	=MIN(1,SUM(I11:I19))

Balance Sheet

Description	Cell	Formula
Error Checks	G4	=Overall_Error_Check
Months	J5	=Timing!J5
Start Date	C6	=Timing!C6
Cash	J14	=IF(J$9=1,'Opening Balance Sheet'!$I$14,I14)+'Cash Flow Statement'!J37
Accounts Receivable	J15	=Calculations!J34
Other Current Assets	J16	=Calculations!J333
Total Current Assets	J17	=SUM(J14:J16)
PP&E	J20	=Calculations!J121
Deferred Tax Assets	J21	=Calculations!J274
Total Non-Current Assets	J22	=SUM(J20:J21)
Total Assets	J24	=J17+J22
Accounts Payable	J27	=Calculations!J60+Calculations!J89
Interest Payable	J28	=Calculations!J157-Calculations!J177
Dividends Payable	J29	=Calculations!J322
Tax Payable	J30	=Calculations!J283
Other Current Liabilities	J31	=Calculations!J344
Total Current Liabilities	J32	=SUM(J27:J31)
Debt	J35	=Calculations!J138
Deferred Tax Liabilities	J36	=Calculations!J236
Total Non-Current Liabilities	J37	=SUM(J35:J36)
Total Liabilities	J39	=J32+J37
Net Assets	J41	=J24-J39
Ordinary Equity	J45	=Calculations!J298
Opening Profits	J46	=IF(J$9=1,'Opening Balance Sheet'!$I$49,I49)
NPAT	J47	='Income Statement'!J27
Dividends Declared	J48	=-Calculations!J320
Retained Profits	J49	=SUM(J46:J48)
Total Equity	J50	=J45+J49
PF Error Check	I55	=MIN(SUM($J55:$N55),1)
PF Error Check	J55	=IF(ISERROR(J41-J50),1,0)
Balance Check	J56	=IF(J55<>0,0,(ROUND(J41-J50, Rounding_Accuracy)<>0)*1)
Insolvency Check	J57	=IF(AND(J55=0,J56=0),(J41<0)*1,0)

Cash Flow Statement

Description	Cell	Formula
Error Checks	G4	=Overall_Error_Check
Months	J5	=Timing!J5
Start Date	C6	=Timing!C6
Cash Receipts	J16	=-Calculations!J33
Direct Cash Payments	J17	=Calculations!J59
Indirect Cash Payments	J18	=Calculations!J88
Cash Payments	J19	=SUM(J17:J18)
Interest Paid	J20	=Calculations!J156

Description	Cell	Formula
Tax Paid	J21	=Calculations!J280
Net Operating Cash Flow	J22	=SUM(J16,J19:J21)
Interest Received	J25	=-Calculations!J176
Purchases of Non-Current Assets	J26	=-Calculations!J119
Net Investing Cash Flows	J27	=SUM(J25:J26)
Debt Drawdowns	J30	=Calculations!J136
Debt Repayments	J31	=Calculations!J137
Ordinary Equity Issuances	J32	=Calculations!J296
Ordinary Equity Buybacks	J33	=Calculations!J297
Dividends Paid	J34	=Calculations!J321
Net Financing Cash Flows	J35	=SUM(J30:J34)
Net Increase / (Decrease) in Cash Held	J37	=J22+J27+J35
NPAT	J43	='Income Statement'!J27
Depreciation	J45	=-'Income Statement'!J20
Interest Expense	J46	=-'Income Statement'!J23
Tax Expense	J47	=-'Income Statement'!J26
(Inc) / Dec in Current Assets	J49	=-SUM(Calculations!J32:J33, Calculations!J331:J332)
Inc / (Dec) in Current Liabilities	J50	=SUM(Calculations!J58:J59, Calculations!J87:J88,Calculations!J342:J343)
Interest Paid	J52	=J20
Tax Paid	J54	=SUM(J43,J45:J47,J49:J50,J52:J53)
PF Error Check	I57	=MIN(SUM($J57:$N57),1)
PF Error Check	J57	=IF(ISERROR(J37+J54),1,)
Reconciliation Check	J58	=IF(J57<>0,0,(ROUND(J22-J54, Rounding_Accuracy)<>0)*1)

Timing Worksheet

Description	Cell	Formula
Timing	A1	=IFERROR(RIGHT(CELL("filename",A1), LEN(CELL("filename",A1)) -FIND("]",CELL("filename",A1))),"")
Case Study Model vLB1.02.xlsm	A2	=Model_Name
Error Checks	F4	=Overall_Error_Check
Months	J5	=J$7
Start Date	J6	=IF(J$9=1,Model_Start_Date,I$7+1)
End Date	J7	=EOMONTH(J$6,MOD(Periodicity+Reporting_ Month_Factor-MONTH(J$6),Periodicity))
Number of Days	J8	=J7-J6+1
Counter	J9	=N(I$9)+1
Timing Assumptions	B11	=MAX($B$10:$B10)+1
Reporting Month Factor	H21	=MOD(Example_Reporting_Month- 1,Periodicity)+1

Index

Second Edition Addendum

Whilst I put together a companion book on Financial Modelling, it occurs to me that we should pass on a few more "tricks of the trade" regarding building financial models. May I suggest that you take the time to look at the website of our company (SumProduct) www.sumproduct.com and avail yourself of daily tips, tricks, ideas and blogs.

For example, I talk on several occasions of copying a formula consistently across a row. That's fine when there are just a few columns, but when there are more rows, it can become cumbersome. Well, here's a useful trick.

Sometimes when modelling you need to copy a formula across many columns (e.g. building a 20+year monthly forecast model). Dragging a formula across using the mouse on a regular basis could lead to a claim for Repetitive Strain Injury. Unless these cells are already non-blank keyboard shortcuts such as CTRL + SHIFT + Right Arrow appear useless. However, all is not lost. The following trick can be used on many occasions.

Imagine you needed to copy formulae across columns J to XZ (say):
- Select the column TWO columns to the right of the last column required (here, this would be column YB)
- A quick way to get there would be to press the F5 function key and then type YB1 + ENTER to go to cell YB1 and then press CTRL + SPACEBAR to select the column YB
- Next, highlight all columns to the right (assuming these are all blank) using CTRL + SHIFT + Right Arrow
- Right click on the mouse and select 'Hide' (this will hide columns YB to the end)
- Now return to where the formula will start (say, cell J9)
- Type the formula in and press ENTER
- Select the cell again and then use the keystroke CTRL + SHIFT + Right Arrow which will highlight cells J9:YA9 inclusive
- Having removed all fingers from the keyboard press SHIFT + Left Arrow which will reduce the range to cells J9:XZ9 inclusive
- Having removed all fingers from the keyboard once more, press CTRL + R to fill the formulae into all cells simultaneously.

Practice will make this second nature!

Three points to note:
1. On first glance, there appears to be no reason to retain a blank column. However, if column XZ is the final column, CTRL + SHIFT + Right Arrow will take you straight to column XZ. However, if you fill in this point, in some versions of Excel, all of the hidden columns will have formulae copied into them too, leading to potential model errors and needless file size bloating.
2. Some modellers will hide or group columns of populated data instead of using the above technique. The problem with this approach is that whilst these columns are hidden, errors may occur in these columns which are only picked up when the fields are made visible once more. This can lead to tremendous re-work which could have been avoided if the developer had inspected ranges periodically instead.
3. CTRL + R will not always retain all formats. If this is important, copy the formula (CTRL + C) before highlighting the whole range and then paste in the usual way (CTRL + V) instead.

Finally, let me end on an extremely pragmatic note. I quizzed my colleagues about what we considered to be the most useful keyboard shortcuts for financial modelling (on a PC). This is what they came up with. Yes, it's an entirely subjective list, but hopefully, you'll find one or two useful shortcuts below. Enjoy!

Keystroke	What it does
ALT + ;	Select visible
ALT + =	Sum selection above or to the left
ALT + Down	Opens AutoComplete, data validation or filter dropdown list
ALT + F1	Insert chart on current sheet
ALT + F11	Show VBA IDE
CTRL + ;	Insert current date (in Edit [F2] mode)
CTRL + 0	Hide column
CTRL + 1	Format cells
CTRL + 9	Hide row
CTRL + ALT + F3	New name
CTRL + B	Bold (toggle)
CTRL + C	Copy
CTRL + D	Fill down
CTRL + Down	Select the last cell in the area down
CTRL + End	Selects the last cell in the sheet
CTRL + ENTER	Fill value in edited cell into all cell and do not move
CTRL + Escape	Bring up Start Menu (overriding an Excel command)
CTRL + F	Find dialog
CTRL + F1	Show / hide Ribbon
CTRL + F3	Open Name Manager
CTRL + F12	Open
CTRL + G	GoTo
CTRL + H	Replace
CTRL + Home	Select cell to reset window (or pane)
CTRL + I	Italic (toggle)
CTRL + K	Insert hyperlink
CTRL + Left	Select the last cell in the area left
CTRL + Multiply (*)	Select current region
CTRL + N	New workbook
CTRL + O	Open workbook
CTRL + P	Print
CTRL + PageDown	Next sheet
CTRL + PageUp	Previous sheet
CTRL + R	Fill right
CTRL + Right	Select the last cell in the area right
CTRL + S	Save
CTRL + Space	Select column
CTRL + Subtract (-)	Delete cells
CTRL + T	Insert Table / convert selection to Table
CTRL + U	Underline (toggle)
CTRL + Up	Select the cell at top of region
CTRL + V	Paste
CTRL + W	Close window
CTRL + X	Cut
CTRL + Y	Redo
CTRL + Z	Undo

Keystroke	What it does
F3	Paste names
F4	Redo / edit (F2) mode: toggle $ references
F5	GoTo / refresh file list
F7	Check spelling
F8	Extend selection mode
F9	Calculate now
F11	Insert chart on new sheet
F12	Save As
Home	Select the first cell in the row
SHIFT + ALT + F1	Insert new sheet
SHIFT + ALT + Left	Ungroup
SHIFT + ALT + Right	Group
SHIFT + Backspace	Collapse selection to the active cell
SHIFT + CTRL + -	Remove all borders
SHIFT + CTRL + =	Insert cells
SHIFT + CTRL + 1	Fixed decimal and comma format
SHIFT + CTRL + 3	Date format
SHIFT + CTRL + 4	Currency format
SHIFT + CTRL + 5	Percentage format
SHIFT + CTRL + 7	Outline border
SHIFT + CTRL + 9	Unhide row
SHIFT + CTRL + Down	Extend selection down to last cell in area down
SHIFT + CTRL + End	Extends the selection to the last cell in the sheet
SHIFT + CTRL + F3	Create names
SHIFT + CTRL + Home	Extend selection to the cell that resets the window or pane
SHIFT + CTRL + Left	Extend selection down to last cell in area left
SHIFT + CTRL + PageDown	Extend selection one sheet down
SHIFT + CTRL + PageUp	Extend selection one sheet up
SHIFT + F2	Insert / Edit Comment
SHIFT + F3	Function Wizard
SHIFT + F9	Calculate sheet
SHIFT + F10	Activate context menus (right-click)
SHIFT + F11	Insert new worksheet
SHIFT + SPACE	Select row
SHIFT + TAB	Tab backwards (previous cell to edit)
TAB	Tab forwards (next cell to edit)

There are over 540 keyboard shortcuts in Excel. For a comprehensive list, please download the Excel file at http://www.sumproduct.com/thought/keyboard+shortcuts.

Also, as I mentioned before, check out the new daily Excel Tip of the Day feature on the www.sumproduct.com homepage.